ISLAND ~~JOTTINGS~~ Joggings

MICHAEL BENNING

Published by

MELROSE BOOKS

An Imprint of Melrose Press Limited
St Thomas Place, Ely
Cambridgeshire
CB7 4GG, UK
www.melrosebooks.com

FIRST EDITION

Copyright © Michael Benning 2011

The Author asserts his moral right to
be identified as the author of this work

Cover designed by Matt Stephens

ISBN 978 1 907040 74 0

Printed and bound in Great Britain by:
CLE Digital Solutions. St Ives, Cambridgeshire

FSC
Mixed Sources
Product group from well-managed
forests and other controlled sources
Cert no. TT-COC-003115
www.fsc.org
© 1996 Forest Stewardship Council

DEDICATIONS

To Lesley for packing the travel journal, without which I could never have started the book.

To Mel and David for inviting me and my travelling companions, Jan, Carrie, Caroline, Danielle, Fran, Carl, Ted, Sue and Vicky, without whom the book would never have been completed.

ACKNOWLEDGEMENTS

I would like to thank *The Caymanian Compass*, *Cayman Free Press*, for providing additional material in respect of Captain Marvin Ebanks and allowing me to include some of that information in compiling this book.

I would also like to thank the *Cayman Net News* for information they published, particularly in respect of Hurricane Ivan and its aftermath, without which I would have been unable to portray an accurate picture of events and life on Grand Cayman.

As Hurricane Ivan progressed, for some days *Cayman Net News* were the only source of communication with the island that enabled family and friends to glean some news of the situation on Grand Cayman prior to making personal contact days later.

I am indebted to them for allowing me to use some of their material.

Whilst 'The Good Wife's Guide' has been claimed to come from a woman's magazine or home economics book from the 1950s the origins of the text remain something of a mystery and as research has failed to trace the original document it remains unattributable.

CONTENTS

CHAPTER 1

'W' Day – Saturday 10th July, 2004

I started to write this on the Sunday morning. Yesterday had been Melanie and David's wedding day. It had been a long day and even longer night of celebrations. I'm not sure I will remember everything but here goes.

We had now been on the island for five days and at last the big day had arrived; this was the real reason why so many of us had travelled the best part of five-thousand-odd miles across the Atlantic to Grand Cayman. A total of ten of us, family and friends, had crossed the Pond, the majority flying direct with British Airways from Heathrow but a couple with Virgin Atlantic to Miami and then Cayman Airways into Georgetown. Other members of David's family, his sister Cynthia and nephew Jose, journeyed from New York and one guest from even further afield. Diane had travelled from Sydney, Australia, via Los Angeles, Mexico and Cuba. I've been to my share of weddings back home in England that have entailed overnight stays or included long weekend breaks but they pale into insignificance when compared to Diane's marathon covering two continents and an ocean, which included four changes of plane together with the consequent stopovers. I bet she didn't envisage that journey when she became Melanie's godmother all those years ago.

The morning was relatively straightforward. Up early, but no running today, as all sorts of preparations were in hand for the afternoon. Weather was warm and humid. The ironing board was out already and Jan, the bride's mother, was continuing with alterations to dresses that she had started yesterday, following last-minute fittings for the bridesmaids. I hoped we didn't run out of needles and cotton!

My shirt, socks and handkerchief were all checked over and passed muster. Mid-morning and we had a break. All the girls went off to Cimboco's for a hen party brunch – we guys thought that was an omelette or eggs and bacon, but suspected the girls had different ideas. Ted, Melanie's father, who was recovering well from his visit to A&E the previous day, joined Carl and I who had already made ourselves comfortable on two sunbeds by the side of the pool at our Indies Suites hotel, just off Seven Mile Beach. The weather was a little cloudy to start with, but this soon passed over and, as promised on the weather forecast, it became bright and sunny and seemed the hottest, and most humid, day so far. Lounging in swimming trunks and taking the occasional dip in cool water was a very relaxing, and unusual for me, way of preparing for a wedding. We were able to watch some of the one-day cricket final from Lords on the television by the poolside bar. The locals were interested in how the West Indies were progressing. Having defeated England to reach the final they were finding life against a very lively New Zealand side much more difficult. My West Indian cricket sun hat, which I acquired in Trinidad some three years earlier, had by now become a regular topic of conversation, with the resident cricket lovers wanting to know where they could purchase one. Surprisingly we were all feeling nice and calm but the hotel was starting to fill up with a number of noisy Americans carrying their diving equipment and this was even more noticeable in what had been, until their arrival, a haven of tranquillity. One in particular seemed to have more hot air than he was likely to find in his underwater cylinders. Within our little group he quickly gained the nickname of Dick the Diver, which seemed, in his case, wholly appropriate.

After five days we had just witnessed our first outbreak of that virulent and infectious disease, HOLS. I originally thought this to be a purely British phenomenon but experience has taught me that it is trans-continental, although fortunately it has not yet reached pandemic

2

proportions. The British variety is normally alcohol-induced and prevalent on the coasts of Spain, the Canary and Balearic islands, and tends to mainly affect males under the age of thirty.

The American strain of Holiday Overseas Loutish Syndrome seemed to infect a slightly older generation but was again male-dominated and didn't appear to need immense amounts of lager to be ingested for the symptoms to appear. A self-belief that 'I'm the biggest, the best, the most successful and the loudest' was the minimum required to ensure every guest became aware of their presence in the hotel. Why is it that a vociferous minority become stereotyped as the typical tourist abroad and spoil the reputations of some great nations?

On this particular occasion, it might not have been a symptom of the HOLS epidemic but a unique case of diverdickulitis. Time would prove that this was just one individual who, as my grandfather would have said, was inebriated with the exuberance of his own verbosity. Whilst at times it would be annoying and totally unnecessary it did provide us with some amusing entertainment later in the week when even his own friends had become tired of his boorish antics.

As time passed the day was gradually but persistently getting warmer. It was time for a swift coating of suntan cream to prevent any unnecessary sunburn.

The girls eventually arrived back at the hotel bringing with them some pasta and salad for the three of us for our lunch. This was very nice and welcome and washed down with an ice-cold beer. We were also drinking lots of water to avoid dehydration. The pudding consisted of rum cake (choc banana and pina colada flavours). Fortunately, Caroline, the noisiest of the United Kingdom guest party, who was staying with Danielle in the adjoining apartment, came in to do some ironing and she managed to devour most of the cake. As a group we had long since decided that whilst she's about, there is every chance that we will manage to eat all of the seven rum cakes in the fridge – even if she is a noisy eater, at least it will get rid of the cake! – nothing personal intended, she's just always noisy.

It was now getting hotter and the sun was beating down on those around the pool. I decided not to go for a final swim before the wedding but to take my time and get ready in a quiet relaxed atmosphere. An overly ambitious plan that in the circumstances was doomed to failure.

By now the bride's mother was interchanging between dress alteration and hairdressing until the girls disappeared back into town in our minibus to help Mel with make-up, hairdo and dress-fitting etc., or whatever else brides need to do in the final hours leading up to their nuptials. This seemed to be a securely kept secret known only to womanhood and even the father of the bride wasn't privy to this preparatory conference that was exclusively for the female species and only those twenty-somethings were allowed anywhere near the inner sanctum of the bride's home for this well-guarded ritual.

The time was advancing steadily, but the atmosphere still remained calm, which was surprising. A rota system started for shaves, showers and baths etc. with Carl and I being early on the list to complete our necessary ablutions and vacate the bathroom and allow ample time for the girls to carry out all their cleansing and beauty treatments without interruption. Our rationale was that this might encourage them to spend less time than is normal in such circumstances but logic told us that this was going to be more in hope than expectation.

It was getting hotter so I was hit with the realisation that anti-perspirant would need to be liberally applied. At least this would be a change from what had become the norm of a coating of suntan oil. I was also hit with a blast of oven-like heat whenever I left the air-conditioned apartment to wander onto the balcony.

4

The bride's mother was still sewing!

We suddenly realised that the clock was now ticking all too quickly and the first signs of panic began to appear as Caroline and Fran had not yet arrived back with the minibus. I think we were more worried about the minibus, our only form of transport to the wedding, than we were about Caroline and Fran who are both very capable of looking after themselves. In fairness to Carl he was worried about Fran. (That was something I had to write otherwise she would have hit both of us.) Phone calls revealed that they were on their way back with Caroline driving 'like a tourist' according to a local motorist who shouted at her when she started 'burning rubber' from a standing start at a road junction. Although to be fair to Caroline, and we all tried to be throughout the holiday albeit unsuccessfully, it would probably have been more accurate to describe her driving as 'like a local' from what we were to experience on the island's roads.

It was still getting hotter and I decided to return to the bath-room for a cold shower in order to cool down!

The bride's mother had not yet quite finished sewing. At last the girls arrived and suddenly the pace seemed to quicken and the decibel levels increased considerably. It's amazing how quiet Carl, Ted and I had been whilst in our own company. The bride's mother needed to revert to hairdressing; this time Caroline. Why do girls throw talcum powder over their hair? Fran appeared much quieter but this was deceptive as she then started flashing her boobs about before forcing them into her dress. I was seeing a side to Fran on this holiday that I had not experienced before.

It was definitely getting hotter! I might need another shower.

I thought I had a good idea. I decided to take an additional shirt and pair of shorts for the evening, but it was difficult to find a pair which matched with the socks and knotted hankie. I can hear the questions as I write. Why the socks and knotted hankie? For some reason, that I cannot comprehend, I've never been renowned for my sartorial elegance. I don't think I could be described as scruffy but I do like to be comfortable. Bearing in mind the climate, the dress code for the wedding was much less formal than one would expect at home. Tailored shorts and smart casual summer shirts were to be acceptable. Lesley, my wife, was aware of this and in an effort to ensure that I didn't appear too out of place had accompanied me to endorse the fitting and give her approval to the design and colour coordination when I went on my annual shopping expedition for clothes. Strangely enough I was convinced that I wasn't the only man to be escorted on such an adventure. Others seemed to be receiving similar encouragement, advice and in many cases instructions.

I'm sure I could have achieved a similar result on my own but at least this satisfied her that I looked the part, provided I remembered to dress in the right clothes on the day. I had threatened to become the stereotypical British holidaymaker abroad by dressing in sandals, white socks and braces together with knotted handkerchief on my head. In addition to threats to disown me, and that was the least of them, she had arranged for Jan and the girls to put me on dress parade before leaving the hotel. She obviously envisaged that this would be on a par with the old-style daily military parade in front of the regimental sergeant-major where everything from bulled boots to tunics with polished buttons and trimmed haircuts were minutely inspected and the slightest speck of dust or dandruff resulted in additional duties. Jan and Carrie had been given strict and specific instructions about what I was to wear and how it was to be worn. These were to be ignored under pain of death. I didn't think this was necessary but if it satisfied her that there was at least a chance of me arriving in a presentable state then I was prepared to be inspected by Jan, Carrie, Caroline, Fran and Danielle. Being on holiday, and in a somewhat mischievous mood, I arranged to have a photograph taken of me masquerading as the old-fashioned and traditional Cockney grandpa on Southend-on-Sea beach. The only thing missing was the braces and jellied eels. Once the picture had been taken I was then able to dispose of the socks and knotted handkerchief and change quickly into my wedding attire but I could look forward to her initial reaction when she first saw the photographs. The reality was that I am nowhere near brave enough to go to any wedding dressed like that. The consequences are too painful to imagine.

By now there was a combination of hairdressing, sewing and ironing all progressing at a frantic pace plus lippie and make-up being carefully administered. Carl and I remained calm and decided on days like this, it's better to be a fella.

> *It was getting even hotter and that was just in the apartment! In an effort to cool down I opened the freezer compartment and squeezed in as much of my head, arms and torso as I could. Surprisingly this was very effective although once removed wasn't as long lasting as one hoped. Short term, however, it was very comfortable.*

I decided to move the minibus into the shade and leave the air-conditioning on. Hopefully this would make the journey more comfortable. I realised that I needed the ignition key and couldn't find it. Don't panic. We swiftly carried out an orderly search. That didn't work. We now thought about panicking. Jan solved the mystery. Did Caroline still have the key? I went next door and knocked. (Had to be careful here as you never knew what you might see when the door opened. Their apartment appeared to be in a regular state of disarray and permanent organised confusion if that is not a contradiction in terms. The girls were often in the same state but much of that resulted in an inability to decide which dress, or outfit, to wear with which pair of shoes and the consequent discarded footwear and clothing that littered the furniture prior to making final decisions. I decided this was a purely female phenomenon.)

The door was eventually opened and Danielle was ready and waiting. However, from the background noises, it was apparent that Caroline was now dressing, 'like a tourist', and, in a not dissimilar fashion to Fran, had yet to force her boobs into her wedding outfit. I grabbed the keys and went to move the bus into the shade under the awning at the front of the hotel. I decided to leave the engine running – this seemed a good idea, as the air-conditioning unit would keep the interior cool.

> *The heat as I walked back to our rooms was stifling and I was*
> *already beginning to leak.*

It took another fifteen minutes, due purely to the delay whilst we waited for one noisy guest, before we all met up in hotel reception and after the statutory photo calls, boarded our tiny charabanc to transport us to the wedding. The minibus, with me driving and nine passengers, set off from the hotel and turned left along Seven Mile Beach Road towards the south of the island.

> *It became apparent very quickly to all inside the van that it*
> *was getting hotter and hotter. We realised we had a problem*
> *with the air-conditioning. It wasn't working!*

Oh to be able to go back to the apartment and put our hands and heads back in the freezer. (Not sure it was meant for that but it certainly had the desired effect in keeping us cool following hot and cold showers taken to both keep clean and try and cool down and in my case prevent me breaking out into another sweat.)

With lots of advice from the now gently poached passengers, most of which cannot be repeated in a diary of this nature, Caroline came up trumps and realised that the air-conditioning wasn't switched on. A flick of the switch did the trick. Who had turned it off was to remain a mystery for the duration of the holiday although accusing glances were aimed at me as the driver. I pleaded my genuine innocence and hinted, very discreetly of course, that the last two in the bus, who had been in a terrible rush to return and beautify themselves, may have inadvertently pressed the wrong button, as they were unfamiliar with the controls. Traffic proved to be the best of the week so far and by now I was getting used to the traffic lights in the sky that had nearly caught me out earlier in the week. At least in daylight I could see which gear we were in. We dropped Jan and Ted off at Mel's house and moved on to the Grand Old House, where the wedding was to take place. I found a parking space under the shade of some overhanging branches and we alighted from our now comfortable bus into a wall of humidity.

Whilst it might seem impossible to anybody sitting reading this in a cold climate it really was still getting hotter.

I had, however, sensibly worn a different shirt for the journey and kept my smartly pressed and pristine shirt on a hanger for the wedding. This proved to be a shrewd move and ensured that at least I would look relatively smart for the wedding ceremony. I changed into my wedding shirt and actually appeared spic-and-span and attempted to look cool. The last part was just not possible despite my best efforts!

I have to say, all the girls looked fabulous in their outfits and David the bridegroom, Mike the best man and Ted the bride's father looked the business in their more formal dinner jackets. The Grand Old House is in a beautiful setting with the waves lapping against the informal register office. This is not a UK-style wood panelled register office that you tend to find in town halls up and down the country, but much more exotic. Alfresco, on a pier surrounded by palms, a clear turquoise sea that meets a cloudless blue sky on a horizon that is difficult to distinguish in the distance. Unfortunately the palms weren't of the gently waving variety, as there wasn't any breeze and the sun was now high in the sky and beating down on the guests as they arrived and alighted from their air-conditioned automobiles.

Unbelievably it was still getting hotter! The first sign of leaks began to percolate through as one or two, and not just me, were beginning to feel the heat.

The artists who were top of the bill were now going through their final preparations in the Wine Room – the coolest room in the house. I could have spent some time in there!

On reflection – a lot of time. The temperature was a great attraction but the enormous and varied selection of fine wines could have kept my attention for some hours, or even days. I attempted to linger but was gently persuaded to leave as I was captured spending too much time eyeing the wine and the stars of the show needed to complete changing into their wedding costumes.

The remainder of guests had now all arrived and prior to gathering on the pier, were all to be found trying to assemble in a tight circle under the one air-conditioner in the bar. It was beginning to resemble a Caymanian Ring-a-Ring-o'Roses, only the posies hadn't yet arrived and some of the guests were already wilting – me in particular!

Ah, we at last had progress on two fronts. The bride's mother had completed dress alterations and was – at last – packing away the needles and cotton, and the groom's father, Ray, had arrived, resplendent in dinner jacket and dickie-bow. He appeared to be quite a character, and had the physique of a Wayne Sleep or Michael Flatley but with even more energy. As the day wore on we were to see and understand why there were such comparisons in more ways than one. Whilst he may have been small of stature, he was big of personality.

The time had arrived for all of us to be ushered into our seats. David the groom and best man, Mike, took their allotted places, followed by the bridesmaids, Carrie and Cynthia. They looked as pretty as a picture against the beautiful backdrop of the translucent Caribbean Sea. Mel then arrived with Ted, looking radiant. Mel that is, not Ted, he just looked a little hot at that stage of the proceedings. I guessed that more than one or two of us were a little concerned for him following his trip to hospital on the previous day.

We were then called to attention for the wedding ceremony. It was fairly brief but very moving and it was obvious that David and Mel are very much in love. The pastor achieved a lovely blend of formality and friendliness with a hint of Caribbean charm, but not a rum cake in sight. I had never been to a wedding quite like this one before.

Sue, Ted's wife following his divorce from Jan many years earlier, provided an excellent and very suitable reading. Once the vows were exchanged and David and Mel were now formally Mister and Missus, we prepared for the photographs. Everybody was snapping away merrily but the 'official' photographer was Ken, a Methodist minister from Wigan. He was carrying two cameras and a variety of different lenses and had acquired a catchphrase, 'It's not like this in Wigan pet,' which is repeated at regular intervals, in a Geordie accent, between each shot. He was becoming the star of the show and with his ready wit was keeping everybody on their toes and lining up the different groups with the best views, and there was no lack of those with the sea, sand and rocky outcrops providing picturesque backdrops.

In fairness, it was very well organised, with his capable assistant, Nic, his daughter, who was later to become Mistress of Ceremonies, in charge of the running order, and manoeuvring the various participants into their designated places for each shot. Nic was a teaching colleague and friend of Mel's. They had travelled to the island together for their first teaching experience overseas some four years earlier and were original flatmates once they had acquired posts at the same school and had forged a firm friendship in that time.

> *It was now very hot and I had definitely sprung a leak. Two dark damp shadows were beginning to appear on either side of my chest and the back of my shirt had become attached. Who needs Velcro?*

I was not the only one in that situation but did seem to be leading the race to increase the flow of liquid into the Caribbean. Lord only knows what David, Mike, Ted and Ray must have been feeling like in their dinner jackets and bow ties, which in Mike's case could easily have been mistaken for a very stylish wetsuit!

I was only thankful that I was dressed in shorts and a lightweight short-sleeved shirt. If I had been required to wear the more traditional suit and tie I think I would have expired in the heat and would have become the second in our party to require medical assistance from the Grand Cayman health service.

If only somebody could invent an external air-conditioning bubble they would find their fortune and never have the need to work again.

It was at this stage of the proceedings that the England football team mini electric fan, bought for me by Lesley from Marks & Spencer for Euro 2004, came into its own. Jan also had a similar one. They were in great demand. If only I had known and anticipated such demand I could have bought a job lot and sold them on at a vast profit. I would have made a mint!

> *By this time Carl was looking at my chest in a most peculiar fashion. It worried me until he asked why I had a map of the world on the front of my shirt.*
>
> *On the left were Europe and Africa whilst on the right sat North and South America with the dry bit in the middle resembling the Atlantic Ocean. I came to the conclusion that the leak was changing into a meltdown by a process of hydroponic evolution.*
>
> *And wait for it... yes, it was getting hotter!*

At least the bride's mother seemed to have lost her penchant for sewing but continued to fuss around the girls, titivating the bridesmaids' hairdos and making sure that Mel remained cool by holding the mini electric fan so close to her that it would not have surprised me had we suddenly encountered a bride with an amputated ear. Now that would have made an interesting story and could even have made the national newspapers.

(In writing up the notes of the wedding on the Sunday morning, or what remained of it, I've now got to the stage where I know the speeches came next but am having difficulty in remembering. It is just possible that the champagne had a detrimental effect on my memory.)

I do remember it was still getting hotter!

Nic, in her capacity as Mistress of Ceremonies, started with a description of what a good wife should be and demonstrated that she had a wicked sense of humour. This was an extract taken from an article claimed to be written in a 1950s' home economics textbook entitled *The Good Wives' Guide*. For some unknown reason the author wished to remain anonymous, or in any event Nic's research failed to identify the writer – or culprit, depending upon which camp you sat in.

With tongue firmly in cheek and in her best schoolmistress manner Nic then proceeded to enlighten Melanie, and the rest of the guests, on the characteristics a good wife was expected to display as David arrived home from work. The gist of the lesson went something like this: "Have dinner ready. Plan ahead, even the night before, to have a delicious meal ready on time for his return. This is a way of letting him know that you have been thinking about him and are concerned about his needs.

"Most men are hungry when they come home and the prospect of a good meal (especially his favourite dish) is part of the warm welcome needed.

"Prepare yourself. Take fifteen minutes to rest so you'll be refreshed when he arrives. Touch up your make-up, put a ribbon in your hair and be fresh-looking. He has just been with a lot of work-weary people.

"Be a little gay and a little more interesting for him. His boring day may need a lift and one of your duties is to provide it. Clear away the clutter. Make one last trip through the main part of the house just before your husband arrives home. Gather up school books, toys, papers etc. and then run a dust cloth over the tables.

"Over the cooler months of the year you should prepare and light a fire for him to unwind by. Your husband will feel he has reached a haven of rest and order, and it will give you a lift too. After all, catering for his comfort will provide you with immense personal satisfaction.

"Prepare the children, take a few minutes to wash their hands and faces (if they are small), comb their hair, and if necessary, change their clothes. They are little treasures and he would like to see them playing the part.

"Minimise all noise. At the time of his arrival, eliminate all noise from the washer, dryer and vacuum. Try to encourage the children to be quiet. Be happy to see him. Greet him with a warm smile and show sincerity in your desire to see him.

"Listen to him. You may have a dozen important things to tell him, but the moment of his arrival is not the time. Let him talk first. Remember, his topics of conversation are more important than yours.

"Make the evening his. Never complain if he comes home late or goes out to dinner or other places of entertainment without you. Instead try to understand his world of strain and pressure, and his very real need to be at home and relax.

"Your goal. Try to make sure your home is a place of peace, order and tranquillity where your husband can renew himself in body and spirit. Don't greet him with complaints and problems. Don't complain if he's late for dinner or even if he stays out all night. Count this as minor compared to what he might have gone through that day.

"Make him comfortable. Have him lean back in a comfortable chair or have him lie down in the bedroom. Have a cool or warm drink ready for him. Arrange his pillow and offer to take off his shoes. Speak in a low, soothing and pleasant voice. Don't ask him questions about his actions or question his judgement or integrity.

"Remember, he is the master of the house and as such will always exercise his will with fairness and truthfulness. You have no right to question him.

"A good wife knows her place."

Nic delivered her gospel, not just by a straightforward reading of the words, but by emphasising certain words or phrases in much the same manner that Joyce Grenfell used to deliver a monologue. A pause here or a raising of the eyebrows there added a little theatre to her delivery so that by the time her lesson was finished the whole audience were convulsed in laughter.

All the guys seemed to agree with the opinions being expressed and I'm sure there were some who were wishing they could be transported back to that bygone age. Equally many of the girls present were unconvinced of its authenticity and certainly didn't appreciate the sentiments. Many were of the view that it was a spoof that must have been written by a man. However, I'm assured that it was a genuine article extracted from a book written back in the early 1950s. Political correctness and equality obviously did not feature very highly back in the post-war years. How things have changed in just two short generations. The result was a hubbub of conversation on each table with the merits of the article being hotly debated between the male and female species in a very humorous manner. Neither side seemed to win the argument but somehow I couldn't imagine any of the girls present following Nic's advice however persuasive husbands and partners tried to be.

After a short delay to allow the guests to quieten down there then followed speeches from Mike, Ted and David. All three speeches were very good and each had the elements of good public speaking. Amusing, brief and on this occasion, moving. Needless to say, the essential ingredient of every good wedding then arrived – tears. I think it started on Table 1, you know that mad group from the UK, but the images and mixed emotions of smiles, tears and hugs seemed wholly appropriate.

Mel and David then cut the cake. This was the cue for the next round of photographs. Amongst the happy 'snappers' with their table cameras was the David Bailey of the Methodist ministry declaring, "Wye hai pet, we doon't have keeks leek this in Wigan." He seemed to be in his element. I bet his sermons don't send the congregation to sleep!

Disaster struck me twice at this juncture. Firstly, my camera decided to come out in sympathy with me as it was too hot. Whilst it wasn't displaying the same symptoms it just would not take any further photos. Try as I might I could not make it work. Even new batteries wouldn't revive it! In fairness I'm not sure they would have worked on me either.

> *At the same time, the heat had ensured that the patches of moisture on my shirt had expanded to the extent that the Atlantic Ocean had disappeared and Africa and South America had become conjoined just below my sternum. The Gulf Stream had become a jet stream so that New York and London were now on the same continent. I was definitely in meltdown. Is this what global warming will be like when it finally takes over?*

One of the more memorable highlights of the day then occurred, one of many I might add, but the majority of the guests missed this as they were on their way to the buffet. It didn't involve any of the main players but I'm sure you can guess the guilty party. For those needing a clue – it was noisy! Yes, you've guessed it; she couldn't contain herself any longer. Caroline, who obviously has a sweet tooth, attacked the strawberry pavlova and demolished three whole sections, as if it were her favourite rum cake. Okay, I exaggerate a teeny bit! – but not a lot. I bet they don't have a Caroline in Wigan either, or if they do they must have a warehouse stacked full of imported rum cake.

> (By now, on the note-writing front, it was Monday morning and I was sitting on the hotel balcony wondering where Sunday had gone and in the interests of accuracy trying to remember the remainder of Saturday evening. The girls had seen me

scribbling these jottings and some fool, or it might have been a combination of Carrie, Danielle and Caroline, came up with the bright notion that these notes should be printed and provided for the guests at the reception in Suffolk in three weeks' time. My personal view was that they should watch the video and not bother with the dashed-off scribble of a hung-over, suntanned and wrung-out merrymaker whose memory was at best suspect and at worst totally inaccurate. A picture's worth a thousand words and would be likely to be far more interesting – and no I'm not on a commission for the film producers! All this was brought about because following their honeymoon David and Mel would return to Grand Cayman via England so that family and friends who were unable to attend the wedding could celebrate with them at the second reception in the UK in three weeks' time. In any event the girls persuaded me, against my better judgement, to complete the written record of the wedding and print it for the guests at the repeat event back home.)

Now, where was I? Oh yes, grub's up and what a banquet it was. The Grand Old House did us proud with a veritable feast. If they eat like this in Grand Cayman, I've got to return for more.

I'm placed between Diane and Carrie on the refined UK and Commonwealth Table whilst Table No.1 is now becoming rowdy. Not surprising considering who's on it and the amount of wine that is now being consumed!

It's a small world. In chatting to one of the waitresses it was readily apparent that she and Diane were fellow Australians. She originally came from a suburb of Sydney that was very close to Diane's home and her parents still lived there. Ironically, earlier in the day at breakfast Ted and Sue had bumped into a couple from Braintree in Essex, who we were to see more of as the week passed.

After a superb pudding, or in the interests of accuracy puddings in the plural – there wasn't any strawberry pavlova left. I wonder who ate it all? No prizes for those guessing the culprit on this occasion. The clues were all too obvious. Caroline was still wiping the debris from her cheeks. – We then joined a disorderly sprint back to the air-conditioner in the bar where the tightly knit throng resembled a bedraggled rugby scrum after a downpour. By now jackets and ties had been discarded and David, Ted and Mike were beginning to look a little more relaxed. Ray, meanwhile, was mingling with those guests he had not yet met, particularly the ladies, and enthralling them with tales of life on Grand Cayman. He made a beeline for Jan and informed her that as mother of the bride it was his duty as father of the groom to ensure that he took her onto the dance floor for her first dance of the evening. He later proved that he was as good as his word and we all gained the impression, even in that early part of the evening, that he was renowned for his dancing ability.

Even Diane, who's used to the heat, believed it was getting hotter. She and I found an upright electric fan, which had thoughtfully been brought onto the terrace by a couple of waiters. We commandeered a couple of chairs and manoeuvred them into what we thought was the most advantageous position before turning the fan on to full power and sitting there in an attempt to find a cool breeze. Impossible!

Having lasted until the end of the banquet, the time had arrived to disappear quickly back to the minibus and change into my dry shirt. I also decided to lose the hankie, which had never been on my head but used all too frequently to wipe my brow. It now appeared more like a well-used dishcloth, but at least I managed to dry off with some 'borrowed' paper towels from the gentlemen's bathroom. I had forgotten to bring the anti-perspirant and although my holiday version is of the 'intensive care' variety, it had already proved to be quite useless in these conditions over the past couple of days. I made a mental note to remember to ask the 'locals' what they use as they appeared to be coping far better than me in the humidity. After using the best part of a carton of paper towels following a liberal, if careful, splash in a basin full of cold water, at least I was now feeling fresh, cool and dry. Well, for five minutes at least!

For all too brief a period I resembled the relatively smart individual who had arrived for the wedding some hours earlier, with the possible exception of my hair which remained damp and more slicked down than normal. As I wandered back through the bar, to join our group who were gathered under the canopy on the pier, I was as smart as any of the other guests and certainly drier than many. Equally I knew this would not last.

Ken the peripatetic photographer from Wigan was wandering amongst the groups of guests and snapping away at unsuspecting victims to add to the wedding album. Meanwhile the disc jockey had arrived and she started to play the music. With a fairly wide age range at the reception, she had an eclectic taste (that's especially for Caroline with her word of the day that she had introduced early in the holiday in which we had all participated in trying to find a word that she didn't know) in music. Well, to be more accurate, it covered the entire second half of the last century which at least meant that I knew a good proportion of the songs and dances even if I couldn't remember all of the words or some of the artists. Although we had been seated in our own groups for the wedding breakfast (why do they call it a wedding breakfast? It's a dinner) it didn't take long to break the ice once we all started to mingle. We got on particularly well with Mel's school chums, many of whom we had met on the Stingray excursion earlier in the week. They are a young and lively lot who obviously like to party. It augured well for a good evening. In addition to Ken's official portraits there were lots of 'happy snappers' flashing away with the complimentary table cameras. Fran seemed to be leading the way and was determined to take more snaps than anybody else, Ken included. I didn't realise it at the time but it was an early indication of just how competitive she is. Dare I say it, even more so than me.

As the music got under way Mel and David called us over to the far end of the pontoon where we were then given an unexpected and impromptu exhibition by the tarpon leaping out of the sea to catch the darting midges, skimming just above the surface. The flying fish kept an ever-increasing audience entertained under floodlights for the rest of the evening.

The bride and groom started the dancing and were soon joined by Mike, the best man, and Carrie and Cynthia, the bridesmaids.

We didn't appreciate just how talented David's family are on the dance floor. Young Jose Amaudi, his nephew, was a cabaret act in himself. Words cannot do justice to his act. He ranged through Charlie Chaplin, without the hat and cane, Sammy Davis Junior, Michael Jackson's Moonwalk, and a very passable impression of Huggy Bear who had found fame in the detective series *Starsky and Hutch*. From that moment on, young Jose became known as Huggy Jnr.

> *Oh, by the way, it was still getting hotter and Newfoundland and the UK and Western Europe were beginning to emerge on my new shirt. Iceland was just a small dot at the moment but I just knew it was going to gain control of the whole North Atlantic within the next half hour. Thanks to Tom Clancy and The <u>Hunt</u> for Red October I was well aware of how strategically important Iceland had been to NATO during the Cold War years but I bet even they couldn't have envisaged how much it was likely to expand when mapped out on my shirt at a time of increased global warming.*

The dancing and singing from the Three Degrees or Three Musketeers, take your choice, quickly moved into full swing. This was, of course, Fran, Caroline and Danielle who were taking the dance floor by storm and persuading everybody to join them. The bedraggled group seeking solace under the air-conditioner in the bar had soon joined the seething mass and the damp-looking rugby scrum now reformed on the dance floor and were swaying and rocking to the music as sunset turned into dusk and dusk became night. The Three Suffolk Stompers dictated the tempo from centre-stage. Talking of which, in the middle of one dance, Fran took over the dance floor and managed to do the splits, as she was encircled by a foot-stamping and hand-clapping audience offering a degree of encouragement that was barely needed. She, and we, are still recovering from the experience.

Let me state quite categorically that the old saying 'horses sweat, men perspire and women simply glow' is not true, although I've been ordered to write that the bride and bridesmaids glowed beautifully. The rest of us were positively dripping!

Which brings me to David's father, Ray. There were a few occasions, no to be honest a lot, when we found David hiding his face. For some unknown reason he appeared to be just a tad embarrassed by his father's circumnavigation of the dance floor.

Ray approaches dancing in the same manner that a World War II pocket battleship would approach the enemy; with gusto and all guns blazing. He took no prisoners. The dances that he didn't know, and there weren't many, he improvised – eat your heart out Fred Astaire. His favourite phrase gave us the quote of the evening – 'Shake what your Mama gave you' – and he shook every bit of it with all his partners in all his dances over the entire dance floor, although we all think he was in his element dancing the more contemporary dances from the jive onwards. His perambulations with Jan began with the immortal words, "You do your thing, I'll do my thing, let's see where it takes us." In Cockney parlance he was ''aving a right ol' knees-up'. If he could be persuaded to travel to the UK he would prove to be both an able and entertaining entrant to *Strictly Come Dancing*. His dress sense and propensity to take the dance floor by storm might even make him a cult figure to rival the winning trio of Mark Ramprakash, Darren Gough or Tom Chambers, although I'm not sure what they would have made of him in Darren's home town of Barnsley. While somewhat older he would have been a very capable understudy for the diminutive Chris Hollins.

The Reverend Ken, our intrepid snapper, was meanwhile patrolling the perimeter of the dance floor attempting to capture one of Ray's more exotic dance movements for posterity to add to his fast-growing portfolio that would be presented to David and Mel in due course. I don't know if he attends many discos back home in Wigan but he would be unlikely to witness such a performance anywhere in the dance halls of Lancashire. Ray had boundless energy and appeared totally at home dancing in such humid conditions whilst some of his younger dancing companions were beginning to wilt as they tried to keep pace with him.

I liked Ray. Firstly, he was a much better dancer than me. My jigging, bopping and fancy footwork have been previously described as being something akin to 'a frog in a blender'. I've never been convinced that is a totally fair analogy – and certainly not to frogs – but equally I do have to accept it is not entirely inaccurate. If I were to be marked on the Torvill and Dean type ice dancing scale I suspect I would score 9.5 for effort and zero for technical merit.

More importantly, I also liked Ray because by the end of the evening he was also just as damp me!

> *Needless to say, in my case and as I had reasonably antici-*
> *pated, Iceland had now succeeded in taking over both the*
> *North and South Atlantic, the polar ice cap had melted and it*
> *hadn't even taken the thirty minutes I'd expected.*

At my age I should know better than to twist the night away in such a climate.

Who said you grow wiser as you grow older? As they say, growing old is mandatory but growing up is optional.

All good things come to an end and the night had passed so quickly that David and Mel were waltzing the last dance before many of us realised that it was time to leave the dance floor for the final time. Blinking through the body brine, all that was left to see was a mass of dripping humanity, forming a long chained archway for Mel and David to swim through and bid their farewells to all their guests, before they departed for their first night of wedded bliss in the Hyatt Regency.

All that was left for the party from the Indies Suites was to start loading the minibus with all the pressies yet to be unwrapped, three discarded dinner jackets of assorted designs and sizes, a variety of differently coloured, sized and shaped shoes that had been abandoned, various travelling apparel, balloons of differing colours and shapes that were inflated, deflated or still in pristine condition in their plastic bags. To this miscellany could be added half a dozen un-sprinkled boxes of confetti, forty-five used table cameras, fork handles (or even four candles as in *The Two Ronnies* sketch. It's amazing the effect drink has at a wedding reception), assorted flowers and table decorations and finally to be able to squeeze in ten lubricated bodies was a minor miracle. Our little minibus was bursting at the seams and my initial reservations when I saw its well-battered body were unfounded. It had done us proud to date and was to continue to do so. Lo and behold my original shirt, draped over one of the seats, was now dry and I quickly exchanged shirts for the final time that evening, or morning to be precise. Of all the occupants I had the most comfortable ride back to our hotel. As we passed through an almost deserted Georgetown, we could see the grey outline of a large container ship at one of the wharves that was being unloaded under floodlight by the dockside night shift. The stevedores and lorry drivers were rushing back and forth, building mountains of containers on the quayside that would be transported to their eventual destinations later in the day. Having passed this solitary hive of activity the remainder of the journey back towards Seven Mile Beach, and our hotel, was free of traffic for probably the only time during the whole of the holiday.

The hotel bar was also deserted and closed which was also a first for us so we were all left to climb the stairs to our rooms, which we managed surprisingly quietly, before diving into our respective rooms and heading for a well-deserved night's rest. As was my custom I poured myself a large glass of water and sat on the balcony with Jan and Carrie as we reflected on the events of the day. I suddenly realised that I was smiling broadly to myself as I pictured in my mind's eye the Peter Pan-like Ray twirling Jan around the dance floor whilst Ken was dodging in and out of tables trying to position himself for a decent shot of the dancing couple. This would be a wedding that we would all remember for a long time. Jan and Carrie were both very tired having had a long and exhausting day and left me to finish sipping my water as I sat gazing at the starlit Caribbean sky, although one or two storm clouds were by now scudding across the sky as predicted by the local weather forecasters. I decided not to wait for the rain and tiptoed across the room to my bed which was waiting to welcome me to my best night's sleep so far. I drifted into my slumbers dreaming of the day and what the rest of the holiday held in store.

David and Mel would be leaving for their honeymoon in Hawaii. Fran wanted us all to go to another wedding – Carl will make his own mind up in his own time. Caroline, being egged on by Carrie and Dani, could become our secret weapon against Dick the Diver and his noisy diving mates. Whilst Jan, the bride's mother, will have to open a dress alteration shop called 'Darn It' in Bury St Edmunds.

Poor Old Ted, Sue and Vicky would need to return to the UK to make sure their insurance companies (in the plural) didn't make a drama out of a crisis.

As I started to doze into that cosy pre-sleep semi-conscious state I remembered that we would have a repeat performance on dry land. We were to meet again in three weeks' time at a country hotel in East Anglia to have a second reception for the benefit of all the family and friends back home in the UK who hadn't been able to make it to Grand Cayman. Would I be able to survive another night like that and how many shirts would be required second time around?

CHAPTER 2

Fat Boy's Suitcase

My trip to Grand Cayman, which was my second visit to the Caribbean, had started some four days before the wedding with an early morning dash around the northern sector of the M25 from the A12 in Essex to London Heathrow Airport's Terminal 4. Somewhat surprisingly this was an accurate description of the progress we made, arriving in about seventy minutes. I have known the same journey take considerably in excess of two hours and that's on a good day.

I was driven to the airport by Les, a good friend and golfing partner of mine, who unfortunately has since died and passed on to the great golfing heaven in the sky. Some three years earlier, in March 2001, he and I had travelled the same route prior to setting off for Trinidad and Tobago. Not unnaturally, our conversation took us back to those islands and watching the Test Match between the West Indies and South Africa at the Queens Park Oval in Port of Spain, where we saw Courtney Walsh take his five hundredth test wicket.

The ground is conveniently positioned adjacent to the British High Commission for those diplomats and attachés who are ardent cricket enthusiasts. I had also taken the opportunity to talk to Curtly Ambrose, that giant of a bowler, in every sense, who had recently retired from international cricket. For somebody who was so hostile when hurling a cricket ball at you at over ninety miles per hour, he was very laid back and relaxed whilst talking about his sport. He was happily leaning against the pavilion rails chatting with the spectators and willing to pose for photographs with the youngsters, and some not quite so young. I wasn't brave enough to ask for his views on the current team who were struggling against the South Africans. Unfortunately, Brian Lara, the hometown hero, was going through a sticky patch, as can happen to any exceptional talent, and the team were in a transitional stage where they could no longer match the performances of their predecessors over the past two decades. Lara was struggling to score runs and at the time wasn't flavour of the month. Hardly surprisingly, in due course he regained his form going on to record the highest ever Test Match score of four hundred runs against England and four years later against the same South African opponents, back in Port of Spain, he held the West Indies batting together with a score of 196 to move effortlessly from the role of villain back to hero. How fickle are the whims of sporting fans and journalists?

Ironically, we also bumped into some players from Danbury Cricket Club in Essex, not far from where we both live. They were touring the island and taking the opportunity to watch the cricket. It was a very different experience to Lords or the Kennington Oval in the more formal and built-up surroundings of Central London where many of the spectators arrive by the Underground network which isn't needed in Port of Spain. The majority seemed to arrive by car and find a parking spot close enough to the ground, walking the last few hundred yards to soak up the atmosphere before entering the stadium to find their seat. Many others arrived by local taxi-buses that were ferrying their passengers back and forth across the city. Some of these looked as if they had seen better days and I'm not sure I would have fancied travelling in one as they wove in and out of the traffic jostling for position in the lines of vehicles approaching the many junctions on the way to the ground. The remainder made their way from different parts of the town on foot. The beat of the music and dancing from the Trinnie Posse gave each day a truly carnival and calypso West Indian atmosphere and even during the slower periods of the cricket, the game was never dull.

We had also played some golf on both the islands and I was looking forward to comparing the courses with those on Grand Cayman. The golf on Tobago was memorable less for our golf than for our somewhat eccentric caddie who joined us on the second tee dressed in trilby hat, wellington boots, grey suit, belt and braces and carrying a somewhat wind battered umbrella, with one unattached spoke, which was now substituting as a makeshift parasol. He quickly explained that he was 'unofficial' but that he knew the course well. Due to the heat, we had taken the option of hiring a buggy so strictly speaking were not in need of a caddie. However, we accepted his offer but neither of us could say that he assisted in improving our game or shot selection. We were left very much to our own devices in deciding which club to use and estimating the distance to the green. I deliberately say the green and not the pin as at our level of handicap we were more than satisfied to hit the green no matter how far from the pin the ball eventually came to rest. His particular forte was in locating our balls, if one might use that expression, and on a course containing its share of blind shots his expertise was such that we didn't lose a ball between us. Not bad for a pair of high handicappers on their first visit to the course. However, the sight of our suited and booted caddie trotting off ahead of our buggy with brolly held aloft to protect him from the sun remained etched in our memories, whilst our recollections of two very average games of golf became vague to say the least.

Tobago itself, with its Scottish connections, was much more memorable. Somehow, it was difficult to imagine that back in the seventeenth century Tobago had been acquired by the enterprising ruler Duke Jakob of Latvia following a neutrality deal with Oliver Cromwell. Latvia at that time renamed their colony New Kurland and had a thriving trade with Europe under their distinctive flag, a black crab on a red background. All of this is now a distant and very faded memory.

The attractive old wooden plantation properties, that have now been renovated and rejuvenated as holiday homes, were reminiscent of a totally relaxed 1950s beachside holiday but with the additional appeal of cocktails and calypso bands. The variety of birdlife that you could almost lean out and touch whilst sitting drinking in the roadside cafés was truly amazing. It was an ornithologist's paradise. The coastline on both the Atlantic and Caribbean sides of the island offered something for everybody, from wild rocky tree-lined outcrops to long sandy beaches and bays. Our own beach at the Grafton Resort, together with others like Stonehaven Bay, were uncrowded and welcoming. How long they remain like that, with Tobago becoming more of a tourist magnet, must be a matter of conjecture. A new hotel and golf complex was being developed between the airport and Scarborough, the capital, and I'm sure that will not be the last as the island becomes more popular. At the moment Tobago provides a snapshot of laid-back life on a Caribbean island where you are just as likely to encounter a leatherback turtle as you are another human being.

Tobago also scored for Les and myself because of the friendliness of the people. Nothing was too much trouble. This was exemplified on our arrival on the island. We had sat next to Shaka Hislop, the Trinidad and Tobago, and at that time West Ham United, goalkeeper, on the flight in. He was returning home to visit his family briefly, prior to a training session, back in Port of Spain, with the national team before two World Cup preliminary games. Having all passed through Immigration Control we were unable to locate our hire car that had been pre-booked. Although his own transport was ready and waiting to whisk him off home for his whistle-stop visit he was aware of our predicament and immediately contacted the hire company on his mobile and remained with us until our transport arrived, before wishing us a pleasant stay on the island. He didn't have to do that but his friendliness and courtesy ensured our all too short stay on Tobago got off to a fine start. Many international professional football stars have gained a stereotypical reputation for being aloof and self-obsessed. He was the exact opposite. Friendly, polite and willing to help out two strangers who were visiting his home island for the first time. A fine role model for any aspiring young sportsman.

Having experienced the hustle and bustle of Port of Spain against the relaxing and olde world charm of Tobago I was eagerly anticipating their comparison with Grand Cayman. Although they are all in the

Caribbean and generically considered to be the West Indies they are some one thousand miles apart on a north-west/south-east axis. On a geographical scale, it would be the equivalent, perhaps, distance-wise, to comparing London with Bucharest. As capital cities, they might have some similarities but they would, inevitably, have enormous differences.

So there was I about to embark on another adventure with some preconceived notions of where I was going but not really knowing quite what to expect. Naive I may be but I've always found this mindset makes travelling much more interesting, certainly less boring, and normally ensures that time does not pass too slowly. I'm not sure that I agree totally with Robert Louis Stevenson's 'to travel hopefully is a better thing than to arrive' but it is a fine philosophy and I always try to look upon the journey as part of the holiday. In that respect, I guess that I am different to many of the passengers who now have to tolerate the delays and inadequate facilities at many major airports. For some strange reason I seem to have developed an immunity to the frustration and angst that afflict so many as they negotiate their passage through the organised chaos of airport terminals. I can totally understand the irritation of so many passengers with the overcrowded and cramped conditions they have to endure at many airports.

Exactly why, I don't know, but my tolerance levels in these situations seem much higher than usual. I'm not always the most patient of people but travel, particularly when on holiday, seems to bring out the best in me. It is almost the exact opposite of my mental state when I'm subjected to a shopping expedition, where I'm far more likely to lose any self-control and at which I've become adept at escaping at the earliest opportunity. Put me in a similar crowded situation in a supermarket where the queues are endless and the staff can be less than helpful and I know that I become just as exasperated and I find it impossible to hide my feelings, normally venting my spleen at whichever unfortunate assistant happens to be within earshot. I am yet another of those individuals who, in that particular environment, can be identified as a sufferer of irritable male syndrome. Unfortunately, experience has taught me that this affliction is extremely contagious and unless controlled very quickly is likely to spread to the female variety of the species who, due to a lack of understanding, will undergo a disproportionate mood swing that will impact upon her partner for at least the rest of the day and in some situations even longer.

I am well aware that I can be impatient, intolerant and have even been described, I thought a little unfairly at the time, as irascible. At an airport though, even passing by their shopping malls, I am able to let it all roll over me and I become calmness personified. I have to admit that I have been lucky. I've had my share of delays; the worst was on a foggy night in Hanover when a group of colleagues and I had to spend a night in a local hotel and sample some of the local beer. It was no great hardship and we arrived home at Saturday lunchtime instead of Friday night. Other than that and a five-hour delay in Newark, New Jersey, again due to fog, the worst I've suffered is the odd hour or two on internal or short-haul flights into Europe.

Research suggests that struggling through Heathrow is more stressful than being mugged at knifepoint and could even prove fatal. I'm not sure that I agree with the comparison and I would certainly prefer to navigate my way through the concourse and walkways of any airport than face a blade-wielding mugger. The experiment indicated that four passengers fitted with heart monitors experienced an immediate increase in their heart rate as soon as they entered the airport. At times during the four hours' wait to board; their aircraft, their heart rates soared to almost four times healthy levels, at one stage some recording two hundred beats a minute. Such a condition, known as tachycardia, can prove fatal.

I can understand the frustration and anger that many suffer as their trip turns into a nightmare experience with queues and delays that eat into holidays or lead to the postponement of important business meetings and possible loss of contracts and jobs.

This isn't helped by a lack of adequate seating which results in many lounging on the floor with their heads resting on any piece of luggage available. Many airports were not built to cope with today's passenger numbers and are buckling under the strain. Add to that the government's security response to the terrorist threat and delays have become endemic.

It isn't just the interminable shuffling through the zigzag posts and tape in order to reach the check-in desks. This is followed by immigration or border control and then the never-ending security cordon. Having safely, if slowly, negotiated all these hurdles you still have to throw the equivalent of a double six to pass Go. The luck of the dice is now baggage handling which was already working at capacity. The government's decision to confine passengers to one small piece of hand luggage has resulted in confusion for passengers and the mass of luggage that people used to carry into the cabin themselves has now been transferred into the cargo holds. This has resulted in baggage handling now working on the point of collapse. Arriving at your destination with your luggage has become more of a lottery then ever. It is hardly surprising that many regular passengers believe that a number of our airports are in terminal decline. Whilst the approach to public safety is understandable, there is a need to balance that against what is obviously going to be a long-term problem. The terrorist threat is likely to be with us for years to come and with the anticipated increase in passenger traffic, unless there is a different approach, there is a danger of our airports grinding to a halt. In many ways that would at least be a propaganda victory for the terrorists. There perhaps needs to be a three-pronged approach to ease the current log-jam. Improved identification techniques to fast-track the millions of genuine passengers through terminals, allied to increased staffing to speed up the physical searches that will still be necessary for those unwilling to undergo body scanning technology and those randomly selected for the comprehensive luggage and personal search. Add to that a review of the current hand luggage restrictions that would see passengers being able to sensibly increase their one small piece of hand luggage and this might go some way to relieving the present burden on passengers. This might also ease the stress levels and temper tantrums on both passengers and staff.

For whatever reason I have still retained that primary-schoolboyish excitement and anticipation as I approach any holiday, particularly when I'm heading somewhere new, and this was no exception as I arrived at Heathrow on that sunny July morning. Even though I knew I had to endure the now compulsory three-hour wait at the airport whilst ensuring that the security and baggage checks were satisfactorily and safely completed. I suppose in this respect I'm lucky, as I'm one of those strange characters who find airports intriguing and people-watching fascinating. I tend to look upon this as the first chapter in a new adventure and can be quite calm and laid back and have not yet allowed delays to upset me. It is possible to observe all forms of human life passing through a terminal building, the good, the bad and the ugly. Families squabbling, frazzled parents, fractious children, babies crying, frustrated business travellers, passengers searching for lost passports, tickets or luggage, other travellers just plain lost. Taxi drivers waiting impatiently for their fares with names written, scribbled or sometimes printed smartly on a variety of different pieces of coloured cardboard. The more professional chauffeurs carrying laminated and labelled A4-sized business cards to assist in identifying their human cargo. Grannies struggling with overloaded suitcases, students with bulging backpacks that they try to pass off as normal hand luggage, husbands buying last-minute duty free presents for their wives or girlfriends, indispensable businessmen (you know, the sort you see in graveyards) rushing to catch a late flight because they're always too busy to be on time, and beleaguered ground staff trying to be pleasant to their multitude of customers who are always right. Plus, of course, the small army of society's twenty-four-hour shiftworkers who keep our airports running with their labours. Cleaning, fetching, carrying and being general dogsbodies to the numerous harassed supervisors who seem to need six jobs completed at once and most of them done yesterday. Not to mention the anoraks who demand answers to the most stupid questions. Perhaps there should be an 'Idiots' Board' displayed with answers to the most frequently asked questions. Such a solution might make passage through the airport more efficient and assist the equilibrium of everybody passing through and those working there.

None of this can equal the stress and tension on the faces of those who have a pathological fear of flying but just accept, in today's world, this mode of transport as a necessary evil. It's almost possible to detect the rise in their blood pressure as they wait in the snaking lanes to reach the check-in or security desks. Once through these obstacles and having progressed to 'Airside' even if they manage to locate a vacant seat, you will rarely find them sitting down. Their anxiety will tend to make them hyperactive, checking and rechecking their passports and boarding passes, fidgeting with the straps and clasps on their hand luggage, some popping pills prescribed by their doctors to calm them during the ordeal of the journey and others taking to drink in the vain hope it will ease their fears. Others will be constantly on the move, walking up and down the aisles of the terminal building, anything to take their minds off the fate that awaits them. I've often wondered, with such large numbers frightened of flying, quite why airport authorities decided to call their buildings 'terminals'? Why not just leave it as 'airport'? I know it's just a word but the terminology can make a difference and it might just ease some of the stress.

It is also possible to see that stress transferred to their travelling companions. These unfortunate individuals are doing their unsuccessful best to ease any fears, in addition to coping with their own travel arrangements, whilst attempting to calm the nerves of their anxious partners. You only have to look at them to see that they have been treading on eggshells for anything between the past twenty-four hours and the last week. Is it any surprise that by the time they reach the boarding gate tempers can become a little frayed around the edges and they might just appear the teeniest bit tetchy?

I can speak with some degree of expertise on this type of situation. My wife, Lesley, unfortunately has a morbid fear of flying. Mere mention of the idea has a marked effect upon her so that any response can appear to others to be irrational. Although we all tried to persuade her to come to the wedding, it was not possible to overcome her fears. This is not something that you can force somebody to do. She has flown in the past but really had to steel herself to board the plane. Twice we have flown to the United States together, the last occasion to New York with Virgin Atlantic, back in December 1995. Whereas the outward leg of the journey was in brilliant sunny weather and as smooth as could possibly be, even I have to admit that the return flight was the most turbulent that I have ever experienced on a Jumbo 747.

It did not get off to a great start as we were delayed for over four hours at Newark which is never a good omen for the nervous flyer, allowing them more time to sit and stew over all the possible disasters that could befall them during the flight. A number of other flights were cancelled so that our plane did not have one spare seat, which added to the usual combination of apprehensive passengers together with a number of impatient businessmen who were berating the crew about the delay. In all, a volatile mix which only added to the anxiety of the aviophobics on board. As we took off there was a distinct smell of burning rubber within the cabin and although nobody said a word, it was possible to see numerous noses twitching uncomfortably. Having been in the air for a few minutes there followed an announcement over the tannoy inform-ing those passengers who had been concerned about the smell that there was no need to worry as we had merely ingested the smell of the tyres of a plane landing on a parallel runway as we took off. Apparently a not unusual phenomenon at airports with adjoining runways, although I personally had not experienced it previously. I'm not sure that I believed it but it did appear to put minds at rest. The flight proceeded comfort-ably for about an hour until the captain came back on the loudspeaker to announce that we would be hitting some difficult weather conditions and it was not possible to avoid it. He told us that he would inform us again as we closed on the storm and that was immediately followed by the flashing 'Seat Belt' warnings. Within ten minutes the next advice over the public address system was simply, 'All crew to jump seats, all crew to jump seats.' I had been on the odd flight in the past that had been a bit bumpy but had never before experienced this sort of alert and it did cause some alarm even amongst accomplished travellers. My approach had always been if the crew are going about their normal tasks serving food and drinks then we didn't have anything to worry about. This was differ-ent. The stewardesses followed instructions immediately, talking to and calming passengers as they did so. The aircraft was soon being buffeted by very strong winds and the turbulence was the worst that I have ever encountered. Lesley was by now gripping my left wrist so tightly that the blood supply to my left hand was fast being cut off and I could see other couples in similar situations. Strangely the young teenager to her left was sleeping soundly, oblivious to the distress that was spreading through the plane. As from time to time we dropped seemingly hundreds of feet and the whole airframe appeared to be vibrating as it coped with the intensity of the storm it was possible to hear a number of screams accompanying each descent with a considerable proportion of passengers crying and hugging each other. I genuinely cannot remember how long it lasted. Looking at my watch was the last thing on my mind. I would estimate that it must have been about thirty to forty minutes although it seemed a lot longer. As the aircraft stabilised and the crew left their safety seats you could almost hear a collective sigh of relief.

As a degree of calmness gradually returned and the flight became much smoother the crew went out of their way to reassure everybody and took extra time and attention with those who had suffered the most. This included Lesley. Their customer care was first class. They could not have been more considerate or caring, and a number of passengers who had been crying as we were being buffeted in the airstreams were allowed on to the flight deck once we had left the stormy weather way behind us. I joined Lesley for this visit and the Captain and First Officer exuded a calm authority that soothed everybody's nerves, allowing them to return to their seats if not full of confidence then at least believing they would get us back to Heathrow in one piece. As they said themselves they also had wives and families to return to and with Christmas a matter of a couple of weeks away would not have been flying if they considered it unsafe. If all those reluctant fliers could have spent some time in the cockpit with these two guys then many more of them would be likely to board a plane without the worry lines etched on their faces and their companions could relax a little and enjoy the flight.

The reality is that crossing the Atlantic in December can be a bit bumpy from time to time. Although we were promised and were given one of the smoothest landings I've ever known, from that day I've not got Lesley back on a plane. For one brief moment, I did think that she might consider the trip to the Cayman Islands but once she realised that they were returning to Suffolk for a second UK reception then I knew that the opportunity had passed. To those who are able to fly without a second thought it can be difficult to understand what to them is an illogical but for others an overwhelming and debilitating fear. I am able to empathise to an extent although I remain a fairly relaxed and laid-back air passenger.

I realised some years ago that I don't like heights. I was involved in a policing operation which necessitated another officer and I having to climb to the top of a floodlight pylon with a video camera to film and record the surrounding area. This was back in the days when the camera and recorder were transported separately and were much heavier and far more bulky than today's hi-tech equipment. Having scaled the metal ladder fixed to the outside of the tower we reached the top where I made the stupid mistake of looking down. I was rendered totally useless and my sergeant colleague Ken, who actually seemed to be enjoying the experience, had to carry out the filming, panning and zooming to scan and capture the whole area on tape. Meanwhile my legs had turned to jelly and I was now grasping the rail around the lighting platform with a vice-like grip that was not going to be easily moved. Whilst I was crouched there, holding on for dear life, I knew I could survive and would not fall. It was the thought of having to return back down the metal ladder on the outside of the gantry that I was not sure I could manage. Ken had to use all of his considerable powers of persuasion to get me back onto the ladder to cope with the descent. Eventually, step by careful step, I reached terra firma and breathed a huge sigh of relief. This was my first experience of what is popularly known as 'vertigo' but is more accurately described as acrophobia or a fear of heights. It was not pleasant and not something that I wished to repeat. How my sweaty palms had held on so tightly I will never know. Fortunately, for the remainder of my career, I was never required to go near another floodlight pylon or at least climb one.

Now I know that is not the same as flying but I'm not sure anybody could force me into climbing any sort of metal tower ever again. Even watching crane drivers climb up to their glass-surrounded cabins on the jib makes the hairs on my neck stand on end, so I can appreciate to a small extent what it is like to have a fear of something that others consider natural. Who knows, one day I might be able to persuade Lesley to get back on a plane and take to the air but to date all ideas and efforts have failed miserably.

As we arrived in the parking lane near Terminal 4, well prepared to face the Heathrow hassle that bright July morning, unusually for me I could easily have been mistaken, albeit briefly, for another stressed and troubled passenger. Having removed my holdall and suitcase from the boot of the car I leaned onto the back seat to put on my jacket. (Didn't wear it once whilst on holiday and on reflection I don't know why I bothered to take it.) On checking the inside pocket my heart missed a beat as I realised my passport and travellers cheques were missing. I was convinced I had put them in that pocket before leaving home. A swift search of every other pocket and the holdall revealed nothing. Had I actually forgotten them and left them on the dining room table? I was beginning to feel a little hot under the collar, which you will gather happened more than once on this trip! Was there time to travel home, retrieve them, and return in time to catch the flight? Would the authorities allow me to do this? What would the traffic be like on the M25 as we were now fast approaching rush hour, which in M25 terms has been known to last all day. Would there be a vacant seat on tomorrow's flight if I didn't get back in time? Could I contact home and get somebody to rush them to the airport? It's amazing just how much detail can flash through your mind in a matter of seconds when you are caught in this sort of situation.

Les saw the obvious alarm on my face and pointed into the gutter underneath the nearside of the car. They were lying precariously perched across the top of a storm drain, one passport and one plain brown envelope containing enough US Dollar travellers cheques to keep me afloat for the next fortnight, having slid out of my jacket as I removed it from the car.

Fortunately neither had slipped between the gratings to a watery grave in a damp and dirty gully. I quickly retrieved them, before we had need of assistance from a sludge gulper, and breathed a very heavy sigh of relief. Was this to be a good omen for the holiday? What my search did reveal, or on this occasion didn't, was the key to the padlock on my suitcase. In my haste, I had actually left this at home. This minor mishap might mean I would need to find a pair of bolt croppers on arrival at the hotel or alternatively if Customs wished to search the suitcase they would do the job for me. For once I wouldn't object to being delayed in the Customs Hall as I'm sure they wouldn't believe that I had forgotten the key and such an excuse would almost certainly ensure that they would want to search my suitcase.

With all of this going on around me at least I was now more relaxed and relieved having renewed my acquaintance with both identification and solvency but the experience helped me understand why television companies have found their fly-on-the-wall airport documentaries to be so successful. They have a ready-made human interest story every day encompassing all emotions imaginable. Add this to the spicy tabloid mix of all manner of celebrities who pass through airports at all hours of the day and night; and they are also relatively inexpensive television. They've even produced a film, starring Tom Hanks and Catherine Zeta Jones, about life in an airport terminal building, although I've yet to see it so cannot make any comparison with reality.

Having arrived much earlier than anticipated, thanks to the unusually empty M25, I found that the flight gate was not yet displayed on the departures monitor. I therefore took the opportunity to grab a quick carton of piping hot coffee for my early morning injection of caffeine and then spent the next hour watching the world pass by, whilst hoping Les had a similarly uneventful return journey around London's orbital car park. I was equally certain that he would find the return leg much more congested.

Heathrow at that time of the morning is reminiscent of a large town coming to life. People arriving for work, not yet fully awake whilst rubbing the sleep from their eyes, some like myself grabbing a quick coffee to kick-start the body into action whilst others had time for a more substantial breakfast. Shops opening for the day as shutters were wound up and lights turned on to parade a wide variety of goods that adorned their window displays in the hope of enticing the thousands of transient residents through their doors. Heathrow currently handles some sixty-seven million passengers a year through its now dated arrival and departure lounges that were designed to cope with forty-five million. In daily terms these millions transpose into about two hundred and ten thousand passengers, thirteen hundred flights and fifty thousand vehicles arriving and departing the world's busiest international airport.

Terminal 5 has now opened and is fully operational, catering for British Airways short and long haul flights to and from the capital; it should, in theory, ease the burden on travellers and staff alike. With room enough for fifty football pitches under the largest single-span roof in the country, it has capacity to cater for at least thirty million of those passengers, allowing the redevelopment and refurbishment of the rest of Heathrow. With more than thirty planes landing each hour, each two and a half miles and ninety seconds apart, and a similar number leaving on a parallel runway, the airport is working at close to its maximum volume. At that operating level any number of minor mishaps can cause disproportionate chaos. Adverse weather conditions, industrial action or inaction, a security threat or even clouds of volcanic ash can cause delays that can have a knock-on effect into the following day and also cause disruption at other international airports as planes miss their allotted slots and end up in the wrong place at the wrong time. The disorder and confusion experienced in its early weeks, with computer software problems, the failure of the baggage handling system and lack of knowledge and training of staff led to massive cancellations and delays. I only hope that those early 'teething problems', and I think I'm being generous in describing them as such, will have been ironed out by the time I need to use Terminal 5.

When you add together the increasing demand for air travel together with the multitude of problems that can create disruption it is hardly surprising that the airport operators BAA wish to build another runway at Heathrow. But, in company with a growing band, I have a genuine empathy with the publicity-conscious and media-wise environmental lobby who are campaigning against such further development. We even try, in our small way, by composting garden waste and sorting glass, paper, cardboard, tins, plastic bottles and silver paper into an assortment of different coloured containers for collection and recycling. However, the great inconsistency is the increasing proportion of the public who are clamouring to find a seat on a plane whether it be for business or pleasure reasons whilst at the same time acknowledging the need to reduce their carbon footprints. There is no doubt that the cheaper 'no frills' airlines have added to the problem in the UK but they have also brought some much needed competition to the market and enabled today's families almost unlimited travel into continental Europe that previous generations could only dream about.

It is vital that the debate about the environmental issues continues but whilst there are two wildly opposing camps both relying upon different analysts speculating as to the potential increase in airline emissions and the proportion of the country's overall discharge of greenhouse gases for which they are responsible they are likely to keep an army of lawyers occupied at public inquiries for the foreseeable future. In the short term governments are likely to impose more green taxes which may discourage a small number from flying but such is the thirst for this form of transport the effect, in common with vehicle excise duty and fuel tax, will be minimal. Meanwhile, Heathrow's reputation continues to go downhill and as the gateway to the capital city can only be creating a poor impression on the businessmen and tourists who arrive daily to queues and hassle just to gain entry to the country. That can only be bad for both London and the country as a whole so the dilemma for the government is to find a solution that will appease both parties. I suspect the result will be a mixture of fudge and compromise but that is what governments are best at in those circumstances.

Whilst I do have an interest in the global warming debate and from time to time discuss it with friends and colleagues I must admit that nothing was further from my mind as I sat sipping my coffee watching passengers and staff scurry to and fro across the concourse as they made their way to the multitude of destinations that awaited them. My mind was firmly fixed on my forthcoming holiday, wondering just what Grand Cayman had in store for me, and I suspect that is an attitude I have in common with numerous others as they transit airports in similar situations.

Eventually British Airways 09.50 flight to Grand Cayman found its way onto the bottom of a lengthy list of worldwide departures. I learned for the first time that we were flying via Nassau, Bahamas. This was not a destination I had ever visited or, until that moment, had even anticipated visiting. Whilst for some, learning of this stop for the first time, this may have been viewed as an unnecessary delay, for me it became an additional item of interest to break up what was likely to be a long and boring journey. I knew I was only likely to see the runway, taxiways, aircraft apron and the terminal building at close quarters with, perhaps, an aerial glimpse of the islands as we descended and took off. No matter, I was now on holiday. Why rush?

I made my way towards the check in desk to meet up with the gang that were to travel together to Grand Cayman for Melanie and David's wedding on the following Saturday.

I have known Melanie since she was a baby and am considered to be a sort of honorary godfather (whatever that may be) to her and her younger sister Carrie. In the interests of accuracy my wife Lesley is Carrie's godmother. As we have known both sisters all their lives we are firm family friends and have attended significant birthday parties and family celebrations. In fact, Lesley and Jan lived less than a hundred yards apart, in the same street, as schoolchildren, and travelled to London together on the train when they both worked in the City as teenagers. Coincidentally I also got to know Jan's father Les very well in my early days as a policeman. He was an ambulanceman and we would regularly be working the same shifts together. The police and ambulance stations were next door to each other so that in addition to coming into contact at the scenes of serious accidents and the like we also got together for the odd cup of tea.

We first met, before I joined the job, when he and his partner Jim stretchered me from the football pitch and conveyed me to hospital with a fractured tibia and fibula. In his off-duty hours Jim also doubled as the town's chimney sweep and although they didn't receive the extensive medical training or gain the qualifications of today's modern paramedics and technicians they were real old-fashioned professionals at their job with a sound knowledge of first aid and, importantly, had the ability to provide their victims with reassurance and confidence that everything would be all right. They possessed the gift of making people laugh even in the most difficult of situations.

Mel is a schoolteacher and had left England four years earlier to commence a contract teaching Business Studies in the Cayman Islands. David is a local Royal Cayman Islands Police officer, whom I met for the first time a year earlier on his initial visit with Mel to England. Having retired recently after serving thirty-one years as a policeman I had a lot in common with him, although he was much quieter than me and obviously much younger. We had got on well together and I was looking forward to meeting him again on his own patch.

At that stage there was little point in me joining the queue for flight BA253 as Carrie had my tickets. In fact she had everybody's tickets. She had made all the arrangements for us to travel, negotiated discounts, booked the holiday, reserved the hotel apartments and even organised the hire vehicle. Although that was to prove more interesting than we could have envisaged as we arrived at Heathrow that first morning. Additionally she had also taken care of a number of the wedding details, which we learned would include a surprise suite at the Hyatt Regency for the bride and groom on their wedding night, before they left for their honeymoon in Hawaii the following morning.

All I had to do was turn up at the airport on time and go with the flow. This was another big attraction for me. No hassle, no details, no route planning, no decisions, just enjoy the holiday. Later in the week we joked that Carrie should set up her own business as a wedding co-ordinator. If ever she gets fed up with her present job I'm sure she could turn her natural talents to a successful and profit-making venture. As I watched the queue start to grow in that time-honoured Disney-style air travel concertina formation I firstly bumped into Ted, Melanie's father, who was with his wife Sue and step-daughter Vicky, all of whom had like me travelled from Essex that morning. They were coming for the first week whilst the remainder of us were staying on for a fortnight in the sun.

Ted had been an old sparring partner of mine both on the badminton court and at the cribbage board many years ago. He and Mel's mother, Jan, had been divorced for some years and I had only seen him once in the intervening period, at an eighteenth birthday party which he had attended alone. Ted introduced me to Sue and Vicky and whilst we were all chatting, with Ted and me catching up on what we had both been up to, I learned of their recent disaster. A week earlier their home had been burnt out following an electrical fault in a power shower. At the time, nobody had been at home, so the fire had been able to catch hold throughout the house. The result being that the combination of fire, smoke and water had destroyed or ruined everything in the home and it was unlikely that they would be back there in less than six months. All their possessions were either lost or damaged. They literally had what they stood in. They were currently staying at a hotel whilst waiting for their insurance company to find them some temporary rented accommodation. Not exactly an ideal preparation for a daughter's wedding. Bearing all this in mind, they were in remarkably good spirits when I met them. I'm not sure I would have been as chirpy in the same circumstances but as Sue said, "We've used up all our tears" and perhaps the opportunity of a week in the Caribbean with a wedding to look forward to was just what the doctor ordered.

Some considerable time later, I was given the opportunity to discover just what they had endured when my own family were placed in a similar situation. My mother-in-law's home was badly damaged in a fire that had originally started in the adjoining bungalow. This is something that you always think happens to other people and not to your own family. She is an eighty-eight-year-old widow and she moved there with her husband when it was built over fifty years ago. It was much more than a semi-detached bungalow; it was her own little home that she had saved and paid for and kept clean, neat and tidy so that the decorations and possessions represented her character and personality. It was her little haven where she would cook her traditional cakes and entertain her many friends who lived locally. The impact upon her was quite devastating. Initially, the wait whilst the surveyors and building inspectors decided whether it needed to be demolished and then, when the decision was made that the shell and skeleton could be saved, the long wait for the new roof to be in place before the builders could start on the restoration inside. She stayed with us until the insurers could find suitable alternative accommodation on a short-term let for six months. It then becomes a matter of arranging to beg, borrow or hire enough furniture and household implements so that you can survive in a strange environment for the foreseeable future. Simple things, like a toothbrush or a kettle for a cup of tea, just aren't there. Whilst family and friends might come up trumps and the insurance company might respond speedily and effectively to requests, with the loss adjusters doing everything they can to ease you through the trauma, it is difficult to put into words the impact such a disaster can have on an individual. The emotions run very raw and range over frustration, depression, anger, helplessness and a feeling that there isn't any light at the end of the tunnel. Reactions aren't necessarily logical and minor delays seem to become major problems that build into a conspiracy to prevent you returning to your own home, even when they are not. For any family to suffer the misfortune of losing their home it is heartbreaking so although I sympathised with Sue, Ted and Vicky I just wasn't able to appreciate exactly what they had been through. On reflection I became full of admiration for them turning up in the way they did and not letting their troubles have any bearing on the wedding or any of the party about to embark on their trip across the Atlantic.

As we stood and talked on the concourse that morning I'm sure we were all wondering how we would gel as a group over the next week. I just had a feeling that there was, understandably, some apprehension on all sides but during the holiday it never manifested itself and if anybody was worried they need not have been. Later in the holiday I quietly congratulated each one of them on their attitude and approach to each other throughout that week, before Ted, Sue and Vicky had to return to England as citizens with no fixed abode. It cannot have been easy and I'm well aware of other wedding parties that have either been quite acrimonious, with both sides trying to score points, or where one party doesn't turn up at all. They say blood is thicker than water but some family disagreements and splits can have far-reaching repercussions.

On this occasion everybody was determined that nothing would occur to spoil Mel and David's wedding, which, as we have seen, went swimmingly. This was not just the ceremony itself but also the events leading up to the day and the following few days when as a gang we were left to our own devices. Although as individuals we were vastly different in ages, personalities, likes and dislikes, fortunately we all blended as a group. This was probably assisted by the informal and certainly unwritten agreement that although we all ate together each evening we did our own thing during the day. Sometimes this would be as a crowd, or in smaller groups, sometimes alone. This approach suited all. If you wanted to swim, read, walk, sleep, sunbathe, sit in the shade, shop, play golf or watch television you did so without feeling you had to do something you were uncomfortable with just to remain part of the group. Is this an essential ingredient of any successful family holiday?

An example was the contrasting tastes in music between the different generations. With personal Walkmans this was never a problem other than when we travelled together in the minibus with the radio on. The easy resolution was whoever drove selected the radio channel. For the most part they were fairly short journeys so it was easy to tolerate others' preferences even if one didn't always appreciate the finer points of their music. What did become noticeable was the decrease in volume when the 'Wrinklies' were driving. The other binding feature was a sense of humour, fun and mischief that didn't go away throughout the whole fortnight. There became almost an expectation that somebody would be thrown into the pool on a daily basis. In fact I think some were positively disappointed on the days it didn't happen.

Back at Heathrow it didn't take too long for the remainder of this section of the party to arrive. They had left home even earlier than I, having been taxied down the M11 from the East Anglian countryside of Bury St Edmunds.

Jan, Melanie's mother, Carrie her sister, who was to be a bridesmaid, and Caroline and Danielle, two old friends from school in Bury, still lived close together in the town and have always remained good friends.

Caroline was making a remarkable amount of noise struggling with her suitcase, that seemed to be bulging at the seams, and she was destined to become the extrovert of the team. Danielle appeared more reserved but, as we learned towards the end of the holiday, is a well practised mimic, particularly of farmyard animals.

We slowly worked our way towards the head of the queue, where I now kept a firm grip on my passport and travellers cheques. We were being processed smartly and efficiently until I placed my suitcase on the baggage belt. It shuddered to a halt, as a uniformed official behind the desk alternately transferred his gaze between me standing in front of him, my luggage on the scales and the computer screen blinking out its information.

"What's the problem?" I asked, smiling nervously.

"Your weight," said the check-in clerk. I was aware that I was carrying a little too much around my middle and looked down past my paunch but I could still see my feet. I was pleased to see that my midriff hadn't grown further overnight without warning.

"Not you," said the assistant who fortunately was now also smiling broadly, "your case. But don't worry, you're not over the limit, it's just to inform the handlers who have to lift it, it's on the heavy side."

Much to my amazement they then attached an additional 'Heavy' label to it. I basically only had shorts, tee-shirts, swimming trunks, washing and shaving kit plus two pairs of trousers, one of which I was wearing. In common with all of the party I was also transporting some table decorations, four candles (which in true Two Ronnies fashion became 'fork handles' for the remainder of the holiday) but no more than anybody else.

This suddenly brought back memories of an unfortunate experience I had undergone back in the spring. Some three months previously I had been declared clinically obese by my doctor following a cat bite during a trip to France. We had been staying in a gite in Brittany, and the resident cat had seemed friendly enough for the first few days. One evening, towards the end of the holiday, whilst sitting on the patio and drinking a glass of wine before our evening meal I was peacefully minding my own business when suddenly, and for no apparent reason, this French ball of fur took a liking to my right calf muscle and sank in a couple of molars. Needless to say the remainder of the assembled company thought this was hilarious and couldn't understand why I was making a fuss. From that day on the French Felix became known as Fang. Although you could detect two small puncture marks it didn't really hurt at the time. However, back home the following week, I had acquired a badly infected, swollen and rather painful leg. My GP put me on a course of antibiotics and prescribed some ointment to massage the infected part daily. As she hadn't seen me for some time, and I hope the next visit is delayed just as long, she decided to carry out a swift medical. They say prevention is better than cure so I readily agreed. The examination progressed smoothly enough until she placed me on the scales. All I could hear was some tutting from below and behind my left ear. I turned around to see her examining a sheet of paper that appeared to be some sort of graph. Physically she is a diminutive figure and whilst standing on the scales I seemed to tower over her but there was no doubt who was in command of the situation. What she lacked in inches she made up for in spirit and confidence. I decided that she probably didn't lose many arguments.

"You're obese," she declared, fixing me with a steady and unblinking stare. My doctor was obviously not one to mince her words and being presented with such information wasn't so much egregiously insulting as surprising and disappointing bearing in mind the amount of jogging I subject myself to in an effort to remain fit. Obviously my exercise regime was to no avail or not strenuous enough. Alternatively, it was just possible that my liking for food and drink was putting on more calories than I was ever going to burn off. I was well aware that I was overweight and had been for as long as I could remember but I had never considered myself to be grossly overweight as was now being indicated by the short trim figure who had returned to her desk to ensure this latest revelation was added to my medical notes.

"Are you sure?" said I. She could obviously sense I was somewhat taken aback.

"Absolutely, according to my chart your body mass index indicates that you are clinically obese," she stated with some certainty. She showed me and I couldn't deny that I was just the wrong side of the oblique line that slanted upwards toward the top right hand corner of her graph. I don't know who invented this body mass index chart but I would hazard a guess they were a group of medics or dieticians who were stick thin. I've previously been described as chunky or stocky and in my blissful ignorance have always made the excuse of heavy bones or muscular density to explain away any weight issue. This would not wash on this occasion and I had now been medically and officially designated as obese. In other words, fat.

"But it's only marginal," I said, looking down at this chart, more in hope than expectation.

"The chart is accurate, it doesn't lie and you're obese," she insisted, stabbing her finger at the point on the scale to prove her point. I needed to try a different tack in an effort to persuade her that I really was a borderline case.

I stepped off the weighing machine, eyeing it with some distrust and responded, "No, the problem is with my legs."

She eyed me rather quizzically and replied, "No, no, no, I've sorted out your leg, that will take about a week to respond to treatment, look the chart says you're obese."

I dare not say what I was thinking of her damned chart, this medical was now becoming serious, so I thought I might add a little wit to lighten up the atmosphere in the surgery. "No, my legs are too short, they always have been," was my swift riposte.

I'm sure she really didn't appreciate my attempt at humour as she looked back at her chart to confirm her diagnosis. At that moment I knew I wasn't going to change her mind. She took her job seriously and wasn't going to be messed around by a cheeky, fat, middle-aged patient who obviously ate and drank too much for his own good. One of us was going to get their money's worth out of this ad hoc medical and at that moment in time it certainly wasn't me. I do appreciate just how busy doctors can be and consequently try not to bother them too much. Now I knew why. This visit had been a necessity due to my swollen and painful leg and look where it had landed me. Although we have three cats at home they have never bitten me. However, on future trips to France you will see me taking a wide berth around all furry feline creatures no matter how cute and cuddly they may appear.

Nonetheless, this doctor's no-nonsense approach must have struck a chord as over the next two months I lost half a stone by eating more sensibly. Whether I could avoid putting it all back on, particularly on holiday, was another matter. I was soon to find out.

Now, three months later, my poor old suitcase had suffered the same indignity, and this time in full public view, of being declared aerodynamically obese. Was somebody picking on me? Did I have a case for unfair discrimination against the manufacturers of scales? Could I argue that my human rights had been infringed as I still counted in old money? Stones and pounds were a currency I understood, as opposed to these metricated or decimalised scales and charts that were now calibrated in kilograms.

I wasn't alone in being declared overweight, or at least my suitcase wasn't. The only other person to attract a 'Heavy' label was Caroline but we learned later that in addition to a wardrobe-load of summer dresses, she had packed ten pairs of shoes plus three of flip-flops, so that she always had a pair to match her bikinis. How can you wear ten pairs of shoes in just fourteen days? She did. I learned later that whilst we were on holiday there had been an ongoing survey that confirmed women pack a lot more than men, yet half their garments remain unworn. A leading psychologist said that over-packing shouldn't be seen as a fault as it demonstrates women's ability to plan for every eventuality. I'm not sure if the psychologist was a man or a woman. The survey discovered that for a two-week break a woman would pack twenty-one pairs of knickers but five pairs would not be worn. They would also pack nine bras and use only five, twenty tops (eight not worn), three evening dresses (one not worn), six pairs of trousers (three not worn), five skirts or pairs of shorts (two not worn), ten pairs of stockings or tights (four not worn), two hats (one not worn) and normally only wear half the pairs of shoes carried onto the plane. Caroline proved them wrong on that count. Almost two thirds of the women surveyed admitted only wearing half the clothes they took with them. Just think of the amount of luggage that could be saved on each flight. The survey concluded that women packed too many items because they had greater foresight than men and an ability to plan for every eventuality. A third of women even admitted packing a waterproof jacket when heading for a sun-kissed beach resort, 'just in case'. This all amounted to packing an extra suitcase of unused outfits. Girls seem to adopt my grandmother's old maxim, 'It's better to be safe than sorry.' In her case she never failed to enquire if one was wearing a clean pair of underpants, 'in case you have an accident', as you left the house. Whilst I'm sure she had the best interests of the family's reputation at heart I'm equally certain that the doctors and nurses in the casualty department of the local hospital would be far too intent on concentrating on your injuries rather than worrying if your drawers were fresh from the laundry. Not that Grandma would ever be convinced that was the case.

For today's modern miss it means taking a waterproof coat when going on a beach holiday in midsummer, together with one or two evening dresses. She will be thinking, 'What if it rains – I'll have to pack for that. What if we're invited to a smart restaurant for dinner – I'll have to pack for that.' Their motto being, 'It's better to pack too much than too little.' The survey also revealed that women tend to plan their packing and start a week in advance of the holiday whereas men are more likely to leave it until the last moment and normally start the day before, with a fair proportion of them leaving it until the very last minute. The exception, of course, are the live-at-home bachelors whose mothers do it all for them. In fairness to the girls the results also indicated that men normally arrived at their destination to find they had forgotten something. The most popular items regularly left at home were cameras, razors, toothbrushes and socks. Although I could not find any mention of suitcase keys in the report, perhaps there was some accuracy in its findings and it was trying to tell me something.

Now I don't know if Caroline was part of the survey but with her ten pairs of shoes and numerous dresses, tops and skirts she certainly would have confirmed the results. The only saving grace was that she isn't one of those girls who pack the first dozen dresses at size eight and the remainder at sizes ten and twelve to allow for over-indulgence on holiday and any consequent increase in weight and waist circumference.

If the survey was restricted to the UK then I'm sure the results were accurate. However, if they had ventured 'Down Under' then I'm convinced their findings may have been very different as we were to learn later in the week, when Diane arrived on the island. The survey obviously wasn't commissioned by a psychologist from the southern hemisphere. We were soon to appreciate that Aussie rules are very different. Quite what practical purpose the survey played I do not know but perhaps that merely reflects me entering the Victor Meldrew stage of my life. There now seem to be a plethora of surveys that only prove an individual or group are able to interpret a quantity of empirical data and reach an academic or theoretical conclusion that is of no use, and of little interest, to the man on the street, other than the individual gaining a master's degree on the back of their research which would then gather dust in the university library for years to come.

For my part I remained aggrieved that I had been picked on once again to join the 'Heavy' mob. I wouldn't have minded but I only had two pairs of shoes plus the ones I stood in. It became my firm intention to avoid any set of scales for the foreseeable future. Silly me, I was forgetting I would need to submit to them again on the return leg in a fortnight. Yes, they would be waiting for me with their 'Heavy' label once again.

Having progressed through the check-in and baggage clerks to obtain our boarding cards we could move towards the departure lounge. A physical examination of tickets, boarding cards and passport photographs enabled us to enter the hand and personal luggage search channel. Hoping that we had removed all sharp and metal objects we then joined a further queue. The security staff were polite but thorough. One of the girls was asked if she was willing to be a guinea pig on a new type of x-ray machine that they were piloting. This was situated in a small cubicle to the side of the main channel, with female security staff scanning a different monitor. Suddenly a further three young ladies were volunteering to 'trial' the new equipment. What is it about women and closets? If one goes they all have to go together. This 'powdering nose' ritual must be something females inherit from their mothers' genes. Why the need to disappear for a confidential committee meeting in the ladies' washroom? I don't doubt that one day a professional student will carry out the necessary research and obtain their doctorate in one of the social sciences by listening in to, timing and analysing these womanly conversations. Needless to say all four of them ended up trying out the latest technology and passed with flying colours. It wasn't possible to see what was going on but from the noise and giggles emanating from this sideshow it obviously wasn't a painful experience and proved to be a quicker process than the conventional skim and search that the rest of the party were subjected to.

This was mainly due to one awkward passenger, immediately in front of me in the queue, who couldn't understand the reason, and was unwilling to remove his shoes. Once it dawned on him that he wouldn't be boarding his plane unless he was willing to submit to the same scrutiny as everybody else he succumbed, albeit reluctantly. The remainder of us eventually completed the conventional metal detector scans so that at last we could join the four girls and all make our way to breakfast.

To hell with my doctor; I went for the full English breakfast, with HP sauce. This was easy to rationalise, I didn't know at that stage what I would have for breakfast for the next two weeks, you're never too sure what the food will be like on the aeroplane, or when you would get it; and finally, I was on holiday.

There then followed the inevitable wait for our flight to be called. This enabled everybody to wander through the different duty free shops to see what bargains could be found. It was reasonable to anticipate that perfume and some drink would be purchased. What I should have foreseen, and didn't, was the amount of new clothes the girls managed to buy in such a short time!

If we had been required to undergo further baggage checks the 'Heavy' labels would have been in much greater demand.

Whilst we were enjoying our enforced retail therapy (well some appeared to be) two other friends, Carl and Fran, were in the same situation on the far side of the airport. They had travelled down with the Suffolk contingent and been dropped off for their flight with American Airlines transiting Miami. We would all meet together again in about fifteen hours' time in Georgetown. Carl and Fran were again long-time friends of the youngsters who together with Carrie and Caroline had all worked together in the local sports centre and swimming pool and were all qualified lifeguards. Not only did I not have to worry about my limited swimming skills but I was also going on holiday with *Baywatch*. Well at least a British edition.

At last, flight BA253 was called and we joined our coach to be taken to the aircraft, a Boeing 767. The flight was fully booked although the vast majority of passengers seemed to be travelling only as far as the Bahamas.

There followed the normal introductions from the flight and cabin crews, compulsory health and safety announcements, life jacket demonstrations with the stewardesses standing in the aisles giving an imitation of an old-fashioned policeman on point duty as they indicated the emergency exits. This was accompanied by a video together with final checks to ensure seat belts were fastened properly before we eventually taxied to the end of the runway some thirty minutes late. We were all in economy class, euphemistically called World Traveller. Jan, Carrie and I were all together in the middle aisle whilst the others were about a dozen rows behind us and already you could detect increasing volumes of noise from the rear compartment.

We took off and, somewhat unusually, headed due east towards London. The majority of flights seem to arrive and depart at Heathrow towards the west; heading in over central London and out towards Windsor, Slough and Maidenhead, due, I believe, to the prevailing winds. Quickly banking to starboard we started our turn that would direct us towards Ireland and the long Atlantic crossing over Bermuda and then initially into Nassau. As the Captain gave us this information it was just possible to detect the more nervous amongst us prick up their ears at the mention of Bermuda. I'm sure I heard the word 'triangle' whispered during a muted conversation from the row in front.

Coffee was served promptly and I settled down to watch the BBC World News video and then started to read the first of the two daily papers I had bought at Heathrow. I've got into this strange habit when flying: I take two newspapers with me, one broadsheet and one tabloid. I suspect that in the not too distant future it will be two tabloids. Although the major stories will be duplicated you can also get a rich mix of articles and usually a fair share of gossip to pass the time. You can also learn things you never knew about the dead from their obituaries, although why I want to read these whilst on a flight I've never quite fathomed. This normally keeps me occupied for the best part of a couple of hours. The two films being shown didn't particularly appeal to me so I spent the remainder of the first leg of the flight reading one of the four books I had brought or trying to grab an hourly leg stretch. With the publicity surrounding deep vein thrombosis, I, and others, were following this sensible precautionary advice. I had also taken a Baby Disprin for the past two days as I had read somewhere that this assists circulation in such circumstances. I unsuccessfully attempted to snatch an occasional doze in my reclining seat. However, this always coincided with visits from the girls in the rear offering a variety of cakes, biscuits or sweets or just wanting to chat. I'm sure this wasn't a coincidence and there was a conspiracy to prevent me catching up on my sleep on this longest leg of the journey.

My one other source of exercise was to visit the lavatory. I have come to the conclusion that whenever I fly there are groups of passengers on board whose bladders work to identical timetables. I never found a queue of less than four whether going fore or aft (or is that only on a boat?) and they always seemed to be the same faces. You could almost time your watches by this two-hourly ritual. We had become a distinctly friendly quintet by the time we were flying over Bermuda.

These visits also gave me the opportunity to chat to the stewardesses who were busily working in the galley. I never cease to be amazed at how much is crammed into a space so small yet ergonomically designed to allow up to three staff to carry out different tasks at any one time. In a curious sort of way they remind me of my grandmother's scullery in a terraced house in London back in the 1950s, where she seemed to spend the majority of her waking hours cooking, washing and even ironing. It was tiny with everything stacked neatly and tidily in cupboards and on shelves all within arm's reach. What did seem to be missing on the plane was the larder in one corner, the copper boiler in the other corner, the wooden wringer by the back door and there certainly wasn't an aluminium bath hanging outside on the fuselage that was brought in on Friday nights and filled with boiling water and Radox crystals before we children were forbidden to leave the dining room whilst our grandparents took their weekly bath. The one other similarity was the length of walk to answer a call of nature. The difference being at my grandparents' house it was an outside trot, facing all the elements, until you reached a brick outhouse that contained a water closet and overhead cistern with the usual length of chain attached to operate the flushing system. Fortunately it was rarely necessary to queue, which was a blessing during the winter months.

On the plane, by the time you reached the front of the queue for the lavatory cubicle you had kept your legs crossed for so long that you could fill a bath the size of my grandparents' without any undue effort. The secret must be to try and time your run for relief at least ten minutes before you think you need to be there, or is this just an affliction that affects men once they reach the age of fifty?

The stewards and stewardesses must gain regular amusement from the pained expressions on travellers' faces as they reach the front of the queue, eagerly and patiently awaiting their turn to gain entry to the comfort break cupboard, only to find that the one person in front of them remains ensconced for much longer than anticipated. Even on this flight, reactions in such circumstances ranged from the first few polite taps on the door to a frenzied shaking of the handle once the crossed legs remedy had started to wear off.

Whilst talking to the crew it was fairly obvious that this was one of their more popular trips, although they were lucky if they were rostered on it more than twice a year. It was apparent that they were unlikely to encounter large groups of young men with the sole aim of drinking the bar dry and for the most part the passengers were polite and undemanding. There could always be the exception to the rule but these seemed to be few and far between. The Cayman Islands are not yet a popular group holiday or travel company destination when compared with the Costas in Spain. Nassau is certainly not a regular stag or hen party venue for a weekend jaunt as some of the Eastern European capitals have now become following the arrival of the cheaper no-frills airlines into the market.

The other big attraction for them on arrival in Nassau is a crew change and the benefit of a two-day break. They then take on the second leg of the next scheduled flight to Grand Cayman and return journey to Nassau where they have another two-day break before a return night flight back to London. This paints a superficial and misleading picture of an attractive and glamorous job with more than its fair share of perks. Having seen just how hard they work on board and what they have to tolerate on some flights it's neither as easy, exciting, romantic nor as fascinating as it may appear on the surface.

Arriving in Nassau it was disappointing to learn that we were not allowed to leave the aircraft. It would have been pleasant to be able to wander around the terminal and get a breath of fresh air. We were on the ground for about an hour and the crew were kind enough to make a pot of fresh tea whilst we were waiting for them to change. We did manage to venture as far as the top of the aircraft steps for an airside view of the terminal building and what hit us immediately was the heat when compared to the temperature we had left behind in England. It was the equivalent of stepping into a sauna. Whilst standing there I was intrigued at the amount of interest the ground staff were taking in me. Realisation dawned; four pretty young ladies accompanied me. Having slowly unloaded the Nassau-bound baggage they seemed reluctant to leave and reunite luggage and owners. This was prolonged when they decided one of the carts had become overloaded which ensured they had to transfer half of the cases onto the next trolley in the line. Whether this was caused by inattention or was deliberate we will never know. However, three very happy young baggage handlers eventually departed to waves and smiles on both sides. Human nature is the same the world over. I don't know if the alighting passengers ever found out why their baggage seemed unnecessarily delayed at a quiet airport with no other inbound flights. I'm equally sure the weight of the suitcases or identifying those with 'Heavy' labels was the last thing on the handlers' minds.

We took off for Grand Cayman with a new crew and not many more than fifty passengers left on board looking forward to what was a very comfortable last seventy-five minutes of the journey. We headed west, over the Bahamas, and as we climbed through the light clouds it was possible to glimpse an aerial view of the archipelago. I hadn't realised there were quite so many of these small islands dotted chainlike along the western fringes of the Atlantic. We continued on a south-westerly bearing flying on across Cuba and the Caribbean Sea towards our destination in the Cayman Islands.

The approach from the north-east into Grand Cayman provides you with a wide-ranging panorama of the island and at the time of our arrival a fine bird's eye view of two huge cruise ships anchored in the harbour just off Georgetown. We were to see many more of these, at close quarters, over the next couple of weeks. In common with some other airports the last few minutes of the flight path into Owen Roberts International Airport can give you the impression that you will be landing in the sea. Should you overshoot the runway then your arrival could be rather damp. Our landing was as smooth as the flight itself. Having left Heathrow a little late we arrived over forty minutes early. Well done British Airways.

The immediate sensation on leaving the aircraft was identical to Nassau. We were hit with a brick wall of heat. One could expect a race to the swimming pool as soon as we arrived at our hotel.

Baggage handling seemed much more efficient than that experienced at our stopover but then there weren't any attractive young female passengers left watching proceedings from the top of the gangway steps. Within ten minutes we were moving forward with suitcases into the Immigration and Customs Halls. Signs were displayed that the Immigration officers were undergoing training but I've been delayed for far longer at other ports of entry where the staff were not trainees. They were polite and friendly and we quickly had our passports stamped and entry cards attached. I reluctantly handed over my passport for examination but kept a beady eye on it until it was safely zipped back into my pocket.

From the air-conditioned terminal, we moved back outside, into the heat, for my first experience of the dampening shirt routine. As the two weeks progressed, I realised that I had not travelled with enough casual shirts. This resulted in a couple of additional trips to the laundry to cater for my regular changes of tops, which amounted to a minimum of three on an average day.

We met up with Mel on the airport concourse. She was more than a little excited and still had a hundred and one things to do before Saturday's wedding. The reunions took some time before our 'Tour Guide' Carrie took charge and ushered us to the 'Tropicana' mini-coach that was to transport us to our hotel. Once again the driver was charming, which was to become a feature of those we met during the holiday, and fortunately the coach was air-conditioned. The trip to the Indies Suites Hotel took about fifteen minutes and we experienced Grand Cayman driving for the first time. Much more was to come once we collected our hired minibus. What was noticeable on this initial journey was the ubiquitous Caribbean taxi bus that I had last seen in Port of Spain. Whilst there certainly weren't as many as I had seen in Trinidad they were just as busy, packed to the gunnels with locals, and darting in and out of the traffic as the drivers spotted any available gap to speed up their journey. We were to see a lot more of these over the next fortnight as they ferried their passengers to and from Georgetown.

Driving along what appeared to be the main coastal road to the west of the island I was able to glimpse Seven Mile Beach for the first time. I learned later in the holiday that it is actually somewhere between five and a half and six miles long depending upon exactly where you start and finish. How it derived its 'Seven Mile' name I do not know but to argue about the odd mile and a half in such surroundings would be pedantic. This long curving shoreline with its wide expanse of sand was white and perfect, fringed with palm trees, and stretched into the distance as far as the eye could see. Beyond the beach was a bright blue sea, shimmering in the late afternoon sun and even from our air-conditioned coach the crystal clear waters looked most inviting. It appeared idyllic. It is said that first impressions are important although they can be misleading. We quickly learned that this one was not misleading.

CHAPTER 3

The 'Caymanian' Right Turn

We found our hotel situated in Foster Drive just off Seven Mile Beach. The neat white two-storey rectangular building with blue roof provided the guest accommodation. The buildings enclosed an open swimming pool that was overlooked by the apartments' internal balconies and patios and surrounded by trimmed grass and shrubs. Indies Suites was one of the more established hotels on the island and the sweeping driveway around a well-tended flowerbed to the canopied entrance to the hotel indicated that this was a well-run establishment. Reception was bright and airy with the décor leaving no doubt in one's mind that they gladly accepted diving enthusiasts. The staff were courteous, obliging and helpful.

Following the formalities of booking in and completing the necessary documentation we were escorted to our rooms. Those of us staying here were occupying four different apartments and I was sharing one with Jan and Carrie, which we found on the top floor. It was light and spacious with one balcony looking down on the already inviting cool blue water of the swimming pool and the entrance lobby and kitchen giving a fine view of the beach to the west. My immediate reaction was that I would feel very comfortable living here for the next fortnight and as proves the case on many occasions initial perceptions tend to be accurate barometers of the situation. We were placed between Ted, Sue and Vicky on the one side and Caroline and Danielle in the other adjoining apartment. Peace and tranquillity to the right of us, noise and chaos to the left of us, but in the midst of such jocund company we already knew we were going to enjoy the next two weeks. We found enough essential provisions in the fridge-freezer to keep us going for the first two or three days. Before we did anything else everybody had dived into their luggage for swimming togs and headed straight for the pool to cool off and relax following our long transatlantic journey. Everybody but me that is. Without a key I couldn't undo the zip on my case let alone dive into it. I was about to return to reception to supply them with my first stupid request of the holiday. Would they have such a thing as a pair of bolt-croppers? Surely they must have had previous guests who were just as forgetful as me. It can't be that unusual to arrive with a padlocked suitcase. Can it? Just as I was about to go Jan said that we should perhaps try all the different keys we had between us. You never know, one might be the same and it would prevent damage to the lock. Anything was worth a try. We inserted Jan's key first, turning it in the lock, which sprung open at the first attempt. It makes one wonder how many different keys the manufacturers of suit-case padlocks use. However, was this a further good omen? Somebody up there was smiling on me at the moment. I was able to join the others in the pool for my first of many relaxing dips in the cool water and I also took the opportunity to chill out with a brief visit to the poolside bar.

By now it was close to six o'clock in the evening. Allowing for the time difference, most of us had been travelling for the past nineteen hours. For me, this also followed a brief and interrupted sleep the previous night.

I'm not sure what it is about my subconscious, and I've met others who suffer similarly, but whenever I know I have to be up very early in the morning I habitually wake up every hour or so to ensure that I don't oversleep. My alarm clock and radio alarm have never let me down but for some unexplained reason a little gremlin in my sleeping brain doesn't trust them. This has always been the same whether it be a pre-dawn departure on holiday, a five am cross-county dash to Stansted Airport, the early morning ferry to France or what used to be the regular early turn shift (six am to two pm) particularly during my first few years' service in the police. It was little wonder that on the old-style conventional shift system at the end of a full week of seven early turns you really would feel like a wet weekend. It was not dissimilar to having jet lag for the three rest days before you switched to night shift. This was particularly prevalent with officers young in service. Early Turn was the only shift where you could have any sort of social life and it inevitably meant burning the candle at both ends and sometimes in the middle as well.

It wasn't unusual to go straight from a night out on the town directly back to the station to start the shift. In common with others I followed this pattern and wanted to spend most of my one weekend off a month in bed. This I rarely achieved so consequently would commence a night shift more fatigued than when I ended it seven nights later. Thank goodness in the twenty-first century we at last have a variety of systems that are being trialled in an effort to enhance the life of shift workers, although I don't believe a perfect system exists to cater for those emergency services staff working 24/7 for 365 days a year. The dilemma of having adequate numbers of staff on duty at times of peak demand balanced with achieving a reasonable family and social life are just not compatible. At least, at long last, the traditional and rigid system of seven early shifts, followed by seven nights and then seven late turns, has been recognised as being unhealthy for the individual and not particularly effective for policing.

Colleagues on shift seemed to fall into two categories. Those like myself who fortunately only occasionally overslept, having turned the alarm off only to drift back to sleep again, or those who were regular oversleepers. The penalty for this misdemeanour normally was to buy a bag of fresh doughnuts from the local bakers for the rest of the shift members at mid-morning tea break. Not particularly healthy eating but the shifts seemed to enjoy them. Perhaps that's why there used to be so many overweight bobbies on shift work, and it was something that I had conveniently forgotten to mention to my doctor. I can only imagine what her likely response would have been had I been foolhardy enough to tell her!

I recollect on one such rare occasion when I overslept, I did learn a lesson the hard way. One cold and bitter January morning the warmth and comfort of my bed induced me back to the land of nod, having switched off my alarm. Fortunately my partner on shift telephoned to re-awaken me from my slumbers. He informed me that our duty sergeant covering from another station was due to meet me at the local railway station for a seven am point. These were the days when personal radios had not long been introduced and mobile phones weren't even a distant dream. We were issued with the original two-piece light blue radio sets. One for receiving radio traffic and the other to send messages. You had to be very careful with the latter as when pressing the transmitting button a telescopic aerial would shoot out so that if you were holding the microphone too close to your mouth it could poke you in the eye or disappear up one nostril. These radios did not always work and consequently were not yet trusted, certainly not by some of the older officers who viewed them as a rather intrusive piece of new-fangled equipment that they could well do without. Police forces, therefore, continued with the long-established and old-fashioned hourly 'points' system of visits to different local telephone kiosks – or in the large city forces the Dr Who Tardis-type police box – for contact, until the radio system became more sophisticated and reliable. You were allocated a daily beat with a different coded letter and number that determined the order in which you visited the telephone kiosks and whether they were to be on the quarter, half, three quarters or actually on the hour. When on a cycle beat some of the points dictated a furious hour's pedalling to arrive on time at the next point, in case the sergeant decided that he would meet with you at that stage of your patrol and sign your pocket book. There was one particular sergeant that you knew with certainty would be there waiting for you, knowing how difficult it would be for you to make it on time. He was more interested in catching out young bobbies than catching criminals. Those days are long since confined to the police history books.

On this particular morning I only had fifteen minutes to spare and this did not allow me time to get to the police station, book on duty, and retrieve all my kit from my locker. My colleague arranged to collect me in the patrol car, bringing my helmet from the top of my locker, and hopefully drop me at the railway station before the sergeant arrived. This allowed me just enough time to throw on a spare summer tunic, which I kept at home, jump into the car for a hurried race against time and be thrown out in front of a group of startled early morning commuters.

The sergeant turned up at about ten past seven and from the heat of his area car wound down the window a few notches to chat to me whilst he grinned and watched me shivering.

"You must be hardy, don't you feel the cold?" he said as we watched the London-bound passengers wrapped in their hats, scarves and over-coats scurrying and skidding along the frost bound pavements to catch their trains to Liverpool Street. He kept me out there for a good ten minutes talking about nothing in particular and everything in general.

At long last he said, "Come on, jump in, let's go for a cuppa. Haven't you learned yet, boy, that a good copper never gets wet and never gets cold?"

I didn't need to be asked twice. In I jumped and started the slow process of thawing out. My teeth took some time to stop chattering but we returned to the nick for a mug of hot tea and a couple of slices of toast, which in those days was a seven o'clock ritual and still is in many stations.

Now, he knew that I had been late for work and I knew that he knew and he knew that I knew that he knew but he didn't utter one word about it until he was due to return to his own station, which was some six miles away.

As he was leaving he turned to me with another broad grin and said, "Oh by the way, you forgot to sign on duty when you arrived at six this morning. don't forget in future will you?"

"No Sarge," said I, as the blood was now beginning to re-circulate towards the extremities of my limbs. With that he disappeared out of the back door and I opened up my locker to enable me to return to my beat, this time properly dressed for the conditions. He was an experienced and old-style sergeant and an ideal role model for young policemen. He had his own approach to discipline that today some might consider unconventional or even harsh but he was scrupulously fair and you always knew exactly where you stood with him. He treated everybody as an individual and earned respect for that style.

Another colleague from the shift that regularly followed us on duty was of the other school. He was a regular late attendee and the doughnut sanction did not have any affect. It mattered not that we dropped hints, were openly rude and blunt, it did not bring about any improvement in his timekeeping. In those days, at a county station, on a shift of three it was not unusual to be depleted to just the one officer for early shift. Even now, forty years later and having entered the twenty-first century, things haven't really changed. When 'Rip van Winkle' didn't arrive on time it meant one of us from the night shift had to remain on duty until he arrived. Alternatively, and at worst, it resulted in an hour's extra duty waiting for the seven am station officer to turn up and open the front office to the public. The result, inevitably, was that one of the three of us would regularly finish night shift an hour later than normal.

Enough was enough, we decided the time had arrived to try and teach him a lesson. We made sure that we had agreement to our cunning plan from our sergeant, the same sergeant who had persuaded me that it wasn't worth sleeping in on cold winter mornings, and put our plot into action. It was a bright and sunny midsummer June morning as we dashed around the police station moving every clock forward two hours. At four am we drove to his house, banging and rattling the front door until a bleary-eyed Rip opened it.

"Come on,' we said, 'you're late again and we want to go home to bed, jump in and we'll drop you off."

Rip, an outspoken, wiry little Yorkshireman, rubbed the sleep from his eyes and said, "Nay, bloody 'ell, sorry lads, gi's two minutes, I'll git drissed."

True to his word some two minutes later we watched from the car as the unshaven Rip emerged from the house carrying collar and studs in one hand (this gives you an idea of how long ago this happened – in those days you were issued with three shirts per year, each coming packaged with two detachable collars and enough slyly hidden pins to ensure your fingers needed a blood transfusion to recover from the multi-punctured blood loss) holding his trousers at almost half mast with the other whilst his braces dangled and flapped around his ankles. He got into the back and we raced to the nick, shoved him through the back door before we jumped into our own cars and roared off home to bed.

Our one regret was that we never saw his face at the moment comprehension hit him. We learned in due course that apparently at about half past four a somewhat bewildered Rip had wandered out of the station and into the middle of the main London Road looking all around for traffic and pedestrians that should be making their way to work, where there were none to be seen and all that could be heard was the dawn chorus. He remained there for some minutes totally bemused until along came the local Co-op milkman. Exactly what was said we will never know but within seconds of the milk roundsman showing Rip his watch there were enough expletives to waken the whole neighbourhood.

I can't repeat what he said to us when he turned up, on time, the following morning but for some reason, after that day, we were never again delayed in finishing night duty.

I digress. Back in Grand Cayman, having freshened up in the pool, showered and changed we took the opportunity to continue unpacking and hang up our wedding outfits to ensure any creases would drop out. The only potential problem was that the three of us were sharing just the one bathroom. This was quickly resolved with an unwritten house rule that on entry you closed both doors to avoid any possible embarrassing moments. It worked well throughout the holiday.

There was already a lot of noise coming from the apartment next door. It was Caroline searching for additional storage space for shoes that wouldn't fit into the cavernous wardrobe and extra hangers to accommodate the numerous additional items of clothing purchased at Heathrow.

We all met up at the poolside bar to open our accounts and see how swiftly we could use up the complimentary fifty-dollar drinks vouchers. David and Mel joined us, together with Carl and Fran who had landed about an hour after us following their transfer in Miami. They were staying in Mel's flat on the south side of the island.

Food seemed to be the dominant theme of the conversation as the majority had not eaten properly since breakfast and that now seemed like yesterday. Allowing for the time difference, back home it *was* yesterday!

Whilst Mel and David took Carrie and me back to the airport to collect our rented minibus the others decided to take a short trek to a local restaurant where we would have our first Caymanian meal together. We agreed to meet there in thirty minutes, when we would also meet Mel's friend Nic and her family. Nic and Mel had travelled out from the UK together to further their careers with a new and different teaching experience in Grand Cayman. They had quickly become firm friends and rented a flat together, close to the school. The thirty minutes turned out to be a Caribbean thirty. We rendezvoused an hour and a half later. There were two reasons for the delay.

On arrival at the car hire company it became apparent that our reserved vehicle wasn't available. There had been a misunderstanding earlier in the day about collection times and it had been re-allocated elsewhere. The clerk did her best to resolve it there and then with a mixture of computer checks and phone calls to trace a suitable alternative vehicle immediately. All her efforts proved to be abortive but she made arrangements for us to pick up our people carrier the next morning at a depot much closer to our hotel.

Having been delayed for some time we rushed back to the restaurant. This was unnecessary as it transpired that the short trek from hotel to eatery was not so short. By the time the remainder of the group had arrived, at the end of their two-mile route march, fatigue had started to take over from famine.

Nonetheless, Caroline led the way and we didn't need any persuasion to follow her through the menu although the gigantic American-sized portions eventually beat most of us. Why is it that some people can eat such enormous amounts of food and remain so thin? Whilst there are others, myself included, who merely have to look at food and the calories gather around our waists.

There were brief introductions to Nic's family who by the time we arrived had finished their meal. They hail from the north-east and her father, Ken, is a Methodist minister who I learned had been both a prison and police chaplain at different times in his career. On second thoughts perhaps that should be calling and not career. Ken is also an avid and very good amateur photographer and he was to be the official photographer on the following Saturday.

Although by now it was close to midnight, once again the heat and humidity hit us as we left the restaurant to be ferried home by Mel and David.

The cool and airy apartments were a welcome relief as most of us hit the sack to try and catch up on some sleep. Being unused to the air-conditioning I found the constant hum distracting but the swift insertion of two cotton-wool buds to serve as homemade ear plugs cushioned any noise and I certainly didn't need to count sheep that night.

Our holiday had started. Strangely enough nobody slept particularly well on that first night. Whether it was overtiredness, excitement or a mixture of both the result was that we were all up and about much earlier than expected for our first breakfast the following morning. By seven we were tucking into fruit juice, coffee, croissants, bagels and Danish pastries together with a variety of fruit that was always available. Eating was already playing a noticeable part in our stay and this didn't change for the duration. Caroline had enough breakfast for two and also managed to acquire a collection of fresh fruit for her mid-morning snack. This, we learned, was a girl who will never go hungry.

Returning to our rooms to finish unpacking and tidy up the bits and pieces we had deposited throughout the apartment on first arrival (it's amazing how untidy I could be after just one night) it was pleasing to find more than sufficient bath towels, face towels and flannels for all of us with still some to spare. The hotel also provided beach towels that could be changed daily, which meant that we needn't have carried our own all the way from home and I might just have avoided the 'Heavy' label had I been privy to this information before setting out. With the amount of towels and linen being used on a daily basis I hate to think how hot it must have been working in the hotel laundry.

I was actually very pleased with the towel and flannel situation as I'd had this premonition of the bathroom being overrun with them. I've heard of some women who take hygiene to the extreme, needing four of everything with them when they are on holiday. They carry flannels and towels for all eventualities including four of each for zits, tits, pits and bits. Now I do like to be clean but that is going a bit too far. Fortunately, Jan and Carrie did not fall into this category and we all remained clean for the whole time, without the need for extra towels and flannels, even if on occasions we were regular occupants of the pool and the shower just to cool down. Me more than most, due to my propensity to become a little damp once I had been outside for any length of time. In any event, can you imagine what the additional towelling would have done to our baggage allowance? The heat did ensure that I paid more visits to the washing machine than I had anticipated but it prevented tee-shirts and shorts becoming too smelly, taking on a life of their own, and walking to the laundry themselves.

As I finished the unpacking, I found amongst my clothes a travel journal that Lesley had managed to secrete without my knowledge. It must have been this booklet that had tipped the scales into the heavy zone, although on picking it up I had to acknowledge that this was improbable. I consoled myself with the thought that it could have been just the straw that broke the camel's back. Unlikely, I know, but like me, my case had been just the wrong side of borderline. She had bought it for me the previous Christmas and mentioned that I could use it to make notes about my trip to the Cayman Islands. I must admit I had completely forgotten about it. She patently hadn't. Over the last few years she has always kept diaries when we have been on holidays and when we revisit them some time later they do serve as good memory-joggers over events that have been forgotten or been muddled in the mists of time. Although I had my trusty camera I decided that I would utilise the journal and for the first time in my life scribble up a daily log of the holiday. If it served no other purpose at least it would help remind me of events that I could describe to Lesley when I got home. I'm equally sure that she never expected me to use it, thinking it would be returned to Essex in the pristine condition it was in on departure. This, therefore, became the origin of my pre-lunch jottings that, following the comments on the wedding and some gentle if sometimes unwanted and ribald encouragement from the girls once they had seen my literary efforts, became an extended record of the holiday. Much to my amazement the result, dear reader, is my first effort at a book, which you are now ploughing through and probably wondering why on earth you started in the first place. Who would be interested in another family's wedding?

It's not as if there are going to be another three and there certainly isn't a funeral! Try as I might I cannot find any sign of Hugh Grant skulking about, although I don't think the girls are too disappointed. At this stage even I'm not sure why I'm still writing it.

Our first full day inevitably progressed into a lazy morning around the pool, chatting, reading and finding our bearings around the hotel.

Liberal amounts of suntan cream are already being applied to avoid sunburn so early in the holiday. I seem to be coating myself with far more than anybody else. It must be my delicate skin!

Mel and David arrived mid-morning to take Carrie and me to collect the hired minibus.

The local office and garage was much closer to the hotel and it didn't take long to complete the local paperwork for us to be presented with our temporary Cayman Islands driving permits which were valid for six months, if we had been able to stay that long. We moved outside to the forecourt to examine the bus and sign off agreed previous damage prior to starting our rental. Working from front to rear around the diagram on the hire contract we managed to agree and insert so many lines and dots, for dents and scratches, that not one side was left unblemished and all four corners had also been involved in their share of scrapes. On eventually reaching the back of the van, displayed for all to see was the sign 'Prestige Motors'. Now if this was a prestige car, I would eat my sun hat, and we were thankful that we were not collecting one that was less impressive. I'm sure it had seen better days. Although it was not the minibus originally allocated to us it was nonetheless clean, tidy and had been thoroughly valeted inside and out so that they were all clean dents and scratches. It could carry nine comfortably and ten at a pinch, and we consoled ourselves with the knowledge that it was relatively inexpensive and should we become involved in a minor collision they would be most unlikely to notice any resultant damage as one additional dent wouldn't have made a jot of difference to the bodywork. In the event the vehicle never let us down and did more than its fair share of fetching and carrying us around the island without the slightest hint of mechanical failure or accident. As far as the latter is concerned this may have been more due to luck than judgement. It also had the one essential piece of equipment needed in a Cayman Island vehicle, air-conditioning, and it was in good working order. My first impression of our prestige motor proved to be unfair as it was totally reliable and the odd dent and scrape were irrelevant. Additionally the hire rates were particularly attractive, so well done Prestige Motors. As my old granny used to say, 'Don't judge a picture by its frame.'

I offered to be the first one to take the wheel. Why do I do these things? Didn't I learn that important lesson from many years ago: never volunteer. In I jumped, only to find the steering wheel on the other side. I shuffled across to discover that I would also be driving an automatic. So here we were with a left-hand-drive vehicle, driving on the left-hand side of the road which could make overtaking interesting, exciting or even scary. I also had to remember to keep my left leg locked in position, in the footwell, to avoid slamming it on the footbrake instead of the non-existent clutch, thus bringing us to a sharp, unexpected and unnecessary halt and any car travelling too close behind us into our back seat. When I originally offered to take my share of the driving duties, I thought it would be just the same as driving back home in dear old England. This was to become a very different and memorable experience.

Trying to remember the pre-driving ritual from all those years ago, I acquainted myself with the controls, checked mirrors, adjusted the seat and made myself comfortable prior to releasing the handbrake and selecting 'drive'. We edged gingerly forward to the roadway. It was a three-lane highway and we needed to turn right to return to the hotel. I learned for the first time that the local custom to carry out this manoeuvre is to drive into the central lane, accelerate, and then filter into the traffic flow in the nearside lane when you find a convenient gap. In itself this is not particularly difficult unless, as I found on this occasion, my first ever effort in Grand Cayman, that another car was doing exactly the same. Unfortunately for both of us he was travelling in the opposite direction. There we were, eyeball to eyeball and speeding towards a head-on collision at a combined speed of about sixty miles per hour. I had this vision in front of me of an American-style sedan being driven by a baseball be-capped driver whose head just about perched above the steering wheel and we were both about to become enmeshed in a heap of tangled metal. Suddenly he veered left into what I thought was a non-existent gap but which he had measured with some precision, obviously being used to such a manoeuvre. He gave me a huge toothless grin as we passed each other with just a few feet to spare and continued on his way quite unconcerned. I was already braking, with my right foot, and then spotted my opportunity to slide into the flow of traffic and continue slowly if not serenely to Seven Mile Beach. Within fifteen seconds I had experienced my first, and I'm glad to report last, near accident and decided if we were to survive I would just have to smile and drive like a local. I'm still not convinced that their mode of turning right is the safest and, perhaps, is a contributory factor in their high casualty rate. With more time and interest I might have bought their equivalent of the Highway Code to see exactly what it recommends. However, as the week progressed we became used to turning right in this manner and accelerating into the nearside lane to avoid further potential mishaps. I tended to make sure there was almost no traffic about, to provide some sort of guarantee that I could complete the manoeuvre safely. This sometimes meant we sat at junctions watching passing traffic for some minutes. This wasn't a problem until a queue formed behind us at which stage I would target my gap in the traffic and aim for it hell for leather to escape from any potential danger.

Having safely managed to navigate the remainder of the journey back to the hotel we joined the others by the pool where Carrie told them of our first driving escapade of the holiday.

Now that we had the transport it was time to go on our first shopping trip, although it wasn't strictly necessary as there were still ample provisions in the fridge. Jan, Sue, Ted and I made our way to Foster's supermarket leaving the girls by the pool to ensure they didn't miss any opportunity to work on their tans.

I'm not an ardent shopper back home; in fact I avoid it whenever possible. I can normally remain fairly even-tempered but being jostled by recalcitrant shopping trolleys with front and rear wheels that are determined to steer in opposite directions, having difficulty in finding what I want and then having to join an endless queue to pay is not my idea of fun. It is one of the rare occasions when I can feel myself becoming stressed. When I do need to shop, I know what I need, go out to buy it and get out of the shop as quickly as possible. I think this must be unique, as the vast majority seem to search around the store before they make up their mind what they need. They also actually seem to enjoy it. To me, this seems an enormous waste of time and effort. Consequently, I do my husbandly duty and try to take the trouble to assist with the Christmas shopping but don't feel my labours are really appreciated. My annual excursion to the supermarket has therefore become something of a pilgrimage with me being the martyr. The cashier on the till, whom

Lesley sees weekly, has got to know me over the years and at least she is always cheerful and chatty, which is more than can be said for some who don't seem to have the slightest interest in what they are doing. She always wishes me the season's greetings and with my usual grimace I respond and remind her I will see her again at the same time next year, whilst rushing to the exit to escape. I'm sure that I cannot be the only husband faced with this situation.

My dislike of shopping and supermarkets in particular can perhaps be attributed to an experience in a Key Markets store, as a spotty-faced adolescent. It was my turn to do the weekly shop and off I trotted with plastic bags and shopping list. This was a chore that I shared with my two younger brothers and from memory I can't recollect that we enjoyed it but we just got on with it. Having walked the mile, mainly downhill, to the store I started collecting the groceries. I can't remember exactly what was on the list but it was a fairly heavy load (I had a habit of heavy loads even all those years ago) and joined one of the half-dozen or so queues to pass through a checkout till. After some fifteen minutes I arrived to take my place at the head of the line to unload my shopping on the cash point conveyor belt only to be told by the cashier in a Cockney smoker's croaky voice, as she finished serving the customer in front of me, "You'll 'ave ta join anuvver queue mate, it's me tea break."

All the other queues had at least five or six people already in them and it would mean at least another quarter of an hour or more before I would be able to make my way home. Why on earth couldn't she have told me that when I first joined her queue?

I said quite politely, "But I've already been waiting fifteen minutes and I don't want to start again, you could have told us that before we started waiting."

"Look luv, like I said it's me tea break an' I ain't gonna miss it. You gotta join anuvver queue," she said, slamming the till shut with an air of self-importance and adult superiority as if to say who is this young teenage upstart questioning me, I'll show him who's boss. She was going to have the final say.

As I've said, on most occasions I'm fairly mild mannered but for some reason I wasn't prepared to accept this and I certainly wasn't her 'love'. What made me say it I don't know but there I was, for probably the first time in my life questioning some sort of authority, if you could call her authority.

"Look, you either serve me or you can put this lot back on the shelves," I said in a loud enough voice that all around began to look in our direction, as I started unloading all of my goods in front of her. I wasn't going to let this crab-faced old biddy get away with this. Alas, it was a confrontation I was always going to lose. She got up from her seat, locked her till and stomped off to her cup of tea, which by now I was hoping would choke her.

I wasn't prepared to lose face so left all the week's groceries at her cash point and walked out of the store with everybody watching me but nobody saying a word. I admit I left the shop very red-faced with a mix of both anger and embarrassment but felt I had made my point.

The reality, of course, was I had cut off my nose to spite my face, as I had now to go to the only other supermarket in town and start the shopping all over again before then carrying it uphill for a mile to reach home.

I'm sure the old witch had a good laugh at my expense at her coven's tea party and I will never know if she, or somebody else, returned all the items to the shelves.

The end result was that I nearly missed being picked up for football that afternoon and for a youngster who had just got into the local town team that would have been a minor disaster, but somehow my protest still seemed worthwhile. It was the first time I had ever been involved in any sort of public confrontation and exactly why then I still do not know. Perhaps it was the beginning of the swinging sixties and I realised that hidden well below the surface was a bit of a rebellious streak in me. It was still the right thing to do. Key Markets, by the way, soon ceased trading in the town. I wonder why?

I'm sure that's not the only reason I don't like shopping and it certainly coloured my view so that ever since I've avoided it whenever possible.

However, I am human and so do have to admit to one weakness on this front and that is when I'm on holiday. For some inexplicable reason my psyche changes and I almost become a normal shopper and start doing strange things. Whether it's because I'm more relaxed or do not have to adhere to any sort of time constraint I don't know.

This first became apparent on French vacations when I would be found in hypermarkets, mainly collecting bottles of vin rouge or latterly, in Provence, vin rosé. I've progressed from the shelves into the local 'caves' and vineyards where one is able to sample the goods prior to purchase. If I'm not found there then look no further than the charcuterie where I could well be buying up their tomate farcies, or in a boulangerie obtaining my daily ration of croissants and baguettes. Perhaps it's just the difference in foreign shops but I start acting abnormally and buy both greater quantities than we need and also items that we probably don't need at all. I've no logical explanation for this behaviour and can only equate it to wives on shopping expeditions who come home to husbands to tell them they have saved some money. The downside normally being for every twenty pounds they have saved it has cost the joint account one hundred pounds to do so.

I do accept this is now also a flaw in my character but it does only manifest itself during holidays.

It did so on our first shopping expedition in Grand Cayman. Foster's supermarket wasn't to blame, although their delicatessen, patisserie and fishmongers seemed far more interesting, with greater variety, than those we see back home. All we bought here were some picky bits to have with drinks on the balcony and ham, cheese, bread, salad and fruit to cater for lunch. We also brought back a dozen bottles of water, which we soon realised would be totally inadequate. Again, the staff were delightful and nothing like my Key Markets experience.

No, my problem arose when we walked across the square to Blackbeard's Liquor Store. Ted and I intended to buy some wine and beer, which we did. I then saw the rum cake and having been asked to bring some back for the girls I took advantage of their offer to buy six small ones, all different flavours, and get a further large one free (pina colada flavour). I know small is relative but Blackbeard's 'small' provides enough portions for four and the large cake will cope with treble that number.

I don't think I realised what I had done until we got back to the hotel and I was looking for somewhere to store the cake. I hadn't been forced into buying them; there was no high pressure sales pitch; in fact on reflection the sales assistant seemed surprised that I had bought so many. She obviously didn't have too many idiot English shoppers visit her store. I eventually squashed them into what would normally be the vegetable compartment of the fridge, which was now loaded to the rim so that care needed to be taken when opening the door. I was convinced that I had bought too many and that they would not be eaten, whilst the girls, particularly Caroline who proved to be the Galloping Gourmet of rum cake cuisine, seemed quite pleased and were confident they would go. They had sampled rum cake on their previous visit and were later to display their expertise in detecting the variety of flavours, proving my initial concerns unfounded as the cache slowly and surely diminished. In fact additional cake was needed to take home as presents for families and friends.

We all lunched around the pool where we continued to relax and drift into holiday mode. Most of us were quietly catching up on some reading, with the odd one or two having a catnap, when suddenly Caroline casually asked anyone who might be listening, "What does 'sphincter' mean?" That instantly brought everybody out of their slumbers. Ted and I explained, as best we could, and asked her what she was reading. By now the audience were fascinated, particularly those who were bored with their own books. She told us it was a book she had brought on holiday. According to her it wasn't very interesting but was quite rude. There followed a fair degree of mickey-taking with Caroline giving as good as she got until we threw her in the pool. Once she dried off she decided we would have a word of the day for the rest of the holiday but none seemed to be as stimulating or create as much interest as the word on the first day.

By late afternoon we were on our way back to the airport to collect Diane who was due to arrive on a Cayman Airways flight from Cuba, the final leg of her journey from Australia.

I was already getting used to the left-hand drive and did not intend to do much, if any, overtaking. It was necessary to remember that some of the traffic lights are perched thirty feet above the road on cables. They are similar to many you see in France but without the mini lights at eye level to assist the driver and prevent muscle strain from having to crane one's neck, giraffe-like, to obtain a view of the lights as they change colour. Although my confidence was improving I continued to drive ultra-carefully and was hoping to avoid the toothless Michael Schumacher coming the other way. In fact, during the fortnight I only missed a red light in the sky once and fortunately there was little traffic at the time and nobody noticed my error, or if they did they were very polite and didn't say a word. On second thoughts this group would not have been polite in those circumstances so they must have missed it.

Owen Roberts International is a busy little airport and in the twenty minutes we were waiting for Diane to arrive there were two departures and four incoming flights including another British Airways from Heathrow. With Miami less than five hundred miles north the airport welcomes trippers from the United States on a daily basis and despite the Cayman Islands' British history there are many more Americans on the island than Brits. Consequently the majority of the hotels and restaurants cater predominately for their tastes with service, portions and prices targeting the American market.

From the open-air spectator verandah on the first floor of the terminal building we saw Diane's plane touch down and taxi onto the terminal apron before watching her and the other passengers traipse across the tarmac to the Arrivals Hall following the path we had taken twenty-four hours previously.

The atmosphere at the airport gives the impression of organised informality and the nervous traveller has one huge advantage. You are able to mingle with the aircrew in the departure lounge as they take advantage of the duty free shops during their brief stopover time on the ground. Being able to chat to the captain and first officer on a one to one basis can give enormous confidence to the reluctant flyer. It's a shame that this is just not possible at the majority of the busier terminals.

Within ten minutes we all met up at the front of the terminal. I had last met Diane at Mel's christening about twenty-eight years previously and wouldn't have recognised her. I'm equally sure at that stage she didn't have the foggiest idea who I was until we were introduced. She impressed me immediately. This lady was some 'Sheila'. Firstly she wasn't carrying any hand luggage and her only suitcase was half the size of mine. I was able to carry it to the minibus with ease. I knew that we would get on and was already considering asking if she would give the girls instructions on what essentials are needed to take on holiday. I'm sure they could learn a valuable lesson. She had travelled almost twice the distance we had flown, with a number of mini-breaks in the journey, and appeared to be coping easily with less than half our baggage. I don't know if Diane is typical of the Antipodean traveller but if so then Qantas will never be carrying excess baggage and they certainly would not have need of any 'Heavy' labels. The drive back to our hotel was uneventful other than the fact that we were all surprised at the amount of traffic in what passed for a Caymanian rush hour. It was essential to keep a wary eye on the scurrying taxibuses as they dashed in and out of the traffic, collecting and dropping off passengers at random, or at least that's how it appeared to the uninitiated. I'm sure they do have predetermined routes and you get to know these if you are a regular user. Compared to our first journey earlier in the day the trip to the airport and back was totally uneventful.

There was just time for a quick dip in the pool to cool off before getting changed for the barbeque arranged by the hotel for all their guests. We had a long table at one end of the pool, which was surrounded by groups of brightly decorated tables. To one side of us was another large party of a local family and their friends celebrating a fiftieth birthday. Everybody joined in the celebrations, and the singing and dancing started early in the holiday, accompanied tonight by a local band. It was also apparent that the poolside bar was a popular rendezvous for local residents on their way home from work, many of whom also ate here on barbeque night. There was a wide selection of fresh meat and fish that was cooked to order and with vegetables and/or salad overflowing from the ample sized plates. This became a feature of all our meals to the extent that I never needed a pudding, rum cake notwithstanding. This was all washed down with a readily available supply of beer, wine and local cocktails which helped lubricate the vocal cords.

During the meal we met Mike, the best man, for the first time. He is a traffic police motorcyclist, and could only stay briefly as he was due to go on night duty. He is a colleague and good friend of David and was the officer who accompanied and tutored him on his early patrols as a police officer. During the evening we gave David and Mel their wedding cards and presented them with an engraved plate signed by all of us who had travelled to Grand Cayman. They were obviously delighted and are a very happy couple. The band finally stopped playing just before midnight and I think by that time tiredness was creeping up on most of us and we were all content to climb the one flight of stairs back to our apartments before jumping into our beds. The two exceptions were Jan and Diane who were both still going strong and catching up with all their news since they had last seen each other some years earlier when Jan had visited Australia.

CHAPTER 4

Early Jogging with the Girls

'W' Day minus two had dawned and amazingly most of us were up bright and early and looking forward to the day ahead. It must be something in the Caribbean air. Diane was walking the beach and having her daily early morning swim in the sea. Quite extraordinarily, Carrie, Caroline and myself were off exploring the island. So what's unusual about that, you might ask? We were on holiday and nothing could be more natural than seeing what delights the different resorts had to offer. This was different.

It was a quarter past seven in the morning and there were the three of us in our training kit running along Seven Mile Beach road towards West Bay. Now I wouldn't dream of doing that at home, why do it on holiday? I normally run – no, to be more accurate, jog – five miles at least twice a week. This tends to be late afternoon or early evening, having returned home from work. Although I've been in the habit of this training routine for many years, starting when I used to run marathons back in the eighties and nineties, I've never got up before seven in the morning to go jogging. I'm not a morning person.

Caroline had recently completed a half-marathon in Norwich, Norfolk, and trains regularly with Carrie and Fran who had run her first London Marathon just over two months earlier, whilst it was Carrie's intention to run her first London Marathon the following year, provided she could gain an entry. What we didn't realise at the time was that Carl and Fran, who were staying with Mel, were doing exactly the same on the southern side of the island. Carl, a sports centre manager, is a good footballer, an excellent swimming coach and is very fit. I suspect their pace was somewhat quicker than our progress along Seven Mile Beach.

Before we started I had to apply my first coating of suntan cream for the day, on neck, shoulders and arms. Even at this early hour I wasn't taking any chances with my delicate skin! Although I didn't see the girls taking the same precautions and I have to admit that their skin did look a lot more delicate than mine.

We slowly got into our stride and our tempo could best be described as steady as opposed to speedy and I'm probably being generous. We had agreed to run as a trio at the speed of the slowest so that we remained together. As a team we were not going to break any records but the girls had a considerable age and weight advantage and we were all reasonably fit. This, our first real venture on foot, could be expressed as interesting and taught us a few lessons about running in such a climate, even in the early morning. Bearing in mind the time of day, the heat and humidity were already overbearing. Fortunately the sun was still rising, so for much of the trek we were able to run in the shade of the trees and tall bushes that had ample foliage and lined much of the route. Caroline, thank goodness, had the foresight to carry a bottle of water which proved to be invaluable as we reached the halfway stage, and we shared it equally between us. On a run of this distance I wouldn't normally bother to take on liquid but in these conditions it was essential. As we turned around to head back to our base my running vest was already so wet that it was possible to wring it out. I was leaking profusely and even the two girls were looking a little warm.

Our route had taken us past the fire station and Cemetery Corner and we were gaining considerable attention both from the passing motorists, who I thought were hooting encouragement, and the passengers jumping on to the taxi-buses. This was quite unusual as when I'm out jogging back home everybody ignores me and I can meander along at my own slow pace oblivious to the outside world.

This was different and it didn't take long to realise why. At home I run alone, here I was accompanied by two pretty young ladies in their running kit, and the Nassau experience was being repeated albeit in a somewhat different scenario. I'm sure some of the onlookers must have wondered what on earth they were doing running with that silly old codger. I suspect the girls were also thinking that themselves!

Nevertheless the toots on various horns, together with the odd ear-shattering klaxon from some lorry drivers, were encouraging and as our pace gradually slackened we needed all the encouragement we could get. What did amaze us was the amount of traffic on the road at that time of the morning. The commuters into Georgetown were early starters and proportionately the traffic was busier than when I drove around the M25 to Heathrow. It really was nose to tail and it wasn't just the scenery that was slowing them down, but the heavy traffic conditions. I learned later in the week that per capita Grand Cayman has one of the highest car-owning populations in the world, which for a small island creates problems of its own.

About a quarter of a mile from the hotel we passed a sign that said 'Beat the Heat' and wondered if it was someone trying to tell us something or having a joke at our expense. It transpired that it was some sort of billboard advertisement for air-conditioning, which every driver would see on his or her way into the office each morning.

We arrived back at the hotel within forty minutes but the return leg had taken almost four minutes longer. It was obvious that we just weren't acclimatised to exercising in those conditions. If we were to continue with this regime we could not afford to leave it any later in the morning. The alternative was to run in the late evening, as was the practice with many local residents, but this would have been too disruptive to the wining and dining we had planned for the remainder of our stay. We knew where our priorities lay and Caroline was always likely to put food ahead of exercise.

Eventually as we made our way past the hotel reception and breakfast bar the facial expressions of the other guests who were already tucking into their breakfasts were a mixture of amazement and amusement. From the quizzical glances coming from a group of rather overweight Americans I'm sure they were convinced that we were a bunch of mad Brits. They were probably correct.

The three of us jumped straight into the pool to cool off and relax our aching muscles before yet another of many refreshing cold showers and off to breakfast with healthy appetites from our morning exertions. As was the norm Caroline managed to outpace us in the breakfast stakes.

It transpired that the morning runs were initially to continue on alternate days but after that first experience the girls opted out and I was left to compete with the heat on my own. The reason was twofold. Firstly, they were more sensible than me but they also tended to keep somewhat later, and more irregular, hours than the remainder of us 'wrinklies' who were normally tucked up and fast asleep before they even thought about coming home. Perhaps, being female with that inborn sixth sense, they also had a premonition that I would experience events on my future solo rambles that I would be unlikely to come across back home and that they had no wish to be any part of. At that stage I was not to know what pitfalls lay in wait for me on my early morning perambulations. Had I done so I suspect I would just have turned over and had another hour or two in bed as opposed to subjecting myself to a chapter of early morning adventures and mishaps.

We split up after breakfast, with Jan, Diane and I going for a long walk along the beach, which was pretty much deserted and unfolded for miles in front of us.

Preparations included the day's second application of lashings of suntan lotion, this time accompanied by sun hat, shades, flip-flops and a dry cotton tee-shirt that did not remain dry for very long.

The footwear was unnecessary, as the sand was fine and silvery rather than the usual golden hue which we're used to, and for most of the time we paddled or waded in the clear shallow water as shoals of tiny blue and silver fish darted around our feet, as if playing a game of tag with each other. From time to time, I dipped myself into the bright blue water and its warmth again reminded me of Trinidad and Tobago. For anybody who has never swum in the sea or never enjoyed swimming in the sea then they really should try the Caribbean. It is a very different experience. Unlike elsewhere, or even the Mediterranean, where people say 'Come in, the water's really warm' and the reality is that it's so cold you come out in goose pimples, the sea in the Caribbean really is warm. When you look into the distance, as you paddle in the shallow waters of Seven Mile Beach, the white powder stretches and stretches – and then stretches some more. Without realising it we were merely preparing ourselves for what Mel and David had planned for our afternoon jaunt. We came across the odd small outcrop of rock but pebbles and shingle were non-existent. The gently lapping waves splashing against my shorts, together with my normal propensity to perspire by the gallon, ensured that by the time we returned for lunch the hotel staff saw me for the second time that morning dripping wet with yet another set of clothes ready for the washing machine. They now joined the group of guests who thought an overweight, eccentric and very damp Englishman had infiltrated their beautiful Caribbean idyll. They were probably right.

I suppose we must have walked for the best part of three hours. My doctor would be pleased with all this exercise I was getting!

We nattered about everything and anything, passing the time of day with the occasional strolling beachcomber. Diane was in her element and this was obviously almost a daily routine for her back home in New South Wales. I suppose the residents must get used to strangers regularly peering into their back gardens, but the design and size of some of the villas kept our attention and we were soon playing guessing games about who might live in them and how much they would cost. We found out later in the holiday the going rate for similar properties and it is fair to say that they were some way, in fact a yawning chasm, beyond our price range, but it's nice to dream.

It was also rumoured that Dick Francis, the jockey-cum-author, lived in one of the mansions along Seven Mile Beach but look as we might he wasn't leaving any clues as to which might be his pied-à-terre by the sea in Grand Cayman. I'm not sure what we were searching for but horses, stables or even a bookshop were conspicuous by their absence and there wasn't any sign of elderly short gentlemen in racing colours or even sets of hooves that had been for an early morning gallop, or given the climate and my own first early morning experience, a trot or canter, across the sand. However, it was easy to understand why he would wish to live here and watch the superb sunsets from his backyard, or even, to present a more accurate picture, rolling lawns and beachside terrace, each evening. It is rumoured that the majority of the beachside homes are owned by multi-millionaires and as we wandered past them that morning I could understand why. If you had that sort of money and could afford to buy yourself a little bit of heaven then I've not come across many better places to park the Roller and set to with the bricks and mortar. Albeit I don't suppose many of the residents got their own hands dirty mixing the sand and cement.

Back at the hotel we lunched in the shade on our balcony and if we had known what was in store for the afternoon would not have eaten as much. The girls managed to devour a further wedge or two of rum cake, whilst Caroline managed three slices, but the stack in the fridge didn't appear any smaller at this stage. It was still only the second full day of our holiday on the island and the rum cake and Caroline were to prove to be prominent features throughout although not necessarily in that order.

CHAPTER 5

Cuddle a Stingray! – Carefully

Having completed lunch and thrown all the crockery and cutlery into the dishwasher we prepared ourselves for the afternoon's adventure.

There was just time to change into another dry top and shorts before setting off for the short trip to Captain Marvin's shop situated on the main road from Georgetown to West Bay, the air-conditioning in the minibus proving invaluable for even this brief journey. There we met up with Carl, Fran, Mel and David and some more of their friends for what proved to be another memorable feature of the holiday. Captain Marvin's store had everything for the diving enthusiast and even more. We purchased our tickets for the afternoon's boat trip but could probably also have bought a boat had we been so inclined and had sufficient funds. I learned that we weren't just going on any old tourist boat but our hosts had chartered the boat solely for our party for the remainder of the day.

Having collected our underwater cameras we made our way back past the hotel to the boat, which was to be skippered by Captain Marvin Ebanks himself. He had been born back in 1916 in West Bay, and with his weatherbeaten and bronzed features was the stereotypical salty old sea dog. He was obviously quite a character and he told us he had been working with the stingrays for more years than he could remember, having originally become involved with them as a young boy feeding them scraps in the warm waters of North Sound whilst cleaning fish and learning the early rudiments of good seamanship. In those days you couldn't clean the fish onshore as there were so many mosquitoes so it was all done at sea before taking them into West Bay where he used to sell them for his father. The unwanted food would be thrown into the water and the stingrays would gather for their daily feast. So started the germ of an idea almost eighty years ago that has, today, developed into Stingray City. I would have loved the opportunity to chat to him at length as he knows the waters like the back of his hand and I'm sure he has forgotten more about the island and its seafaring history than most people would care to remember. Unfortunately he was so busy organising the crew and casting off that our conversation was all too brief.

Sitting at the open rear of the boat, in just my swimming trunks, I joined others in applying yet another covering of suntan cream. These tubes had become an essential compo-nent of the holiday. At least on this occasion I was one of many who were daubing themselves in a variety of oils and creams that ranged from the low to the ultra-high sun protec-tion factors.

The boat was larger than I expected and turned out to be a well-used ocean-going motor cruiser. I would estimate that it would carry sixty or seventy comfortably and probably a few more at a bit of a pinch. I suppose in omnibus terms it could be described as a double-decker with its two tiered decks joined by a metal ladder. It provided all the facilities you could possibly need, including a very spacious cabin area in case of inclement weather. It was obvious to all that any use of the cabin was likely to be minimal on such a beautiful day.

Some of the gang had already arrived and were comfortably ensconced on deck so that in total there were about forty of us on board. These included David's friends from the local constabulary, and Mel's school colleagues and their families, all of whom were to be guests at the wedding. What we didn't appreciate until we entered the galley was the variety and amount of food all the girls had prepared. It was to be a veritable feast and they deserved congratulations on their culinary efforts. I know I keep returning to the subject of food but they do eat well in the Cayman Islands.

Ken and his family were aboard and it was the first time we saw him wield his cameras, in the plural, in anger. I would love to be able to tell you that he was pronouncing that, 'Wye hai, we doon't 'ave fish leeke this back hoom in Wigan, pet' but he was far too busy zooming in on us fitting goggles, masks, snorkels and oversized flippers to have time to chat.

We had all heard and read about Stingray City and initially thought that it was the location we were headed to. However, with Captain Marvin at the helm we were steering slightly further east and after about thirty-five minutes' sailing arrived at an area known locally as the Sandbar. He certainly knew his stuff for within minutes of dropping anchor, or whatever it is you do when you park a boat at sea, we could see the stingrays swarming and surrounding the boat.

Both the Sandbar and Stingray City are located in North Sound between Palmetto Point and Rum Point and are one of the Caymans' premier tourist destinations, attracting dozens of trips every day. It is a unique site where the water is fairly shallow and so clear that it offers a perfect view of all the underwater activity. Experienced divers consider the area to be amongst the best diving sites in the world and it's certainly the best in the Caribbean. They acknowledge that the combination of the underwater visibility, the sandbars and particularly the stingrays make it a great attraction not only for the hundreds of tourists on a daily basis but also for the expert diver.

As a non-diver I certainly bow to their expertise. However as a resident tourist it really is worthwhile staying until the sun sets over West Bay. The visiting tourists from the cruise liners will have long since departed back to their floating hotels and watching the sun disappear in the peace and tranquillity of North Sound is worth the wait. Alternatively arrive early in the morning, before the cruisers, and watch the stingrays swarm around looking for their breakfast, and I don't mean Corn Flakes or Rice Krispies. Having said that, from the size of some of them I'm sure they have more than two Shredded Wheat for breakfast.

Although I love being in the water, I've never been confident and try to avoid going out of my depth. It was only five years ago that I learned to swim. I can only do the crawl and still consider myself to be a poor swimmer. Any attempt at the breast stroke flounders after no more than half a dozen strokes which get me absolutely nowhere; I then need to revert to splashing everybody nearby with an uncoordinated flailing of arms and legs in an effort to remain afloat. I am able to do enough to save myself but not much else. To put my ability in this department into some sort of perspective, when compared to the endeavours of 'Eric the Eel' back in the Sydney Olympics of 2000 I would still be bobbing about in the toddlers' pool. In my terms Eric is the equivalent of an Ian Thorpe. It was only twelve months earlier, on holiday, that I had learned to float for the first time in my life. Credit for this is due to the patience and perseverance of Jo, a swimming coach, who happened to be on the same holiday. Until then I would try and lie on my back, and tense up, with the result that I started to fold like a hinge so that bum first I sank slowly beneath the surface taking in vast quantities of water to eventually re-emerge gasping, coughing, spluttering and sucking in oxygen in an attempt to regain some composure. The result was that I sounded something akin to an old diesel engine trying to start on an icy midwinter's morning. This was usually to the great amusement of family, friends and any other interested spectators who had gained the misleading impression that I was some sort of underwater comical cabaret act. Somehow Jo gave me the confidence to achieve what, for me, had hitherto been impossible. Until then I hadn't realised just how buoyant the human body can be in water.

What now astounds me is that once I realised I wasn't going to drown and was persuaded to lie back, relax, and allow my body to float I cannot understand why I couldn't do it before. I used to blame it on heavy bones. (Why on earth didn't I think of that in the doctor's surgery? On reflection I'm equally certain that she would have had a cutting response to such a learned and knowledgeable opinion.) I now know that was not a valid excuse but purely a matter of nerve and trust in my own ability, which took me fifty-odd years to acquire.

I descended the steps at the stern of Captain Marvin's boat with some trepidation. It wasn't the depth of water I was concerned about, as once I had swum on to a sandbank the sea only came up to my chest. In any event Carl, Carrie, Caroline and Fran are all lifeguards so I was in the safe hands of the Suffolk Baywatch Four. It was just that I had never knowingly bathed with a stingray before so I suppose it was a fear of the unknown. Ironically the four brave lifesavers were just as apprehensive as me, if not more so. I don't think any of us fancied risking upsetting one of these potentially dangerous flat fish by unwittingly stepping on one and receiving a nasty sting that could result in a hospital visit. At that stage not one of us believed the reassuring noises being made by our hosts who assured us that despite their vampire-like appearance and the stinger in their long bony tail not one of the hundreds of thousands of tourists had ever been stung by one of these friendly creatures. Although not one of us said a word I'm sure we were all thinking, there's always a first time.

Having taken the plunge it was certainly a strange and unusual sensation to find the stingrays swimming around my feet and rubbing and brushing their wings against me. I know it's unfair, because they can't answer back, but they really are ugly creatures. In their world I'm sure they think the same about us when they see the hordes of strange human frames with limbs protruding from four corners, bedecked with goggles, masks and multicoloured corrugated plastic pipes sticking out of their mouths, entering their natural habitat. Stingrays have broad, flat almost disc-shaped bodies with small ill-defined heads with their beady eyes and blunt snout on the topside and large pectoral fins, commonly, but mistakenly, called their wings. This misnomer is not helped by the stingray's method of swimming, which resembles a bird in flight, so I could understand why some people would think of them as giant black water-bats.

In fact the best representation I have heard of a stingray is that they resemble underwater blackened stealth bombers as a group of them approach silently looking for food. They appear quite innocuous and do not hold any malicious intent for their human company who are swimming, snorkelling and floating together in the water. However, like the stealth bomber, they carry a deadly load on their venomous spine with a whip-like tail that is used purely as a defence mechanism. It pays not to step on one, even accidentally.

As we mingled together we realised just how gentle they are as they glide silently by flapping their wings and waiting to be fed. This was much easier than I ever imagined. I held a piece of squid, in the same manner you would hold an ice cream cone, whilst they approach and effectively suck it out of your hand. I have to admit that on this first occasion I flinched slightly at this unique encounter as the massive stingray with a three-foot wingspan (this isn't one of those exaggerated fisherman's tales, it might even have been wider than three feet), approached and sucked the squid from between my fingers, leaving the famous Cayman love-bite, the stingray 'hickey' on the back of my hand.

Having been provided with their-mid afternoon snack they allow you to stroke their undersides and, lifting them briefly above the surface, spurt water on your chest almost as their way of saying thank you for the grub. As they approach for more food, the larger ones being greedier than their smaller brothers and sisters, it is obvious that there is considerable variance in bulk and size with the average being equivalent to the normal bathmat that you would find as you step from a shower. The largest one that we saw had a wingspan of over four feet and we were told that in the local waters adult females can grow as large as six feet across, whilst the short-tailed stingray can reach more than fourteen feet in length and can weigh close on eight hundred pounds, preying on crabs, mantis shrimps and conger eels. Fortunately we were not destined to see any of these giants in the waters of North Sound.

I soon found that I was losing any fear that I had, as you realise that they do not display any hostility towards those trespassers invading their environment. Before long I'm actually holding one against my chest and floating back whilst cuddling a stingray. It is difficult to describe the feel of their skin. It's obviously soft and wet and is covered with a protective slimy coating. Some in the group considered it to be velvety but the most accurate description I can conjure up is to equate it with a damp chamois leather being dragged across your skin. It wasn't an unpleasant sensation and you soon become used to it. As another one brushed up against me, and with the help of one of Captain Marvin's friendly and knowledgeable crew it was placed across my back to subject me to a free, and after my early morning exercise, very welcoming massage as I floated lazily in the tranquil waters. Ted, Carl and I had become quickly acquainted with our new piscatorial friends and any fears we had soon disappeared. The spectacle of my 'hug a stingray' experience amused everybody present and brought forth a fair degree of mirth and mickey-taking from those who were aware of my lack of swimming ability and confidence in the water.

Nobody was more astonished than myself that I had made friends with these waterborne creatures but I was thoroughly enjoying the experience. Much to my amazement one of the 'Suffolk Baywatch' crew was making a terrible fuss and did not want to be seen anywhere near a stingray. It was none other than Caroline who was obviously very uncomfortable in their presence and for probably the one and only time in my life I was more confident in the water than a fully qualified lifeguard. I'm equally sure that would have changed had there been an emergency and she would have come into her own whilst I would have been left floundering and doing my best imitation of a doggy paddle as I gradually submerged from view. Her concern was understandable as for hundreds of years stingrays have been feared. The misconception that they were dangerous was caused by a lack of understanding about their anatomy. They do have long whip-like tails that terminate in a number of razor-sharp serrated barbs located at the tip. The barbs contain venom used to deter predators. They can cause considerable pain and swelling upon contact but stingrays are not aggressive creatures and do not attack man or other mammals unless they are being attacked themselves and are under stress. They use their tails purely as a defence mechanism and these are fairly ineffective against their main predators, sharks, although they can penetrate a man's arm or leg and have been known to cause severe lacerations to divers who get too close and upset them.

We were warned before we entered the water that we were only likely to be stung if we were to tread on one by mistake should we not see it lying on the sand whilst feeding. The chances of this occurring really were minimal as they are in perpetual motion in the water as they circle their visitors in search of a free handout of squid. Perhaps, if Caroline had not been given this warning she may not have been quite as apprehensive. The only wonder was that the fuss and noise she was making did not scare them off. Strangely, as when many pet animals detect fear in a human, it had the opposite effect and seemed to attract them to her in greater numbers. She became one of the first to return to the safe haven of the boat. The rays that we encountered had whitish underbellies and a variety of shades of grey, brown or black backs that were easy to distinguish in the crystal clear waters of the Sandbar so that, in reality, the chances of stepping on one were slim.

Swimming and snorkelling around the Sandbar it is possible to see shoals of different colourful fish glide past underwater, seemingly unperturbed by their human neighbours' playtime with the stingrays. I spent much of the remaining time in the water, with Ted and Carl, drifting on or just under the surface watching the antics of the stingrays as they hovered and slid from one source of food to the next. Diane was thoroughly enjoying herself and seemed almost as much at home in the sea as the fish. All four of us had lost any fear that we might have had when we first entered the water and were now quite at home swimming with the stingrays. Whether Diane had any previous experience back home in Australia I don't know but if she had she was remaining very coy about it. It was perhaps fortunate that our holiday was before her compatriot, the fearless Steve Irwin, was to be fatally stung by a stingray whilst filming in the waters of the Great Barrier Reef off the coast of Queensland.

The world-renowned 'Crocodile Hunter' as he had become known had earned a global reputation for his daring exploits with dangerous reptiles and it was a tragic irony that he should meet his death in a freak snorkelling accident when he had escaped from far more perilous escapades, which involved enormous risks, with hardly a scratch on his body. Unprovoked attacks from stingrays are unheard of so what caused this particular one to stab him through the chest will forever remain a mystery. It appeared that the barb went into his chest and penetrated his heart. If it had stung him in any other part of his body he would probably still be alive to tell the tale. Knowing him he would have laughed it off in his typical laddish Aussie humour that had endeared him to so many of his army of viewers. The publicity surrounding his death indicated that it was only the fourth such known stingray fatality in Australian waters. Now I'm sure that if any of the four of us remaining in the water, feeding our friendly and docile Cayman stingrays, had been aware of that information then our approach may well have been similar to Caroline's and it's even possible that one or two of us would have been more than reluctant to leave the security of Captain Marvin's boat. Nonetheless, ignorance is bliss and we continued to enjoy our underwater adventure swimming with, and in my case cuddling, stingrays.

Eventually we ran out of food and made our way back to the boat, scrambling over the stern to be hosed down with fresh water by Captain Marvin, who seemed to be amusing himself spraying his passengers from tip to toe with his onboard high-pressure hose of fresh water.

This was very welcome and we hardly needed to towel ourselves down as the heat and sun were drying us off without the need of any external assistance. It was an unbelievable experience that I wouldn't have imagined in my wildest dreams and I enjoyed every minute of it. However, knowing what I know now about the unlucky Steve Irwin I'm not sure that it is an encounter that I will ever participate in again.

Once again, time for more sun-block application. The sun was now burning brightly and my pale skin was taking on a pinkish hue. I wasn't taking any chances and continued to protect my naked extremities with another generous coating of cream.

Surprise, surprise it was time to eat again. Our afternoon dip in the warm waters had done nothing to harm our appetites and we managed to do justice to the buffet laid on by our hosts. Plates were overflowing with selections from a vast array of different mouth-watering dishes. The only item of food that was missing was rum cake and needless to say Caroline soon spotted this serious omission. In deference to our location and new-found friends, that we were now leaving in our wake as we set sail to the far side of North Sound, fish dishes were notable by their absence. A wide choice of wine, beer, fruit juices or mineral water was also available to assist digestion.

I sampled the locally brewed Stingray beer for the first time and certainly not the last. We spread ourselves around the decks and tucked into our onboard Caribbean picnic as we headed towards land and welcomed the cooling sea breeze as our octogenarian captain opened the throttle. This only masked the real power of the sun and it was easy to burn without realising it.

There was just time for a quick top up with the protective lotion before disembarking for a brief interlude at a beach-side cocktail bar.

Mooring on a wooden pier at a mini slip marina at Cayman Kai, we split into three distinct groups. The children remained playing on the beach, whilst the young fit things, who didn't want to miss any opportunity in the sun, swam out to a floating pontoon to practise their diving skills. We wrinklies, who didn't need any further exercise, made our way under the palms to the Kaibo Cocktail Bar where we found it necessary to try just a small sample of the numerous tropical cocktails available on the menu. Over the course of the next ninety minutes it was fair to say that the sample was no longer small. The youngsters joined us at regular intervals and then provided some additional waterborne cabaret by taking it in turns to swim back to the pontoon trying not to spill any of the drinks they carried with them. They managed this delicate operation with a marked degree of success and no little skill. It seemed to be a matter of considerable personal pride that they should not waste any of their cocktails, swimming with one arm whilst balancing a tray of drinks above the water's surface with the other. This matinee entertainment then became the subject of a little bar-side gambling, with wagers on the most likely 'waiter' to spill the drinks. Our expert lifeguards demonstrated their lifesaving skills with the trays and not one drink was lost. Equally this may well have said as much about their appreciation of the cocktails as their swimming ability.

At last our friendly skipper made his way from the boat, back towards us, along the pier and shoreline, with the rolling gait typical of a man who has spent a lifetime on the waves, He motioned that we should join him at one side of the bar where he seemed to find a comfortable position that he was obviously used to. This gave me the opportunity to have a slightly longer chat with him and I learned that he had acquired his skills on a sailboat with his father. He had learned how to handle a boat the hard way; they hadn't had motor boats in those early days, almost the best part of a century ago. It was obvious that he enjoyed his job and loved the sea and his surroundings. He remained full of enthusiasm and liked nothing better than to see his guests enjoying themselves and marvelling at their experience in his very capable hands. He had already demonstrated his prowess as a sailor although we didn't experience his culinary skills for he regularly cooked for his parties on the beach. We had already eaten so much that any more and I'm sure we could have sunk the boat. Our skipper hadn't spent all his life in the Cayman Islands. He had travelled the world on board various liners and with different shipping companies and during the Second World War he had worked for the United States on a tugboat patrolling the area of the Panama Canal. He then lived on a houseboat in that region for a short period of time following the war. In due course the call of home was too great to ignore so he returned to his birthplace. The lure of the sea was such that he started taking tourists to snorkel and dive for conch and lobster in 1951 and initially did this from the area now known as Morgan's Harbour, where on their return they would have a cook-out, now called the ubiquitous barbeque, over a wood fire on the beach. When he later switched to Rum Point he started to stop off at the Sandbar to let his guests feed the stingrays, although he hastened to add that in those days you would have been lucky to see another couple of boats out there.

For a while he pursued some land-based ventures, including a bakery and grocery store, before returning to his first love back on the water and resumed taking landlubbers like myself out to the stingray site. At the time of writing, our veteran sailor continued to go out on four or five trips a week and had yet to find the word 'retirement' in his vocabulary. His love of people and love of the sea kept him young at heart and I only hope that I'm as active when I manage to reach his age. Whilst he loved his work his family were just as important and you would never find him working on a Sunday.

He had been married twice and outlived both his wives and fathered a total of fifteen children, four of whom had also died. He was now the proud grandfather to thirty-one, together with a further fourteen great-grandchildren. Whilst I could have sat and chatted to him all day and learned so much more about the island he eventually decided that it was time to embark for the homeward leg of our afternoon journey. Before we set off on the short walk across the sand we had to wait whilst the girls prepared themselves for the homeward trek. Us guys didn't see the need for any preparation – the girls seemed fine as they were – but it was something we were to become accustomed to as the holiday progressed. We eventually and reluctantly quaffed the remainder of our Kaibo cocktails and joined the crew on board where the now awesome Captain

Marvin Ebanks again took control to steer us back across the bay to the west arm of the island.

Oops, I almost forgot. Time for a quick rub down with what remained of this tube of suntan lotion. Fortunately there was enough left to see me through to the end of the day. Must remember to check supplies when we got back to the hotel. At this rate I would need to replenish stocks at regular intervals.

Whether he had an urgent evening appointment or not, I do not know. Whereas the first stage of our afternoon cruise, to the Sandbar, had been quite serene, and the next to Kaibo slightly quicker, our return journey saw us steaming home at full speed. Our legendary leader was demonstrating there was life in the old dog yet. Standing in the wheelhouse he opened the throttle and skimming his boat across the waves, he left a considerable wake to our stern that rocked the smaller craft that were moored close to Kaibo. He looked to be thoroughly enjoying himself. We certainly were.

Sailing back to harbour it was possible to see the new Ritz Carlton building against the skyline. This was to be a six or seven storey hotel complex, the tallest structure on the island, being constructed on Seven Mile Beach. Also visible were a couple of cruise liners anchored on the other side of the island prior to setting sail with their hundreds of passengers for wherever was to be tomorrow's destination. Both the hotel and the cruise liners dwarfed all the other buildings as we scanned the horizon towards Georgetown. This was hardly surprising as no building is allowed to be more than seven storeys so perhaps this is one reason why the island remains relatively unspoiled.

Our view as we crossed North Sound bay gave a good indication of how flat Grand Cayman is compared to my earlier impressions of Trinidad and Tobago, both of which are positively mountainous by comparison. It wasn't long before we were being piloted, much more sedately, into Governor's Creek as we watched the island ferry plying its way into the channel before crossing the Sound to its destination at Rum Point. Crossing Governor's Harbour we entered one of the canal-like waterways before Captain Marvin navigated his boat into its position at the quayside.

This cheerful senior citizen had provided us with a wonderful afternoon's enjoyment whilst letting us learn something of Caymanian culture and marvel at the wonder of those placid and even-tempered stingrays as we joined them in their habitat. If somebody had suggested to me, just a year earlier. that I would spend an afternoon snorkelling in warm ocean waters feeding and cavorting with stingrays I would have thought they were insane. We thanked our master mariner for giving us a memory of The Stingrays of Grand Cayman that we would not forget for a long time. Although it had not been completed at the time of our visit a bronze and stainless steel Stingray Trio sculpture has since been erected in the Bayshore Mall opposite the South Terminal which I'm sure will be seen and appreciated by all the cruise passengers as they disembark. Enjoy the artwork but then go and mingle with the real McCoy. It was one of the most memorable features of the whole holiday and that comes as a recommendation from a real landlubber. I wonder if one day they will also erect a memorial to Captain Marvin?

Following the short walk back to the hotel there was enough time for a final evening dip in the pool to cool off before a shave and shower prior to changing into some smarter togs for our evening dinner. The bathroom roster was working well and much to my amazement the girls didn't seem to be taking any longer to get ready than us fellas. There was the usual exception to the rule. I'm aware that good rules are not supposed to have exceptions but they clearly hadn't counted on – yes, you know who – Caroline, when they adopted that principle. It wasn't that she was slower than everybody else. She just couldn't make up her mind which shoes to wear with which dress, of which she had many. She came into our apartment at regular intervals seeking advice on the different matching outfits. Even to my inexperienced eye she looked fine in all of them, but still she needed Jan and Carrie's views before making a final decision.

The result was that we would all meet for our evening rendezvous at the poolside bar, before moving on to the restaurant selected for that night, with Danielle and Caroline usually being the last to arrive. They looked as beautiful as ever with Caroline inevitably wearing the outfit that she had first started with and taking not a blind bit of notice of the guidance she had sought only minutes earlier. Now, I can understand her ignoring my pretty worthless opinion but Jan and Carrie did seem to know what they were talking about. I'm not sure I will ever understand women and clothes or that I should even try. I don't somehow think I'm the only bloke in this position. It's obviously a girl thing, that is inherited in the female genes of the species.

On this particular night a table had been reserved at Café Med, a restaurant that was on the road back towards Georgetown. Fortunately it was not an early booking so we were able to linger at the bar, which became something of a ritual as the holiday progressed. A number of us weren't particularly hungry at that stage. This was hardly surprising as our efforts at lunchtime and mid-afternoon had taken their toll. This was a lesson that we should have heeded there and then but in common with many whilst on holiday we continued to eat, and drink, more than we should. I would either have to avoid my doctor for at least the next year or make sure that I tried to stick to my early morning regime of jogging along the west coast regularly. At this early stage of the week it was already distinctly possible to see another diet looming on the horizon when I returned home, having gorged myself for the duration of the holiday.

Eventually we loaded ourselves aboard our prestige motor and Carrie volunteered to be the driver for the night, allowing me to drink. This was an eminently sensible suggestion as following my consumption during the day I may not have been under the limit and it would have been foolish, to say the least, to get behind the wheel. I'm not used to afternoon cocktails containing generous amounts of rum, but I'm equally sure that it's something I could become used to without too much effort.

Café Med was another excellent restaurant off West Bay Road. I'm not sure I did their menu justice as I wanted something fairly light and only needed the one course. Feeling very guilty I had a fish dish and it was delicious. I had to endure some unwarranted abuse from the rest of the party but I was able to remind that them that our friends from the afternoon also ate dead fish and they kept coming back for more. I didn't feel any less guilty but couldn't think of a better excuse at the time.

During the meal the small dance floor was being used for group salsa lessons. This in itself provided some further amusement, watching different shaped and sized couples trying to master the intricacies of this popular dance routine. Amongst the willing learners was a young man who later in the holiday we learned was named Brian. He was very nimble on his feet, appeared ultra-confident, almost extrovert, and was at least ten years younger than any other participant. He was evidently enjoying himself, very quick on the uptake and willing to lead much older partners on the dance floor. In fact the instructor used him for some of the demonstrations. We were to bump into him again, both literally and metaphorically, during our final week on the island, when we were to learn there was much more to him than being an accomplished salsa dancer.

On this particular night we returned to Indies Suites together. I think we were so exhausted from the day's adventures that we all just wanted to get to sleep. For once the youngsters decided that they didn't want to go clubbing into the early hours. Climbing into bed I reflected on just how much we had crammed into the first couple of days. I was hoping that tomorrow would be more relaxing as all the main players in the wedding ceremony would be taking part in a rehearsal at the Grand Old House, Petra Plantation on South Church Street. We had a wedding to go to on the Saturday and from what I could see as I hung my clothes in the wardrobe the bride's mother still had a little bit of sewing to do before the big day.

CHAPTER 6

The Loneliness of the Short-Distance Jogger

'W' Day minus one and astonishingly I was wide awake by seven in the morning, having slept really well. I decided that I probably wouldn't get the chance for the next couple of days so prepared to take myself off for another run. This time, having learned the lesson from Caroline on the first run, I carried my own bottle of water which I collected from the freezer on the way out of the apartment. I knew that it would take only a matter of minutes for the iced water to defrost to enable me to refresh myself with the cool liquid. There wasn't any sign of the girls rousing themselves from their slumbers and I wasn't brave enough to try and wake them, so it was likely to be a much quieter run than our first trip.

Only a small amount of sun cream needed at this early hour, on neck, shoulders and arms, as I prised open a new tube. I had already realised I would need to purchase additional supplies and made a mental note for the next shopping trip. I also rubbed a little embrocation into my leg muscles and carried out a few perfunctory stretching exercises before setting off on my first solo run.

By the time I hit the road I could see Diane already disappearing across the beach. She had outdone me by being up by six o'clock for her usual early morning swim and long walk across the sand.

Once again the traffic was chock-a-block on the highway. I was still having difficulty in believing so many commuters drive into work at this time of the morning. Today, however, they didn't seem to be taking any notice of me. Normality had returned. I was wholly used to running in my own company although I missed the girls' encouragement. The fittest among the inhabitants were to be found cycling to work and without exception all those I had seen the previous day gave me a cheery 'Good morning' or 'Hello' as we passed each other at the start of our day's labours. Well, it was for them, whilst I intended to be relatively lazy for the rest of the day.

What I was not used to was the heat, particularly at that time of the day. I tried to keep in the shade as much as possible. As I was jogging along at my own steady pace I began to think of the forthcoming Olympics to be held in Athens. If I was struggling at my gentle speed what must it be like for the athletes training both in humid conditions, and at altitude, to prepare themselves for what, in some cases, could be the pinnacle of their sporting careers?

I was experiencing just a small amount of the effort, pain and discomfort they were enduring to represent their countries. They must have tremendous stamina and be really super-fit just to achieve the required level of competition to attain the qualifying times for the Olympics. That was a level that I could only dream about but many of them are an inspiration to aspiring young, and not so young, athletes to achieve dreams of competing in and completing a marathon.

A name that came to mind, as I brushed yet more sweat from my eyes, was Paula Radcliffe as I visualised her pounding the pavements with her unique and distinctive 'nodding head' and permafrown expression style of running. We all now know that she didn't meet her own high expectations or reach the standards to which she aspired and ran out of steam after twenty-two miles in the Athens heat, earning herself much opprobrium in the British press. Perhaps she was unwise, or ill advised, or just plain naïve in not wishing to disappoint her supporters to then attempt the ten thousand metres only five days later. We all would have liked to see her finish the race but she didn't deserve the unwarranted and ill-informed criticism that she was subjected to at the hands of the national press. They filed their copy taking little or no account of her injuries or the stomach complaint that she suffered and her reaction to anti-inflammatory medication that sapped her of energy.

What I find is an extraordinarily British trait is how the media love to belittle our heroes when they lose a race or a match. The vast majority of the so-called journalists who castigated her following her performance had never been near a running track in their lives let alone covered the distances that she does in training to enable her to win marathons in record-breaking time. She remains an exceptionally gifted runner as her achievements have proved. We all have bad days at the office and one bad week, however disappointing, does not turn her into a figure deserving of so much derision. Legitimate constructive analysis from fellow former athletes is acceptable but not the demeaning of a sporting icon by supposed professional journalists who are seeking a cheap headline. Just a year earlier they were lauding her as the greatest ever British marathon runner and backing her for the 'Sportsperson of the Year' trophy. I hope she returns to make them eat their words. Already she has, yet again, proved her ability in winning both the New York and London Marathons, achieving a world record along the way. Almost a year after Athens she won the World Championship Marathon in the manner that she had hoped to win the Olympic Games. From the front for 26 miles 385 yards, at a pace no other woman has ever been able to run, she entered Helsinki's Olympic Stadium entirely alone and finished one minute and a few seconds ahead of her great rival Catherine Nderaba.

Radcliffe proved conclusively that she is the supreme marathon runner of her generation. Not only was her time a record for the world championships but, ironically, was also faster than any woman has ever run the distance at the Olympics. To place her achievement in some perspective she ran the race faster than the famous Emil Zatopek's marathon triumph in Helsinki at the 1952 Games and was quicker than any man who won the Olympic gold up to 1960.

Although she was unable to regain peak fitness for the Bejing Olympic Marathon in 2008 she was determined to finish despite carrying an injury. After two years away from competitive athletics where she suffered a series of injuries, including a stress fracture to the base of her spine, and giving birth to her first child, her determination and guts were just not enough to even gain her a podium place in Bejing where she was beaten by many excellent marathon runners who on her day she would normally have left in her wake.

If she can eventually retain the fitness she achieved to win the New York Marathon, less than a year after giving birth, she might just be a contender for London 2012 although that is now asking a lot of her. Unfortunately, she will be four years older and, if I'm objective, will possibly be past her peak, but it would be a brave man to bet against her and I'm not in that camp. I hope I'm wrong and her sheer willpower and single-mindedness keep her going for one valedictory race to cap a great career. In New York that day, against the odds, for twenty-six miles she had to race another great rival and was able to out-sprint her over the final few hundred yards. Once again she was a sporting hero. How fickle can be the great British sporting public or is it really the not so great sporting media who influence public opinion and who after the tears of disappointment in Bejing were quick to criticise her performance, labelling her a 'drama queen'. The reality is that competitive sport is a great leveller and in the elite international arena the margins between success and failure can be minute. They can be dictated by minor stresses and strains, or even a slight chill, so that on the day one opponent might just gain a slight advantage that is the difference between winning and losing. That alone should not make the winner a hero and the remainder also-rans or villains but comparisons over a whole career are a much better barometer of an individual's standing in any sporting discipline. Regrettably such stories rarely supply the editors with an eye catching headline so I suspect that we will continue to see our sportsmen and women being hyped to the heavens when they do well only to then suffer unfairly at the hands of the scribes following an off day. Hopefully the majority of our sportsmen and women are level headed enough to do a Kipling and 'treat those two impostors just the same'.

Whatever the result in London, Radcliffe will, I am sure, remain one of the greatest ever British athletes, who had the courage and determination to take on all comers, leading from the front from start to finish. She took marathon running to a different level. She was not run of the mill and the vast majority will remember her for her willingness to break the mould and break her opponents from the front. She was a winner who represented everything that is best in British sport.

I wonder if their successors will say the same of the journalists who found it so easy to criticise her?

My own daydreaming and somewhat more pedestrian progress continued until I reached the halfway mark near Dolphin Point where I paused for water. I've never been able to run properly and drink at the same time, as natural marathon runners tend to do. So I turned and headed for home walking for a hundred metres whilst I took on board the necessary liquid refreshment. My return lap became much more sluggish than the outward half and whereas at home I can run at a consistent, albeit slow, pace, out there in the heat and humidity of the Cayman Islands it's alarming how the temperature swiftly saps your energy. My pace could be reasonably compared to the tortoise against the likes of Radcliffe's hare. Running on Grand Cayman does have one distinct advantage. It's totally flat and that does make life easier for the runner or cyclist. Back home, Essex is regularly described as a flat county and for the most part that is a fairly accurate description when compared with other counties. On my training runs I've found hills and inclines that you don't expect in Essex and will certainly not come across on the island. Weeks later watching the marathon on television I couldn't possibly experience the emotions that Paula Radcliffe went through but I could relate to her plight on that hot and sultry August evening in the Greek capital.

I arrived back at the hotel to find them cleaning the swimming pool so I leapt into a cold shower and quickly rinsed and wrung out my running kit before joining Jan and the girls for breakfast. Diane was also back so that over the coffee and croissants we looked at the photographs of her new home near Sydney where the views across the water are quite exceptional. This is somewhere else I will have to visit. Jogging on Bondi Beach or on a hillside track in the Blue Mountains as yet remains an unfulfilled ambition.

Carl and Fran arrived in time to join us for coffee and muffins and it's no surprise to learn that they were also up bright and early and running around the island's athletics track before eight in the morning. I told them I'd completed my five miles before they started their run but omitted to tell them how slow I had been today. At that stage I think they were quite impressed with my efforts, for an old codger, and I had no wish to expose my true athletic ability, or to be more accurate, lack of it. I was happy to keep my limitations to myself.

Diane, Carl and I decided we needed to improve our cash-flow situation so we headed for the Cayman Islands National Bank to change some travellers cheques. Having gained entry following scrutiny by two uniformed security guards we were met by a very helpful and talkative customer advisor. We didn't need any advice – our transactions were simple and straightforward – but to reach the cashier everybody had to follow the same procedure. There were four counters open and about half a dozen customers waiting. The staff were genuinely interested in their clients' needs and took their time with each one. You didn't gain the impression that you were just a numbered account on a conveyer belt progressing through the system but were treated as an individual and valued customer. The old-fashioned courtesy was somewhat disarming as one rarely finds this back home. The downside to this was a twenty minute wait to get some cash into my pockets. On holiday this is unimportant but I'm not sure I would always be as patient if this delay were to be the norm. Perhaps two more tellers at the cash desk would have achieved the right balance. The wait did give me the opportunity to chat to a very friendly American lady who was also on vacation. This was her sixth visit and she was now considering purchasing a property on the island that she had 'fallen in love with'.

All the staff were wearing their name badges and one name that was conspicuous was Bodden, which was a name that I hadn't encountered prior to my arrival in Grand Cayman. It quickly became obvious that it was a prominent name on the island and later in the holiday we were to pass by Bodden Town on the south side of the island. I learned in due course that the name had originated on the island after one of Oliver Cromwell's soldiers named Bodden settled there. Over the centuries the family expanded with the majority originally living on the south side of the island which over the years gradually developed into the community of Bodden Town. One other name that we encountered regularly was Ebanks; I think I first noticed it at Captain Marvin's and had seen it a number of times since. It was another name that I was not familiar with although it made me wonder if its derivation might be similar to that of Chris Eubank, the boxer? Both names are common, with established families, in the Cayman Islands and we were to see them regularly throughout our stay although I had seen neither prior to this holiday.

As the island accepts and deals in two currencies, both Cayman Island dollars and United States dollars (and if you proffer the latter you will receive change in the former) I was now more than a little confused as I was also carrying pounds sterling and the travellers cheques. The locals didn't have any problem converting the currencies, as they regularly proved in the evenings when we would pay for our joint meals with a mixture of CI dollars, US dollars or the convenience of the omnipresent plastic credit card and sometimes a combination of all three. Ted had tried to ease the situation by giving each of us a computerised conversion chart that he had printed back home in England. This should have helped matters but for me it became more confusing and difficult. Firstly I had to carry it in my spectacle case. The print was so small that without my reading glasses it was impossible to decipher. My next problem was to find my glasses case. I'd only needed them over the past six months and continually put them down and forgot where I last had them. The young-sters also put this memory loss down to my age! I was beginning to think they might be right. Finally and fatally he had transposed the conversion rate incorrectly so that CI and US dollars read the wrong way round and both were inaccurate when compared against the pound sterling. It took us about a week to realise this, when we eventually happened upon an accurate conversion table in a local gift shop. The one advantage to this major error came at the end of the holiday when on returning the minibus we found the converted bill to be much more modest than we had originally estimated, leaving a sizeable sum in the kitty.

Anyway, I received CI$210 for each of my US$250 cheques and clutching my passport and different denominations of notes in various currencies left the bank and rejoined the others back in the bus without dropping any of it in the gutter or forgetting my spectacle case which was tucked into the back pocket of my shorts.

I was now becoming used to driving an automatic with left-hand drive on the nearside of the road and also making sure my left leg didn't move from the footwell. The three of us decided to go and seek out the local golf courses as we were determined to test our golfing prowess in this wonderful Caribbean environment. After all, it's not often one has such an opportunity. We wanted to make it into an occasion that we must not miss. As keen golfers, of limited talent, we were full of optimism and were sure the new experience would only improve our golf. As is normal for such individuals the reality was not to match our own high and unrealistic expectations. We quickly found the Britannia course at the rear of the Hyatt Regency Hotel complex. We took a leisurely drive through the estate. It didn't take us long to realise that even if we pooled all our resources we couldn't afford to live here. You needed to be seri-ously rich to own any of these houses, although we learned that some are available for holiday lets.

Amongst the huge detached mansions, with beautifully manicured lawns and gardens that backed onto the golf course, you would catch the occasional glimpse of a buggy sliding across the verdant fairways transporting its driver to his or her next attempt to achieve both distance and accuracy. The estate was tastefully designed and the whole area had a sense of opulence. In addition to the multi-garages there were also carports that housed the parked golf buggies. A number of the properties had the advantage of a waterside location with their own ocean-going yachts moored alongside their kitchen windows. The three of us in our commonplace hired minibus were given some strange looks by the small army of gardeners who were busy mowing, clipping, pruning and planting the well tended roadside gardens. We did not appear in harmony with the neighbourhood, were obviously strangers and probably looked more than a little shifty as we drove slowly around the leafy avenues, apparently casing the joints. In reality we were trying to view as many holes on the course as possible to assess how difficult it might be for us relatively high handicappers. There were lots of traps for the unwary golfer. The fairways were narrow and although generally flat also contained a considerable number of undulations that I suspect were manmade. In addition to the numerous bunkers there were also more than a fair share of water hazards that experience had taught me tended to be a magnet for any wayward shot of mine. In any round, on a course that I had not previously played, I normally managed to play a high proportion of these and where there was water you can be reasonably sure that I would find it.

We watched a few games in progress and although we were unaware of the quality of the golfers it was readily apparent that the greens were lightning fast. Overall, we were unanimous that the course was difficult and probably too daunting for the likes of ourselves. Parking the bus amongst the limousines we entered the clubhouse with some trepidation. We found the pro shop and enquired of the resident professional details of the course and terms for guest players. As was the norm on the island he proved very helpful and provided a comprehensive explanation of how the course was played. On odd days in the week it was set as a nine-hole championship course played twice from different tees with a total distance of six thousand yards. On even days it was played as an eighteen-hole par fifty-seven executive course with Sundays used as both, changing at midday.

We told him we had watched a little of the golf and from what we had seen it looked very difficult, allowing little margin for error. He told us the course had been designed by Jack Nicklaus and was beautiful but very challenging for players of all abilities. Apparently even a visiting professional at a pro-am competition was heard to remark after a particularly trying round that 'Nicklaus must have designed this on a bad day'. We ascertained that it was possible to hire clubs for the day and the fact that they were TaylorMade indicated the standard expected. Obtaining the necessary brochures we made our way back to our conspicuous minibus, parked in a row of smart limousines, rather in awe of the golfers who were unloading their bags from the rear of their electric buggies. The expressions on their faces and the overheard snatches of conversation indicated that they had all had good rounds of golf. It was obvious they were much better golfers than us and must have been regulars on the course. This was one impressive golf course that, as it turned out, we were not destined to play.

Our next port of call was the Safehaven Links Course, which is situated adjacent to the Ritz Carlton Tower Hotel, at the time a monolith under construction and growing by the minute. Every time we drove past it there seemed to be hordes of tradesmen in hard hats, swarming around the building like bees around a honey pot, fetching and carrying bricks, concrete and other assorted building materials or construction equipment. Situated on the edge of Seven Mile Beach, as the edifice gradually rose and took shape its progress resembled a giant concrete-grey gun emplacement but this merely represented the shell of the building. There was a long way to go before the finishing touches could be applied and if the finished article were to match the plans, which Fran and I saw later in the holiday, it would become an impressive feature of the Grand Cayman landscape. In due time they were going to offer competition to the current two courses on West Bay. They were having their own course designed by Greg Norman and from the marketing brochures I was sure it would be just as impressive as both its neighbours.

At first sight Safehaven looked a little more inviting. The first hole is a relatively straightforward par three. Beware first impressions, they can be misleading. This course is a par seventy-one at over six thousand six hundred yards and with the prevailing winds can equal over seven thousand yards on a calm day, according to the marketing literature. Again it is relatively flat but has water abutting or crossing the majority of holes. Following our initial recce we decided to give this course the opportunity to test our golfing skills the following week. Although this appeared to be the less demanding of the two golf clubs that we had inspected we did only have time for a brief look at the course. The moral here is not to rely upon just a cursory examination. Do your homework before making final decisions. Having come to our decision I therefore decided that I would need to buy some additional golf balls in view of the amount of water I needed to avoid. What I didn't realise at the time was that the other two were thinking exactly the same. Experience was to prove that I, and they, needed them.

Making our way back to the hotel we dropped Diane off at Governor's Beach to allow her to wander off on one of her beach trekking expeditions. Not having any need to hurry Carl and I decided that we would explore further north along West Bay. We drove off towards the turtle farm and did a circular tour in the direction of Hell and back – Hell being a small hamlet located in the north-west of the island. We were to return to both with the gang after the wedding.

A number of things struck us about this part of the island. We found a few palm-fringed coves and parking areas that were totally unoccupied, giving the west coast of the island the impression of serenity. The sea was calm and inviting with the sun glistening on the gentle waves as they rolled onto the sandy beach that sloped gradually into the clear blue water. The balmy scene was enchanting and as good as any I've seen in any Caribbean tourist pamphlet. This proved to be a disastrously inaccurate description some two months later.

Property, or realty as it's described locally, varied from the beachside mansions and hotels to the almost shanty-town appearance of some of the corrugated roofed bungalows slightly further inland. This reminded me very much of parts of Tobago; very laid back and commercialism hadn't yet been allowed to spoil the character of the island. Another prominent feature was the number of churches and chapels we passed on our travels. I don't know the size of their congregations or whether they are attended only on high days, holidays and the Sabbath but they certainly give the impression of a very Christian country, with more places of worship than seemed viable for such a small population. There is no doubt that many that we met were true Christians and regular attendees at their own churches of whatever denomination. Very different to back home where congregations are falling and many now visit church only for births, deaths and marriages and even those numbers are diminishing.

Driving out in the vicinity of The Shores and Morgan's Harbour provided fine views across the tranquil waters of North Sound towards Stingray City and the various boats taking their mix of diving enthusiasts, sightseers and inquisitive tourists to their aquatic adventures for the day.

We eventually made a slow and circuitous return to our base where Carl and I were going to join the girls on the beach. On arrival we were met with a mini crisis. Linking up with Sue and Vicky they told us that Ted had been taken to hospital earlier in the morning with a suspected heart attack. Fortunately the electrocardiogram tests had not revealed any heart problems. Ted had experienced a very restless night and there was a possibility that he had an ulcer or even kidney stones which can be excruciatingly painful. The heat, dehydration and any possible anxiety over the following day's wedding may also have been contributory factors. Ted was still at the hospital awaiting discharge whilst completing yet more insurance forms. On this occasion they were of the medical variety. He was becoming something of an expert at the intricacies of insurance claim applications. He didn't need collecting at that time and was to return later in the afternoon in time for the wedding rehearsal, armed with a prescription for enough medication to keep him going until well after the holiday. In fact, we could probably have opened our own pharmacy.

Meanwhile Carl and I were despatched to the beach to inform the girls of the morning's happenings and allay any fears. This was made much easier as we now had the test results and the situation was under control. Nonetheless this resulted in a prompt return from the beach, as everybody wanted to see Ted and make sure for themselves that he had made a full recovery from his ordeal. By the time he returned, although not exactly looking a picture of health he was still a little flushed but then so were most of us in the heat; he was feeling better and appeared relaxed. He was very complimentary about his treatment which had been swift and very professional. We had previously passed a Medical University on our excursions which, bearing in mind the size and situation of the island, was surprising. For any budding medical students I would certainly recommend Grand Cayman. From our limited, and what happily proved to be our only, experience the medical facilities appeared to be more than adequate.

Whilst the immediate family attended the dress rehearsal, all being transported by Carrie in the minibus, the remainder of us enjoyed a lazy afternoon around the hotel pool.

Copious amounts of suntan lotion continued to be applied as there was no let up in the afternoon sun. The temperature appeared to be increasing with each passing day and I was already spending more time in the shade. Fortunately the weather forecast for the weekend was not displaying any great change other than a further increase in temperature. The omens for the wedding were good but I would need to ensure lotion and spare tee-shirts were readily available.

As I lay on the towel-covered sun loungers reading, daydreaming and sunbathing, the surroundings of the apartments' arched balconies and patios were reminiscent of the cloisters of a medieval monastery or one of the more eminent public school quadrangles, and just as peaceful. Our idyll was to last for another twenty-four hours. We were not to know, at that time on that gloriously sunny and tranquil Friday afternoon, that the vocal Dick the Diver must have been preparing for his vacation at that very moment. I'm sure any near neighbours of his back home in the United States must have been well aware and were looking forward to some peace and quiet for the next week.

Following the rehearsal Ted was already looking a lot better. Some of the girls had gone back into town with Mel for a pedicure and whatever else girlies do to beautify themselves. They all wanted to look their best for the wedding. They were away for some time and us guys jokingly wondered whether we should cut our toenails by the pool. We unanimously decided against it.

The entertainment for the afternoon was provided by Indie, the hotel cat. I had seen her for the first time that morning and although I was prepared to approach and stroke her I remained wary and was unwilling to turn my back on her or, importantly, allow my legs within biting distance. She had six kittens and all were being well fed and looked after by both the hotel staff and many of the guests. She was clearly a caring mother and naturally concerned for the wellbeing of her offspring who had been the subject of numerous visits from all and sundry. Such were the frequency of these well meaning, but in feline terms intrusive, visits she obviously decided that she needed to move her brood to a better protected residence that provided increased camouflage and an improved and safer environment. Over the course of a couple of hours she moved all six kittens from their original lair at one end of the hotel to a new home underneath a large shrub that had ample foliage in which she could hide them. Although you couldn't see them ensconced in their leafy den everybody knew exactly where they were. The whole operation had been patiently planned and executed by Indie, displaying her maternal instincts, and carrying each baby in her mouth the entire length of the swimming pool to the fresh hideaway. From time to time she stopped and paused for breath but on each occasion took advantage of overhanging bushes to protect her tiny furry mouthful from prying eyes. Although there must have been thirty or more spectators they were all enthralled with this display of animal magic and not one person tried to interfere with her labours whilst carrying out her family house move. Having completed the final journey with her sixth kitten she joined them under their leafy canopy where she then took advantage of a well-earned rest. Pickfords could not have made a better job of it themselves.

Later in the afternoon we were joined by David and Mike who arrived with Cynthia and Jose together with Ray, David and Cynthia's father, who we were introduced to for the first time. There was still time for all of us to take advantage of another dip in the pool and with Jose joining us in the water our swimming coaches, and Carl in particular, went into teaching mode and gave him the first of what was to become a number of swimming lessons. Once again we didn't want to leave the pool, which made the showers a rushed affair before we met up at the bar for drinks and nibbles prior to heading off for our evening meal. In other circumstances I think many of us would have been happy to remain at the bar as we saw the hotel's complimentary regular Friday night buffet being prepared.

Tonight was to be special as we were all to rendezvous at the Sunset Bar, which was where David and Mel first met. It was my turn to drive so I was sticking with the fruit cocktails, which I found surprisingly refreshing and looked no different to the vast array of alcoholic mixers that were also on offer. I enjoyed these so much that it was no hardship to drink these on my driving nights. I would save my wine allowance for the meal. The Sunset Bar is on the south of the island and is a popular venue for all age groups. I had to park in the road but this didn't present a problem.

The bar and open-air restaurant were crowded and although we were a large group it didn't take too long to secure our tables which provided a panorama over the rocks and semi-circular bay back west towards Georgetown. We also had a fine view of the late evening incoming aircraft as they completed their finals with a long arcing sweep around

West Bay before straightening and zooming down to the runway that was about a mile from where we were seated. Having been up there a few days earlier it was now interesting to watch the manoeuvre from the ground and gain a different perspective as these giant metal birds seemed to float past overhead to land safely on the tarmac at Owen Roberts International. We must have watched a dozen or so of these international jets glide in bringing their cargoes of divers, bankers and tourists, all of whom would be exceedingly well catered for by the fine restaurants, chic villas, smart hotels and sublime submarine adventures that were awaiting their arrival. As the planes approached it became obvious that the majority were owned by the local carrier, Cayman Airways. This was an airline that, until a few months previously I had never heard of, but as the national carrier they ran busy daily schedules into and out of Grand Cayman. Little did anybody realise that just a few weeks later this relatively small airline company, in worldwide terms, would become one of the few lifelines for the islanders.

Yet again the food at the Sunset Bar was plentiful and there were so many of us that we tended to split into smaller groups at the different tables. This had the effect of making us a somewhat raucous and merry group as conversations across the tables became louder in direct proportion to the amount of wine and beer being drunk. The meal finished just in time to watch the firework spectacular that illuminated the bay from Georgetown. We were assured that this wasn't in honour of David and Mel's wedding but is a fairly regular event on the island. The brightly coloured rockets and starbursts lit up the night sky and I'm sure could be seen from almost anywhere on the island. Strangely enough we must have been too far distant, or the prevailing wind protected us from hearing the obvious bangs as each pyrotechnic ignited and exploded in the distance. Although there was still the noise of the restaurant and bar it still seemed strange to see the rockets zoom into the darkness without being able to hear their screech and whizzbangs as they did so. It was as if the display took place in an eerie silence that somehow didn't appear normal. Perhaps it was just the school-kid coming out in me again. I was on holiday and wanted to be a part of it as opposed to being just a spectator on the sidelines.

The boys at this stage had decided to take David off to a local club for his final night of freedom and give him a stag night to remember. Ted and I were not convinced that this was the wisest course to take on the night before his wedding – Ted perhaps more so than me, but this was understandable being the father of the bride. Over the years we had been to more than our fair share of stag dos and whilst at their age this was the obvious thing to do, experience had taught us both that it is probably more sensible to arrange it for the weekend before the wedding. I'm equally sure that when we were in our twenties, and certainly as teenagers, we didn't see it this way at all. The group made their way to their taxis having made numerous promises to the girls to the extent that I was sure there were far too many to keep. I'm also sure from an equal number of whispered threats from the ladies present, into their shell-likes, that they would suffer unmentionable consequences should David meet any unforeseen hazards that prevented him from turning up bright eyed, bushy tailed and on time on the morrow. I also recollect Mel whispering sweet nothings – well, at the time I presumed that's what they were – into David's ear before he left. Now I'm sure they couldn't have contained any sort of menace, but by this stage of the evening the girls had persuaded her to partake of the odd tequila so she may just have been reminding him to enjoy himself as she had already had her hen night a week or two earlier.

This is a slightly misleading description – well a wholly misleading description – as the hen night with her girlie friends from the school had lasted a week. It had been on board a Caribbean cruise liner that they had boarded in Georgetown and then island hopped in the lap of luxury for the next seven days and nights. I know, I've seen the photographs!

Back home I know hen and stag nights have progressed from a Friday night patronising the local boozer, night club and Indian or Chinese restaurants to weekend breaks at a wide selection of far more interesting European destinations. The imperative being to demonstrate to our continental cousins that we don't want to be on the fringe of the European Union but genuine partners in entente cordiale at the top table drinking their wine, beer and spirits in true Anglo-Saxon fashion.

Why is it that the Caribbean equivalent appears a lot more appealing? It might just have something to do with the climate. The sun, sea, shimmering sand and thought of lying on the deck of a cruise ship sipping one of the hundreds of ice-cold cocktails mixed by a friendly bartender as you anchor off yet another exotic palm-fringed island, for a lazy day in the sun.

As the boys left, Ted and I could just about understand why the girls didn't seem in the slightest bit envious of the lads' night out. We had remained behind with the girls as he was still recovering from his hospitalisation earlier in the day and I had volunteered to be bus driver for the night. If I'm also honest the thought of staying in the smoky atmosphere of a night club until the early hours is no longer as appealing as it was thirty years ago. We both got into a somewhat philosophical conversation with Ken, the Methodist minister-cum-official photographer. His ministry had been anything but dull. At different times he had been both a prison chaplain and a police chaplain. On the face of it that may appear contradictory but the reality was that they were complementary and he learned from each experience. Listening to him talk I could imagine him being both respected and effective in each role. As he said, he was attending to people encompassing the good, the bad and the indifferent. All of them had similar problems whether they were financial, domestic, addictive dependencies or something else that they had difficulty coping with. What was different was how they coped with them and their ability to learn from their experiences and if necessary make changes in their lifestyles. Everybody is different and some are capable of facing difficulties and dealing with problems far better than others. He was not being judgemental but merely relating facts as he saw them. Somehow the conversation gradually progressed until we found we were discussing paedophiles, their lives in prison, and how they should be supervised and monitored when they are released. Should they ever be released and how do you protect further potential young victims or prevent the paedophiles re-offending? As I mentioned, it was a fairly philosophical conversation and I think at that point we all agreed that it was something to which there are many different, sometimes polarised, views without being able to find a solution that would be acceptable to everybody.

The debate was getting much too heavy to be having the night before the wedding. We moved swiftly on to the merits of our favourite football teams and their chances of winning the Premiership in the coming season. This actually created much more division between us and was far more suitable to our environment. Having been born virtually opposite their ground and supported Chelsea Football Club all my life I was full of my usual pre-season optimism and confident they would win the league for the first time in fifty years. For the first time in half a century my optimism was to be rewarded with a record number of Premiership points. As a young boy, back in 1955, my memories of the Blues' first Championship triumph are vague, although I can still remember the names of all the players. Media coverage at the time was poor due to a newspaper strike and *Match of the Day* was still some years away whilst satellite and cable television were not yet even a distant dream. How technology has changed in just over a generation. Ted and Carrie were singing the praises of Arsenal, having just won the Championship without losing a game, but Chelsea were to prove to be their masters over the coming season with their brand of English grit and determination together with a generous mix of continental flair that was blended together and given fresh impetus by the introduction of their new outspoken, some would say outrageous, 'special' Portuguese manager and one or two foreign imports.

On returning to our minibus I suddenly realised this would be the first time I would be driving it in the dark. This didn't concern me unduly until I got in and switched on the lights. On the very few occasions I had previously driven a car with an automatic gearbox the panel is normally illuminated to enable the driver to see which gear the car is in. Our panel was unlit. What I didn't want to do was inadvertently place it in park or reverse when we should be moving forward. Apart from the distinct possibility of suddenly shooting backwards and shunting the car behind us, selecting the wrong gear could have quite devastating consequences for the cogs in the gearbox. I had this mental picture of teeth shearing off in a grinding mass of whirring metal and us coming to a premature halt as our trusty motor met a sudden and early demise half way home. They must have the equivalent of the AA or RAC on Grand Cayman. Fortunately, thanks to an overhead light I managed to locate 'park' and 'drive' and decided that I would rely on just these two for the journey home. Much to my amazement it was uneventful with very little traffic about and no need for any right turns into oncoming traffic. We arrived back in time for a nightcap at the hotel bar before preparing for the big day. A quick look at the weather channel on the television before going to bed indicated the possibility of a stormy night – this wasn't a surprise as we could see lightning in the far distance in West Bay – but tomorrow's forecast had not changed and was predicting another very hot and sunny day. This proved to be totally accurate. Eat your heart out Michael Fish.

Before finally retiring to my bed for the night I had to make sure that the suntan cream and deodorant were readily available in large containers. At the time I did not know that the anti-perspirant would need to be administered by the gallon to be of any benefit. A quick dab, or even a prolonged rub, with a roll-on would prove to be as effective as King Canute holding back the waves. For me beads of perspiration were to become waves of sweat. At least it was good honest sweat and I don't think there is any anti-perspirant yet manufactured that would have been the slightest use in the circumstances.

Chapter 7

Anti Climax Day – 'W' Day + One

As you may have noticed from the first chapter, my memory of the Sunday, 'W' Day plus one, particularly the morning, was rather vague. This is probably attributable to the wedding celebrations and our return to the hotel, where we sat on our balcony and talked through our memories of the day whilst consuming a final drink. In my case it had been a glass of water. Honest guv.

Although I started my jumbled jottings of the events at the marriage ceremony and reception of 'W' Day, on the Sunday morning, by the time I had completed these initial scribblings a couple of days had passed by and a quantity of liquor had passed my lips. Jan and the girls told me this was the day after the day before but I was writing about the day before yesterday. Consequently, I was more confused than usual and that particular Sunday remains a bit hazy. I cannot, therefore, vouch for total accuracy. I do remember the day started with a late, leisurely and light breakfast with Jan and Diane where I drank more than my usual amount of fruit juice to counter any dehydration.

Sitting by the pool in the morning sunshine I started to gather my thoughts and pen the first few notes about the wedding day on what had been a very memorable Saturday. At least my recollections of it, which were quite reasonable to start with, needed some memory-jogging and assistance from the girls on some of the finer detail as the morning wore on. As I've said I eventually completed my scribbled notes over two days later as I was not at my best on the Sunday morning, which still remains somewhat obscure. I therefore have a ready-made excuse if I have included any inaccuracies. Any such error would have been based upon what the girls told me as I faithfully recorded their version in the certain knowledge that they wouldn't have dreamt of misleading me and their younger memories were bound to be much more accurate than mine.

First and foremost I had to administer the first of the daily applications of the suntan cream which together with sunhat and shades remained close to my sun-lounger for the duration.

The remainder of the party gradually assembled around the pool with the youngsters, not unusually, being the last to arrive. We all settled to what was to be a lazy morning around the pool, reading, sunbathing and dozing, which proved to be the dominant pastime, with me jotting down my recollections of 'W' Day.

Lying there with the sun rising and glinting on the inviting blue water of the swimming pool I could understand why Mel had been attracted to working in Grand Cayman.

It is the largest of the Cayman Islands lying in the Western Caribbean just less than ninety miles south-west of its smaller sister islands of Cayman Brac with the appropriately named Little Cayman situated to its north-east and separated by a channel five miles wide. In Caribbean terms they are a small isolated group of islands one hundred and fifty miles to the south-west of Cuba, one hundred and eighty miles north-west of Jamaica and a little less than five hundred miles south of Miami. Cayman Airways run flights between the islands on one of their smaller aircraft carrying no more than twenty passengers. From their base at Owen Roberts Airport in Georgetown it's no more than a forty minute hop to the two smaller islands.

In addition to the now famous underwater attractions the islands boast a wealth of flora and fauna that do not get the recognition that the efforts of the local preservationists and environmentalists deserve. For example, Grand Cayman hosts the great natural wonder of the blue iguana which, until recently, was close to extinction with a mere thirty creatures left in the wild. A recovery programme, run by the island's National Trust, has not only ensured their survival but they are now beginning to thrive again. The blue iguana, in fact a very distinctive iridescent blue, is a giant dragon-like lizard that can grow to more than five feet in length and weigh as much as twenty-five pounds can now only be found on Grand Cayman. They are much less hardy creatures than their cousins the common green iguanas native to Central and South America. The successful recovery programme has seen their numbers rise to over one hundred and forty. They are all tagged and released into the Botanic Gardens but recently there have been reports that they have now managed to wander further afield and been spotted on one of the golf courses where it must be quite disconcerting to see one basking in the sunshine and then start bobbing its head up and down just as you're about to putt for a birdie, which I have to admit was unlikely in my case.

Away from the sophisticated hotels, million-dollar villas, palm-fringed beaches and shopping arcades the island is made up of marshy flatlands, mangrove forests and tropical woodland. In between the wooden boarded dwellings of the interior grow huge mahogany trees and red, orange and tangerine-yellow poincianas that provide a vista of colour to attract any artist or photographer anxious to capture a portrait of nature in full bloom. I'm not sure if the Rev Ken found time to focus his lens on such pictorial delights but I don't doubt for one minute that if he had it would have been an accurate and lifelike portrayal of natural beauty.

Geographically, the Cayman Islands are part of the Cayman Ridge, which extends westward from Cuba. The Cayman Trench, the deepest part of the Caribbean at a depth of over four miles, separates the three small islands from Jamaica.

Cayman Brac is the most rugged of the three islands with windswept and deserted beaches and a few tiny settlements that belong to a bygone age. The Brac Bluff stretches like a spine for the length of the island and affords magnificent uninterrupted views over the waters of the Caribbean Sea. It is home to a variety of parrots and its limestone cliffs provide a haven for brown boobies and frigate birds. Their natural habitat attracts ornithologists and tourists alike. In short it's a twitcher's paradise.

The eponymous Little Cayman is the smallest of the archipelago with a population of about one hundred and twenty. They are either local Caymanians or visitors who fell in love with the island and never went home. It is no more than ten miles long and a mile across and had been a haunt of Ernest Hemingway. Its airport is the antithesis of Heathrow. A small landing strip and wooden shack, which doubles as both check-in counter and island post office, is all that is required as terminal building, fire station and air traffic control. The island has yet to experience even a semblance of a hassled passenger in a security queue. A short distance away is a video rental store which must do some trade in order to exist but quite who would want to rent videos in such numbers to make it a viable enterprise in such a location I do not know.

In common with its sister islands Little Cayman has its share of deserted beaches where the little beachfront bungalows have become the small and private resorts catering for discerning holidaymakers. Moving away from the beaches much of the remainder of the palm-fringed island is a flat ten square miles of nature reserve which houses diverse breeds of birds. Visiting twitchers could find anything from white, green or tin-toned herons, frigate birds with nine-foot wingspans to the red-footed booby plus a few more in between.

The islands enjoy temperatures of seventy to ninety degrees Fahrenheit all year round. As you can see I'm of the generation that understands 'old money'. In modern parlance it is the equivalent of twenty-one to thirty-two degrees centigrade or Celsius although I have never learned or bothered to find out why the same temperature is referred to by two different names. I know that the temperature scale was introduced by the Swedish astronomer Anders Celsius in the eighteenth century but why it can also be referred to as centigrade I do not know. The conversion is difficult enough by having to subtract thirty-two, multiply by five and divide by nine without then having two names for the same thing. The reality is that, whichever denomination you wish to use, you needn't take your winter woollies on holiday to Grand Cayman. Unless, of course, your name happens to be Caroline or you are willing to pay unnecessary excess baggage charges. Lying south of the Tropic of Cancer the islands do not experience the frost, ice and snow of British winters.

Grand Cayman, at seventy-six square miles, is the daddy of the three islands, is a major international financial centre and is also becoming more popular as a tourist destination aimed presently at the luxury end of the market but also specialising in holidays for diving enthusiasts. Wherever you swim in the Caymans you are never more than a dozen breaststrokes away from beautiful and exotic coral reefs which are home to numerous tropical fish such as the parrotfish or even the fairy basslet which you will not miss due to its being the most vivid shade of purple you are ever likely to see either on land or underwater.

The islands are recognised as the birthplace of the modern sport of recreational scuba diving following the opening of the Caribbean's first diving shop in Grand Cayman by the legendary Bob Soto in 1957. Whilst I'm not a diving enthusiast, the experience with snorkel and stingrays being the limit of my waterborne adventures, I can understand the attraction of diving in this colourful kaleidoscope of underwater charm.

The offshore financial market and the tourist industry form the foundations of the Caymans' prosperity and strong economy and they combine to provide the local populace with the highest standard of living in the Caribbean. This financial stability seems to make a significant difference to visitors because it removes that uncomfortable feeling, sometimes experienced elsewhere, that while you're spending a very lazy and relaxing holiday, the locals are living a far less pleasant lifestyle and are, consequently, full of resentment at the good time you are having. This certainly wasn't the case with the locals that we met. The Caymanians greeted us with broad smiles and appeared genuinely pleased to welcome visitors. They are proud of their territory and happy with their way of life. They hold family and community values above all else and there is a tangible sense of wellbeing that greets you at every turn.

It wasn't until 1966 that the islands started to take tourism seriously and the initial Tourism Board was formed. The potential for attracting overseas visitors was then recognised and developed and the Cayman Islands Department of Tourism was created by the Tourism Law of 1974.

Grand Cayman, if it were to be stretched out straight, would be somewhere between twenty-five and thirty miles long and I would estimate a maximum of five miles across at its widest point. It is very flat, with its highest point no more than sixty feet above sea level, if that. It has a total area of approximately seventy-eight square miles and its most striking feature is the shallow, reef-protected lagoon, the North Sound, which itself has an area of about thirty-five square miles. To describe the island as crescent shaped is, in fact, inaccurate. Its long narrow arm to the west starts to give that impression as its sweeps around to the south past the capital Georgetown leaving the immense bay of North Sound behind as you move towards the east. At this stage the curve straightens out and becomes wider providing the flat eastern underbelly of the island. There is just the one main road around the coastal perimeter of this eastern peninsula that is bisected at approximately the halfway point by the Frank Sound Drive which links the Queens Highway to the north with Eastern Highway that skirts the southern boundary of the island. This is the only road that leads to the Queen Elizabeth II Botanic Garden which is pretty much in the centre of the island and seems to be surrounded by a mangrove swamp. The road system is easy to follow and according to my tourist guide has five 'A' class roads covering the length and breadth of the island. For the most part these provide a pleasant driving experience unless you hit Georgetown during the rush hour, particularly if you need to turn right.

My early impression from this first visit to the island, particularly from the architecture, was predominantly of a colonial British influence but with an undoubted move towards a more modern American style, which was gathering increasing momentum but fortunately seemed to remain sympathetic to the more traditional buildings. The Cayman Islands elected to remain a British Crown colony in 1962 when Jamaica gained its independence. Until that time they had been a dependency of Jamaica. The islands, as a United Kingdom Overseas Territory, received their first governor in 1971 and their constitution was adopted in 1972. At the time of our trip the incumbent governor was Mr Bruce Dinwiddy, although there is now a large measure of self-government. The government leader was Mr McKeever Bush, dubbed locally, and somewhat irreverently, by some as 'Big Mac'. This doubtless has something to do with the size of the man. His Excellency the Governor, who is directly appointed by Her Majesty the Queen, retains responsibility for the civil service, defence, external affairs and internal security and the Commissioner of the Royal Cayman Islands Police Service reports directly to the governor's office. The police force for the islands was first established back in 1907. Prior to that time there used to be a number of locally appointed district constables who received the princely sum of ten shillings (fifty pence in today's decimalised currency) for a day's duty. The current police service now has over four hundred and fifty police officers and support staff and bears little resemblance to those early days. Having said that the concept of district constables has stood the test of time and today's community-based neighbourhood officers forging contacts with their local residents remains the bedrock of successful policing. Since our visit the governor completed his term of office and he has been succeeded by Mr Stuart Jack, who coincidentally was brought up in Essex and as somebody who had been involved in scouting since his youth also took on the role of Chief Scout of the Scout Association of the Cayman Islands. The general election, which was postponed due to the disaster in September 2004 was eventually held in 2005 and returned Mr Kurt Tibbetts as the new government leader.

With a population of around fifty thousand enjoying one of the highest standards of living in the Caribbean there is just about one percent unemployment in this small but thriving Caribbean community.

The resident population consists of ninety different nationalities thus making it a multi-cultural and highly diverse society.

The tax free status of the islands dates back to the late eighteenth century and for generations the reason for its introduction was one of the most often told stories in the island's history. The tale relived the night of 'The Wreck of the Ten Sails' which was the biggest shipwreck in the history of Grand Cayman. Legend indicates that one night in November 1788 the lead ship in a convoy of merchantmen bound from Jamaica to Britain ran aground on a reef to the east of the island. She gave off a distress signal to warn the other ships, but this was misunderstood as a call to follow with the result that nine more ships sailed straight onto the rocks. The people of East End are reported to have demonstrated great heroism in ensuring that no lives were lost and folk-tale further states that one of the lives saved was royalty. For this, King George III is said to have granted the islands freedom from conscription, while another report claims that freedom from taxation was bestowed on the people of the islands as a reward. However, actual records do not entirely support this story.

In recent years a different version of this story has been accepted and officially recognised as the definitive history of the event following some detailed research which uncovered further evidence which proved to be far more convincing. Whilst there are many similarities there are also major differences between the two accounts, not least being the date when the tragedy occurred. The basic scenario remained the same with ten vessels from a large convoy of over fifty merchant ships en route to England and Europe from Jamaica being wrecked off the eastern tip of the island, close to Gun Bay. It was in February 1794, not November 1788 as was long believed, that this courageous and historic saga unfolded. Contrary to enduring and popular myth the convoy did not carry Prince William, the future King William IV, or any other member of the royal family. Quite why their route from Jamaica to England took them past Grand Cayman I do not know.

Local people, as soon as they realised there was a potential disaster occurring just offshore left their homes in the middle of a treacherous night and commenced a brave and difficult rescue operation. The fifty-eight merchantmen, sailing in poor weather conditions, were accompanied by the Royal Naval frigate HMS *Convert*. Many of the ships in the convoy were forced off course by strong winds. It was shortly after midnight and a number of the convoy's ships drifted past the frigate. In the darkness there was an outbreak of gunfire and some of the ships thought they were being attacked by pirates.

These waters had gained a reputation for such attacks during the previous century. At one time this had been a constant threat from a variety of ne'er-do-wells ranging from the Spanish conquistadors to ordinary ocean-going maritime muggers and robbers if they could be described as such. Some of the pirates gained considerable notoriety and included the likes of Sir Henry Morgan, Sir Edward 'Blackbeard' Teach, Neal Walker and the famous female pirate Ann Bonney who was linked to 'Calico Jack' Rackham and his gang of seafaring rascals, all of whom continue to be part of the romantic but historically questionable folklore of this western Caribbean island. Whether they resembled the likes of Johnny Depp as an erstwhile Pirate of the Caribbean is open to debate but probably unlikely.

Amidst the confusion ten of the fleet, including HMS *Convert*, decided to get closer to the shore to afford themselves greater protection. Without today's navigational aids, global positioning satellites and modern radio telecommunications the gales and strong sea forced them into the coral reef where all ten ships went aground in the rough waters and were lost. HMS *Convert* herself would probably have avoided the disaster had it not been for a merchant ship crashing into her bow. By the time the *Convert* had cleared the vessel, the frigate was too near the breakers to avoid them. She struck the reef and bilged. Winds and rough seas continued, preventing the rest of the convoy from coming to the aid of those who had been wrecked on the rocks. A number of intrepid island fishermen took to their small boats and rowed out to the fast sinking ships to carry out a heroic rescue. They were undaunted by the atrocious weather conditions returning time and again to pluck the exhausted sailors from the waves as they crashed against the reef. Hundreds of crewmen were saved that night due to the courage of a few local gallant Caymanians in their tiny fishing boats. It is amazing that the death toll remained as low as eight. This was one of the most memorable events in the history of the Cayman Islands and today there is a memorial to this unique and tragic maritime accident, roughly three miles south of the Reef Resort in Gun Bay, at a vantage point called Queen's View overlooking the scene of this dramatic rescue.

The master of HMS *Convert*, Captain Lawford, described the dawning of the following day as 'A most melancholy scene; seven ships and two Brigs on the same reef as the Convert'. Thus it became known as The Wreck of the Ten Sails. Lawford requested the remaining ships to sail around to Georgetown to pick up those who had managed to come ashore. He and others set off on a day and a half trek across country into Georgetown. Eventually the surviving ships set sail to continue on their original course to Europe and the salvaged goods and remaining crew were transported back to Jamaica in another navy vessel, HMS *Success*.

As the *Convert* was a Royal Navy vessel the wrecking became the subject of a court martial. Captain Lawford, his officers and crew were tried for the loss of the HMS *Convert*. During the trial it was revealed that a current had unexpectedly carried the fleet some twenty miles north of its course. It was concluded that the *Convert*'s loss was 'occasioned by a strong current setting the ship very considerably to the northward of reckoning'. Lawford and his crew were honourably acquitted and the Captain continued a long and prosperous career in the navy.

The incident underscores how common shipwrecks have been in the history of the islands, and how much Caymanians themselves have depended on the sea. Ironically, today, one of Radio Cayman's communication and transmitter masts stands prominently with a commanding view over the whole rescue site.

This area has now become one of the most popular diving sites on the island and its reputation brings divers from around the globe to plunge into the waters and swim around the remains of eight of the sunken vessels in their resting place on the seabed. During the nineteenth century Gun Bay became one of only two legal ports of entry to the island with authority for maritime trade and traffic together with the additional, and apparently totally unconnected, legal burden of registration of all births, deaths and marriages on the island.

As a mark of his appreciation King George III granted the islands tax free status and this has continued to the present day. On my income and limited capital, the Caymans' reputation as a tax haven was purely of academic interest. I would never be likely to benefit from an ability to avoid such things as corporation or capital gains tax so my visit to the island was strictly for leisure and pleasure and not for financial gain.

Following the split with Jamaica the island enacted specific financial legislation in 1966 that safeguarded and formalised the tax-free status of the islands and enabled the banking community to develop and thrive, providing economic stability for the islanders. Today there are over five hundred international banks operating in the Caymans together with over four hundred insurance corporations making it the fifth largest financial centre in the world. This together with tourism provides the backbone of Grand Cayman's commercial success and economic independence. What effect the credit crunch and worldwide banking crisis will eventually have on the Grand Cayman based institutions remains to be seen. The Cayman Islands are not yet as popular or as well publicised a holiday destination as many of their Caribbean contemporaries. They are also much smaller than the majority of the islands and have very limited natural resources. Although, in common with our small party, many holidaymakers now stay in the excellent hotels and rented villas, but it is the day-trippers who generate a large proportion of the tourist income.

I'm not talking of the sort of day-trippers that you would encounter at Blackpool, Brighton, Skegness or Southend, having travelled to those coastal resorts by car, coach or train from large inland conurbations. You will not see the 'kiss me quick' hats or children with lips and cheeks covered in the sticky remnants of pink fluffy candy floss that you might find on Marine Parade, Southend on Sea where there is opportunity aplenty for families to enjoy the cheap and calorific loaded fast food, from the many and varied outlets, having been disgorged from the coaches bringing their annual beanos from London and the suburbs down to their seaside playground for the day. In fairness to Southend on Sea, although the fish and chip shops, the public houses and penny arcades haven't really changed over the years, the majority of their clientele no longer arrive in the 1950s-style charabancs or on the two main railway lines from the capital. Large numbers now travel by car and enjoy the thrills and spills of the family accessible Adventure Island and Sea Life Centre, sensibly developed by a local businessman who is attempting to regenerate the seafront in a responsible and family friendly welcoming way that will attract crowds back to the town. Others stay on late, patronising the numerous nightclubs into the early hours, and giving their support to a thriving night time economy. Many of them join the cruisers circulating the seafront from the Kursaal roundabout to Pier Hill and beyond, along Western Esplanade to the Casino and back. This started purely for the owners of some superb and artistically decorated custom cars that enabled them to display their pristine vehicles in a slow moving parade to an admiring public once a month. Over time this has turned into a weekly, and sometimes nightly, event that now includes any souped up factory model and some that are just plain ordinary production line bog standard cars. As opposed to the original intention they are really not much more than nuisance value that have brought the cruisers a bad name amongst local residents and are now unwelcome by many in the town. Albeit there is now a belated attempt to return to the original concept.

Grand Cayman is a very different island to Adventure Island and its cruisers are a completely different variety being welcomed with open arms by traders and residents alike. These visitors arrive in huge ocean going cruise ships that anchor just outside Georgetown and are ferried into the port by the small tenders that buzz back and forth like busy floating worker bees. The liners can carry over two thousand passengers and are probably busier than many small towns and certainly generate more income. In peak season there will be as many as six liners a day, six days a week, heading into Grand Cayman with their passengers adding to the hustle and bustle around the port area searching for the many duty free bargains in the numerous jewellers all within easy walking distance of the port. Even in the low season, on five days each week, it's possible to see up to four liners resting in the bay, whilst their cruisers look to spend their dollars or flash the plastic in the shops as others take advantage of the many coach trips around the island or take an excursion to Stingray City. Whilst you cannot find the candy floss sellers the Cayman equivalent are the rum cake vendors with their offers of free samples of every flavour imaginable to whet the appetites of their many customers, hundreds of whom you can see weighed down with their cartons of cake that they will take back to the staterooms on the floating hotels. Knowing what the cuisine is like on board I am sure that many of the cakes are not eaten until the revellers all return back home from their holidays or are then given to family and friends as presents.

In fact Tortuga rum cakes have been declared the 'Best Cruise Souvenir' as these tropical treats are also sold in the onboard gift shops of nearly a hundred cruise ships throughout the Caribbean. Baked fresh daily, at three different bakeries on the island, using a four-generations-old secret family recipe Tortuga rum cakes were introduced in the Cayman Islands nearly twenty years ago. We learned that they are made from only the finest natural ingredients and a special, five-year-old blend of Tortuga Gold Rum. It is impossible to mistake the sweet smell of the rum cakes being baked as you enter the bakery. They are now recognised as the leading export from the Cayman Islands and franchise bakeries have opened in Jamaica, Barbados and more recently the Bahamas. Produced in a variety of flavours including original golden with walnuts, chocolate, coconut, Blue Mountain coffee, banana, key lime and pineapple all using natural ingredients and a specially blended Tortuga Gold Rum each cake is hand-glazed before being vacuum-packed and heat-sealed. This provides a six-month shelf life that can be extended by storing in a refrigerator which was an experiment that we were testing to the maximum, as the fridge/freezer in the apartment was packed to capacity. However, with the ever-hungry Caroline making regular and furtive visits to the kitchen we were never likely to be able to test the true extended life cycle of the local rum cakes.

As lunchtime approached on 'W' Day plus one, the majority of the wedding guests were recovering from their partying of the previous twenty-four hours and were beginning to look a little more lifelike. This manifested itself with the girls trying to lift me from my sun-bed and deposit me in the pool. In trying to save my notes from a damp and watery grave they asked what I was doing. I showed them that I was attempting to write up a chronicle of the previous day's events at the wedding in my travel journal.

They insisted on reading my efforts to date, although I did have to assist with deciphering some of the less than legible handwriting. They seemed genuinely pleased, and surprised, with my efforts and asked if I would print them up for the second reception back home in England.

I duly obliged so that in addition to the photographs and video on display at the second reception I had penned a few pages to try and paint a picture of a Caribbean wedding from a visitor's perspective. Copies were left on each table. The result was that I received a not wholly unexpected number of derogatory but amusing comments from my travelling companions but one or two other guests suggested that I should turn my wedding day memories into a book. Rather foolishly I decided to take on the challenge so that once I had started I followed Magnus Magnusson's mantra and continued until I finished.

Our Sunday lunch back at the hotel included, unsurprisingly, the obligatory rum cake for pudding, but our ample and varied menu, together with I suspect the after-effects of the wedding banquet and liquid refreshment, meant that on this occasion our refrigerated cache showed little sign of diminishing. Unusually, not even Caroline could be persuaded to nibble on a small slice and by now I was beginning to think we would need to start offering it to other guests at the hotel if we were ever to get rid of it. I was to be proved wrong on that score.

Early afternoon saw us all jump back into our reliable little bus for Carrie to take us to Smiths Cove, a local beauty spot on the south side of the island, and within a couple of minutes' walk of David and Mel's home. We were all eagerly looking forward to this trip as those who knew it described it as one of the most beautiful little inlets on the island, a sandy palm-fringed beach surrounded by rocky outcrops with the warm sunkissed sea lapping at your feet. We were then going to meet up with the newlyweds to see their wedding presents before having a final dinner with them prior to their departure the following morning for their honeymoon.

Driving through Georgetown, it was much quieter than usual without any cruise liners in town. We could see the large container ship that we had first seen docked in the wee small hours when we were returning home from the wedding, which at that time had been bathed in floodlights for the night-shift dock workers. It was still being unloaded and the mountain of containers was growing on the quayside as the ship started to sit higher in the water. The articulated lorries lumbering around the docks couldn't seem to keep pace with the speed at which the enormous bulky metal trunks were being offloaded. Bearing in mind this was Sunday afternoon, in an overtly Christian community, it was a stark reminder of how reliant Grand Cayman is on imports. Literally everything has to be shipped onto the island and there are proposals for a completely new cargo terminal to be developed leaving the present port available for just the cruise ships.

We soon arrived at Smiths Cove and the first thing that struck me was the number of cars parked there. It was a good indicator that the beach was packed solid. Obviously a popular Sunday afternoon haunt for the locals. What did surprise me was the amount of rubbish that had been discarded and left to rot where it lay. This unwanted detritus littered the beach and surrounding area to the extent that you had to pick your way around it to reach the water's edge. Remnants of unfinished barbecues and even evidence of drug paraphernalia were all too readily apparent. We eventually found a spot to park ourselves but all the shaded areas were already jam-packed with families trying to take advantage of yet another sunny Sunday afternoon on the beach.

> *The sun had reached its zenith and without a cloud in the sky it was probably the hottest it had been since our arrival on the island. If this trend continued I would be roasted by the end of the holiday. Yet more lashings of suntan cream were applied to all naked parts. This time everybody seemed to be daubing themselves and each other with a little bit extra. For a change it wasn't just me!*
>
> *I decided to make a mental note to consider buying shares in one of the manufacturers of these protective coatings. It must be a profitable investment.*

We split into two groups, half going into the water, which seemed rougher than that we had become used to on Seven Mile Beach, and the remainder sitting and reading or just sunbathing. I decided to be a bit of a wimp and avoid the water around the rocks. I tried to find somewhere to lay my towel to sit and read but ended up perched on an unoccupied rock. It was exceptionally hot and even my sun hat was soon bathed in perspiration offering little protection against the sun and the heat. I was beginning to feel quite uncomfortable and it was apparent I wasn't the only one. Three or four of us edged nearer to some bushes to try and take advantage of the little shade available as we saw a family get up and leave rather hastily. We settled again in the recently vacated spot but within ten minutes we realised why the other family had moved. Ants!

We had unwittingly discovered an ants' nest or to put it more accurately they had found us. Having already been disturbed they now started to crawl around us. Now I've nothing against ants. They are quite harmless little creatures and as you see the lines of them scurrying around they appear to be industrious and busy little workers. I don't mind flicking the odd one off me when I'm in the garden and it has inadvertently taken a liking to my skin. I'm even normally careful in swatting them away as I wish them no harm. That was not the case on this sunny July afternoon as a whole company of them had decided to launch a pincer movement and attack both my legs at the same time. Initially the attacks appeared to be spontaneous and sporadic but Regimental Sergeant-Major Ant soon marshalled his troops and a concerted effort by the stormtrooper ants was now focused on effecting a strategic and synchronised assault on both feet. It was obvious it had been planned and they were well trained and veterans of many previously successful campaigns against innocent and unwary visitors to Antland. My efforts to brush them off gently with the palms of my hands were comparable to attempting to rebuff a tank regiment with a water pistol. The coating of suntan cream was proving a particular disadvantage as it was assisting the ant army to cling, limpet-like, to my limbs and foil my brave attempts to repel the invaders. I was going to come off second best in this particular skirmish as they encroached even further in their attempts to swarm all over us. I wasn't the only one to be suffering from this antkrieg as yet further battalions of this well-oiled military machine had now found other unguarded victims and their advance guard were reconnoitring the beachhead to target the unsuspecting, vulnerable and defenceless humans who were minding their own business. I definitely knew I was fighting a losing battle as the tickling little warrior scouts had now infiltrated into the cracks between my toes. This was going to become unbearable as their antics began to antagonise me. I decided the only antidote was to execute a tactical retreat as I raised the white flag – well, a grubby sweat-stained handkerchief from the previous day's exertions – to dab off my assailants, some of whom were now getting far too close to the gap between my shorts and my groin for my liking. By now my discomfort was such that I was convinced that I didn't wish to remain in this sandy Ant Kingdom any longer.

I was not the only one in this situation as Sue and I looked at each other, both hopping on one leg and repelling all boarders as we tried to retain our balance and discourage the rearguard raiders from gaining any further footing. It was obvious we were both thinking along the same lines.

Eventually the swimmers joined us from the water and seemed quite amused at our discomfort. Why can one person's misfortune seem so funny to onlookers? It is, perhaps, a quirk of the British sense of humour, or even the German equivalent, schadenfreude. After a brief discussion half of us decided to return to the hotel where we would be far more comfortable sitting by the pool with refreshments readily available from the poolside bar. The majority of the youngsters remained behind at the Cove. They were far more hardy than us middle-aged antiquities. Caroline in particular had found a solitary and antisocial sunny spot on the rocks some distance away, out of sight, and it was obvious we were not going to budge her. She was determined to return home with a true Caribbean tan albeit she seemed totally oblivious to the power of the sun with the brisk sea breeze tending to mask its heat. Unless she was careful she would end up being barbecued. We all agreed to meet together at Mel and David's house in the early evening. At that time we were not to know that we were to enjoy a further encounter with the Ant Army a little later in the holiday, when I would have the opportunity to gain revenge on some of those who thought my plight so hilarious.

Having heard how beautiful it was, my image of Smith's Cove did not live up to expectations and this became my first and only disappointment of the holiday. In fairness, we did pass it again later in the week as we were returning home one afternoon. On the second occasion it was empty and all the rubbish had been removed. It was then much more like its original description and I could understand why the girls had raved about it and why it was so popular. Perhaps the moral of this tale is not to visit it on a Sunday afternoon and if you do remember to take a plentiful supply of insect repellent in addition to the obligatory tube of sun cream. I would recommend a minimum of a litre of each with a further readily available reserve stored in the car if you intend to stay on into the evening. The air-conditioning in the minibus was a welcome relief, after our experience on the beach, as we drove slowly back to the hotel.

Ted and I immediately hit the swimming pool and then settled on the sun loungers for a relaxing afternoon, he reading, and I continuing to catch up on my jottings which were by now beginning to take shape around my recollections of the previous day's celebrations.

Having replenished the coating of suntan lotion that the Caymanian ant population had crawled all over, with the odd crushed specimen still being removed from the cracks between my toes, I was now prepared for a more comfortable afternoon.

A mixture of the heat and the previous day's exertions were catching up on us and starting to have a soporific effect. We were both beginning to doze when we were roused from our slumbers by Dick the Diver and his gang of intrepid divers returning to ensure that everybody in the hotel learned of their day's underwater exploits, whether they wanted to or not. It became apparent that it was only Dick, as their self-appointed leader, who found that he needed to holler at a decibel level way above the norm to ensure that all his followers heard him, whether in earshot or not. Regrettably our own noisy secret weapon, Caroline, was five miles away, sunbathing in Antland on Sea, so we were unable on this occasion to launch a counteroffensive. I couldn't decide which was worse, ticklish ants or noisy Dicks. We decided to just accept the fact that this was not going to be the peaceful sunny summer afternoon that we had anticipated. Fortunately Dick and his pals quickly succumbed to pangs of hunger and disappeared from the scene so that equilibrium was restored. We did eventually catch up on some sleep in the sun before cooling off with a dip in the pool and a cold shower, prior to collecting together the 'wrinklie' half of the gang to drive back towards South Sound and meet up with the others at David and Mel's home.

I guess the wedding-present-opening ceremony was not dissimilar to any other the world over. The expensive wrapping paper surrounded by coloured silky ribbons and bows was ripped off with abandon and discarded all over the lounge floor. The bride and groom were trying to meticulously work their way through the pile of presents but amongst the hubbub and 'oohs' and 'aahs' as each package was opened they were being ably assisted, or even hindered, by David's nephew. Jose, 'Huggy Junior', was proving to be a much more enthusiastic participant than the newlyweds and was soon racing up and down the room finding the next brightly covered parcel to be opened. His rationale was simple: if it was large it had to be opened quickly; if it was large and heavy it had to be opened now. If it was large, heavy and extravagantly decorated why wasn't it already open?

I don't know exactly how many presents there were heaped on and around the table but they were considerable in number. If there were an award for the fastest opening of wedding presents there was every chance that the world record would have been broken that afternoon and 'Huggy Junior' would be proudly recognised in the record books. I cannot imagine what he will be like when he is eventually old enough to marry. Somebody should warn his prospective bride well before the event or alternatively contact the *Guinness Book of Records* to provide an Invigilator and create a new record. If *The Generation Game* were ever to return to our television screens they should introduce this as a new game for the contestants. 'Huggy Junior' could become the expert guest displaying how quickly and expertly he can demolish even the most professionally wrapped presents, before going on to judge the competitors' efforts. Although how Bruce Forsyth would be able to control him I do not know. Somehow I don't think 'I'm in charge' would have the slightest effect. I think 'Huggy Junior' enjoyed himself more than the bride and groom.

The bride's mother was yet again making herself useful in listing all the gifts against guests' names to assist with the thank-you letters that were to be written in due course. She also busied herself having found a large plastic bin liner to collect up the waste paper and ensuring that each present was safely stored away, particularly the more fragile china and glass sets that could so easily have been knocked over in all the excitement. At this juncture on the Sunday afternoon she seemed to have forgotten her needle and cotton and none of the girls were in need of her hairdressing talents in the immediate future. We managed to get through the whole event without breaking or dropping one present although there were one or two near misses as 'Huggy Junior' lost interest in each present once it was opened and quickly started to rip the wrapping paper off the next that he had snatched from the diminishing pile before anybody could stop him. What we could not possibly have known at that time was that a large number of these presents would be lost or destroyed in less than two months' time and Jan's efforts to stack and pack carefully would all be in vain.

Our evening meal was a comfortable five-minute walk away to Sunset House, where we had eaten on Friday evening before the wedding. We had all enjoyed our previous meal and the atmosphere and entertainment in the restaurant and were happy to return to sample something different on the menu. More importantly David and Mel had to be up before dawn to catch their flight so this was very convenient for them. I wasn't particularly hungry, which was hardly surprising bearing in mind how much I had eaten over the past twenty four-hours so thought I would have one of the lighter meals, described as a 'snack' on the menu. I opted for a Flipper Burger and salad. I had never tasted one of these before but I was on holiday and in true Michael Palin style decided that as it was a local dish that was on offer I would have to sample it. There are some native delicacies that I have seen him eat on his many explorations that, to be honest, I wouldn't touch with a barge pole. He has sipped and nibbled so many different essences and such a huge variety of ethnic cuisine that his palate must by now be finely attuned to anything remotely disagreeable or alternatively he has the benefit of a cast iron stomach. My Flipper Burger was very tasty, if rather larger than I had anticipated, and despite having to tolerate what were now the customary rude and disparaging remarks from my group of convivial fellow diners about my eating habits in general and penchant for fish dishes in particular. In spite of having to listen to them asking if I had seen the dolphins basking earlier in the day, I still enjoyed my meal.

Much like our previous visit there continued a number of inbound aircraft but tonight there were no fireworks illuminating the night sky. Having finished our dinner we were sitting around the tables sipping our drinks, chatting and listening to the music. I was watching Ted teach Carrie the finer points of backgammon. It was a game I had played only once previously, about five years earlier, on holiday in France. I had tried, unsuccessfully, to learn the rudimentary elements of the game and only had a very vague recollection of the rules. Carrie and I persuaded Ted to attempt to teach us the basics in thirty minutes so that we could continue to play once he had returned home during the next week. He willingly, but foolishly, took on the task. Having just about grasped the essentials he and I decided to play one game before returning to our hotel. With lots of encouragement from our female fans we started to throw the dice. I still didn't really know exactly what I was doing but somehow I kept managing to throw a high proportion of doubles including an unfair share of sixes. At least from Ted's perspective it must have seemed unfair. Me, I was just revelling in my good fortune. The unlikely combination of beginner's luck and Carrie providing the tactical advice from the sidelines proved to be too much for poor old Ted, who was by now beginning to wilt and perhaps needed some more of his medication or even a stronger drink. Whilst I will never know how I managed to beat him, somehow I reached the finishing line first. Ironically Carrie and I never got the opportunity to play again on the holiday and if Ted were to play me today I wouldn't have the foggiest idea of what I was doing having long since forgotten all the tips he gave me. With the luck I was having that night I should have phoned home and bought a lottery ticket. I can't remember who drove back to the hotel that night but know it wasn't me. We arrived back in time to have a final night cap at the pool bar before crashing into our beds to dream about and look forward to a less hectic schedule for the remainder of the holiday.

CHAPTER 8

Machete Man – MM – 'W' Day + Two

Jan and Carrie were up early on this bright Monday morning and had left the apartment before five o'clock to collect the honeymooners and transport them and their luggage to the airport. Although I heard them leave I was still in the land of nod and not yet properly awake. From then on though I seemed to doze fitfully so that by six o'clock I was wide awake and it seemed fairly pointless lying in bed on what was already another warm and sunny day. I changed into my running gear and carried out my compulsory stretching exercises. The older I get the more difficult these become but I suppose they are also more important as the muscles and joints start to creak and groan and need a few squirts of the metaphorical WD40 or in my case some Deep Heat massage cream to warm them up and prepare them for the exercise ahead. In my younger days, as an enthusiastic if not skilful footballer, the smell of Goddard's Horse Liniment or oil of wintergreen was all-pervasive in the dressing rooms and now I have to make sure the odour wafts out of the bathroom window and doesn't infiltrate the remainder of the house. This is not so bad during the summer months but not always appreciated in winter when the window is left open. On holiday it was much easier as I only needed to go onto the balcony, administer the necessary embrocation, and let the smell dissipate in the fresh air.

By the time I was ready to start my run the girls were coming back through the front door and I think were just a tad surprised to see me ready to go jogging at that time of the day. Although I offered to wait for Carrie to get changed and join me she didn't seem to appreciate my offer and was more intent on returning to bed. Neither of us, at that stage, realised just how sensible that decision would prove to be on this particular morning.

In addition to the muscle massage I administered my first daily helping of suntan cream to provide some protection from the heat of the early morning sun.

I was off and running before six-thirty in the morning, frozen water bottle in hand and ready to attack the long flat Seven Mile Beach Road. I think I also amazed myself as I had never been up and running at that time of the day even when I was much younger, fitter and training for marathons. The one and only exception being when I was one of a team of twenty Essex policemen running a non-stop relay from John O'Groats to Lands End for charity. We ran in pairs and covered the distance in less than five days ending up both elated and exhausted but with over £28,000 in the bank for the two charities, but that was some eighteen years previously. I was now over two stone heavier and considerably slower. If my two colleagues at work could have seen me that morning they just would not have believed that this was happening. They are always in the office bright eyed and bushy tailed long before I ever arrive and it's accepted that I don't do breakfast meetings. The only reason I was exercising at that time of the morning was simply because it would be much too hot later in the day.

I started the morning's run at a reasonable pace, which was quite surprising considering my calorific intake of food and drink over the weekend. Being earlier than normal, traffic was lighter than that to which I had become accustomed. I managed to retain my steady pace, past the fire station, the cemetery and Foster's supermarket, out towards Dolphin Point without even a second thought of my Flipper Burger from the previous evening. Having taken most of my water on board at the half way stage I now had to slow down as I turned for the return journey to ensure I got back to the hotel in one piece, or at least not in a state of exhaustion. Unusually for me I had started off too quickly and had no wish to peak too early and have difficulty in completing the run. Having said that, my chances of peaking at all were very slim.

When I set off on my run that morning I had not anticipated meeting MM, otherwise known as Machete Man (I was to learn later it is pronounced locally as 'Mashet' and in the Caribbean for those of a violent disposition is often a weapon of choice).

I had a little over a mile and a half to run, or about twelve to thirteen minutes at my pace, as I continued my gentle trot, in the early morning sunshine, back to the hotel. My running vest was already bathed in sweat and my wristbands were not much better having wiped the beads of salty water from my eyes every couple of minutes or so. Trying to take advantage of what shade there was I was running on the wide verge on the nearside of the road. The remainder of the run wasn't going to get any easier. It was just a matter of gritting my teeth and heading for home. I wasn't specifically timing my run so was probably daydreaming and looking forward to diving into the cool water of the swimming pool to be followed by fresh orange juice and croissant for breakfast and thinking of what delights the remainder of the day would uncover. I could see ahead of me a small pickup truck parked on the verge and realised I would need to step into the carriageway to go past it. As I approached it, a hirsute and muscular young man emerged from the bushes, looking rather dishevelled and agitated. He was wielding a machete in his right hand and momentarily looked towards me before disappearing quickly and somewhat stealthily back into the undergrowth. What was he up to with a machete at that time of the morning? He certainly looked as if he knew how to use it. In fact he looked as if he had been using it. Was there a dismembered body hidden in the bushes or was it still in the back of his truck?

My already slow pace suddenly decreased dramatically. I needed to make a decision and quickly. This was the second time in less than a week that my brain started to perform mental gymnastics in microseconds. A confrontation with Machete Man could prove to be much more dangerous and traumatic than merely forgetting a wallet and passport and could potentially end with me in hospital. Not a pleasant thought, particularly for the local hospital.

What was I to do?

Was this going to develop into a fight-or-flight syndrome that I had read about when you are under pressure and frightened? Which option do I take? Do I turn around and run the other way?

No, I was already tiring and this would only take me further away from the sanctuary of the hotel. Where was all that traffic, or the other joggers, that I had seen on previous mornings? Nowhere to be seen at the moment but I was out and about much earlier this morning. No sign of help anywhere to be seen. Suddenly I felt somewhat isolated. There were a couple of sandy footpaths that led down to the beach. If he were to reappear and attack me could I make them in time and outrun him. If I made the beach I could dive into the sea. I might be a better swimmer than him, although I wasn't that confident, but at least he would have difficulty swimming and flailing the weapon at the same time. Hold on a minute, Caymanian Caveman looked much younger, bigger, taller, stronger and fitter than me and I had already been running for over half an hour. What was he doing with a machete at that time of the morning?

Which would be the preferable option, drowning or trying to disarm Machete Man barehanded? Neither seemed to hold out much hope for little old me. What now, try to front him out if he reappeared? Think, don't panic. Come on, you can talk your way out of this. About twenty-five years ago I attended a negotiators' course. What did they teach me? Damn, I remember now, I failed the course.

What do I do? I'm gradually getting closer to the truck, although now almost down to walking pace, and whilst I can hear wheezing and creaking noises coming from within the trees I still can't see anything. Still no sign of passing traffic, I'm on my own. No radio to call for assistance, no truncheon down a trouser leg to defend myself, no stabproof vest, no slash-resistant gloves, no handcuffs and certainly no CS spray to disorientate a would-be assailant, which was the latest equipment to be issued shortly before I retired.

The last time I had been in a situation bearing any resemblance to this was probably a dozen or more years earlier. It was about one o'clock in the morning and I was on patrol on my own when a radio call went out to a disturbance outside a nightclub on Southend seafront. Three drunks had been ejected from the club and were trying to regain entry. I was approaching the club on Marine Parade as the radio operator put out the call. I pulled up the patrol car, turned on the blue lights and jumped out. I knew that other units were also responding to the call so started to approach the three young men who by then were kicking at the doors of the night club. One was carrying aloft a large metal waste bin that he had removed from its holder whilst another was holding a beer bottle. All of them were shouting obscenities when suddenly the one carrying the bin hurled it through the windows of the club. He was also the noisiest and appeared to be the ringleader so I naturally targeted him. Normally if you can restrain the ringleader the followers tend to calm down. This wasn't to be the case on this occasion. Having grabbed him and dragged him towards the police car it became fairly obvious that he didn't want to come with me and started to object both verbally and physically. We both slid across the bonnet of the police car and fell to the ground, half in the gutter and half on the pavement. As I grappled with him, trying hard to take a firm grip of his right wrist and arm (the moves and arrest techniques they taught you in defensive skills and conflict resolution training never did work in real life, well not for me, anyway) his two mates decided that they would attempt to release him from my now failing grasp. Fortunately the one carrying the bottle had somehow managed to lose it and it resulted in the four of us rolling about the pavement with arms and legs flailing in all directions. It was impossible to get onto my radio and call for urgent assistance but I was equally determined I was not going to lose my prisoner. That would have resulted in an unbelievable amount of mickey-taking from the night shift once I returned to the station. Given the opportunity the younger officers, and probably the older ones as well, would enjoy every minute of it and that was something I wanted to avoid if at all possible. By now my arms and legs were taking a fair battering, not so much from deliberate kicks and punches aimed at me, although there were one or two, but more from them exerting pressure in trying to release their mate. Unless some help arrived quickly I sensed I would come off second best. It initially arrived from an unexpected source. Suddenly the chief steward at the club emerged from the doorway and effectively took one of the three out of the equation by holding him in a bear hug. In my earlier days he would have been colloquially known as the head bouncer but for some reason this particular nomenclature did nothing to enhance their reputation. As efforts were made to legitimise their trade and registration became the norm, door steward became a more acceptable form of address. His unforeseen, and for me fortuitous, entrance into the fray was something of a surprise as I had previous dealings with this particular bouncer some weeks earlier in the charge room at the police station. Fortunately for me, as he said later, "You treated me fair and square guvnor, I wasn't gonna see you done over." This left me holding on to one and fending off the other as a crowd then began to gather around us. At long last the cavalry arrived in the form of a section from the force support unit and they were a group I was always pleased to see, never more so than at that moment. Their restraint methods were far more efficient than my feeble efforts and all three of my assailants were handcuffed and placed in the police carrier in what seemed like a matter of seconds. The whole episode had lasted no more than three minutes but time is relative and for me that was a very long three minutes but I had emerged with nothing more than a pair of badly bruised and grazed legs and a dusty uniform which was probably better than a bruised ego if I had let him escape. Importantly I had avoided the ribbing from the night shift back at the station that I would have had to endure had any of my prisoners managed to escape.

All three of my young aggressors apologised the following morning, once they had sobered up. They were three Londoners who had come to town for a stag party and their drunken antics had got them thrown out of the night club.

My target, the ringleader, eventually appeared in Crown Court and pleaded guilty, receiving four months' imprisonment for his fun on the pavement in addition to a further twelve months for a sentence that had previously been suspended. In mitigation his barrister, whom I had known a long time and who prosecuted as much as he defended, told the court that the defendant would not have resisted arrest if he had realised I was a policeman as I wasn't wearing a hat. For some reason he omitted to inform the Judge that I had arrived in a fully marked police car, with blue lights revolving, wearing full uniform, and the only reason I didn't have my cap on was because his client had knocked it off during the scuffle.

My three minutes that night had been difficult enough, knowing that assistance was on its way and also knowing that I was only up against fists and feet. Nobody had been carrying a machete. This beautiful sunny Caribbean morning was different. It had only been a matter of a few seconds since I had first seen MM and I was now creeping closer to the pickup truck.

I had never been in a situation like this before. I was almost level with the truck and while it is difficult to describe I could still hear what now sounded like a chopping noise coming from somewhere within the bushes. As you have probably gathered from my wimpish retreat from the beach to escape the invading ants the previous afternoon I prefer to be a live coward than a slashed or mutilated hero. Decision time was fast approaching. What were my options? Should I sprint past and keep going as fast as my legs would now carry me, turn back or head for the beach? Come on, be decisive. Whilst a quick escape was the preferable option my curiosity was getting the better of me. What was he up to?

The road and verges were wide along this stretch so at the last second I crossed over hoping that either he would ignore me or if the worst came to the worst at least I would have a head start, even if it were only a short head. I should also get an opportunity, even if briefly, to see exactly what he was doing in the undergrowth. I made a mental note of the number plate and tried to break into a sprint. Although I did manage to speed up I wouldn't, even in my wildest dreams, describe it as a sprint. A fast trot was the best I could achieve. As I started to pass the pickup I glanced across from the opposite verge and as I did so he reappeared still brandishing the machete, but it was now in his left hand and he was dragging something towards the truck with his other hand and making some considerable effort to do so.

What was it? Was it a body?

My brain was telling my short fat hairy legs to run faster but for some strange reason they weren't getting the message and everything seemed to be going into slow motion. At that moment the pickup was masking whatever it was he was tugging across the dusty earth towards the truck. Luckily for me he seemed so intent upon his task that he hadn't appeared to notice me on the far side of the road. By now I was edging further away and with every step putting greater distance between MM and myself and regaining just a little bit of confidence. So much so that I couldn't resist peering back to see if he had yet reached the truck with the body he was trailing behind him. He had. However, the body turned out to be an enormous palm tree branch that he was now hauling onto the back of his pickup. Quite what he wanted with a palm frond at that time of the morning I will never know and didn't stop to find out. Whether he was a local florist selecting some foliage for bouquets and flower arrangements or an out of work insomniac trainee lumberjack practising his trade will remain a matter of conjecture.

It was astonishing how quickly my confidence recovered and returning to the shady side of the street the faltering and stuttering paces of just a few moments ago had now miraculously changed into a brisk run although this didn't last for long, as breathing heavily and leaking profusely I completed my weary and now wary way back to the hotel. Just as bewilderingly traffic started travelling in both directions as if appearing from nowhere. Where had they been just five minutes previously?

Back at base, feeling pretty exhausted but relieved I dived, well okay slid, slowly feet first into the pool to cool off, relax, and wonder how I had let my vivid imagination get the better of me. Jan and Carrie were already tucking into the muffins and I joined them at the table to enjoy a hearty breakfast but no longer as the condemned man likely to die by a thousand slashes on an isolated beachside track on a Caribbean island. They were intrigued by my tale of the morning's run but I'm still not sure if they were laughing at me or with me. The only certainty that it accomplished was that Carrie would definitely not be going on any more morning jaunts with me. Meanwhile Diane had returned from her daily pre-breakfast routine of walking and swimming and her saunter onto the beach had seemed tame in comparison to my own morning jog. Perhaps I should join her in future and avoid this early morning excitement. Her approach to morning exercise appeared to be much safer and less stressful.

> *The time had arrived for the second of the day's applications of suntan lotion as I settled into my regular spot by the pool. This holiday was much sunnier and hotter than I had expected. Perhaps I should forego my early morning expeditions.*

Another hour or so of sitting by the pool and continuing to write up the notes on the wedding before the majority of us went off to Georgetown to explore the sights and the shops. Well, the girls were shopping. I don't think I've ever seen so many jewellery shops in such a small area anywhere in the world. Two cruise ships were in port and their passengers, mainly Americans, were doing their utmost to support the local economy and export some pretty big rocks back to the States. Rum cake was being sampled and sold by the slab. I made a mental note to let Caroline know, when we get back to the hotel, exactly where the cake bargains could be found. Having achieved just a light grilling on Sunday she had decided to remain at the hotel and barbeque herself poolside. She could currently be described as 'medium rare' but was displaying a stubborn determination to be 'well done' by the time we returned home the following week. In this task she was destined to be successful.

Having initially split up we kept bumping into each other as we meandered through the shops. One or two were buying knick-knacks to take home to the UK, others were just window-shopping at this stage. I belonged firmly to the second category. We still had over a week on holiday and I just knew we would be visiting the shops again, and again and possibly even again! As I wandered through the many and different jewellery stores the selection was quite overwhelming and the prices, in comparison with the UK, were very reasonable and competitive. There was a vast array of watches on offer and even I must admit I was tempted. However, on this day I was pleased to see that I had my sensible shopper's head on and was browsing amongst the cabinets in the different jewellers searching for a particular style of earrings that I knew Lesley would like and also match with other bits and bobs that she wore. With just one exception all the staff were helpful and once they knew I was merely on a reconnaissance expedition left me to my own devices to memorise which stores I would need to visit a second time before I made any final decision. The only exception was one shopkeeper who would not leave me alone and followed me up and down the aisles continually looking over my shoulder and trying to persuade me to purchase items that I didn't want and had no intention of buying. Wherever I went he followed and was never more than six feet from my side. Now whether he didn't like the look of me, although I didn't look particularly different from the hundreds of other tourists in town that morning, or perhaps my early morning experience had made me appear suspicious, I will never know but he was determined not to let me out of his reach. The result was that I left his store vowing not to return and to take my custom to one of his numerous competitors who were happy for me to peruse the merchandise in my own time and at my own pace without the hindrance of being shadowed wherever I went. He reminded me of the stereotype second-hand car dealer who hovers constantly with his hard sell technique when a softer more subtle approach is always likely to be more successful. At least it is with me.

I did manage to find a photographic and camera store along one of the side streets where the helpful young man assured me that they would be able to fix my camera and with any luck also save the film that had jammed to a stop in the heat at the wedding. I left the camera in their care and they promised me it would be ready in a couple of hours.

We all met up back at the minibus and returned to the hotel for a lunchtime snack. Food remained a priority. Back at the poolside we found Caroline and Danielle having a fit of the giggles at the noise emanating from Dick the Diver who was unsuccessfully trying to round up his gang of itinerant divers and escort them to his chosen choice of venue for lunch. Was there a hint of rebellion in his camp? Could we detect the first signs of resistance to his authority?

Suddenly a number of them had disappeared and try as he might he could not find them or get any response from their rooms. The longer this went on the louder his voice boomed as he called their names whilst dashing from room to room and knocking on the doors. It was also apparent that he had already started on the pre-lunch drinks. This had become the worst attack of diverdickulitus that we had seen since he arrived as he rushed around the pool becoming more frenzied after each unsuccessful hammering on doors that steadfastly refused to open. The more irate he became the funnier it appeared and now the giggles were no longer contained and it became fairly obvious that he was the source of our amusement. The girls had this vision, whether it was accurate mattered not, of half a dozen Americans crouching behind sofas or lying under beds in order to avoid lunch with their leader. There was an obvious whiff of mutiny in his camp. He eventually realised that we were laughing at him and I could see the beginnings of a minor diplomatic incident in the offing. Fortunately, in the interests of Anglo-American relations, he was far more intent on locating his errant troop of underwater explorers than taking any real interest in a small bunch of puny Brits who obviously weren't there for the diving. They might be able to dive but I could float!

Unless we were careful I could see a US v UK battle of wits building up at the poolside over the next few days. Rule Britannia. Eventually Dick disappeared into Reception and was not seen, or heard, for the remainder of the day, which made the hotel pool much more tranquil.

We all disappeared in different directions in the afternoon. Jan and I drove back into Georgetown as I wanted to return to the photographers to see if they had succeeded in rescuing my film that had become stuck on the reel in the heat of the previous Saturday afternoon. My luck was in. Not only had they retrieved the film but had developed it and printed all the negatives. They didn't know what had caused the camera to snag but had replaced the film and it was now working perfectly. Quite by accident, therefore, I became the first of the guests to have some photographs of the wedding and fortunately the jamming of the spool had not ruined any of them. I was sure they were not going to be as good as Ken's, the snap-happy photographic cleric from Wigan, but he did have the advantage of the Almighty looking after his camera and perhaps some of his influence had rubbed off on my very basic 'point and press' attempts at photography. In any event I was very satisfied with my efforts, for a rank amateur. So satisfied, in fact, that on the strength of it we went straight across the road to an ice cream parlour where we celebrated with two flavoured cornets. Mine was the largest ever triple-filled cone imaginable, and within seconds I realised this was a serious error. Having seen the size of it I wasn't sure that I would be able to eat it, albeit I would give it a good try. More importantly, it was likely to melt away in my hands, creating a gooey sticky mass, before I could get halfway through.

Not for the first time in my life my eyes were proving to be bigger than my tummy. I remember as a young boy my grandfather used to tell me this. He was a wise and patient man and one of the gentlest of people I have ever known. In fact he was a gentleman in every sense of the word. He was a coppersmith by trade and, although working for a company based in London, had travelled all over the country repairing and installing large tanks and vats in numerous breweries. His skills had also taken him across the Irish Sea to Dublin where from time to time he plied his trade in the Guinness brewery. Perhaps this explained both his and my grandmother's liking for a bottle of the black velvet.

I can clearly remember him guiding me around a huge foundry in Wandsworth and, much more interestingly, a tour of the many breweries along the Mile End Road and Whitechapel in the East End of London. I'm sure today's health and safety mafia would frown upon such educational excursions for a seven-year-old but I enjoyed them immensely and he and his colleagues always ensured that I was kept well away from any danger. Grandad Joe could literally turn his hands to almost anything and displayed considerable dexterity. He was an excellent carpenter and had hand-crafted his own tool box that contained a treasure trove of a joiner's tools of the trade. I learned to play shove-ha'penny on a board that he had made as a young man, with such well used halfpennies that one side was so smooth it was difficult to detect that it was a coin of the realm. His ability as a shuffler of a deck of cards never ceased to amaze me as did his memory of which cards, and who held them, remained to be played in a game of whist. As a self- taught pianist, who professed not to be able to read a note of music, although I'm not sure I believed this, he would sit and play the piano for hours at family parties. On Sunday afternoons we would gather in the front room of his rented terraced house where he would entertain us by playing a medley of tunes in the style of the typical pub piano player. He had an ear for music and was the first person I heard use the phrase 'you hum it and I'll play it', way before Morecambe and Wise repeated it on television. Although a working class man, from a humble background, he was particularly erudite and would recount all sorts of tales in his own quiet fashion but he ensured there was something to learn from all of them. Eventually the company he worked for moved from London to a new industrial site on the outskirts of Crawley New Town in the Sussex countryside and at his time of life he had no wish to uproot himself and my grandmother and move miles away from the family. In those days it was a difficult journey by public transport and he didn't have a car or even drive. He retired from the company, which was a blessing in disguise for the family as we all saw a lot more of him. Not one to sit and do nothing his retirement saw him take on the task of school crossing patrol on the busy West Hill, Wandsworth, near its junction with Upper Richmond Road which is where the main A3 joined the old South Circular Road. Why a gentleman in his sixties would want to take on such a demanding post having worked hard all his life I do not know but, looking back, it might just have been necessary to bring in a few more pence to eke out what was a meagre pension. Whatever the reason he took his role of protecting the children very seriously and he loved every minute of it. They obviously also loved him which was evident from the cards and little presents that the children and their parents gave him at Christmas. For me it was a real bonus as I saw him every morning and afternoon on my way to and from school. In fact I would regularly wait and walk home with him to sit and listen to another of his stories before him walking me back to my parents' house which was no more than a ten-minute stroll away.

Every couple of months or so, he would take me on a treat to the museums of South Kensington. We would travel on the top deck, much more exciting for a young boy, of a number 14 London Transport bus from Putney Bridge and alight outside the Natural History Museum. From there he might occasionally wander along to the Victoria and Albert but, without fail, we would always end up in the Science Museum on Exhibition Road. This was my favourite and at that age I would happily have not bothered with the former two. Fortunately he insisted that we spent a little time in both although my attention span in both was always very limited. That was not the case with the Science Museum where I enjoyed my first hands on experience (back in the 1950s I don't think the word 'interactive' had yet been invented and computer games weren't even a distant dream) of the different working models and his ability to explain the mechanical intricacies of the various moving parts as I pressed buttons or turned handles ensured that he always had to force me out of the doors to catch the bus home. From time to time if I had behaved myself, which on reflection was rarely, he would take me down to the tunnel that connected the museum with South Kensington Underground

Station and we would catch the District Line tube train to Putney Bridge. From there it was a short walk over the iron railway bridge that crossed the River Thames. We would stop and either look through the many girders upriver to where the annual Oxford and Cambridge Universities boat race starts or across to Wandsworth Park where as a child I learned to play cricket and football, which could consist of fifteen a side with a rush goalie and coats as goalposts. I could never leave the bridge until a train came along and as they were either entering or exiting the station were usually travelling fairly slowly. Being a boy I thought I could run faster than the train but however slowly the trains were moving they were always faster than me and I came off second best every time. Quite what the drivers and passengers made of the smartly dressed elderly gentleman in his Sunday best with collar and tie and wearing a trilby hat being accompanied by a somewhat unkempt and breathless urchin who kept racing away from him I cannot imagine. Why he never lost his patience with me I'll never know. He taught me an awful lot in my formative years and all I wanted to do was to be able to copy him. I've managed to fail in almost every respect. I'm pretty hopeless with my hands, my efforts at wood and metal work never turning out as intended and my only success on the piano was what he taught me years ago and is a very stilted version of 'God save the Queen' with two fingers trying to tinkle just one ivory at a time. Not easy when you are all fingers and thumbs. I suppose the closest I've come is getting halfway there when I became a copper. I'm sure he would forgive me, and also be smiling at me, for not managing the 'smith' bit. For whatever reason I never did manage to inherit those really useful genes from the male side of the Benning lineage and 'Dexterity' will never be my middle name. In the current information technology world my lack of such skills is even more pronounced as evidenced by my unsuccessful efforts to master the intricacies of a personal computer or even get to grips with the remote control for the television and digital recorder.

Hopefully, though, some of my grandfather's better points have rubbed off and I might even have remembered the odd piece of knowledge or good advice that he tried to impress upon me.

As a youngster I never used to heed his words of wisdom. Now, fifty-odd years later, things hadn't changed. Why couldn't I grow wiser as I grew older? I was reminded of this, as my grandfather used to buy me a cornet, albeit a much smaller one, from an Italian ice cream vendor who set up his stall near the museums and as I had anticipated it became apparent that the stifling heat was now melting my giant ice cream far more quickly than I could eat it.

My newly acquired photographs of the wedding were in imminent danger of being covered in a ruinous sticky mass of pina colada flavoured ice cream that was unlikely to enhance either their artistic or technical quality. We rushed back across the road to retrieve some wet wipes from the minibus and fortunately the pictures didn't suffer any permanent damage. I'm sure Ken wouldn't have made such a basic mistake with his album of wedding pictures.

Georgetown was very different in the afternoon from the Georgetown we had visited in the morning. The cruise ships had departed and were sailing full steam ahead onto their next island destinations. The hustle and bustle of the pre-lunch visitors, frenetically rushing from store to store in search of the numerous bargains available in the limited time allotted to their brief and profitable call at this tiny island capital, had been replaced by a serene and almost siesta-like atmosphere, as the resident tourists drifted around the port area in a much more relaxed mood. The shop staff were able to spend even more time displaying their assortment of wares and I now ventured even further in-store past the windows and started to examine closely the cabinets where the selection of earrings available was not going to make any decision easy. I was totally honest with the assistants, in that I was not there to buy anything that afternoon, merely to look, but they were all extremely knowledgeable and polite in the expectation that I might return later in the holiday to grace them with my custom. They were probably the friendliest group of vendors I had ever encountered. They all wore name tags and in addition to the native Caymanians had travelled from around the globe to enjoy their work experience on the island, and if their demeanour was any indicator, enjoy it they obviously did. On that afternoon alone I met people from around the Commonwealth, Canada, Australia, Belfast, Scotland, Jamaica and other Caribbean islands. In addition the United States had their share of representatives together with a liberal smattering from the European Union including Germany, Austria, Ireland and Holland, not forgetting ourselves in Great Britain. In one of the jewellers I also met a charming young lady named Carol, from Venezuela, who was the consummate saleswoman and who in due course would be the one to persuade me to purchase the holiday presents from her store.

I also found a small antiques shop opposite the embarkation jetty and in browsing amongst the wide variety of reasonably priced artefacts and craftwork came across a piece of sunflower pattern Carlton Ware that was surprisingly inexpensive compared to UK prices. Good quality Carlton Ware at affordable prices is now difficult to find and this was a genuine surprise to have travelled so far to happen upon such a bargain. Notwithstanding, I am well aware that antique dealers normally value their goods at a price where they expect to haggle with their regular customers, or even irregular ones and you don't come much more irregular than me.

Consequently I made an offer that I knew he would refuse and we bartered for a minute or two before agreeing on a price that we were both happy to settle at. I had only managed to achieve a ten percent reduction on the proviso that I was willing to pay cash and not use the universal credit card. For the likes of myself, being a member of that sensible and enormous band of reluctant male shoppers, this capped a worthwhile afternoon and was a real bonus. Not carrying enough currency with me I promised that I would return in a few days with sufficient funds to settle the deal. He, not unnaturally, told me that it may well be sold by the time I returned but not being in a position to settle there and then I was willing to take my chance on nobody else showing an interest in the meantime.

I was extremely pleased with my afternoon's shopping escapade. It had proved to be much more profitable than anticipated.

We took a detour back to the hotel by way of taking a quick look at Mel's school and her first lodgings, which she had shared with Nic when they first arrived on the island and were just a five minute walk to the school gates. I understand that the walking option was rarely taken with sixty seconds by car being preferable. Being in the middle of a holiday period the school was totally deserted so we didn't have an opportunity for a full tour and the silence seemed strangely out of keeping with the environment. I'm sure it would be very different on an ordinary school day. The lodgings appeared just as quiet and were a two storey building that had been divided into flats with their own swimming pool surrounded by a lawn and some trees in a peaceful residential area. A very pleasant welcome if you are moving into a new job, on the island, to find you are starting in such delightful accommodation and surroundings. Although Jan and I were not to know it at the time both the school and the lodgings would present a very different and far more dramatic picture in six weeks' time.

We had a quick stop at the Grand Old House where we recovered a pair of abandoned shoes. We knew by this time that, following the reception, at least two of the guests had left with the wrong shoes but we never did manage to match the proper shoes to their rightful owners. It must be a female thing, removing shoes to dance, but on this occasion there is a faint possibility that alcohol consumption also played its part in the unsolved case of the wandering footwear.

As we were passing nearby I also took the opportunity of calling in at the Links Safehaven's golf course to book an earlier tee off time. As newcomers to the course we wanted to ensure that darkness didn't descend before we had completed all eighteen holes. This proved to be one of my more sensible decisions of the holiday as we were to find out on the following Wednesday.

The rest of the afternoon was spent lazing by the pool, which by now was becoming part of the daily routine. This was the first opportunity anybody had to see some wedding pictures and they were passed around to an accompaniment of 'oohs', 'aahs' and 'Doesn't she look lovely'. Much to my amazement my endeavours as a tropical wedding photographer had turned out to be quite acceptable to my interested audience, to the extent that I was already starting to receive requests for copies. I decided to keep this quiet in case Ken thought that I was trespassing too far onto his turf and we had not yet seen the results of his far more professional images. I had no wish to be thought of as a latter day paparazzi trying to gain advantage with an early exclusive.

> *Another very hot and sunny afternoon. Yet a further liberal coating of suntan cream applied all over. I was now certain that my original quota would not last for the remainder of the holiday! Would need to remember to look out for further supplies on my next venture to the supermarket.*

As the afternoon wore on, with the sun moving across the hotel and gradually disappearing below the rooftop to the west, I continued penning my notes interspersed with reading, swimming, drinking too much and chatting to another group of American divers who were totally different to their compatriots. The verbose and decibel enhanced Dick with his portable and inbuilt loudhailer was nowhere to be seen although some of his gang began to appear rather conspiratorially from their rooms and gathered together to sit quietly around the pool bar and actually appeared to be enjoying themselves without the attention of their leader. Whilst they were laughing and joking it was simply within their own small group and it wasn't intruding upon the activities of other guests. Perhaps my first impressions of them had been misleading and I had judged them a little harshly. Without their esteemed leader they were different people. Probably for the first time since our arrival I now felt totally relaxed. It had only taken the best part of a week and I just wondered if it had anything to do with my miraculous escape from MM earlier in the day? I wondered what he was now doing with his bunch of fronds and why he needed to carry out his lopping and pruning at that time of the morning. Although I could now look back on the episode more rationally and was able to see the funny side of my pre-breakfast stroll we never will know the answer to the mystery of MM, the early morning lumberjack on Seven Mile Beach.

By the time we were ready to depart for our evening meal I had managed to catch up on my scribbled jottings of the wedding. This had taken far longer than I had envisaged but a combination of poor handwriting, writer's cramp, drink, failing memory, unwarranted inter-ruptions from my fellow wedding guests who were intent on assisting or possibly hindering with the task, an army of ants, more drink, and the many events on the day all took their toll.

A travel manual and pen that by now had absorbed a share of the suntan lotion did not assist the process as they kept sliding under the sun beds and disappearing from view, as I regularly needed to top up my protective coating. At least they would not suffer from sunburn.

With my notes now completed and up to date I headed for the pool to be surrounded by cool clear water for a relaxing swim before we washed, changed and set off to taste test yet another of the Grand Cayman selec-tion of fine restaurants.

This particular evening it was Carrie's turn to drive. Very sensible, as I had enjoyed a most relaxing late afternoon and early evening and exper-imented with one or two new cocktails. Having all piled into the minibus and turned south along Seven Mile Beach it seemed that everybody had been caught up in the relaxed mood. With nothing of interest on the radio the minibus became a mobile community singing auditorium. I use that description, as opposed to a choir, as the standard of singing could best be defined as variable. Whilst there were one or two reasonable vocalists in our midst this particular journey resulted in full audience participation so that even though everybody enjoyed the impromptu concert some of the unrehearsed efforts would have been unlikely to impress any independent listeners and certainly would not have won many votes on one of the current glut of television programmes searching for future singing stars. The repertoire ranged through 'Waltzing Matilda', 'My Knapsack on My Back', 'She'll Be Coming Round the Mountain', through to a variety of Cockney classics and even included the odd blander rugby rhyme, of which the girls wanted to learn all the words. I don't think I had heard anything like it since as a youngster I had attended a Boy Scout jamboree gang show where enthusiasm always made up for any lack of quality. I don't believe any judges with a discerning ear would have appreciated our musical production but we enjoyed it. Pre-dinner liquid refreshment may possibly have been a contributory factor. Thank goodness the restaurant didn't have a karaoke machine, as I'm sure we would have spoiled everybody's meal.

This was to be our first visit to the eponymous 'Treehouse' restaurant and yet again it proved to be a popular and excellent choice. There was a selection of tables, undercover or simply under the stars, including one at the end of a wooden decked pier jutting out over the ridiculously blue water with the table placed beneath a thatched straw like canopy and the water lapping underneath your feet. A most romantic setting and this became Fran's favourite restaurant of the holiday. The atmosphere was casual which was appropriate for our mood, as one or two of the younger members of the party were still singing and demanding to have a repeat of one of the rugby songs. Ted and I did manage to quieten them down by promising a reprise on the return journey. The staff were attentive, without being too pushy and the prices very reasonable. The head chef, Greg Trebilcock, hails from Canada although with a name like that I wondered if he had some West Country ancestors? The menu had something for every taste and I eventually selected the evening's 'special', which was grouper, and it proved to be simply delicious. I know I had selected yet another fish dish but vaguely remember an old wives' tale that fish was good for your brains. It's amazing what you believe as a child. The entertainment was again provided by the local tarpon, some of whom must have been almost four feet long (I know it's a fishy tale but I promise I don't exaggerate) as they skidded across and just below the surface snatching at the tasty morsels that were provided for them by the restaurant every evening. I guess that our experience that evening is fairly typical of the majority of nightlife on Grand Cayman. A quiet meal in a classy restaurant seemed to be very much the norm. Although for the younger generation, or the more adventurous, there were alternatives.

On the way home we dropped the girls off at the Royal Palms, an extremely popular nightclub, that we would all visit together later in the week. This was not before Ted and I had to repeat a somewhat flat and hoarse version of what had become Fran's favourite song of the holiday although she never did manage to learn the words. Consumption of the dreaded drink played its part in her inability to come to terms with this fairly simple task. Ted and I were excellent tutors but the same could not be said of our pupil. Carrie didn't join them at the night club on this occasion as she looked very tired and was more than happy to complete her driver duties for the night.

Back at the hotel we found a videotape of the wedding waiting for us. Mike, the best man, had delivered it earlier in the evening. It had been supplied by his sister who had displayed her competence by managing to blend into the background at the wedding whilst she went about her task of filming the event. She runs her own company, on the island, producing such videos or marketing material for commercial organisations. Unfortunately we didn't have a video recorder in our apartments so we needed to be a little more patient before we could watch the action replay. This was probably a blessing in disguise as we were all pretty drowsy and quickly trod our weary paths to bed.

I slept really well but experienced a strange dream of being covered head to toe in suntan lotion and slipping through the clutches of a madman who was trying to kill me before I managed to escape by running away. I don't know what happened after that, as I must have woken up.

Strange things, dreams!

CHAPTER 9

Who's for a Barbecue?

Although a week had gone by it seemed only yesterday that we had all met up at Heathrow looking forward to our trip to the Cayman Islands. For the majority we were almost halfway through our holiday. Unfortunately for Ted, Sue and Vicky their vacation was almost over as they were to fly back home later in the day. They were returning from the tropical climate of sun, sea and sand to the reality of life back in England where they had to face the prospect of getting their home and life back to some sort of normality. Their immediate future would consist of living life from suitcases in a hotel room that was likely to be very different to our apartment in the Caribbean. At least Ted was now feeling much better and appeared more like his old self although he hadn't offered me a return fixture on the backgammon board. I couldn't possibly be as lucky a second time. They were unlikely to be in their own home before Christmas and over the course of the next six months would need to be patient whilst they watched their house being rebuilt and hopefully negotiated a reasonable and final settlement with the insurance companies. One could only pray that whatever temporary accommodation they were offered in the interim at least it would afford them some comfort until they could return to their own home and a more conventional family life to which they were accustomed.

Sitting chatting at breakfast that morning I think we all realised just how rapidly the first week had passed and how much more quickly the remainder of the holiday would now disappear.

Breakfast at the hotel was always a fairly simple affair as we nattered and laughed over the previous day's events, made plans for the day ahead or gossiped with other guests. Pleasantries were always exchanged with the staff who were scurrying to vacuum, dust and tidy the rooms, cleaning the pool, sweeping the surrounding patios or manicuring the grass and plants.

There was always a member of staff on hand to ensure we had a plentiful supply of piping hot coffee, natural fruit juice, crisply baked croissants, flavoured muffins and fresh fruit and the tables wiped spotlessly clean for the next guests, once each group had finished breakfast.

I didn't really appreciate the effective simplicity of the hotel and the courtesy of the staff until returning home and staying in an English country hotel for the UK reception some three weeks later. Hindsight is a wonderful gift but what a difference!

The contrast was so marked and the English competition was so poor it appeared that they weren't really trying. In fact I'm convinced they weren't. It was the first time that I had stayed in an East Anglian version of 'Fawlty Towers'. It is difficult to describe how disinterested some of the staff were in accommodating their guests and the comparison with Basil Fawlty would be distinctly unfair on the manic John Cleese character. At least he tried to satisfy some of the guest's needs even if they generally resulted in well intentioned mishaps. The only accurate comparison was that the audience ended up laughing at Basil and his antics to outwit the dominant Sybil and bully the hapless Manuel; we ended up laughing at the breakfast table at the total incompetence of the staff. If we hadn't been laughing we would have been crying.

Things did not get off to a good start and over time gradually deteriorated. Arriving on the Friday afternoon for a three-day weekend break, arrangements to use some of the hotel facilities that had been booked months previously, we found were delayed until late afternoon due to the hotel hosting a corporate event. The attitude was very much 'like it or lump it'. The commercial imperative of profit dictated that we were to be the 'second class' customers for the remainder of the day.

There wasn't an alternative and it resulted in delaying an evening meal that had been arranged with Mel and David and their family and friends. It was inconvenient but not the end of the world.

However, things quickly got worse. Lesley and I had decided that our contribution to the weekend celebrations was to be the second, or English edition, of the wedding cake. Having carefully driven over eighty miles with it delicately perched on the back seat of the car we wished to ensure that it would be in perfect condition for the reception on the Saturday. When making the reservation we were promised that it could be placed in their cold store overnight. Why wasn't I surprised that the receptionist was unaware of this arrangement? On carrying the tiers to the hotel kitchen we discovered that the cold store was full and the cake was to rest on an open shelf amongst a variety of tins in the heat of the kitchen. We weren't prepared to take the chance that it would remain in one piece so took it with us to our room, which was almost as hot – no air-conditioning here – and cautiously placed it in our wardrobe for safekeeping. If it were damaged now we only had ourselves to blame.

The *coup de grâce* was delivered at breakfast the following morning and the hapless Manuel, *he from Barcelona*, could not have done better, or worse, depending upon your viewpoint. In fact if the actor Andrew Sachs had been given such a script even he would have thought it too far-fetched. Arriving at the entrance to the dining room we waited to be shown to our table. The two young members of staff who were waiting on tables displayed not the remotest bit of interest in us despite some obvious coughing and foot-shuffling. Although they peered across at us they remained totally indifferent and showed not the slightest inclination of making an approach or even enquiring why we might be loitering in their doorway. After five minutes we took the bull by the horns and made our own way, sitting down at a table that had been laid for breakfast. It was readily apparent that either the table had been re-laid following breakfast for other guests or the tablecloth had not been changed since yesterday as there was a liberal helping of marmalade and recently deposited tea or coffee stains visible on the surface. We had placed ourselves at one side of the room so were perfectly visible but not at that stage to the waiter and waitress who had now turned their backs on us to talk between themselves.

This section of the room was by now almost full and a number of other guests were collecting in the bar area waiting impatiently for a table. By this time what appeared to be a supervisor was meandering through the room and preventing the new arrivals from entering the empty half of the room that had already been prepared for luncheon diners. This area was barred to the hotel residents who reasonably required a breakfast to go with the bed they had booked for the night. Some guests were persuaded to return to the waiting queue where there were already mutterings of discontent. It was obvious there were many more guests than available tables and some were now demanding they be allowed to occupy the empty tables in the reserved area of the restaurant. A number of them went to the far end of the room to take tea or coffee from the self-service buffet bar back to the queue whilst they waited for a vacant table.

The hotel must have been aware, for some considerable time, exactly how many guests had reserved rooms and would be attending breakfast. To deliberately restrict the number of tables available, knowing this would be likely to upset their paying guests, displayed a complete lack of customer care and gave the impression that they were more interested in profit margins than looking after their guests.

Having not yet been served I went and collected two coffees and also found some cereals. To avoid further delay I helped myself to a small bowl of muesli and some Weetabix for Lesley. Having returned to our table we could not find any sugar as she wanted just a slight sprinkling over the top of her cereal. Enquiries at nearby tables merely confirmed a lack of sugar throughout the restaurant. At long last the waitress approached the two couples at the table nearest us to take their breakfast order. I caught her attention and requested some sugar. Having completed the order from the adjoining table she promised to 'search for the sugar'. That seemed a strange thing to say but it later became obvious that she and her colleague were trainees. Quite who was training them never became apparent.

After some fifteen minutes, by which time we had drunk the coffee and I had eaten my muesli, she returned with a bowl of sugar. The only problem was that they were sugar lumps and would have appeared somewhat incongruous sitting on top of a Weetabix. On calling her back we learned that was the only sugar they had. We didn't bother to try and grate it over the cereal.

She then had to leave us to try to calm down a young family who were seated patiently waiting for both their breakfasts and some warm milk they had requested some time previously for their baby. There was obviously a problem in obtaining warm milk on a Saturday morning. It was apparent that they had ordered this when first entering the restaurant and had been kept waiting so long that they were clearly and understandably losing patience. At last she returned to us to take our order. We both rarely have a cooked breakfast but the smoked haddock and a poached egg appealed to both of us. She disappeared back into the kitchen and we waited and we waited. I replenished our coffee cups and still we waited. I was beginning to think that it was a mistake ordering the haddock but soon realised that everybody was waiting. It mattered not what you had ordered.

Some forty minutes later the waiter, this being the operative word in this hotel restaurant, arrived at the table of four next to us carrying their breakfasts. He apologised profusely for the delay explaining that they only had one cook in the kitchen. The two couples had travelled down from the north of England to go to the races at Newmarket. They were very pleasant people but were becoming rather dismayed at the unnecessary delay. Their dismay almost turned into anger when one of the men was given a full English breakfast instead of the omelette that he had ordered. The waiter apologised yet again and was about to take it back when the man told him not to bother as he couldn't afford to be delayed any further and he was content to eat the fried breakfast. Ourselves and the other young family were still waiting, the bar area was becoming more crowded, the supervisor hadn't been seen for twenty minutes and further arrivals were now seated in the prohibited area of the dining room and were making themselves comfortable at the tables and collecting their coffee and cereals. They were determined not to be moved. The atmosphere was becoming decidedly moody. It only needed 'Basil' to arrive and order the recalcitrant guests from their seats and we would have realised that we were on *Candid Camera* or being used as unpaid extras in a remake of an edition of *Fawlty Towers*.

At that stage the young waiter re-emerged and for the second time approached the gentleman race-goer, who was now tucking into his fry-up and appeared to be enjoying it, with another plate on which was an omelette. Our northern friend no longer wanted the omelette but the young trainee was obviously under strict orders from Basil, Manuel or whoever the supervisor was imitating in the kitchen, and in one fell swoop snatched the first breakfast from the table, insisting that it was for somebody else, and replaced it with the omelette before exiting stage left into the kitchen. An eerie silence descended over the restaurant whilst one diner now sat open-mouthed still clutching his knife and fork. Whilst everybody waited with bated breath, expecting him to explode with anger, we couldn't help ourselves but started laughing and a number of others began to smile or tried to disguise their emerging giggles. We could all see the funny side of what was in reality not a very amusing incident.

This certainly eased the tension and it seemed everybody decided just to accept their fate and also accept whatever happened to be served for breakfast whether it was what they had ordered or not. The restaurant supervisor had, once again, disappeared and it seemed fairly pointless in complaining to the two youngsters.

We eventually did get our smoked haddock some three quarters of an hour later and ultimately returned to our rooms not quite believing what we had just witnessed.

The Sunday morning breakfast was slightly better organised. They had wisely decided to open the whole restaurant but had changed the format to a serve-yourself buffet-style breakfast but unfortunately not as good as that we enjoyed at Indies Suites. Somehow the ambiance wasn't quite the same. The only delays experienced were whilst waiting for the chef to refill individual hot plates and trays once they had been emptied. Sunday breakfast was in fact relatively swift and uneventful compared to day one.

Monday morning was different again. We had reverted to the conventional waitress service, albeit with different staff. Whilst there were some delays it was a considerable improvement on the Saturday, probably because many guests seemed to have departed and at last they had located a supplier of granulated sugar. We actually completed an uninterrupted breakfast.

Having packed our bags I returned to reception to collect the bill. This was at a different and more expensive rate to that charged for other wedding guests staying in identical rooms. Having had to resolve that misunderstanding I requested to see the manager. I was joined by the father of the young family who appeared to be even more irate than me and was also demanding that he speak to the manager. We were both, unsurprisingly, unsuccessful. The manager was engaged in a meeting and unavailable. We both left contact numbers, more in hope than expectation. In fairness, I was contacted later the same week and received an apology for the unacceptable service. This is a tactic I have used myself in the past, as it is far easier to deal with somebody once their anger has subsided. The main reason given was new and temporary staff and a lack of time to train them properly. I was promised that this would be rectified and although we were offered a complimentary meal by way of compensation, I politely, but firmly, declined the opportunity, as I normally like to start and complete dinner on the same day.

Breakfast and service at the Indies Suites was a positive delight compared to what we sometimes have to tolerate at home.

With half the holiday gone Diane, Jan and myself decided that we would travel back into Georgetown to visit the Cayman Islands National Museum for our share of local history and culture. I had learned by now that apparently the town was originally called Hogsties. Local legend has it that this nomenclature was derived from the wild boar that were penned in sties to provide food for journeying merchantmen who visited the island some three hundred years ago. At that time the islands were used by English, French, Spanish and Dutch explorers, other buccaneers and ships plying the Spanish Main route as convenient ports of rest and replenishment of the ship's stores of fresh water and food. In addition to the wild boar, local sea turtles and wild fowl were part of the staple diet taken on board to feed the seamen on the next leg of their voyage.

It was both fortuitous and far-sighted to change the name to Georgetown in honour of King George III as I'm sure the Grand Cayman Tourist Board would have experienced some difficulty in marketing the island as a holiday destination with a capital named Hogsties. I can just imagine some of the comments if one were to receive a postcard from the neighbours on their annual summer holiday and the postmark depicted was Hogsties.

Equally I couldn't see the father of the bride being very amused if his daughter were to come home and tell him that she was contemplating getting married in somewhere called Pigpens or the like. Yes, the name change was both necessary and eminently sensible. By the way, although I saw small groups of three and four chickens wandering along the roadside on our trips around the island, as you will see later, we were assured there weren't any wild boar. This isn't as far-fetched as it might seem as a number of countries, including England, have numerous reported, if occasional, sightings.

About twenty-five years ago when I was working as a shift inspector in Basildon we spent over a month trying to track and trap a wild boar. There had been a number of sightings, mainly at night, in the Langdon Hills area. At the time a large number of smart and expensive houses were being developed and for the owners to awake in the morning to find that their newly landscaped gardens had been turned into a ploughed field by a hairy beast running amok with its tusks tucked into the manicured turf as it raced across the lawn was quite upsetting to say the least. It did make for a different approach to early shift as patrols were called to the numerous reports of damaged gardens. Having never been trained in animal tracking or wild beast trapping none of us were too sure of what we were intended to do when we eventually came face to face with the nocturnal visitor but our presence did seem to provide some sort of reassurance to the local residents, even if it didn't to us when we were on foot in the area at night. I never did meet up with the animal and to the best of my recollection having dug up and ruined its share of gardens it disappeared back from whence it came. Having made the headlines in the local press and achieved his fifteen minutes of fame this Essex Swine obviously decided to retain his anonymity and return to the wild never to be seen again. This was much to the relief of many officers at Basildon as they prepared for night shift with only their trusty truncheon tucked down their right trouser leg for protection.

My only other experience of wild boar was whilst on holiday in the Var region of southern France about four years earlier. We had rented a property and were already aware that *les Sangliers* inhabited the local forests although we had never seen any on our previous visits to the area. However, the owners of our rented gite told us that it was not unusual to see one, at night, drinking from their swimming pool. Although this was an interesting story, and added to the atmosphere of a French country holiday, having looked out onto the pool for the first two or three nights and not glimpsed anything amiss we then forgot about it. I should add that this was perfectly safe as our cottage was one level above the pool and had a perfect view of the pool and its surrounds. Whilst I still hadn't undertaken any wild animal training I was unconcerned if he did turn up, as to reach me he needed to negotiate a steep paved stairway before then turning back on himself for a further thirty yard dash to the cottage door. I was quite content that

I would be inside with the door locked and bolted before my porcine friend was halfway up the steps. My wimpish traits will always out.

We were well into the second week of our holiday, and had forgotten about the wild boar, when having returned home from a local Bistro one evening I was sitting on the terrace sipping a final glass of wine when we heard some strange noises coming from the direction of the swimming pool. The noises could only be described as a sort of snorting and snuffling. We both moved cautiously and quietly towards the low wall to look down at the pool and there clearly bathed in the moonlight was an adult together with the feral equivalent of a piglet slurping water from the edge of the pool. Neither took any notice of us as we watched from on high and after five minutes both parent and child turned and left their local watering hole before trotting off back into the nearby woodland. By pure coincidence and in confirmation of our sighting we told our story at lunch in a regional vineyard, the Château de Berne, the following day. Having listened to our escapade the waitress returned to the table with a bottle of their wine labelled 'Wild Pig'. I could not leave without sampling it and found that it was a sparkling rosé and it had more of a 'tang' about it than other local rosé wines. As you can see I could not describe myself as a wine connoisseur. I detected a very drinkable wine but my palate isn't sensitive enough to taste some of the other flavours inherent in this local brew. However, I was suitably impressed, so that when we left, after a lengthy and relaxed French lunch, I was carrying a few bottles from their 'cave' although with a name like that could not see it being a popular or profitable vintage at home. Once again my judgement was questionable as I have since seen it on sale in the UK. The waitress went on to tell us that it was not unusual to find the local wild boar eating some of the rotting grapes that had fallen from the vines and literally fermented where they lay. The local boar population obviously enjoyed them as they regularly returned for more. One could see the attraction in being a Provençal boar with wine and truffles being on the daily menu. The waitress had more of an English than French sense of humour. This, perhaps, wasn't so unusual as the Château is now owned by an Englishman so perhaps he had started to stamp his personality and humour on the locals. I wasn't sure whether to believe her or if this was another French rural myth that became more exaggerated with each telling. Having witnessed them with my own eyes the night before I certainly wasn't prepared to question its authenticity. Although we continued to watch out for our nocturnal visitors for the remainder of the holiday they failed to turn up again.

Back in Grand Cayman I didn't see any farmyard pigs during my stay let alone any hogs or sows of the roving variety, and apart from the small groups of domestic fowl scuttling along the roadside verges in search of the odd scrap of food, there was a lack of livestock farming.

Whilst the name Georgetown doesn't conjure up a picture of the most idyllic of holiday settings and any of the monarchs named Charles, Victoria, Edward, Elizabeth or any other royal personage would have been equally appropriate, all of them are far preferable to the original Hogsties.

The National Museum, although housed in only a small detached building, when compared to the likes of the Victoria and Albert, Science or Natural History edifices in South Kensington, London, is an attractively white-painted, green-shuttered, family-style house with a verandah and prominent red roof. It provided a compelling insight into the lives and times of the people of the Cayman Islands. In its earlier days it served its time as the island's courthouse and is one of the oldest buildings on Grand Cayman, having now housed the museum for over fifteen years. It is situated opposite the port at the junction of Harbour Drive, Goring Avenue and Shedden Road. Judging from the numbers inside when we entered it is obviously a popular attraction with the cruise tourists. The museum encourages local artists to improve their skills and awards a scholarship, together with the McCoy prize, to the winning artist of an annual competition. The successful artist's work becomes part of the museum's collection.

We started our visit in the mini-theatre, fortunately air-conditioned, watching the videotape that provides an array of background information about the islands and their progressive passage from barren uninhabited swamplands to the thriving modern day community. I suppose in total we spent over a couple of hours wandering around the various exhibits and it was much cooler inside than on the waterside watching the sun drenched cruisers queuing to await their turn on the tenders that would ferry them back to the floating hotels that were moored calmly in the bay. The museum houses an array of artefacts that provide more than enough interest for everybody, from the expert archaeologist down to the uniniti-ated and fairly ignorant visitor like myself who was merely attempting to gain a basic insight into the history of the islands.

The islands were discovered by Christopher Columbus during his fourth and last voyage to the New World in May 1503. Whilst sailing from Panama to Hispaniola (now Haiti and the Dominican Republic) strong winds and heavy seas (that seems to be a feature of Cayman history) pushed his ships off course and much further west than he intended. His crew eventually sighted two small islands, Little Cayman and Cayman Brac, with thousands of rocks and tortoises on the beaches. His son Ferdinand wrote in his journal that they had sailed by a pair of 'small low islands filled with tortoises'. In fact the rocks and tortoises were breeding turtles – and the Caymans turned out to be three coral-fringed islands and not just the two. Columbus appropriately named the islands Las Tortugas after the abundant sea turtles that inhabited both islands. The islands were later named Lagartos, after large lizards or alligators. An early English visitor to the islands was Sir Francis Drake who reported seeing great serpents or large lizards called 'Caymanas', which were apparently edible, when he visited the islands in 1585-86. One of Drake's crew described them as ten-foot crocodiles and in the early nineteenth century shooting the crocodiles was still recognised as a Sunday sport. Perhaps the original Crocodile Dundee came from the Cayman Islands and not the Australian outback as depicted by Paul Hogan. The name Caymanas is derived from a Carib word for marine crocodile and this name has remained in modified form since the late sixteenth century.

The islands came under British control in 1655 when Oliver Cromwell's army captured Jamaica from the Spanish. Following the Treaty of Madrid in 1670 when Spain recognised British possession of all land, islands and colonies in the West Indies, the islands formally became part of the British Empire and were then administered as a dependency of Jamaica for the next three hundred years until Jamaica gained its independence in 1962.

The first census of the Islands was taken in 1802, showing a population in Grand Cayman of nine hundred and thirty-three, of whom five hundred and forty-five were slaves. Before slavery was abolished they were owned by just one hundred and sixteen families. It was in May 1835 that Governor Sligo of Jamaica landed in Cayman where the proclamation declaring all slaves free in accordance with the Emancipation Act of 1833 was read at Pedro St James and a number of other prominent places on the island. It was possibly this one act that paved the way for the development of Cayman into the society it is today.

Perhaps for me the most interesting exhibit in the museum was a scaled geological model of the islands and their relationship to the Cayman Trench. In similar fashion to the proverbial iceberg nine tenths of the islands are below the surface. To examine the model and see just how deep the water is around the island was quite an eye opener. To think that less than a week ago I had been happily swimming with the stingrays in blissful ignorance of the depth of the water around me and had actually started to feel confident in the water. Not any more, for the remainder of the holiday I would keep my feet firmly on the sand and make sure that I did not venture beyond my depth. What a wimp!

The mocked-up replica of this small area of the Caribbean, with the mammoth rocky outcrops towering and climbing from the seabed so that only a fraction of their peaks were above the surface provided a vivid impression of what the offshore waters were really like. Whilst the actual land surface was tiny in comparison to the surrounding water the popularity of Grand Cayman as a diver's paradise now became totally understandable. We all left the museum feeling that we had, at least, gained a small insight into the Cayman Islands, their people and their history and now hopefully had a better understanding of our environment for the remainder of the holiday.

Having left the comfortable conditions of the museum, and being in the company of two ladies, we headed for a further reconnoitre of the jewellers, to examine the local bling-bling. We managed to find even more stores selling diamonds and gems than on our original sortie into town. The selection of precious stones remained mind-boggling. I was merely trying to shorten the odds in respect of a pair of earrings and had adopted what I thought was a strategic yet simple process of elimination. Jan and Diane had, meanwhile, got into what I might call typical female shopping mode and were inspecting a variety of figurines and objets d'art. I'm not sure whether they had any intention to buy or were just window-shopping but the by-product of their latest expedition was merely to select further sets of ear adornments so that for every one I eliminated they managed to find me a further two, that they assured me were bargains, to add to the bottom of the now ever-growing list. This wasn't being particularly helpful but at least it kept me cool whilst wandering into the climate controlled gem stores. I tended to keep returning to one particular store, probably because I enjoyed the in-house music more than any other. To my simple mind this seemed as good a reason as any to buy from this particular dealer. I knew there was no need to be hasty over my decision as there was bound to be a need to return for further shop-gazing as we still had almost a week remaining on the island. By this stage one set of earrings was beginning to look like any other.

Taking a circuitous route back to the hotel we called into an art and craft-type store called Pure Art on the south-west corner of the island near Smith's Cove. Initial impressions from the outside were of a somewhat down-at-heel ramshackle emporium that had seen better days. Nothing could have been further from the truth. Once inside we were able to explore all the nooks and crannies that were crammed full of a whole variety of articles and mouthwatering foodstuffs that would have had Diane and Jan spending a considerable amount of time and money searching for bargains to take back home as presents or keepsakes but for the numbers of Canadian and American tourists already packed inside selecting from the huge display on offer. The numbers made it a little uncomfortable and limited the time we spent there. Thank goodness. The girls decided to return on a quieter day to delve deeper into the treasure chest. I limited myself to the purchase of one or two small knick-knacks that we could hang as decorations on the tree at Christmas, which over the years has started to take on an international flavour.

Back at the hotel we had a very juicy watermelon for lunch before bidding our farewells to Ted, Sue and Vicky, wishing them a safe return and hoping that their negotiations with the insurance companies would not be too protracted and successfully get them back into their home by Christmas. Carrie and Fran volunteered to drive them to the airport and were then going into town for yet more retail therapy. Probably more sensible than us morning shoppers as the cruise ships would have departed and the stores would be less crowded and frenetic.

This left just Carl and myself to cope with the six remaining women. Hopelessly outnumbered, we decided to have a restful afternoon by the pool swimming, reading and occasionally dozing.

The sun continued to beat down from a clear azure blue sky although there was now a slight offshore breeze that masked the heat of the sun.

> *This dictated that yet more coatings of suntan cream needed to be applied although by now I had started to lose my pink hue and was beginning to turn a slight bronze colour. None of us could compare with Caroline and Danielle who were now getting to the burnt toast stage. I was convinced that they had cheated and gained a head start by visiting a tanning parlour in the weeks before the holiday.*

For whatever reason the girls decided that Carl and I would benefit from a bit of home cooking. Perhaps they were already feeling sorry for us having to cope with the six of them. In order to ensure total accuracy I need to say that for 'home cooking' read 'beachside barbecue'. Jan and Diane decided to stroll to the beach to examine the homemade grilling sites (I don't mean Caroline and Danielle who were being 'well done' poolside) that we had seen on our previous visits. In Grand Cayman they obviously encourage visitors to cook their own meals close to the water's edge. On their return from town Fran and Carrie were immediately dispatched again to obtain sufficient provisions for our evening meal. They were provided with a number of different choices, in fact too many for them to remember although following our discovery earlier in the day nobody opted for pork, whether of the wild or domesticated variety. To make matters easier we eventually decided to let them select the food as their choice of restaurants to date had been excellent and we couldn't see them letting us down over chicken, steak, sausages and lamb chops. We knew, with some certainty, they wouldn't make any mistakes with the wine and beers.

Returning from the beach recce our two senior scouts informed us that the local barbecue sites were not the cleanest in the world and might not be a healthy option. Fran and Carrie were sent on a further errand to locate a 'takeaway' barbecue. This took them some time but they eventually found one at one of the Kirk's Freeport supermarkets.

The two forward scouts remained in the apartment kitchen in charge of the microwave busily defrosting the frozen meat and preparing different salads. The remainder of us, carefully carrying the rest of the food and drink, made our way in the minibus down to the beach with the intention of lighting up and having the embers glowing by the time Jan and Diane arrived with the defrosted meat. Most unusually for that time of the evening we had great difficulty in driving through the traffic which was nose to tail along the main road. Although by now we should have learned not to be surprised by the traffic conditions. As we edged our way into the stream a police car and ambulance, with lights flashing and two-tones blaring roared past in the opposite direction on their way to an accident. We had even greater difficulty in finding a parking space and found a very large crowd had already assembled on the beach.

Ironically and sadly, we learned they had gathered to hold a memorial service and candlelit vigil for a seventeen-year-old boy who had recently been killed in a road crash. The vast majority of those present were his fellow students and a preacher was conducting a solemn reading. We stood and looked on silently for a few minutes before moving to a quiet corner much farther along the beach. We were not at all sure that it was appropriate for us to remain but could not move too far away until Jan and Diane, with the remainder of the food, arrived to find us. We had no wish to intrude on the private grief of all of those present so sat quietly and watched from a distance. It was a moving experience to see so many young people at the memorial service. Eventually Jan and Diane arrived, having searched for us for over thirty minutes. They had encountered difficulty in locating us due to the sheer numbers on the beach and the fact that we had moved much further along than we had originally indicated. As they arrived the congregation started to disperse, initially into smaller throngs and then they drifted away in ones and twos until the vast majority had disappeared.

Although the atmosphere was now rather sombre and very different to that when we set out from the hotel we decided to continue with the barbecue. Unfortunately the barbecue had no desire to continue with us. Whether it had been left outside, to the mercy of the elements, we will never know, but try as we might we could not make it light. Having exhausted our supply of paper napkins in trying to ignite the coals it was apparent that they were so damp that whatever we did was not going to light this particular fire. Perhaps having a beachside barbecue on this particular night was not such a good idea after all. Undaunted Dani and Fran were dispatched to locate more ignitables, whilst Carl and I combed the sand looking for any dry driftwood. Unlike Smith's Cove the beach was so clean we couldn't even find any litter that would assist in starting a fire. Luckily the girls quickly found a bag of fresh and dry coals at a local petrol station and at long last we were fanning some flames to set up our beachside cooker. Jan, who was never afraid of getting her hands dirty, had already taken charge of the candlelit kitchen and at long last the meat was beginning to cook. She had temporarily disposed of her needles and cotton but was just as adept with her culinary skills and some delightful and mouth-watering smells were soon emanating from the homemade oven.

We had started on the drinks and were now looking forward to our evening meal when one or two started complaining that their feet were stinging. We initially thought it was the fine sand getting between their toes and irritating the mosquito repellent that most of us had sprayed on our legs and feet. This, however, was not the source of the discomfort. Suddenly Caroline leapt high in the air, squealed loudly, which was not unusual, and when coming back down to earth started kicking furiously at the sand around her feet. It is very difficult to accurately describe what followed. Caroline then proceeded to produce a realistic imitation of a screaming, babbling, whirling dervish as she took off across the beach and running amok entered the sea in a sudden gush of spray, sand and surf before disappearing in the general direction of Cuba.

Realisation dawned; she had trod on a small ant's nest and disturbed the occupants who were exacting their revenge by crawling over her feet. All that could be heard were some expletives, describing insect life in general and ants in particular, gradually fading into the distance.

Was this the second wave of an invasion force who were landing on a further beach-head to support their colleagues of the First Expeditionary Ant Army which we had attempted to repel at Smiths Cove? If so, they could only be described as the Light Infantry. A cursory inspection revealed their numbers to be much smaller and they would require considerable reinforcements if they were to ruin our barbecue, although by now we were beginning to think that perhaps we had not chosen the best night for our shoreline meal. It no longer seemed quite as attractive an idea as when first mooted. Who was the clown who suggested it anyway? Not one of the group would admit to originally suggesting a beach barbecue. I'm sure it was one of the girls.

We were not about to be deterred by a few ants and the first signs of food began to appear. Jan and Diane had brought some order to their temporary camp-side kitchen, well, an aluminium barbecue tray perched on top of a concrete bollard, whilst the rest of us seemed to have taken to drink. In all honesty this appeared the norm for the majority of us most evenings. In true chuck wagon style a banging together of the utensils summoned us to the kitchen to collect our evening meals. In spite of the disruption it was very tasty and well cooked.

A rather damp Caroline had now reappeared, which purely coincidentally occurred simultaneously with the serving of the food. She has a marvellous sense of timing, that girl, allied to a good nose for food and drink. She was carrying a candle that she was trying to hold upside down and keep alight whilst dissecting an area of sand to ensure it was now devoid of her assailants. If not they were obviously going to be waxed to death. Not satisfied that she had sanitised her part of the dining room she proceeded to perch, on tiptoe, on a wooden bench pulling faces and making strange noises that were intended to frighten away any remnants of the ant army. Despite our inauspicious start we now all had something to eat and were merrily munching. Well done to our beachside Delia Smiths.

We had just about finished when Carl, who had found a comfortable spot in the sand on the far side of the barbecue, unexpectedly leapt ten feet in the air and with arms akimbo did an exact replica of Caroline's 'St Vitus Dance' as he sped across the beach towards the water looking as if he wouldn't slow down until he reached Jamaica. He wasn't as noisy as Caroline – nobody was – but his sprinting was much more impressive. Everybody else was highly amused and roaring with laughter at Carl's antics as he disappeared into the darkness so that he could no longer be seen and all that could be heard was the splashing of water that gradually faded into the distance of the warm night air. Why do we find others' discomfort so amusing? Even I who had been a victim just a couple of days ago was now curled up at the comic scene being acted out in front of me. Danielle became so convulsed with laughter she managed to spill her beaker of wine over the few remaining ants and this seemed to be the final blow that finished them off. They obviously had an aversion to alcohol and had at long last met a weapon that had thwarted them.

The ants had attempted their final assault but with the exception of Carl and Caroline, who was now refusing to leave her wooden perch, they were meeting firm resistance from opponents who had now been well fed and watered and were not prepared to retreat. They aborted their mission and like a defeated army melted away not to be seen again. Carl did eventually return to complete his meal but somehow had seemed to lose his appetite.

Once equilibrium had been restored we settled to another impromptu concert from 'The Three Musketeers and D'Artangan', Caroline, Dani, Fran and Carrie, who serenaded us around the remains of the camp-fire (dying embers of the barbecue) under a beautiful and clear starlit sky. All this sounds awfully romantic but the reality was that Carl and Caroline were still very much in Ant Raid Warden mode and keeping a beady eye out for any stragglers who might return to the beachhead. The star of the evening had to be Caroline who earned full marks for entertainment value. Her silky smooth voice, which always dominated the remainder of the quartet, when allied to her natural dancing prowess across the sand – well we think it was dancing although it included a mix of stamping and kicking at anything that resembled any sort of moving insect life – comfortably outshone Carl's humble efforts. Poetry in motion it was not.

There was still so much giggling and gossiping, and the remnants of a chorus of 'Waltzing Matilda' for Diane's benefit, going on in the minibus as Carrie drove us back to our awaiting beds that she completely missed the turning into the hotel and we saw a little more of Seven Mile Beach at night before finally arriving at our Island Supreme Allied Command Headquarters having repulsed a further invasion. Without exception everybody made for the showers to dispose of sand, ants and insect repellent and in Caroline and Carl's case lick their wounds and regain their composure. For one of them regaining composure was just not possible.

I emerged to sit on the balcony with a nightcap and browse through the pages of a local paper. I came across the story of the young boy who had been killed in the road accident and whose memorial service we had chanced into earlier in the evening. It brought back the much more sombre mood that we had experienced when arriving on the beach and as I read on it was apparent that the casualty rate on the island seems to be much higher than it should be for such a community. The car is a dominant feature of everybody's lives and a very high proportion of the population rely upon their four wheels to take them about their daily tasks. Not to mention the numbers of hire cars that visitors, like ourselves, rely upon to transport us to the island's tourist spots. Having already seen the huge amount of traffic commuting into Georgetown each morning, and mused about where they all disappeared to for the day, I had joked with the others that we should form a consortium to buy a piece of scrubland close to the centre of the capital. Having set ourselves up as Caribbean National Car Parks Limited we could build a multi-storey car park and then watch the money roll in on a daily basis. I'm not sure that it would be appreciated by the local community but it seemed like a good idea at the time, as such ideas tend to do after a glass or two of vin rouge.

Quite why there are so many accidents on such a small island I do not know. Other than my initial ninety seconds of acclimatisation to the Caymanian right turn I found driving around the island to be a fairly peaceful and unhurried affair. One cannot say the same when driving around back home in England. Equally, I should have to accept that I was on holiday so did not have the need to rush anywhere to meet deadlines or attend meetings so that, even subconsciously, I was in a far more relaxed state of mind. The majority of the roads were not vastly different to country roads at home and it was obvious that there had been some recent progress in highway construction. Although these had been intended to improve traffic flows they had brought their own problems. One new road in particular, that we had now travelled along a number of times, was receiving an abnormally high amount of adverse publicity. In the short space of time that it had been open it had already experienced more than its fair share of serious accidents. Listening to the local news whilst driving, it was possible to hear of accidents, almost daily, although most of them wouldn't have warranted a mention back home.

Most of the criticism seemed to be aimed at the increasing amount of traffic on the roads and how long drivers now have to sit in their cars commuting to and from work or just to do their shopping. Although this was obviously creating frustration the snails-pace was only likely to cause minor scrapes as opposed to the fatal and serious collisions caused by far greater speeds. For a small island it has one of the highest per capita ratios of car owners to residents in the world. In excess of thirty thousand cars for about forty-five thousand residents, with more (cars not residents) arriving by the boatload. Apparently there are many houses where every occupier is a car owner. There is an on going debate on the island to find the best solution. There probably isn't one simple answer but I suspect it will be a mix of highway construction and redesign of some current hazards and junctions with traffic calming measures on the faster stretches to reduce accidents. This will need to be aligned to a comprehensive integrated public transport strategy that would persuade motorists to take to their feet or move from four wheels to two. Currently there isn't any incentive to persuade motorists to leave their cars at home. All of this costs money but when measured against the cost of human life and treating the injured may then be seen as a worthwhile investment. In purely economic terms the amount of millions of dollars lost in productivity as employees sit waiting in traffic jams might be a financial inducement for some of the larger commercial organisations to sponsor or at least consider some sort of car pooling or sharing scheme for the hundreds of daily commuters into Georgetown. It could save both them and their workers a tidy sum over the course of a year. The alternative seems to be some sort of restriction upon car ownership but I'm not sure that would be a politically viable option. In fact I'm sure it would be a guaranteed vote-loser. I'm also sure that limiting the age limit for driving, at both the lower and upper ends of the scale, would not be welcome but linked to a stricter driving examination, followed by a twelve-month conviction-free probationary period together with medicals and three-yearly tests for the elderly driver could also reduce the casualty rate. Perhaps the provision of a reasonably priced waterborne bus service from piers constructed on the outskirts of the island into the port of Georgetown might prove to be a popular alternative.

I went to bed thinking of all the students we had seen at the memorial service on the beach and what a waste of a young life. It made me think of the number of fatal collisions I had attended whilst I had been attached to the Traffic division and how many had been totally avoidable but for the reckless actions of one of the drivers. As many experienced Traffic officers used to say, 'The most dangerous nut in the car is the one behind the wheel.' In modern parlance it isn't the car that kills you; it's the driver. I hoped that the impact of the service would make all those teenagers think carefully about how they would drive each time they got behind a wheel. Somehow I think it will prove to be a forlorn hope as that sort of memory, other than for the immediate family, tends to be of a temporary nature and doesn't have a lasting effect on one's driving habits. I dozed off to sleep but awoke the next morning having already forgotten about the death of the young motorist.

CHAPTER 10

Chicken, Turtles and Sex

*A*s was now becoming the norm, I was up bright and early and prepared for my morning run with the usual mixture of suntan cream on arms, shoulders and neck accompanied by stretching exercises for calf muscles and hamstrings. Having seen many fine athletes go through this routine (not involving the application of suntan cream) I had convinced myself that it must be good for me but it never seems to improve my performance, with the only noticeable result being the more I did it the more my muscles ached. They do say 'no gain without pain' and these regular sunrise sorties were becoming more painful and unpredictable as each day passed.

Having collected the essential plastic bottle of iced water from the refrigerator, which I found had slipped down a shelf and was now nestled amongst the cache of rum cake (I made a mental note to ensure that Caroline would stick to her rum cake diet). I set off along Seven Mile Beach Road and having returned to my more customary time of seven am was greeted, with a smile and nod of the head or a cheery 'hello' by the other regular joggers, cyclists and dog walkers who were now getting used to seeing my sun-cream-coated perspiring mass on my morning mini-marathon out towards West Bay and on to Dolphin Point.

After about a mile I came across the debris from the accident that we had heard the police and ambulance services attending the night before. It was strewn across the verge and included jagged pieces of broken bumper, headlamp glass and the remains of some hubcaps. I hoped that the occupants had fared better than their vehicles. I made good progress to the halfway point, where I took on board some liquid refreshment, but my return journey slowed considerably. It was going to be another very hot day.

Although this morning's exercise was much more uneventful, with MM being conspicuous by his absence, I didn't realise quite how much the heat had slowed me down until about half a mile from home as I was daydreaming and looking forward to the cool inviting water of the swimming pool when to my shock, amazement and horror I was overtaken by a chicken. Yes, a chicken and a fairly scrawny specimen at that; although he, or she, did appear to be a very fit chicken and the fastest I had ever seen. I would, of course, have to say that. Over the past week we had become used to seeing small groups of chickens fighting for scraps at the side of the road but I didn't realise they also went out on training runs at dawn. I had learned there was a Grand Cayman Marathon and perhaps this one was preparing for the as yet unknown poultry equivalent. It brought a whole new meaning to the term 'free range'. Back in England I'm used to being overtaken by a whole host of different class athletes, all of whom are much fitter, much slimmer and normally much younger than me. I can live comfortably with this as very occasionally I come across somebody who is actually much slower than myself and I can glide past them with that superior air of the fitter long distance runner. In the interests of accuracy I should say firstly, this is a rarity, and secondly I tend to puff and pant past them and hope that they don't return the compliment further along the road. However, this was my first, and I hope last, experience of being overtaken by a creature more suited to laying eggs. Other than the passing motorists, who hopefully were concentrating on their driving, there didn't appear to be anybody else in the vicinity to witness my embarrassment as my new-found feathered running partner disappeared back into the bushes and allowed me to finish my run in my own company. I wouldn't have minded being overtaken by a dog, preferably a greyhound, or even one of the local Cuban racers. I'm not talking of Albert Juantorina but a variety of fast-moving snake which is commonly found on the island. The Cuban racers can grow to a length of four feet, have small mouths without the normal venomous fangs and whilst they can certainly appear frightening are totally harmless to humans. Although I had learned that they inhabited Grand Cayman I did not meet any during my travels but I think I would have much preferred to be outpaced by such a creature than a wandering fowl. It would have been much less embarrassing and also made for a better story. However, truth will out and for a few metres I had to play second best to a chicken.

Having been suitably chastened by my run-in with 'Roadrunner' my pace became quite sedate. However, as had become my routine, I approached the hotel in the same manner that I left it. I won't describe it as a sprint, but for me it was a fast trot, so that should anybody happen to be watching as they opened their bedroom curtains, I might just appear to be a reasonable athlete. If only they knew. I had already determined that I would not be having hard-boiled eggs for breakfast this morning.

Following my regular early morning dip in the pool and swift handwash and rinse of my running gear I made my way to breakfast. I sat chatting to the family from Essex who were moving out to Grand Cayman and staying in the hotel whilst they searched for a suitable property. He was a surveyor who had been appointed to a government post on the island having recently completed his contract back home in the UK. They had lived very close to my youngest brother, in the rural north of the county, and were now out here on another contract, about to start a new chapter in their lives. Once they learned of what I had done in my previous life they told me of their burglary experience back home in Essex. As a police officer, present or retired, you become used to people telling you of their differing contacts with the police. Unfortunately many of these seem to be related to a bad experience. In this particular case they were one of many victims of a particularly prolific local burglar who had managed to evade capture by the boys in blue for some time before eventually being arrested.

They certainly weren't being critical and I was yet again reminded of the impact that a house burglar has on his victims. I had experienced this all too often over the years particularly with the more elderly and vulnerable victims. The shock of a stranger invading their home had resulted in a number of them having to move house as they could no longer feel safe and secure in their own homes. It wasn't just the loss or damage caused to their property but the psychological effect that occurred every time they walked back through their front doors. All too often they are left with a legacy of fear and anxiety. Those apologist do-gooders who consider burglary to be a minor crime purely against property and are ever willing to mitigate on behalf of the burglars would do well to spend some time with the victims. It might not, intrinsically, be recognised as a crime of violence but they underestimate its significance upon the many thousands of victims each year. Equally those who have the difficult role of judging and sentencing these miscreants, whether they are Magistrates or HM Judges, would be better informed if they had to visit the scenes of a number of these crimes and view the ransacked houses in the company of the victims. If every three or four years they were given a gentle reminder of the reality of such a crime, as opposed to listening to an articulate lawyer's bland and detached narrative in the sanitised environs of a courtroom, they might be better placed to ensure that the victims had greater faith in the justice system giving equal prominence and consideration to the victims' rights as it does to the human rights of the criminals.

My new friends from Essex were to spend the morning house hunting, although they had already spotted one or two that they fancied and were returning for a further viewing. Quite how prices compared with those at home I was not exactly certain but suspected they were likely to be somewhat more expensive than the average Essex three up, three down semi-detached. Meanwhile we were to spend the morning going to Hell and back.

By nine-thirty Carl and Fran had arrived and we were all aboard our trusty people carrier and making our way north, along much of the route of my morning perambulations parallel to Seven Mile Beach. I kept a beady eye upon the roadside undergrowth to see if 'Roadrunner' were to emerge once more but he had obviously completed his morning run and returned to rest in his hatch or training camp for the remainder of the day. We drove past the West Bay United Church, without as much as a second glance, and continued directly on towards the small settlement of Hell. I'm sure the pastor and parishioners would have willingly given their time to counsel us, had we even stopped briefly, but we were determinedly set upon the road to Hell and nothing was going to deter us. Although the singular sign post had seen better days and was in need of a coat of paint and a touch up from a sign-writer, it remained relatively easy to follow the well-trodden path to Hell. We reached this small hamlet that appeared to be not much more than a few well-established gift shops which were selling the sort of memorabilia that you could buy in any Golden Mile seafront emporium back home. The only difference was that most of this came with a brand and label from Hell. The atmosphere was noisy and cheerful with most of the activity occurring around the single storey shop that also doubled as a post office, thus enabling thousands of tourists to send their postcards home from Hell accompanied with the appropriate postmark. This particular store was the focal point of the community as it is situated to the front of the main attraction. It was already packed with tourists. Other than the novelty value I failed to appreciate why so many visitors wanted to send their friends and family a holiday memento from this particular stop on their travels. There were many far more attractive places on the island as I'm equally sure there were on the remainder of their cruises. However, there's no accounting for taste and from the never ending stream of cards being popped into the post-box the appeal of a postmark from Hell obviously kept the local postal sorting office staff busy throughout the holiday season and I suspect also the remainder of the year.

On this particular Wednesday morning Hell's stores were busy with a large number of customers, who had arrived in a convoy of air-conditioned coaches having been collected from the four cruise ships moored back in Georgetown port. In a fashion not dissimilar to a class of schoolchildren on a day's outing they were lining up to have their photographs taken, either in groups or individually, with Satan or Lucifer who appeared rather grotesque in their fancy dress and devilish masks. Not unreasonably I guess that was their intention. The actors seemed very popular with the little groups of diminutive oriental visitors who were busy with their digital cameras laughing and giggling, rushing back and forth as if in a competition with each other to take more snaps of their compatriots with Beelzebub than had ever previously been achieved in thirty minutes in Hell. Perhaps a trophy was awaiting the winner of the funniest photo contest back on board at that evening's after-dinner entertainment in the ship's theatre. Quite what the prize would consist of I do not know but there were numerous images and statues of 'Old Harry' available in the shop any of which would fit the bill. Whatever it was, it was proving a great attraction because although the coach drivers and couriers were trying to round up their passengers to move on to their next destination the snap-happy cruisers were now rushing around in a demonic frenzy determined not to miss any opportunity to snatch that last all important photograph that might see them crowned as King of the Underworld Photographers. Quite what Ken, our photographer/cleric, would have made of all this I don't know, although I'm sure he wouldn't have been averse to visiting Hell, purely on a fact-finding mission. The coach drivers eventually lost patience with their charges who either couldn't, or didn't want to, understand them and were continuing to chatter in their native tongues as they ignored the pleas of the drivers to return to the coaches. Having waited long enough a couple of the drivers started to drive slowly away. That did the trick. We then witnessed the amusing, for us at least, scene of groups of unfit and mainly well-fed overweight cruisers straggled along the road as they started to chase the coaches back towards Georgetown. One elderly, and particularly corpulent, matriarch appeared as if she was on the verge of a heart attack as she waddled up the road in pursuit of her coach. Dressed in baggy linen blouse and matching skirt she resembled one of my grandmother's steamed suet puddings that used to bulge around the middle where the string used to struggle to keep the dumpling-like mass inside the muslin. Just like the puddings as they were taken out of the saucepan, she looked as if she had reached bursting point.

Having made them run for long enough the drivers eased the coaches to a halt to enable their passengers to clamber aboard, puffing, panting and sweating as they climbed, or collapsed, into their seats. I just wondered if the drivers had played this game before as I'm sure I didn't imagine one of them give a knowing wink and a grin as he drove off on his now delayed return journey to the port.

Meanwhile, as I had anticipated on my early morning run the day was already becoming much hotter.

Having only had the opportunity for the single pre-run application of suntan cream I took advantage of the limited shade available to ensure my arms, shoulders and legs were protected from the heat of the enormous golden globe in the sky.

Once the photogenic cruisers had departed, willingly or otherwise, we had time to explore Hell in a more comfortable and less frenetic atmosphere, although as I've said it was already unbelievably hot and only just about mid-morning. Bearing in mind where we were I suppose we couldn't have expected it to be anything other than hot.

Hell gave the appearance of being somewhat neglected although the shop obviously did a roaring trade and was crammed to the rafters with souvenirs to take home to Grandma. Although I don't think any self-respecting grandchild would have taken such a gift within a mile of their grandparents. It's amazing how views differ as the cash tills were continually registering sales and the seaside arcade-type gifts were disappearing like hot cakes or, bearing in mind our location, rum cakes. It was blatantly obvious that this particular outpost in Hell was a real money-spinner. In fairness, the shopkeeper and his assistants were a very happy bunch and the mood had rubbed off on the customers. They were very welcoming hosts and did their devil's best to make all the visitors as comfortable as possible in the hope they might prolong their stay or even return at a later date. I personally didn't feel the need to leave with a tee-shirt, hot chilli powder or assorted crockery all decorated with greetings from Hell.

To the rear of the store and main car park was an area that resembled an arid and desolate moonscape and was wholly uninviting. It was a reasonable imitation of a scorched netherworld of fire and brimstone that stretched away into the distance. Not somewhere that I would wish to spend any length of time. To the front of this barren wasteland was a wooden boarded viewing platform on which we assembled for the statutory group photograph against a backdrop of a deserted godforsaken waste inhabited by a few burnt and skeletal tree trunks with the solitary black ghoulish figure of 'Old Nick' seemingly beckoning you into his habitat. None of us were in any rush to climb over the fence and set foot on the charred remains of this hellhole. Even if we had been so minded the rocks looked so sharp that the slightest slip could have caused serious injury. These rocks are known locally as iron-shore and it is rumoured that from time to time the local residents pour oil across them and then set fire to it to 'enhance' their appearance as a tourist attraction. The desert landscape looked so inhospitable that, to my mind, it wasn't in need of any enhancement which together with the heat of the sun reflecting off the rocks was more than enough to create a very realistic impression of a torrid and bottomless pit leading into oblivion. If one were awarding marks in a manner similar to an ice dancing competition then, compared to Torvill and Dean, it would probably score zero out of ten for cultural merit and a maximum of five out of ten for novelty value. Not an attraction that was likely to become etched in one's memory for a lengthy period of time. There was a certain irony that on an island that was obviously a predominantly Christian community one should find Hell in its midst. Perhaps there is logic to their thinking for it was, for me, the sort of place once visited I would not be rushing to return.

Our three quarters of an hour in Hell was quite long enough and I think we were all happy to move on to our next port of call, the turtle farm, which turned out to be much more crowded than Hell and, unsurprisingly, was a much more popular venue with the tourist trade; both day-trippers and resident holidaymakers alike.

It was a short drive towards the northern tip of the western arm of the island and we found the farm situated roughly midway between North West Point and Conch Point overlooking the sea near Boatswain's Bay. Standing, looking out across the sand and rocky outcrops at the sun-drenched clear blue water the view was vastly different to that we had experienced just thirty minutes earlier. We joined a short and orderly queue to gain entry to the farm and many of those in the line had disembarked from one of the cruise liners moored back in Georgetown. Not for the first time on this holiday I was the subject of some envious glances accompanied by enquiries about the local outlet for the purchase of my West Indian sun hat. Those without any head covering, particularly the follically challenged, were suffering in the heat and it was normal to see the locals carrying umbrellas aloft to protect them from the sun. So far in just over a week in Grand Cayman I hadn't seen anywhere trading in West Indies cricket merchandise; although you could find other wide-brimmed sun hats they didn't seem to have the same attraction as the maroon-coloured headgear with palm tree motif that I had acquired three years earlier in Port of Spain. My trusty hat had been well worn both on that trip and on my week to date and was by now displaying signs of wear. The sun had already started to blanch the exterior which was beginning to fade to a pinkish hue whilst the underside of the brim retained its deep purple tone being screened from the direct rays of the sun. The internal sweatband, originally brilliant white, had become discoloured with a mixture of perspiration and excess suntan cream that even if not intended to blend together was a natural result of my daily excursions into the sun. For some strange reason this only seemed to enhance the appeal of this now weatherbeaten piece of garb. It certainly didn't draw the same degree of fascination when it was in pristine condition back in Trinidad, although in fairness it was one of many on display in the days before, during and after the Test Match. I'm sure there is an opportunity beckoning for any Georgetown merchant willing to obtain some sort of franchise with the West Indian Cricket Board, to meet the needs of the local cricket enthusiasts. I would be willing to provide the necessary distressing to the material if it were likely to increase the value and the profit margin. This could be arranged for a nominal administration fee and the price of a flight to, and accommodation costs in, Grand Cayman. Who knows, we might start a new and lucrative fashion statement. It's certainly no less crazy than frayed jeans with strategically placed holes in the knees and the bum, as modelled by some supposed superstars and sporting icons who wish to set the latest fashion fad as opposed to follow-ing it. I guess there's no accounting for taste and as I wouldn't profess to be the most sartorially elegant perhaps I should be the last to be critical of the younger generation and their dress sense.

Once inside the turtle farm we started our tour at one of the smaller tanks that contained some younger turtles. It was impossible to count how many were in the tank but whilst we were there two keepers were actually filling this round swimming pool with about another fifty young turtles that were excitedly splashing into the water and swimming around amongst their new friends.

The turtles didn't appear to have any fear of humans, in fact quite the reverse. As we leaned over the tank watching their antics they would swim up to us, almost inviting us to lift them from the water. Surprisingly, in this area the keepers were happy to allow us to lift them by their underbellies from the water and hold them in the palms of our hands as they flapped their arms and posed for photographs. We were warned against trying the same with their older cousins that we would see on the other side of the farm.

All of us were comfortable holding the turtles, with one exception. The usual suspect couldn't quite get the hang of lifting them from the surface of the water. Each time she tried and the youngster flapped its wings, splashing her, she would let go and drop it back into the pool. It was actually very pleasant being splashed with cool water, whilst standing in the noon day sun. After numerous attempts, and no little degree of encouragement from the rest of the gang, well if not encouragement then mickey-taking, she found a tame one that was happy to remain motionless as she raised it into her arms and then appeared to hold a conversation with him or her. I must admit I don't know how to distinguish the sex of a turtle. To the casual observer there are no obvious signs or appendages that provide instant recognition. I'm sure if I had asked one of the keepers they would have been willing to tell me or perhaps even demonstrate the difference. I learned later that even the experts have difficulty in differentiating between the sexes until the turtles are much older.

Exactly what was said between Caroline and the young turtle we will never know but they seemed to be holding a meaningful conversation in 'Turtlespeak' and each appeared to understand the other.

What the turtle made of Caroline is anybody's guess but having had its picture taken with this strange young Englishwoman it returned to the water and dived for the bottom not to be seen again. I'm sure it just wanted some peace and quiet.

Caroline meanwhile, had started to regain her composure, if that's not a contradiction in terms, and was excitedly telling anyone who would listen how brave she had been to cuddle a Teenage Turtle, even if it wasn't of the Ninja variety.

I mention the sex of the turtles for two reasons. Firstly, I have not made any proper or direct reference to the subject of sex before. Secondly, and this is the prime reason, is that I've been told that unless I include sex in the story the book is unlikely to be published and less likely to be sold. Being the mercenary individual that I am I therefore decided to abandon my principles and introduce sex into at least one chapter. Not that I am anti-sex. Quite the contrary, but it took me a while to work out how I could legitimately include it in my holiday notes on Grand Cayman.

Now, as I mention above, I am unable to tell the sex of a turtle but sex is a real issue for the turtle farm. It's amazing what one learns on holiday. In my case it's normally a bundle of useless information. In this particular instance the gestation period for a turtle is two months and each female can lay up to seven clutches of eggs, each clutch containing about one hundred eggs. Then comes the tricky bit for the turtle farm, for it is this that will determine the sex of the turtles. If this next procedure goes wrong it will impact upon the creature's sex and consequently upon the next generation of turtles. Once the turtles lay their eggs they are all collected and placed in incubators where the temperature must remain constant as it is this that determines the sex of the turtle. Provided it remains at this set temperature it ensures that an equal number of male and female turtles are hatched. If it drops slightly then the result would be a batch of all-male turtles and alternatively if it were to become warmer a group of all-female turtles would be born. Needless to say the turtle farm takes the sex and breeding business very seriously.

Initially the tiny babies are nurtured in small warm boxes before being transferred to their more natural water environment, in one of the many tanks where they are housed and cared for, so that they can grow up to a weight of six pounds in their first year. As you wander through the farm it is encouraging to see so many schoolchildren taking an interest in the young turtles not just out of curiosity but with a seemingly genuine concern about their environment and their future. A new venture was planned for the turtle farm, which included the creation of a marine park close to Boatswain's Beach and was due for completion in 2006. Attractions incorporate an interactive turtle area, a snorkelling area, an aviary and a nature trail to attract young and old alike. As a world-class research centre it will be a unique experience for all lovers of wildlife. We were all sure that Caroline would just love the interactive turtle area although the turtles might not feel quite the same about her.

The turtle farm is now also linked to a project with the Sea Life Centres in Europe. The initial objective was to raise awareness within Europe of the plight of the endangered green sea turtle. Turtles were being distributed to six aquariums in the United Kingdom, Holland, France and Belgium.

Those housed at the Sea Life Centre in Weymouth, England, would inhabit a new and specially built turtle sanctuary. The aim is for the Sea Life Centres, by the display of the turtles in their aquariums, to contribute to and support the Cayman Turtle Farm programmes to promote conservation of the green sea turtle and raise awareness of the turtle-related culture and traditions of the Cayman Islands which it was hoped would be sustained. Additionally, they intended to raise enough funds to construct a much-needed Sea Turtle Rescue and Wildlife Information Centre on the Greek island of Zakynthos which hosts the vast majority of nests of the Mediterranean loggerhead turtles. Hopefully the link between these different centres will ensure the protection and conservation of the world's turtle population. The initial transfer of twenty turtles to the United Kingdom was accompanied by a veterinary surgeon and they were flown direct by British Airways to the Heathrow Animal Reception Centre before completing their journeys to their new homes.

As we crossed the road into the part of the farm holding the older and more established turtle population I must admit that I did have some reservations about the sheer numbers of turtles housed together in each tank. Many of these turtles were quite enormous and even if you wanted to hold one it would not be humanly possible. A fully grown turtle can weigh in excess of five hundred pounds and that is an awful lot of turtle to cuddle. To my inexperienced eye there did appear to be too many crammed in together, in the confined space of the circular tanks. In some cases they were almost sitting on each other and they just didn't appear to be very happy. Although if you were to ask me the difference between a happy and unhappy turtle I do not have a ready answer and found it impossible to tell if they were smiling or scowling. With over fifteen thousand turtles on the farm I just wasn't convinced that if I were an adult turtle I would be content with my lot. The babies and youngsters seemed to have the space and conditions to enjoy themselves whereas the mature turtles were in more congested and uncomfortable-looking quarters and didn't appear to relish their situation. Although we were assured that between ten and fifteen percent are returned to the wild every year I just had the feeling that some of those on the farm would have jumped at the opportunity to escape. We were not to know at the time but for some of them that moment was just a few weeks away.

A couple of days later we were chatting to a local resident on the beach and expressing our concern about the confined space in which the older turtles were kept and our perception that they would be happier if they were allowed to roam free in their natural environment. She took a totally diametric position and insisted that the majority would not survive if given their freedom as infants, as opposed to being reared in the comparative comfort of the turtle farm. The tanks are replenished with fresh sea water on a daily basis and I couldn't argue with her assertion that the turtle population was fit and healthy. They just didn't look very happy packed, almost sardine-like, together in the tanks. She was adamant that the green sea turtle, which is an endangered species, would by now be extinct but for the efforts of the turtle farm. Although I had some reservations, purely in relation to the housing conditions of the older inhabitants, overall I was very impressed with the turtle farm both in respect of facilities for the numerous visitors to this obviously fascinating tourist attraction but also for their efforts in the field of conservation. It is estimated that about half a million passengers from the cruise liners visit the turtle farm every year and I can fully understand the appeal of these gentle and endangered creatures. Perhaps, in my ignorance, I shouldn't be questioning the acknowledged expertise of those at the turtle farm who obviously have a genuine desire to care for and conserve the turtle population.

The farm is a fitting tribute to the turtles, indigenous creatures of the islands, who were even mentioned by Christopher Columbus when he first spotted the islands early in the sixteenth century and named them

Las Tortugas in recognition of the colonies of enormous green sea turtles inhabiting these small landfalls.

Today the turtle is a national symbol and can even be seen on the tail fins of planes in the Cayman Airways fleet.

For me the last couple of hours had been much more interesting than Hell but unfortunately our visit to the farm seemed all too brief as we clambered back aboard the bus to return to the hotel for a late lunch, before three of us were to spoil a good walk by testing some of the island's fairways with our golfing prowess, or lack of it.

CHAPTER 11

Three's a Handicap

The Inaugural Grand Cayman Caribbean International and Joint World Mixed Handicap Golf Tournament was due to tee off later that afternoon. The heat of the midday sun ensured that an earlier start would not have been a sensible option.

We lunched around the pool with Carl and Diane studiously absorbing the details of the course yardage charts whilst I was busy scribbling my diary notes, to try and keep them up to date, following the morning's trip to Hell and visit to the turtle farm.

The afternoon international golfing event was to feature two of Europe's totally unknown and unheard of golfing non-superstars who are destined to remain firmly entrenched in the category of keen and enthusiastic amateurs. As far as all the golfing journalists and magazines are concerned they will retain the anonymity that has been a feature of their golfing careers to date. Firstly, Carl, who was used to hacking his way around the parkland and links courses of East Anglia. However, he did have youth and fitness upon his side and had received some coaching and advice from his grandfather before leaving England for the sunnier climes of Grand Cayman.

The other contender from the northern hemisphere was yours truly who had picked up a golf club five years previously and then found it to be the most technically difficult and frustrating sport I had ever played. Unfortunately for all the bad shots that I played during the course of a round I normally also managed to play the odd decent one. This persuaded me, against my better judgement, that one day I could become a golfer so that consequently I kept returning for more punishment. I only wish that I had started playing at a much earlier age. At least I now felt confident enough in my own ability to take on the world (well, two of them) and not embarrass myself in the process.

The third and final competitor in this truly international array of anonymous golfing heroes was Diane, that Antipodean wonder golfer who at great personal expense (no sponsorship available) had agreed to meet the two Poms in a head to head three ball to decide who was to become the 2004 World Mixed Open Champion. Diane was probably the most experienced of the field having played many different courses in both Asia and Australia and had also been taking her daily fitness regime a bit too seriously. Even she, however, would admit to being less than Michelle Wie or Laura Davies like in her approach to golf.

Having just heard that the professional circuit was now allowing women to compete in some competitions, that were previously the sole preserve of their male counterparts, we thought that our international open event might just set the tone for those who possess a slightly greater talent than ourselves. We were in the vanguard of truly mixed worldwide golfing competition. Quite what the omnipotent oligarchs of Augusta, Georgia or the more genteel members of the Royal and Ancient at St Andrews on the east coast of Fife would have made of our foray into this arena I hate to think!

I suspect we would not have achieved their wholehearted support and some of their more conservative supporters would have been positively appalled at our little mixed competition. Nonetheless we were determined to enjoy ourselves and also play to the best of our limited ability.

The one thing that we did have in common was that we all appeared to be naturally competitive which was not necessarily matched by an equal abundance of skill. There is no doubt that we were all looking forward to our first holiday game of golf as we made our way to the Links course at Safehaven to pit our wits against both the natural and designed hazards that awaited our best efforts. A number of holes would prove that the traps were deliberately placed to catch out the likes of ourselves, as high handicap golfers.

Safehaven's Links is the only accredited eighteen-hole championship course on the island and is a par seventy-one. The course is over ten years old and as such is now reasonably well established. Compared with many courses at home it is relatively flat although some of the fairways could best be described as gently undulating. In contrast my home club and course, Three Rivers Golf Club, in the village of Cold Norton in dear flat old Essex could be characterised as positively mountainous. As you climb 'Cardiac Hill' on the approach to the fourteenth green and then plod your weary way up a further gradient to the fifteenth tee you would not brand Essex as flat, particularly if you were carrying your bag with a full set of clubs. However, from this high point above the valley of the River Crouch you are able to appreciate the local scenery of the course with its lush greens and sloping fairways to the south together with a generous mixture of majestic oaks, rows of poplars, silver birches, weeping willows and a variety of other trees, bushes and hedges. You are able to glimpse the rabbit population idly munching the grass whilst being spied on by a well-nourished ginger tom cat who has obviously marked out his own territory at the top of the hill. Squirrels searching for hidden acorns are plentiful and can be spotted scampering from tree to tree and ascending them at a considerable rate of knots. A wide variety of birdlife is to be found ranging from the moorhen and duck populations close to the water to the odd pheasants, who seem intent on committing suicide by wandering in front of tees as golfers are about to launch huge drives, to the green woodpecker that shuttles back and forth across the second, fourteenth and seventeenth fairways. The views to the east towards the Blackwater estuary, with the two ugly concrete grey edifices of Bradwell nuclear power station just visible on the distant horizon, and to the south over the green pastures and marshes blending with the golden, amber and brown patchwork landscape to the wide flat valley of the River Crouch and onwards to the conurbation of Southend on Sea sitting near the mouth of the Thames estuary make the trek worthwhile, particularly on a sunny summer's day. As you swivel further to the right it is possible to look across in the direction of Langdon Hills, Basildon New Town and on towards the Queen Elizabeth II Bridge at the Dartford/Thurrock river crossing. Standing on the fifteenth tee I would estimate that as you span this vista across the south of the county you are probably scanning the best part of a quarter of the county of Essex. It is rarely, if ever, described as the most picturesque county in England but this particular view, from the highest vantage point on the course, probably encompasses all that you are likely to see in a panorama of the Essex countryside. All of this is, of course, purely relative as compared to many courses at home in the UK Three Rivers would be considered to be no more than a gentle stroll taking in the odd gradual incline. By contrast I'm pretty sure that wherever you stand on Safehaven you are never more than a few feet above sea level, in common with anywhere else on Grand Cayman.

Driving down Safehaven Drive, the long approach road, to the Safehaven clubhouse, with the course on your left, you begin to appreciate just how difficult this six thousand six hundred and five-yard course could be for the enthusiastic hacker. It becomes even more difficult when you learn that the prevailing winds make this equate to about seven thousand yards on a calm day. As more of the course blossoms into view and the scope of the water hazards starts to become apparent it is easy to understand that any misplaced confidence can easily ebb away. The course was constructed around one massive horseshoe shaped lake that abuts seven of the holes. In case you manage to avoid this stretch of water there are another ten smaller lakes that are ready and waiting as water magnets for any slightly mis-hit shot. For good measure, to one end of the course you have the vast expanse of North Sound stretching as far as the eye can see whilst at the opposite end Mitchell's Creek, leading to the many quays in Governor's Creek, adjoins its western perimeter. We were not to know, and didn't even in our wildest dreams imagine, that in less than two months the water we could now see would be as nothing compared to the raging torrent that would hit the island completely submerging the course and flooding the clubhouse to a depth of several feet.

The local brochure depicts Safehaven as a mature course with lush greens and thousands of tropical shrubs and trees. It also mentions panoramic views of the Island's North Sound and refreshing sea breezes. All of this presents an accurate portrait unless you happen to be trying to hit a two hundred yard shot onto a postage stamp whilst contending with a strong cross or headwind. At such a time I'm not sure that even Tiger Woods would express it as a 'refreshing sea breeze'. I can understand why the pamphlet describes it as 'a perfect day in paradise' but for those on the course when Hurricane Ivan arrived I'm willing to bet it seemed anything but paradise. A wet and windy Hell would have been a far more appropriate description.

Having paid our US$60 (about £35 at the time of our visit) for our green fee, hire of Calloway Big Bertha clubs and electric buggy rental, to the friendly receptionist in the professional's shop, the course marshal ensured that we were properly kitted out, with sets of clubs that suited each of us, before we could make our way to the first tee. He found me a set of left-handed clubs that were in excellent condition. This is easier said than done as less than ten percent of golfers are cack-handed. I'm one of the strange band of individuals who do everything right handed until I pick up a golf club or cricket bat when I then immediately become a southpaw. I just cannot hit a ball if I try to do it in the conventional right-handed manner. When playing cricket I bowl right-handed and play racket sports right-handed. There is no logical reason for this quirk of nature which becomes even stranger when my two younger brothers have followed in an identical fashion. Bearing in mind that neither of our parents did anything left-handed this will remain one of the mysteries of life in the Benning family.

I gained the impression that it was also the role of our elderly and knowledgeable marshal to enforce the strict dress code at the club. If we had not been smartly and properly attired then I'm sure he would have politely, but firmly, made sure we changed into something more appropriate prior to starting our round. Use of the buggy was not optional. I normally would not even contemplate using a buggy but the local rules insist that this is essential for two reasons. It keeps the players on the course moving at a reasonable pace, avoiding delays and queues at the tees, but more importantly helps protect you from the heat. I probably didn't appreciate this until we had almost completed our round when realisation dawned that four hours walking in the sun, carrying a full set of golf clubs, would have ended up being quite uncomfortable if not exhausting and could possibly spoil an enjoyable game of golf. Importantly it was also possible to transport a sufficient quantity of soft drinks on the buggy that proved to be a vital element, as we tended to need liquid refreshment every couple of holes. The marshal made sure we were acquainted with the local rules which included driving the buggies along the meandering paths at the side of the fairways until you were level with your ball. You could then drive to your ball, take your next shot, before retracing your steps to the pathway to drive on to wherever the ball had landed. I hadn't come across this practice previously, as back home it is the custom to drive along the fairways. By keeping to the cart paths it ensured that the fairways remained in excellent condition. Although Safehaven is classed as a links course it belied its nomenclature. It was almost too neat and tidy to be a links course. That is not intended as a criticism but when compared to the dunes, gorse and scrubland that is experienced on such a course in England the impression given here was that it was almost too perfect or tailored to be a conventional seaside golf course. We were fortunate in not finding any of the thick rough found at home but there were more than enough traps for the unwary and those who were unfamiliar with the course layout. We were in for a challenging round of golf. Having assessed the many water hazards I decided to buy six balls to ensure I would have plenty in reserve should I be unfortunate enough to land the odd one in the water. Surely even I couldn't possibly lose six balls in just eighteen holes of golf. Could I?

The three of us made our way to the first tee full of confidence and ready to face whatever vagaries the course or weather conditions were likely to throw at us. You will notice already that as a golfer I will never be the author of my own misfortune. It will always be some sort of freak of nature that sends the ball in the wrong direction or brings it to its final resting place in a position that makes it impossible to play the next shot. Wind, rain, an unlucky bounce, a hidden ditch, a bunker in the wrong position or even a tree that looks much smaller in the distance than it really is can all ruin a perfectly good shot. Why is it, when I'm assured that trees consist of twenty percent branches and eighty percent air, I always manage to find the twenty percent? It is also a fact of my golfing life that having hit the offending branch the ball will come to rest immediately behind the tree as opposed to bouncing back onto the fairway.

This was not the case on the first hole where we all got off to a satisfactory start by bogeying this par three short hole. We had all managed to play to our handicaps but this merely lulled us into a false sense of security. It was not destined to be that easy. We quickly realised that we had just played the second easiest hole on the course and one of only three that did not have a dreaded water magnet.

The second hole was a four hundred and ninety-yard par five from the yellow tee and needed your drive to carry a hundred-yard lake to the front of the tee to land on a narrow tree lined fairway. Reality dawned, this was going to be much more difficult. Diane struggled on this hole, having become enmeshed in some trees and bushes, but Carl and I somehow both managed to again come in at just one over par thanks to two very reasonable putts. As we putted out on this hole we saw a flash of lightning in the distance, and the skies over North Sound were starting to look ominously black and threatening.

Having completed the first two holes without any disasters my confidence was increasing so I took the Calloway Big Bertha driver from the bag for the first time. This was my first of many mistakes. My second in approaching this par four dog-leg right, with two water hazards, was not realising immediately that this was also stroke index one, making it the most difficult hole on the course. I wound myself up and pulled my first shot to the right. I still wasn't unduly concerned. Although I had landed in some light rough I was satisfied that a decent strike, cutting out some of the dog-leg, would see me over the second lake and close to the green. As is the norm with eighteen handicappers I was far too ambitious. I didn't strike the ball cleanly enough out of the rough and managed to plant it firmly in the lake. Having incurred an additional stroke by dropping a new ball I then played my one and only shot with that ball. Trying too hard to ensure that I didn't just clear the water but make the green I topped it and it flew straight into the lake, did a pass-able imitation of one of Barnes Wallis's bouncing bombs skimming very niftily across the surface before deciding that it preferred a career in the navy as opposed to the air force so reverted into submarine mode and on hearing the captain's orders to 'dive, dive, dive' dutifully obeyed and disappeared under the water never to be seen again, leaving just a few ripples spreading on the surface to mark the spot of its demise. From a reasonable position, after two holes, I had now lost a third of my ball supply and hadn't yet reached the third green. Oh, by the way, it was just beginning to rain and the storm clouds, although still some distance away, were gathering and appeared to moving in our direction. Storm clouds were also gathering around me on the third hole!

Fortunately for me Diane and Carl were also experiencing problems of their own; Carl joining me in the drink; so that this proved to be a hole we would all rather forget. Under the Stapleford scoring rules of golf we managed the grand total of zero points between the three of us.

The fourth hole is called Lake Side. This is not inaccurate but why this particular one should be so named when it would be equally appropriate for at least a dozen others I do not know. It is described as a strong par four with a tee shot being the first experience of playing into the prevailing breeze. As we arrived at the tee the wind was getting stronger and the rain becoming heavier. Although it was warm rain, their description was the equivalent of an estate agent describing an overgrown uncultivated and weed infested mud patch as a 'natural English Country Garden with potential'. Having all made a mess of the previous hole none of us were looking forward to driving off, with a lake to our right and jutting out to the front of the tee and both trees and a further lake ahead of us, provided we hit our tee shots straight. The onset of the storm did nothing to improve our confidence levels at that moment in time. We gauged the storm was still about two miles away and quickly decided that should it move any closer we would return to the sanctuary of the clubhouse and wait for it to pass. Why was it that on the one afternoon we decided to play golf we were to glimpse the first sign of miserable weather since we arrived on the island?

For the first, and what proved to be the only, time during my visit I did not need to resort to my supply of suntan cream. Most unusual and a pleasant change!

Without exception we all hit excellent tee shots and played the hole in regulation for our handicaps. Once again golf proved to be that most frustrating of sports when in a matter of minutes you can move from being a total novice into a half-decent golfer and then back again but cannot explain why this occurs.

Our moods on arriving at the fifth tee were much improved and, as with the golf, the weather had changed just as quickly. The rain had stopped, the sun was coming out and the black storm clouds were now disappearing into the distance. Carl and Diane both hit their tee shots straight and true, over the lake, landing on the green one hundred and forty yards away with Carl's ball rolling close to the hole. I selected my club, pictured the shot in my mind's eye, took the usual perfect practice swing before taking aim and hitting my ball straight into the water no more than a yard short of the green. Being in mixed company I didn't swear but smiled sweetly. Whilst they couldn't hear what I was uttering under my breath they didn't need to be Brains of Britain to guess my true feelings. I had now completed four holes, lost half my supply of balls and at this rate wouldn't even reach the halfway point without running out of balls, so to speak. Reaching into my bag I extracted my fourth ball of the day and placed it carefully on the tee peg. I peered into the pocket of the bag just to ensure there were at least two balls remaining. How long would it be before they were to see the light of day? Having gone through my pre-shot routine for the second time I once again swivelled my hips and hitting cleanly through the ball, lofted it over the water, past the pin to the back of the green. Why couldn't I have done that first time around? I still remained furthest from the hole but putted back down a slight slope and tapped in for a five. Diane got her par and Carl putted in for a birdie to take an early commanding lead. If only my first shot hadn't been grabbed by the dreaded water magnet I would have also achieved a par and we would all have left the green as very happy golfers.

The sixth is the second par five on the course and is a long left-handed dog-leg. The fairway is fringed with palm trees and narrows as you approach the green, which has a deep bunker sitting immediately to its front. Lest I forget, the water that had just swallowed my third ball sits to the right of the tee and the main lake to the left of the fairway, although there was enough room for error to avoid both. My tee shot here proved to be my best so far and with my left handed natural fade it took me around the corner onto the left of the fairway. Two more shots took me to the left of the green. I wanted to make sure I avoided the bunker but had left myself with a tricky chip onto the green. Although I managed to land the ball at the front of the green it rolled way past the flag but I still managed to get down in two for a bogey that I would have settled for from the tee. My two playing partners achieved a similar result albeit by very different routes with Carl unsuccessfully trying to decapitate the top of a palm tree.

The sun was now shining brightly whilst the prevailing wind masked its intensity. My West Indies cricket hat, which was becoming grubbier by the day, was again proving its worth. I approached the seventh tee with some trepidation as you again had to clear water from the tee in order to reach the fairway. Having done that if you could hit the ball long enough and accurately enough you could reach the green that was set dramatically on the lake bank. At least there was a bunker to the back of the green to prevent you running into the water if you clubbed the ball too far. There wasn't any likelihood of me reaching the bunker. I ended up tucked neatly against the base of a palm tree to the front and left of the green. If I had been right handed the shot wouldn't have been a problem. I had never found it necessary to cuddle a palm tree before and it is not something I would recommend. My best effort managed to scoop the ball nearer the green. A pitch and two putts gave me a double bogey and I was falling behind my two playing partners who now seemed to be in the groove.

We moved onto to the eighth hole, a three hundred and thirty-five-yard par four, and it was no longer a surprise to be teeing off with water in front of you. Any confidence that I had was now fast disappearing as I lined up my tee shot. For once it went reasonably straight but at the last moment veered to the right of the fairway, leaving me a shot over yet more water. Determined to avoid this hazard I aimed left and was successful until I saw the ball dribble into a bunker to the left of the green. Now I am well aware that professional golfers are normally content to be in a bunker close to the green and have the ability to come out with enough spin on the ball to cut it back close to the hole. I do not have that same ability or belief in myself. However, for once I came out first time, straight onto the green and took two putts to sink the ball. At least I had played the hole to my handicap as did Carl and Diane. We moved on towards the ninth and the turn with a renewed spring in our step.

We then saw the hole which is only a short hundred and ten-yard par three. The hole is called 'Small Island' and this is a slight misnomer as it is only surrounded by water on three sides. The yardage chart introduces this hole with the words, and I quote, 'This hole is reached across the inlet by all golfers.' As the three of us viewed the distant green, surrounded by palm trees, without exception we were all thinking that all golfers do not reach the green. Without the water it would be simple. The psychological effect of the beautiful stretch of clear blue water made a simple tee shot quite daunting. Reading on in our course guide it was kind enough to inform us that there was a drop area for those who didn't make it. It went on to add, 'The front of the green rises gently from the water to hold those shots which are a little short thanks to the prevailing breeze which can sometimes be a three clubber.' This merely added to the uncertainty of which club to select in an attempt to land on the green. The guide concluded, 'The view from the tee is one of the most attractive on the course.' I would wholeheartedly agree with this final sentence; the scene was aesthetically pleasing and tranquil. Indeed on a sunny Sunday afternoon it would have been quite delightful. However, this was scant consolation as I stood there humming and harring over which club to select as the breeze began to stiffen. I eventually made my decision. I would go long for safety. At least there was a bunker at the back of the green to prevent my ball rolling into the water should I overclub it. I can't say I relaxed on the tee but I achieved a reasonable contact and my ball soared high above the water until the wind took charge drifting it away from the green and the bunker. Once it landed I then lost sight of it. Fortunately all three of us reached terra firma and we drove our buggies around the circular path to locate the resting places of our various shots. Carl had left himself a very long putt, Diane had landed a little short whilst I had overshot the green but quickly found my ball where it had come to rest in a position that ensured I would quickly resume my love affair with another of the local palm tree population. I needed to move sideways to go forward but a fortuitous bounce got me to the edge of the green. All of us achieved bogies which left us at the halfway stage in a much happier frame of mind than a few holes earlier. I was bringing up the rear of the trio with nothing to choose between my two playing partners at the turn. Prior to moving onto the tenth I availed myself of the opportunity of paying a quick visit to the professional's shop to purchase a further three golf balls and replenish my supply that had dwindled in and around the water magnets.

I also came to the conclusion at this stage that my decision about an hour earlier that I didn't need to replenish my coating of sun block had been a little premature. Whilst the breeze was now increasing into a reasonable north-westerly it only disguised the heat from the sun, which although it was late afternoon was still very strong. I took the opportunity to take two minutes at the halfway stage to dab a few drops of cream on my face, arms and legs. I would definitely require fresh supplies.

The tenth hole, like the first, tries to lull the unwary into a false sense of security. Neither hole has a water hazard but the tenth makes up for this with a couple of bunkers placed strategically to trap any decent drive that might fade to the right of the fairway. If you manage to avoid these, which we all did, you are left with a view of the green that is surrounded by five bunkers. More sand traps than any other green on the course. This was one of our better holes. My playing partners both bogied the hole. I fortunately managed to land my second shot on the green and two-putted for a par four which set me up nicely for the signature hole of the course.

This is described as 'a seaside hole to remember' and believe me that is an accurate description. Playing from the yellow tees it is only a hundred and forty-five-yard par three. However, the tee is positioned to the rear and side of a rather large lake. Having carried the water you need to propel the ball between two bunkers and onto the green. Should you over-hit your tee shot you will be able to see your ball disappear into the vast blue expanse of North Sound. This is less likely as you are aiming directly into the prevailing wind, which by now in late afternoon was becoming stronger. As you stand on the tee you can understand why they have made this their signature hole. The view across the lake onto the palm fringed green with the sun glistening on the wave capped water of North Sound makes this a very attractive hole. As I'm not a big hitter, and allowing for the very stiff breeze, I selected a much longer club, a five iron, and for once everything was in sync. My rhythm, swing, stance and head all did what they were supposed to do and this time did it together. The ball took off towards the heavens and the arc of its trajectory brought it back down to earth safely on the green when it then proceeded to roll on and on towards the left, coming to rest in some fringe grass to the front of another bunker. My two playing partners were struggling. Both had put their first shots into the water and neither had reached the green in three. I had an opportunity to start catching them. I chipped back onto the green and the ball rolled agonisingly slowly back up the slope, stopping just a couple of inches from the hole. A birdie had been too much to expect but I was on a roll as they say. Successive pars had brought me back into contention in this three competitor inaugural golfing championship. Spectators, television cameras, Peter Alliss, sponsorship and the media circus were all conspicuous by their absence, which was hardly surprising as those taking part, and their friends back at Indies Suites, were the only living souls who were aware of this massive historical event being dramatically played out into the early evening sunshine of the Caribbean.

I approached the next hole full of confidence. I should have known better. Golf has a nasty habit of bringing you back down to earth when you least expect it and it was about to prove to me that I'm not as good a golfer as I was beginning to think. I was again to lead off from the tee. This is a longish par five and as you stand on the tee looking towards the green some five hundred-odd yards away it appears fairly straightforward. Needless to say this was deceptive. Although Diane and Carl didn't experience my problems and went from tee to green in regulation. I managed to clear the water immediately in front of the tee. Just. My second shot from the dry bank of the lake took me into some trees on the left. This was where I stayed for my next two shots. The yardage chart informs you that the gravel cart-path is the highest surface from Georgetown in West Bay. I wouldn't know as I didn't manage to venture anywhere near the path or my intended direction of travel. Having eventually reached the green with my fifth shot and taking another two to find the hole I remained firmly back in third place. Carl and Diane seemed to have inherited the happy mood that I had acquired on the previous two holes. It's a funny old game is this golf.

For the thirteenth hole I was last off the tee following the now smiling Carl and Diane. All three of us carried the water with our tee shots and between us we had surrounded the hole. Unfortunately not one of us was closer than twenty feet from the hole and with the different borrows to read and overcome we all took three putts which was disappointing but on reflection, after the previous hole, I was happy to settle for a four.

The next hole, a three hundred and fifty-yard par four, appeared fairly straightforward provided you can carry three fairway bunkers with your tee shot. Diane wasn't able to and went from a bunker into some trees to the right of the fairway. She was now going through the same experience that I had encountered two holes earlier. As you approach the green the fairway narrows considerably and Carl joined Diane in the trees. My second shot was no better but although I didn't hit it cleanly it skimmed along the grass and remained on the fairway. Both Carl and Diane had to come sideways, out of the trees, before aiming for the green with their fourth shots. Carl had a particularly difficult lie and had to perform peculiar contortions whilst balancing mainly on one leg with his other at an oblique angle, just to chip the ball a few yards backwards and sideways. Meanwhile, I had chipped onto the green with my third and this time only needed the regulation two putts and I was back in contention just behind my two partners, with just four holes to play.

As we stood on the next tee looking towards the green, almost three hundred yards away, we studied the yardage chart hoping to find advice and inspiration. The description merely ensured that any confidence I had acquired on the last hole quickly dissipated. It is described as a short par four which features water off the tee and at the front and rear of the green, which is perched precariously on the edge of Mitchell's Lake. The approach shot to the pin requires some delicacy if it is to hold the green.

Having taken in this information, all three of us looked at each other and agreed that, so far, delicacy had not been one of our stronger points. We were, of course, all being somewhat premature. We first of all had to get to a position where we could play a chip onto the green. If you hit too far right, to be certain of avoiding the water, there were some trees waiting for you. Diane and Carl went right and found the trees, although Carl still had a reasonable shot. I flirted with the water but the ball rolled to a stop just in time, which I think surprised me just as much as the others. Carl and I hit reasonable second shots but both of us ended short of the green. We had taken the advice for delicacy too literally and adopted a safety first approach. Perhaps I should have followed this advice much earlier in my round. Diane meanwhile had needed to come out of the trees sideways before she could play her approach shot to the pin. She, however, was far more adventurous and went through the green, stopping short of the water but next to a tree so that she would also now have to become a tree hugger before she could get back to the smooth putting surface of the green. Carl and I both bogied the hole whilst Diane carded a six and, as we made our way to the sixteenth tee, was to be heard muttering words to the effect of 'unfriendly' Caymanian trees or something in a similar vein. We were sure that in her lovely Australian accent that was the general meaning of the words, even if they had been spoken with feeling. All of us had now become fully paid up members of the Tree Huggers Union. By now we would all have been happy to see MM arrive to hack away at the offending branches and trees.

The course now turned back towards the clubhouse for the final three holes, to initially face another par four described as a 'visually attractive yet tantalizingly right to left hole ... [with] water to the left front of the narrow two tiered green'. This was not inaccurate but failed to give you the whole picture. The water actually stretched along much of the left of the fairway. With my cack-handed penchant to slice my tee shots this was another hazard waiting to claim my ball. I continued with my newly found safety first motto and hit an iron from the tee and much to my amazement landed in the centre of the fairway about one hundred and twenty yards from the green. My two partners also adopted a cautious approach and were both on dry land in some light rough just to the right of the fairway. All of us hit second shots adjacent to the green which left us with a chip and a putt to par the hole. The chips were fine but we all then needed two putts to find the hole. Although we were all slightly disappointed each of us would have settled for that before our tee shots and for once not one of us had got into any real difficulty. Two holes to play and the scores were now quite close.

The penultimate hole is named 'Devious'. Standing on the tee and reading the Yardage Book we could see why. Whilst being the shortest par four on the course at two hundred and sixty yards it was also probably the most difficult. It was described thus: 'Two accurate iron shots into the breeze are needed to reach a small waterside green surrounded by sand grass and waste bunkers.' They had only forgotten to mention some trees that seemed to be perched between the green and water's edge for nuisance value and concluded their depiction with the superfluous sentence, 'Many a good round might founder here.' We had all achieved that distinction much earlier in our rounds.

Their summary for this hole was erroneous in one other respect but this wasn't totally their fault. It was now early evening and the breeze they had mentioned now seemed more like a gale blowing in from North Sound. By now our earlier experiences had made us all much more circumspect in our approach and without exception we were all content to hit medium iron shots onto the fairway. Our second shots were not as accurate. I rolled into the bunker at the back of the green; Carl preferred the bunker to the left whilst Diane, true to form, continued her scrutiny of the local tree population. Carl and I were now sure that she was trying to emulate some sort of Australian David Bellamy and would return home as an expert arborologist. With arms and legs wrapped around the tree she managed to chip to the front of the green. Carl was trapped under the lip of the bunker and needed two to escape whilst, for once, I managed to paddle the ball onto the green. I normally manage to play a variety of shots when I'm in a bunker, none of which you will find in any coaching video or manual, and none of which are normally very effective. Paddle, therefore, is probably the best way to describe how I managed to scoop the ball and a shovel full of sand onto the green on this occasion. Once again I couldn't sink a relatively easy putt but still managed a five which brought me level with Carl and both of us fractionally ahead of Diane.

The final hole is known as 'Waterloo' and as we surveyed the long undulating par five in front of us, with water stretching for the whole length of the hole, and to the right of the fairway, we wondered how many had met their Waterloo in the vast expanse of glistening blue water. The headwind was now beginning to create little whitecaps on the surface of the water. It was now also approaching dusk and the sunlight was beginning to fade. Although we had taken longer than expected our decision to book an earlier tee time was now proving to be one of our more sensible decisions of the holiday. Any later and we may not have completed the round.

The fairway was relatively narrow compared to some others and Carl and I hit our tee shots left to ensure we avoided the water. This put us in some tufty grass and for a change we were closer to the trees than Diane who had decided to take a straighter line and almost drifted into the lake but her ball dribbled to a stop just in time. At this stage the hole took a severe dog-leg right at almost ninety degrees. True professionals would have hit across the water to land close to the green. All three of us decided to play up to the corner to avoid any danger and escape the dreaded water magnet. This still left us a long third shot to the green, with water to our right and a mix of trees and shrubs to the left. Safety first had become the order of the day. Why hadn't I adopted this policy much earlier in the round? We all landed short of the green but this enabled us to chip and run our fourth shots towards the pin without any danger. The large green with its differing borrows was difficult to read and we all two putted for acceptable sixes all round. Well, after our earlier disasters it was perfectly acceptable to us even if Tiger Woods would expect, at least, to birdie the hole.

Much to my amazement, having replenished my stock of balls at the halfway stage, I had completed the back nine without losing a ball. That didn't prevent me from being the overall winner of the competition, for losing most balls. As we returned our buggies to the clubhouse each of us was in good spirits. In common with many golfers we could vividly remember our best shots whilst also thinking that if the 'if onlys' and 'what ifs' had gone in then we would have had quite splendid rounds. Equally we would also have been single figure handicappers. One can but dream. Without exception, having navigated the course for the first time without experiencing too many disasters, we all wanted to return as we all considered that we would actually improve on our second outing, as we now knew what to expect from the course. This is another golfing myth, that most golfers believe they will improve their scores until they do actually return only to discover that their expectations aren't matched by their ability. Unfortunately with so many other items on our packed agenda we never did get the opportunity to return and test that theory.

As we drove away from the course and looked back at some of the holes we had just played I think we all felt reasonably satisfied with our afternoon's efforts. Our golf was not of the highest standard, but bearing in mind it was the first time we had played the course all of us had carded presentable scores and had an enjoyable afternoon's entertainment. We had also provided ourselves with another topic of conversation for the remainder of the holiday. That's the trouble with golfers. To those who don't play the game they can be so so boring. When I thought back to my experiences of golfing in Trinidad and Tobago there were some considerable differences and one similarity. The obvious difference was that Grand Cayman was much flatter and the distraction of the howler monkeys playing and screeching in the hillside forests was missing. That didn't make the course any easier. Also missing was our unofficial caddie and his rather eccentric golfing garb. Perhaps if he had been there I wouldn't have lost as many balls. The one similarity was that my golf was still consistently inconsistent. It hadn't improved one jot.

We had been so engrossed in the golf that we hadn't realised that we were now about an hour later than anticipated. We just had time to grab a swift shower and cocktail by the poolside bar before driving to DJ's, another one of the local eateries, for one of their Mexican meals. In common with the other restaurants we had visited the quality was yet again very good with American-sized portions. For some inexplicable reason much of the conversation gravitated towards golf. The majority of the party managed to display a healthy disinterest whilst three strange people at one end of the table spoke in riddles of swing planes, sand wedges, lob wedges, bunkers, borrows and the benefits of using a driving iron.

The final comment did bring forth a riposte from one of the girls about not being very good with it as the creases on one's shirt tended to indicate that further practice was required. By that stage of the evening Carl and I, and I think even Diane, had no wish nor interest in honing our skills with a smoothing iron, although in Diane's case they didn't look as if they needed improving. In fairness I probably couldn't say the same for Carl and myself. However, all three of us remained casually indifferent to such cutting remarks and continued to relive all the shots that we had played during the afternoon. Well at least the good ones, conveniently forgetting the many poorer efforts, particularly those that came to a watery demise. A deadly serious international golfing competition it may have been, at least in our minds. A golfing master-class it was not!

As we started our puddings the band began playing in the adjoining dining room. It was beginning to look that the remainder of the evening was going to be both noisy and enjoyable. Having completed the meal the three older groovers in the party decided that we should not cramp the youngsters' style so we left them to bop the night away on the dance floor. I'm sure Carl, who was looking as tired as the three wrinklies, would also have jumped at the chance of an early night but the girls were not going to let him escape that easily. He was last seen being manoeuvred into position to demonstrate the intricacies of the rumba, samba and salsa or in whatever combination the girls decided to lead him. As we exited stage left, to find our trusty people carrier, I'm not sure if it was a smile of expectation or meek surrender I saw on Carl's face. One part of me would actually have enjoyed staying on at the restaurant and bopping the remainder of the night away but another part, my sensible head, was telling me that my body would gain greater benefit from a good night's sleep. Thirty years previously I would have been much more of a nocturnal creature and enjoyed every minute of it. Perhaps that was always why

I preferred working the night shift as opposed to early turn although once the old age clock reached fifty recovering from even a short set of nights became far more problematic and was very different to my experiences as a twenty-five-year-old. In those days, following a night shift, I would be in bed by seven and it wasn't unusual to sleep through until seven in the evening before getting up and preparing to go back on nights. I can even remember one colleague who overslept before a night shift. Thirty-plus years on I did well to sleep until nine in the morning and was normally up by lunchtime although still feeling tired by the time I went back to work in the evening. Recovery from a set of three or four nights was akin to having jet lag from a long-haul flight for the next three days.

By the time we arrived back at Indies Suites I was feeling quite tired but had enough energy to drag myself to the poolside bar for a swift nightcap before climbing the stairs to hit the sack and dreaming of a Tiger-like golf swing, or in my case as a left-hander I would happily settle to be even a poor imitation of Phil Mickelson. Dream on!

CHAPTER 12

Tropical Paradise – Rum, Sun, Sea and Sand

I had slept very well and by now had become accustomed to the faint hum of the air-conditioning in the background. This still did not prevent me utilising the homemade earplugs that completely masked any sound. I had permanently borrowed a couple of the girls' cotton wool and lint pads that they use to remove unwanted make-up at the end of the day. Split into quarters and neatly inserted into the ear they were as good as the genuine moulded plastic article used by the military. I would have been quite happy to return them to the girls at the end of the holiday but I suspect that they were no longer fit for use and even if they were the offer would have been declined bearing in mind they had been stuffed into a pair of wax-laden orifices each evening for the past fortnight.

I awoke to the sun already glinting in through a slight gap that I had unwittingly left between the curtains. I did not rush to climb out of bed as this was a morning when I could have a lie in as I was going to allow the commuters from West Bay a peaceful journey to work without having to watch an overweight sweaty old jogger meandering along their highways and byways in an attempt to avoid gaining too much weight and trying to retain a modicum of fitness.

I had time for a swift dip in the pool before breakfast. The local contractor had just completed his daily cleaning duties and I was joined by a young man who settled into a rhythmic crawl up and down the pool. I use the word 'crawl' to describe his swimming stroke and not his speed;

otherwise 'sprint' would have been a more appropriate description. He was managing to complete over two lengths of the pool to my one, and that was not accounting for my occasional rests at the shallow end to regain my breath. His elegant swimming stroke was considerably smoother, faster and created far less wash than mine. In fact in comparison it was express-like and he made my endeavours appear very laboured, even tortoise-like, as he seemed to be able to swim length after length without any effort and also without the apparent need to lift his head out of the water to breathe. He was a much more accomplished swimmer than me but that was not very difficult. As we came to the end of our morning exertions, he had done probably six times as much as me but I'm sure I had expended double the energy. We both stopped for a brief chat as we towelled ourselves down. He was a student and on holiday with his parents visiting friends on the island. He also had a dry sense of humour. As we were both about to leave he looked around the pool and remarked, 'There aren't any Germans staying here then.'

I didn't catch on immediately and said, "Pardon? I'm not with you."

He spread an arm and motioned around the poolside. "Look," he said, with a big grin on his face, "all these sun-beds and not a towel on one of them. Like I said, not a German in sight."

I hadn't seen any obvious signs of German holidaymakers at the hotel so I guess the reputation of the stereotypical German holidaymaker continues to go before them and will be difficult to live down. We chatted briefly for a couple of minutes before disappearing in different directions. I didn't think about it at the time but I had not seen him prior to that morning and didn't see him again for the duration of the holiday. Who he was and where he came from I'll never know but he was an excellent swimmer.

Having shaved, showered and found a clean tee-shirt and new pair of shorts I wandered downstairs and joined everybody for breakfast. The fresh orange juice was very popular and a generous glass together with a croissant and cup of coffee was quite sufficient. As was becoming the norm the youngsters had danced the night away but looked none the worse for wear and Caroline's red hue of a couple of days previously was now turning into a golden tan.

As we finished our coffees Carrie explained to Diane and myself that she was going to take us on a tour of the island, right around the coast road, ending up at the delightfully named Rum Point, on the northern tip of the island, for the day. I had heard Jan, Carrie and Mel all talk of Rum Point and it was obviously a popular spot that they had visited previously. I didn't get too excited as they had also sung the praises of Smith's Cove and I had been singularly disappointed.

We packed the beach bags with towels and in my case a ready supply of suntan cream and set off for the far side of Georgetown to collect Carl and Fran. It wasn't too long before we were heading for the coastal perimeter road and passing the island's Stingray brewery as we made our way towards Bodden Town. We continued to head easterly past the Lighthouse Club and onwards around Half Moon Bay towards East Point and the East End Lighthouse. Carrie was driving very steadily giving us the opportunity to view the superb sandy coves and beaches that dot the south eastern coast of the island as you progress along the Eastern Highway. It was possible to view the pounding breakers crashing against one or two of the rocky promontories. Compared to the western side of the island, where we were boarded, the sea appeared somewhat more energetic on this side of the island. It wasn't as rough as the sea we had experienced at Smith's Cove on the Sunday but it was decidedly lively. I had yet to see anything other than calm flat waters off Seven Mile Beach. This trip reminded me of a similar journey around one of the coastal roads in Tobago, some three years earlier, although Grand Cayman is much flatter.

We stopped for a short time near Gun Bay and looked out towards the Wreck of the Ten Sails, before moving on in the direction of Long Coconut Point and Spotters Bay. Although you could see the surf and the white horses skimming the waves as they rolled toward the shore I had experienced much rougher and heavier seas in the English Channel, on the many ferries I have used as they plough back and forth between Calais and Dover. Looking out across the waves it was possible to imagine how cruel the sea could be and how brave the local fishermen had been on that heroic night hundreds of years ago as they set off in the total darkness of the storm tossed waters attempting to rescue their fellow seafarers, without a second thought for their own safety. Perhaps they were a very early Caribbean manifestation of the UK's own courageous volunteers in the Royal National Lifeboat Institute.

Having skirted the southern and eastern boundaries of the island we then started to turn back on ourselves and headed westerly on the Queens Highway passing Anchor Point and Little Bluff Bay. The road classifications were a little confusing as having left Bodden Town on the A3, somewhere towards East End it had become the A4, and we now found ourselves back an the A3 and heading towards the A4 on the northern side of the island. This didn't really make any difference to our progress and although there appeared to be at least two different roads with the same numbers we couldn't get lost as we had never left the one and only coast road as we headed towards our destination for a day at the seaside. What a satellite navigation system would have made of the changes to the road numbers I do not know (as a self-confessed IT dinosaur I don't possess one of these technical whizz bang gadgets as they were not made for my computer blank brain; I've always managed to get by with some assistance from cartographers and perhaps an over-reliance on following my nose, although this has been broken on more than one occasion and now tends to steer towards the left) but it wouldn't have mattered as it was impossible to get lost, with or without technology. Whether we were on the A3 or the A4 didn't really matter as we made steady progress with the occasional stop to admire the coastal scenery. Traffic was minimal and this route was in stark contrast to the A3 and A4 that I was much more familiar with as they head west out of London. Those on the island were much more pleasant and stress free. There wasn't even anywhere to practise the dreaded Caymanian right turn, unless you wanted to end up in the drink.

The journey so far had provided me with conflicting reactions. We had passed a number of new developments that were in various stages of construction and comprising mainly very plush and expensive villas and condos. One in particular looked very impressive and appeared to have been completed fairly recently. From the numbers and types of car parked outside the developers obviously didn't have any problem in selling or renting the apartments in this particular condominium. As we drove past slowly we all joked that we could happily live here on the island although not knowing the price I suspect it was more than a little out of our reach. Having driven past these modern structures, within half a mile they were replaced by little groups of old-fashioned bungalows and shacks that were in need of a coat of paint and had been built many years earlier on narrow dirt tracks just off the main road. Huddled together in little groups they gave the impression of a somewhat dilapidated community that had experienced better days.

Driving on along the north side of the island the development here was much less sporadic as we passed Grape Tree Point and Bouse Bluff before eventually arriving at Rum Point.

It is said that first impressions are important and my initial view of Rum Point was that it lived up to all the expectations that the girls had indicated.

Firstly it provided the sort of scene that you expect to see in the glossy holiday brochures that you can pick up from the shelves and coffee tables in the many Travel Agents that are now established on our High Streets. It was possible to imagine the fine sand, ultramarine sea and matching sky looking back at you as you opened the front page of the travel journal. There was, of course, one huge difference. The magazines and pamphlets were unable to replicate the kind of dripping heat and humidity that by now had made me leak more than a rusty colander on a wet day in Manchester.

Secondly, I found the cleanest changing rooms and lavatories I have ever seen on a beach. They were spotless and I was able to change into my swimming trunks both in comfort and with my feet on a dry floor. Most unusual for changing rooms and something I had rarely experienced at home.

Importantly, and I hadn't mentioned this yet today as up until then we had been protected by the comfort of the air-conditioning in the hotel and the people carrier, I was able to cover myself with the usual liberal coating of protective cream. It wasn't yet even close to midday and the sun was blisteringly hot in a cloudless sky.

We split into the normal two groups. The youngsters made their way to the water's edge on the beach to soak up the full glare of the sun in order to improve their already bronzed bodies. Diane, Jan and myself found some beach chairs that were provided together with a number of hammocks that were strung under some palm trees and made ourselves comfortable where we could also have the benefit of a little shade.

I settled down to read my book and enjoy what was to be probably the most relaxing day of the holiday. It was a matter of no more than a dozen or so paces (ok large ones for my short legs) to the beachside restaurant and bar for liquid refreshment. We took it in turns to pay regular visits throughout the day. Equally, for those wrinklies taking advantage of the shade it was no further to walk across the sand and into the clear blue water to float and cool off or swim out just a short distance and watch the shoals of small colourful fish darting in all directions in the water. Lying there on the surface watching the kaleidoscope of marine life glide gracefully by, so close that you could almost reach out and touch them, was so relaxing that it was almost possible to doze off and float away. Except in my case I still wasn't confident enough to go that far. Floating I could now manage, floating and sleeping were multi tasking that were far too advanced an enterprise for me, a mere man, to take any chances.

Diane, however, was a totally different kettle of fish, no pun intended, and spent much more time in the water than she did on the beach. Our cousins from Down Under just seem naturally more at home in the water than us Poms.

The girls continued to roast and build up their tans by just lazing on their beach towels. Not unnaturally, they were also attracting a fair degree of attention from a couple of guys who were hiring out kayaks further along the beach. They did not have too many customers for although the beach was reasonably well populated it wasn't crowded and the majority wanted to relax as opposed to exerting themselves under the blistering sun. For some unknown reason they found it necessary to walk the same route across the beach at regular intervals. Their circuit inevitably entailed walking past the girls in both directions. They tried to make it appear that they were touting for customers. This may have been true to a degree but I suspect they also had an alternative motive. Initially the girls treated them with a degree of disdain and indifference. I don't think this was deliberate but just the girls catching up on some sleep.

Carl meanwhile was in his element and had found his forte in looking after Huggy Junior and trying to teach him to swim. He had loads of patience and it was possible to see Huggy growing in confidence in the water. Fran and the girls joined them from time to time in the water and the kayak guys, who had become self-appointed lifeguards, were never too far away whenever the girls ventured into the water to cool off. If only they knew they were in the company of some real lifeguards. They were obviously there for the day so were content to play the long patient game as far as the girls were concerned.

Not being one who can lie on a beach and do nothing all day, and not having had my morning constitutional, I decided to disappear on one of my regular treks, albeit walking at a slow and regular constabulary pace.

Firstly it was essential that I paid a return visit to the changing rooms for a top-up with the suntan lotion. I hadn't used any for at least two hours and was beginning to get withdrawal symptoms. The beachside facilities remained just as clean and dry as my first visit on arrival. Quite amazing. Ten out of ten and a gold star to whoever looked after them.

On with the shades and I started to wander along a beachside lane that bordered a number of holiday bungalows. To refer to them as merely bungalows is something of a misnomer and does not accord them their true credit. Tucked away between the azure waters of the Caribbean and a palm fringed track leading to nowhere, many were like single storey villas with gardens that rolled onto the beach providing a westerly outlook across North Sound. I guess that their evening views of the setting sun at dusk must be quite spectacular. The only sounds to be heard were the birds singing and the water gently lapping onto the beach. To be able to live here must be akin to finding a hidden corner of paradise.

As I meandered down the lane it was apparent that a number of the properties were unoccupied and available for holiday rental although there wasn't any indication of the weekly fees. I took the opportunity to take a closer look at some of them and wandered across the beach as opposed to the roadway. I quickly came to the conclusion that I would have no difficulty in spending a fortnight's, or preferably a month's, holiday in such a location and with the restaurant and bar within a stone's throw; provided the likes of Freddie Flintoff was throwing it, I would be content to set up camp here and not move for the duration.

Having completed my recce I started back down the track and literally bumped into one of Grand Cayman's boys in blue. He was the local community policeman and on patrol, taking a stroll around his beat, making sure that the empty houses were secure. It was fortunate for me that he hadn't arrived ten minutes earlier otherwise he would have found a nosy, oily and rather scruffy holidaymaker walking across the back gardens of the unoccupied houses and that might have appeared just a little suspicious. Now that would have been embarrassing. Trying to explain my innocence and avoid being arrested whilst on holiday.

Walking back towards the roadway made me appear much less guilty but it was obvious that I was not one of his local residents and not recognising me he decided to stop me for a friendly chat. At least that is the way he made it appear and very good he was too. I was equally sure that until he was happy with me I was unlikely to be making my way back to our group on the beach. I would have done exactly the same in his situation. Who was this unkempt individual coming away from the dead end of a cul-de-sac and trying to pass himself off as a West Indian cricket lover by having a battered and sun bleached Caribbean sun hat perched on his head? Could he be Burglar Bill who was casing one or two of the villas available for renting to see if there was anything worth stealing? I was not to know at that stage whether or not somebody had seen me wandering along the beachside of the houses and alerted the local police.

Having chatted to me for a few minutes he was satisfied that I was not on the island to break into any houses and it transpired that he was just out on a normal patrol of his neighbourhood. Why was it that I never had a beat like this in paradise to patrol? Southend High Street or Basildon town centre bore no resemblance to this beat and both would come a very poor second best in comparison.

As we got to know each other I learned that he was Canadian and had only been a police officer on Grand Cayman for less than four months. He had been a policeman in Toronto for twenty years previously before he and his wife decided to up sticks for a fresh challenge. They saw an advert providing an opportunity to move to somewhere quite different and sample life and policing in the somewhat sunnier and warmer climes of the Caribbean.

We compared verbal notes of our differing experiences but as he said, "Some things in policing do not change, wherever you happen to be. You are still dealing with people, the good, the bad and the ugly and drunks are drunks whether you happen to be in Toronto, Georgetown or London."

Although he had found many differences to his previous life back home in Canada he had already encountered many similarities. I guess domestic disputes are much the same the world over with police intervention very rarely solving a couple's problems and sometimes exacerbating them. Arresting the violent partner and affording some protection and support to the victim in the short term to prevent any greater harm, until other agencies and the lawyers and courts become involved, is about the best that can be achieved in the immediate aftermath of that type of incident.

One occurrence that he had not expected was the number of fatal accidents that he had already encountered compared to his previous patch back in Toronto. Like me he was surprised that for such a small island there were so many unnecessary fatalities. Neither of us had any ready answers but both speculated as to just how stringent the local driving examinations were and wondered whether they should be made a lot tougher?

We strolled back down the lane together keeping step in regulation Mr Plod style and pace, which wasn't difficult for either of us, but to the casual observer we must have appeared an ill assorted pair; he in his smart lightweight uniform and me looking like a beach bum yet managing to march together pace by pace albeit slowly. As we reached the pathway to the beach we stood and chatted for some time. It was readily apparent, from the many greetings he received, that he had got to know a number of the inhabitants very well in the short time he had been based on the island. It would have been very tempting for the pair of us to have bent our knees in unison and greeted the locals with a stereophonic 'Hello, Hello, Hello', but whilst it might have been amusing to both of us at the time our humour may not have been appreciated by the neighbourhood and could have diminished the respect he had built up since his arrival. We resisted the urge to act the fool. He was obviously very happy in his work and had fallen on his feet in being posted to such a delightful beat.

Although the majority of the police officers were Caymanians there were a number of UK, currently around fifty, and Canadian officers in the local police force. Some were on short two-year secondment contracts whilst others arrived intending to benefit from a temporary career attachment to an overseas policing experience and were then able to extend their stay until they retired. I was aware that a number from my own force back home in Essex had taken advantage of such an opportunity and whilst some had returned one or two had stayed on the island for the remainder of their policing careers. As the majority tended to opt to extend their contracts there was now talk of introducing five-year secondments. One of the attractions was the tax-free salary together with free healthcare provision and a pension after twenty-one years' service. Officers on shift worked a twelve-hour tour of duty with two days on and two days off although the force were about to experiment with eight-hour duty rotas. Another throwback to my early years as a police officer was unpaid overtime which was only compensated as time off in lieu which could mean officers accruing additional annual leave.

In common with the United Kingdom, policing was undergoing a period of transformation and rapid change. The island's police force was trying to keep pace with the demands of the twenty-first century whilst at the same time continuing to develop a neighbourhood policing philosophy. In comparison with what I had become used to, crime levels seemed relatively low, although in common with the UK the fear of crime appeared disproportionately high. Recent trends had indicated that crime was now falling and the police had held a number of community meetings to reassure the public, increase confidence and reduce the fear of crime.

One major difference in policing procedure was the lack of anything resembling the Police and Criminal Evidence Act 1984 (in legal circles referred to as PACE). Obtaining evidence still relied upon the old Judges Rules that existed when I first joined the job back in the Sixties and now seems to belong to a bygone age. Interviews were not yet tape-recorded and were conducted contemporaneously although there were plans to move to taped interviews in the foreseeable future. Pre-trial disclosure remained a distance down the road and the file submission system basically consisted of witness statements and a summary of the offence, again somewhat akin to the process in England back in the Sixties. Suspects could be initially detained for thirty-six hours and this could be doubled with authority from a superintendent.

The police cars that I saw seemed to resemble the United States version of a patrol car that I had seen in the popular television series

Hill Street Blues and *NYPD Blue*, and seemed fairly old-fashioned compared to what we are now using in England. Radio communications also seemed a bit hit and miss with the majority relying on their mobile phones, although this didn't seem to hamper them unduly.

Having previously had long conversations with David about our differing policing experiences and now listening to my new-found friend, I was left wondering why I hadn't taken more notice of the occasional adverts that the Royal Cayman Islands Police Service place in the policing magazine, *Police Review*. Being happy in my role back home in Essex I hadn't really taken very much notice of them, but on reflection and experiencing the reality of Caribbean life made me wonder if I had missed an opportunity earlier in my career. Like many things in life that was a question that would remain unanswered but whilst I was enjoying my sojourn on the island I needed to remind myself that was all it was and I was happy with what I had done and what I had achieved with few or no regrets. A fortnight's holiday could be a very different experience to a permanent posting and I'm not sure that I would have coped with a two-year secondment. That is no reflection on either the islanders or their police service. It is more a pragmatic approach to my likelihood of survival given my propensity to perspire and my need for half the world's supply of suntan cream together with a demand for at least half a dozen fresh shirts or tops a day. I could well have broken the police force's annual uniform budget with my stockpile of shirts in the first three months. I'm equally sure the local laundry and dry cleaners would have found my secondment a very profitable experience, until I eventually melted away.

Looking at my Canadian/Caribbean colleague in his well-turned-out and neatly pressed summer uniform I decided that I could never have remained that smart for more than ten minutes away from the air-conditioning. Perhaps I was better suited to the more moderate English climate, even if only from a professional viewpoint. We chatted for a while longer before eventually bidding each other farewell and I wished him the best of luck in his change of career path before I made my way further along the beach towards the small headland and he carried on his patrol. Little did either of us know exactly what was in store for him and his colleagues in six weeks' time and the impact it would have on the island and its emergency services.

Prior to continuing my walk I took advantage once again of the spotless changing rooms to obtain my ritual top-up of protective suntan lotion on those parts that the sun could reach and believe me the sun was doing its level best to reach them.

Progressing on my way past the small pier, where the ferry to the Hyatt Regency departed every two hours or so, I made my way across the sand and around a rocky outcrop where there were a small number of groups swimming and sunbathing. I couldn't make up my mind if this was a private beach belonging to the smart-looking apartments that were scattered among the palms as the majority of the bathers seemed to come from them. There wasn't any sign preventing access and nobody approached me to check if I should be there so I continued my aimless meanderings.

Suddenly a voice from the sea said "Excuse me" in what was immediately recognisable as a soft Irish brogue. I looked to my side and just behind me to see two young ladies emerging from the water. Not unnaturally I stopped. "Yes?" I said, wondering what on earth they wanted. One of the girls was carrying a camera and in her Irish lilt replied, "Would you mind taking a photograph of us together please?"

"Not at all," I responded, coming to the conclusion that they obviously felt quite safe giving their camera to this grey-haired elderly beach bum wearing a weird sweat-drenched hat. I must admit I also considered it would be even more interesting chatting to these two attractive young ladies than it had been to the local bobby. No offence intended to the local constabulary, with whom I had spent an interesting and informative half-hour and with whom I had a lot more in common, but I'm sure he would have felt exactly the same in my situation.

Having mastered the intricacies of the zoom lens and attempting my best imitation of Patrick Lichfield I managed to take a couple of shots, whilst thinking if only Ken the photographic parson from Wigan were here to advise me. At least then I may have been able to make a decent fist of pretending to know what I was doing with a camera. In any event I managed to get both girls, together with a backdrop of sand, sea and clear blue sky, reasonably proportioned in the frame. Well at least both girls were very reasonably proportioned. What the finished article would turn out like, I would never know. I'm also sure that a professional photographer would have taken much more time over it and made sure that everything was positioned correctly.

The Irish girl was from Dublin and her friend from Arizona and they were taking advantage of a short break together in the Caymans. They were indeed staying in one of the nearby apartments and intended to return later in the year for the week of the Pirates festival.

I had already learned something of this unique Caymanian festival from Mel and David. It is held during the last week of October and is the precursor to the winter tourist season. It is the autumn equivalent of the spring Batabano festival and attracts a larger number of visitors. Pirates Week commemorates the Island's early days when the Cayman Islands were plundered by bands of pirates who landed to bury their treasure and, I am told, make merry. Quite what making merry was in those distant times compared to the current festivities I'm none too sure and whether the local inhabitants were as comfortable and welcoming with the merrymaking as today's residents one can only hazard a guess. I think it reasonable to assume that many of the islanders considered their freebooting guests to be unwelcome and undesirable. Equally for any Robin Hood-like buccaneers there may well have been a genuine and pleasant offer of hospitality from those who benefited from their sea piracy.

The whole week now has a very much carnival atmosphere and could perhaps be best described as a sort of Caribbean Mardi Gras. The islands celebrate their colourful seafaring past with great pride throughout the week-long event. It is possible to party from morning to night through the pirates' parades, costume contests, music, fireworks, sports competitions and local craft fairs. The festival commences with a mock pirate landing by bands of rowdy pirates who hijack His Excellency the Governor in Georgetown harbour. Today the spectators can be just as boisterous as the sea-borne raiders. The kidnapping is followed by a parade of colourful floats and local steel drum bands. Georgetown virtually closes down for the day as the whole island parties the night away, dancing under the stars to local and guest bands and enjoying the numerous culinary delights on offer.

On different days during the week the districts of West Bay, Georgetown, Bodden Town, East End and Northside take turns in hosting a district heritage day, with local skills and crafts on display followed by an evening of live music, entertainment and a mixture of barbecue or buffet-style eating.

As we stood chatting on the beach little did the girls, or I, imagine that they would not get the opportunity to return later in the year to sample the delights of Pirates Week and the friendly Caymanian hospitality.

I took far more interest in the Irish girl than I did her American friend. There was nothing personal in this; although on reflection it must have appeared to be rather rude as I almost ignored her. It was simply that I have never been to Dublin and it is a city that I have always intended to visit. Perhaps one day I will make it, having heard lots of stories about the place. Unfortunately I had never met anybody from Tucson or the like and I have never had a yen to visit Arizona.

I was able to learn where to find the best hotels, at a reasonable price, and some of the attractions and hostelries that I must not miss when I eventually arrive in Dublin. Unfortunately not being in a position to make notes and having a head like a sieve I have since forgotten most of the advice so that when I do eventually arrive I will have to start from scratch. A mixture of alcohol and anno domini does nothing to assist the memory, as my colleagues back home in the office often remind me. I did remember, however, that a tour of the Guinness brewery was a must and I should also take the opportunity to leave the city and visit the countryside of the nearby Wicklow Mountains.

I guess we must have chatted for twenty minutes or more before I started to make my way back to my hammock under the palms. As I did so I saw the small ferry chugging into the jetty at the end of its thirty minutes or so crossing of North Sound. No more than half a dozen passengers disembarked, if that's the right description for getting off a small boat, and made their way to the beach carrying beach towels and bags. I joined Jan and Diane, who had managed to drag herself from the water, and we decided it was time for a snack and a drink. I didn't appreciate just how thirsty and hungry you could become doing absolutely nothing.

We wandered across to the beachside restaurant and bar, underneath the palms, to sample one or two of their non-alcoholic fruit cocktails that were just what the doctor ordered. In fact I enjoyed mine so much that I had to refresh my palate with another one or two. I needed to be careful – I was beginning to enjoy these just as much as their slightly stronger variety of mixtures that were on offer in all the bars. So much so I had to try a few more as the holiday wore on. The youngsters drifted over in ones and twos for the odd bite to eat but mainly to quench their thirst before we all meandered back to the beach to read, doze or, in Carrie, Caroline, Cynthia and Danielle's case to continue to top up their tans and studiously ignore the two lads working to rent out their kayaks from the beach. Carl and Fran were continuing to teach young Huggy to swim and improve his confidence in the water. They had acquired a job for the duration and were both very patient teachers.

However, even the best teachers deserve a rest and Huggy Junior wasn't going to give them one. Carl found an ideal and alternative solution a little further along the beach. It came in the form of a kayak that he swiftly hired, from two guys who did not have many customers, and sculled back to his very enthusiastic student. This was a new experience for Huggy who scrambled up and over the gunnels and made himself comfortable sitting opposite Carl before they spent the rest of the afternoon floating around in the sunshine and jumping in and out of the boat to cool off. I'm not sure that this was any more relaxing for Carl but as they say, 'a change is as good as a rest' and he still seemed to be enjoying himself keeping his young charge occupied. At least it gave Fran the opportunity to return to the beach and join the girls lapping up the sun. Carl's approach for the kayak seemed to break the ice with the two attendants and the girls had now also decided that the time was appropriate to demonstrate at least a passing interest in the two 'fit' young fellas who were renting out and providing lessons in the kayaks and also on jet-skis.

The two guys were not particularly busy on this sunny afternoon and they had spotted that the girls sunbathing further along the beach were at long last looking in their direction. Thus commenced some harmless flirting as the girls then decided to display their interest by once again appearing totally disinterested. Strange creatures women, but this group seemed to know what they were about. This was reciprocated by the two guys who were well aware of the rules of the game as they gradually edged closer along the beach with their collection of boats in tow. The fact that Carl was out in one of their boats gave them the ideal excuse to let them make the first positive move in displaying their obvious interest in the female form that was sunbathing nearby. Although from time to time they wandered back into the water to anchor a returning kayak, well if not anchor it then at least lash a number together. I'm not at all sure of the collective noun for a number of kayaks or even if there is one. Perhaps in this case a lashing of kayaks seemed to be appropriate and the two guys seemed to know exactly what they were doing. Their chores on this day were not particularly arduous so they still had ample time to chat to the girls, which appeared to them to be far more interesting than looking after their waterborne craft.

I meanwhile had wandered back into the water to try a spot of snorkelling, and drifted aimlessly about in the calm clear water viewing the shoals of tiny but brightly coloured fish as they darted back and forth playing what resembled an underwater game of tag.

I learned, much later, that Rum Point is also the venue for an exotic evening experience. Known as the Bio-bay tour a guide takes you out in kayaks where the bay has an abundance of bioluminescent creatures that in the darkness provide a spectacular oceanic light show. If I had known at the time I would have wanted to return to witness this underwater display of fireworks and tiny flashing Christmas tree-like lights. As the fish dart about in the water they leave trails of light, not dissimilar to an aircraft's vapour trail, and as your oars swish in and out of the water they create luminous droplets that seem to hang in the night air before falling back to the water's surface. Apparently this is all due to the presence of huge amounts of bioluminescent marine plankton, in local waters, to find food or as a defence mechanism against predators. This was one show that I missed but when I return will be high on my list of 'must dos'.

As the afternoon wore on from time to time I surfaced, removed my snorkel, and lay floating and daydreaming in the warm water. It was amazing just how confident I had become knowing that Carl was close by keeping Huggy Junior amused jumping in and out of the boat and the remaining Baywatch Three were within shouting distance lying on the beach. I'm sure they would have left their little game of 'Are we interested or are we not' to come and rescue me had the need arisen. Fortunately the need didn't arise so they were able to continue teasing the two guys who had by now manoeuvred the whole flotilla of jet-skis and kayaks to a point right opposite the girls and were busy, pretending to be busy, parking or even mooring their craft. I could anticipate that at any moment the girls were going to receive an invitation to come on board and enjoy the pleasures of being swept across the water to paradise. Knowing them I was also aware of how easily and dismissively they would be able to resist such temptation.

As I lazed in the water I was able to get a much closer look at the ferry that had been plying its trade across North Sound all day. Until that moment, as it slowly drifted past me to its berth at Rum Point, I hadn't

Island Joggings

taken too much notice of it. There was an awareness that from time to time it appeared in the background and then disappeared again but I would guess that it arrived at the concrete jetty about every couple of hours or so, although I certainly wasn't timing its arrival and departure. This was not a ferry of the roll-on/roll-off variety that you see criss-crossing the English Channel carrying huge container lorries, coach-loads of tourists, family-packed cars and even the booze cruisers to and from mainland Europe. The Grand Cayman Ferry was much smaller, about the size of a reasonably large ocean-going yacht, which carried foot passengers back and forth between Rum Point and a pier adjacent to the Britannia golf course and Hyatt Regency complex. I would estimate that the trip across the bay would take about thirty minutes or perhaps a little more sailing into a stiff breeze. However, for those who lived permanently, or were just holidaying, at Rum Point what an ideal way of getting to work or travelling for a game of golf rather than having to jump in a car and drive halfway around the island. It also had all the advantages of missing the Georgetown rush hour traffic, the traffic lights in the sky and the suicidal Caymanian right turn not to mention the grinning gummy Michael Schumacher impersonators. I've no idea how much a return fare was likely to cost but it must have been worth it just to avoid the stress.

As the latest set of no more than twenty passengers disembarked to make their way along the jetty and onto the beach they appeared to be a very mixed bunch indeed. There looked to be two or three youngsters returning from school, a handful of holidaymakers with beach-bags slung over their shoulders that included the odd brightly coloured corrugated plastic snorkel poking out of the top and a family of four carrying or wheeling suitcases along the pier seemingly playing the part of new arrivals, looking somewhat bemused, very hot, perspiring under the afternoon sun and giving all the appearance of the travel weary parents who have all but given up hope of trying to pacify the kids with their oft repeated and monotonous query of 'Are we nearly there yet?' At long last it appeared they were reaching the end of a lengthy and uncomfortable journey. If they did not fall into this category then I apologise for doing them a grave injustice but if not then they can claim the consolation of giving a first class acting performance for which I was their singular, and not very appreciative, audience. This boat did not carry any golfers back from the Britannia but bringing up the rear were two incongruous middle-aged gentlemen dressed smartly in suits, each carrying a briefcase. In contrast to the suitcase carrying family slightly ahead of them they were a picture of serenity and didn't even appear to notice the heat. They walked along in unison quickly skipping around the struggling family, continuing through the gently swaying palms, on past the restaurant and disappearing in the distance towards the roadway leading down to the Kaibo Yacht Club.

They could possibly have passed as brothers, even twins, but who they were, where they had come from and exactly where they were going dressed like that on a scorchingly hot afternoon we will never know. If they were Georgetown office workers who had finished early and were making a quick getaway on an afternoon ferry then they were the most formally dressed office personnel that I had witnessed on the trip. (Even the bank manager that I had spied sitting in his glass-panelled and air-conditioned office was wearing smart tailored shorts and an open-neck shirt.) They may possibly have been local debt collectors coming to enforce a bad debt but surely they would have been more likely to arrive in an air-conditioned limousine. Insurance salesmen or even rent collectors could have been a possibility although double-glazing salesmen were even less likely in this climate. I was now playing mental guessing games with myself on a puzzle to which I would never know the true answer. Whatever and whoever they were they did give the impression of men on a joint mission as they appeared oblivious to all around them before passing out of view, not to be seen again.

The whole scene was more reminiscent of the sort of sketch one might see in a Monty Python programme. As the pair disappeared across the sand I was watching and smiling to myself as I envisaged John Cleese and Michael Palin in their office suits on a Caribbean island. All that was missing were the bowler hats, umbrellas and the pair marching away from the Ministry of Silly Walks.

I made my way out of the water giggling away to myself and anybody who saw me must have wondered what on earth I was laughing at. Jan was laying on a hammock reading her book whilst Diane, the Antipodean Waterbabe, was back in the water on the far side of the pier.

Meanwhile, the two young boat wardens had come up with a cunning plan to demonstrate to the girls their honourable intentions. Carl had now worn himself out and had rowed Huggy Junior to the shore. Huggy was still full of life and as opposed to inviting the girls for a trip on one of their boats one of the guys offered to take Huggy out on a jet-ski. At this stage they were still adopting the cool indirect strategy when, in my view, a more direct approach might, by now, have been more appropriate and achieved the desired result. Even if rebuffed it would have put them out of their misery. Boat Warden No. 1 approached the girls who continued to display a healthy disinterest but were more than happy for him to keep young Huggy occupied a while longer. Carl was ecstatic.

Huggy disappeared in a jet of foam with his new found friend, to be followed skimming over the surf by the other young buck, where they both then proceeded to give a master-class in jet-ski aquabatics the like of which I have never witnessed before or since. We saw the equivalent of handbrake turns, sea-borne looping the loop and if it had been humanly possible a barrel roll. I'm sure they felt this would impress the girls. It certainly impressed Huggy Junior who didn't stop talking about it for the remainder of the day. Unfortunately the girls weren't in the slightest bit interested and promptly lay back on their towels and went to sleep in the sun. All that macho effort, totally in vain.

Well, in fairness to one of the guys, it wasn't totally in vain. On his return to the beach he did manage to wheedle our hotel telephone number out of Caroline but this was in exchange for taking a photograph of the whole group of us sat with our feet dangling over the jetty. He was a pleasant young man who was trying to eke out his student grant with some additional funds from part time work during the summer vacation. He was an English student from Warwickshire and obviously smitten with Caroline. He would happily have taken pictures of us for the remainder of the day if she had asked him. Regrettably for him I think she considered he was a little too young for her.

He did try and make contact with her over the next couple of days but was unsuccessful. Although he had the correct hotel number she had cunningly given him the extension to our room and not her own. On two occasions I had to disappoint him as each time Caroline was, predictably, unavailable. I tried to let him down gently and after the second abortive attempt he obviously got the message. Caroline denied giving him the wrong extension number and was sure he had made a mistake in transcribing one digit incorrectly. As plausible as this may have been to some people I have to say that the smile on her face and wicked glint in her eye did not convince me that she was telling the whole truth. I came to the conclusion that our Caroline could be a bit of a rascal but obviously a very appealing young rascal.

The group photograph, sitting on the pier, was an integral and mandatory part of the holiday. When the youngsters had visited Mel on previous occasions they had always taken group photos in this particular spot. I had seen these snaps prior to leaving the UK and at that time had not regarded them as anything more than another picture of a party enjoying themselves on holiday. To now actually be here and be included in the shot was almost surreal. I know it was the schoolboy coming out in me again but I still get excited about inconsequential and silly things on holiday that on a normal day would not rate a second thought. What was now all too obvious was that the photographs did not do justice to our location. We would have needed a very wide-angled lens to capture the idyllic scene and even that could not have conveyed the true character of Rum Point on that glorious July afternoon. This was another highlight of the holiday and our time there had passed all too quickly. I would have happily remained until dusk and beyond.

Having completed the statutory photos we bundled our beach paraphernalia together and started to make our way back to our trusty wagon.

I use the word 'paraphernalia' deliberately as I could not believe just how much was being packed into the variety of canvas beach bags and rucksacks before we were ready to leave. We had only spent a day by the seaside but to my mind we had carried enough for a week's holiday and all eventualities that might arise during that time. I'm not sure that an army would go to war carrying as much kit. Carl and I knowingly raised our eyebrows as we watched all the 'essentials' being carefully stored by the seven girls but in fairness I should absolve Diane from this criticism as she continued with her happy knack of travelling light. It must be a female southern hemisphere phenomenon. There was still no sign of this sensible habit catching on with the girls from good old England.

Before departing I had to pay one final visit to the 'Gents'. It may appear that I have developed a morbid curiosity with gentlemen's lavatories but the reality of the situation is, in common with other men who reach a certain age, I find it far more convenient, and comfortable, to pay a quick visit to spend a penny before setting off on a journey, rather than having to waste time looking for a toilet en route. Fortunately this isn't always necessary, or possible, but better safe than sorry and it can be rather disagreeable and irritating to have to sit cross-legged for an inordinate length of time waiting for relief. Perhaps the French have the right approach where the rule seems to be if you've got to go, you've got to go. Their culture allows them to find the nearest field, point Percy at the hedgerow before continuing on their journey in a more enjoyable and relaxed state.

The changing room and toilets were in an identical state to that when we arrived earlier in the day. Clean, dry and absolutely spotless. If there were such a thing as an equivalent Egon Ronay Guide for Grand Loos (and there might be for all I know) then I would have to recommend these for a five-star rating.

Trekking back across the sand I volunteered to drive back to the hotel having contentedly stuck with the non alcoholic fruit cocktails all day. Carrie readily agreed. One also got the feeling that there were two pairs of rather disappointed and sorrowful eyes watching our departure from the water's edge. It's lucky that they couldn't hear some of the amusing but disparaging remarks that the girls were making about 'juvenile young students' as we jumped aboard the minibus. These girls could be so hurtful, but wicked.

I took a slightly different route home by turning right at Old Man Bay (turning left was not an option unless one wanted to get very wet) and cutting across the middle of the island on the north/south Frank Sound Drive. This took us directly past the entrance to the Queen Elizabeth II Botanic Gardens. We paused here to seek a glimpse of the flora and fauna on display although from the roadway it was not possible to achieve a decent sight of the many different specimens that are growing in the park.

There are sixty-five acres of woodland trails overhung with almost every variety of tree on earth, lakes and flower gardens that attract butterflies and hundreds of exotic birds. The Caymanians have long had a tradition of plant medicine and among the native plants is the 'headache bush' and the periwinkle that for years was used locally to slow the growth of tumours and has recently been discovered to contain two cancer fighting elements.

The Caymans boast twenty-six indigenous orchids and the fabulous banana orchid is the national flower. It is also possible to find the fragrant ylang-ylang tree whose perfume I'm told is the basic ingredient for Chanel No. 5, although I have to confess that I cannot personally vouch for this.

Unfortunately we didn't have time to explore the gardens and continued on our cross-island route which probably chopped about eleven or twelve miles off our homeward journey. Back on the coast road we travelled on through Bodden Town past the unusually named Reef Song Condos before diverting around South Sound Road to drop Carl and Fran off at David and Mel's house. This was a much more pleasant drive rather than heading straight into Georgetown. Passing the Tennis and Rugby Clubs gave us the opportunity to stop and inspect a very impressive detached house that was being built overlooking the beach. Mel had previously pointed this out as her ideal home on the island. To be more precise it became apparent that this would be Carrie's dream home and she would be trying to persuade her big sister to buy here so that she could spend her holidays in this ideal setting. We could all understand exactly why she had chosen this spot and this house. A magnificent traditional Caribbean beachside villa featuring its own swimming pool, fringed by gently swaying palms and with a southerly aspect that guaranteed dawn till dusk sunshine. I suspect even if we had pooled all our resources we still wouldn't have been able to afford it. It would have been interesting and informative to have perused the estate agent's brochure and their valuation of the property. Just a cursory inspection seemed to indicate that on this occasion there wouldn't be any need to exaggerate the finer characteristics of this particular holding. We didn't imagine that within weeks of returning from their honeymoon nature would dictate that the newlyweds would be forced to start searching for a new home, although this dream home that was now almost complete and awaiting occupation was also destined to be badly damaged.

We moved on, thinking that a lottery win might go some way to affording such a home but realistically knowing that our chances of that were less likely than those of Southend United winning the FA Cup. Both bordered on the impossible. Driving on we ignored the strangely named 'Pull and Be Damned Point'. There must be a story attached to such a sobriquet but I never did have time to enquire into the reasons for this particular moniker.

Having previously moaned about our uncomfortable visit to Smith's Cove Carrie insisted that we stop briefly to see if I would reassess my opinion in different circumstances. I would have to admit that I was reluctant to do so and requested, somewhat tongue in cheek, if the girls had any ant repellent amongst their baggage that was littering the rear of our holiday bus. The response was not what one would expect from refined young ladies but I understood the gist of it.

On this occasion I was able to pull into the small car park that was empty. How different to the difficulty in finding a parking spot on our previous visit on the Sunday. The contrast could not have been more marked. If I hadn't seen it with my own eyes I would not have believed I was in the same place. This time I strolled through the shade of the trees and shrubs and onto the blindingly white sand looking toward the rocky outcrop of the cove as the sun was beginning to set on the aquamarine sea and it was all ours. Not another person in sight. No concessions, no litter, and surprisingly no ants. I could now understand why the girls loved this cove and why they thought it so romantic. Yes, even an old cynic like me could now relate to their original description and appreciate why they would wish to return. What a shame that the locals allowed this impression to be spoiled at the weekend. A litter-clearing team on a Sunday morning would make the cove so much more inviting to the afternoon visitors. Little did we know at that time but we were to hear more of Smith's Cove as our holiday drew to a close.

Having dropped Carl and Fran off at their holiday home we chugged slowly into Georgetown where we joined the rush hour traffic as it left the capital. I've often wondered why it is called the rush hour? My experience of travelling at that time of the day, both in the mornings and early evenings, is that the pace of the traffic is anything but a rush. It has mattered not where I have been, London, Berlin, Paris, Rome or even more locally in Southend on Sea, Colchester or Chelmsford, with large numbers of disgruntled and frustrated drivers slowly simmering away until they reach boiling point as they sit in the stationary traffic which is normally nose to tail and crawling slowly nowhere. At least we were unlikely to be accosted by the mad Michael Schumacher impressionist racing to turn right. It wasn't possible to race anywhere in these conditions. Tonight was no different as we progressed at a snail's pace toward West Bay Drive and onwards tortoise like along Seven Mile Beach until we eventually reached the haven of Indies Suites.

As had become the norm there was time for a gentle swim in the pool followed by a relaxing ten minutes in the jacuzzi before showering the day's dirt away and changing for the evening meal. For the first time since we arrived on the island Caroline and Danielle were ready and waiting before the rest of us. Although they had snacked during the day they were obviously hungry and looking forward to their dinner. They were wearing summer dresses that had come out of the wardrobe for the first time and looked as pretty as ever, having taken an hour less than normal to get themselves ready for the evening's adventures. Okay, so I am prone to a little exaggeration but it must be a girlie trait to take three times as long as necessary to prepare for an evening out when the end result is no different. For clarity, and the need to save myself from a female verbal battering or worse, I need to stress that my comments are not critical but quite the reverse, they are complimentary, or at least they are meant to be.

Tonight the girls decided to pay a return visit to Cimboco's which was where they had taken Mel for her pre-nuptial hen party brunch. This was to be my first visit and was less than a ten-minute drive from the hotel. It describes itself as a Caribbean café but this is somewhat understated and doesn't do sufficient credit to the varied menu at very reasonable prices. The atmosphere was friendly and informal and I was to experience what was now becoming my usual nightly problem in coming to a decision about selecting my meal from the many delicious options available. Having chosen a light Caesar salad for starters I opted for one of the day's fresh fish specials which was grilled Mahi-Mahi. I wasn't disappointed and in common with our other meals it was very filling. The girls chose a variety of different dishes ranging through pastas, caramelised sea scallops to lime marinated grilled shrimps. I was the only fella in the group that evening as Fran and Carl wanted a romantic evening on their own at a restaurant in Georgetown. This seemed perfectly normal and the rest of us thought nothing more of it until we were to learn later in the holiday that they had an ulterior motive in wishing to be alone.

Having taken our time over completing our main courses, which was assisted by one or two bottles of chilled white wine and plenty of chat over the day's trip to Rum Point, which without exception everybody enjoyed and wanted to pay a return visit, the waitress returned with the pudding menus. For some strange reason, possibly the amount of wine consumed, Caroline and I both complained that we couldn't find rum cake anywhere on the menu. This was a surprise as literally everything else was available on this comprehensive list of desserts including such calorific delights as Caribbean Crème Brulé, Full Moon Chocolate Pecan Pie, Cayman Lime Pie and something called 'Up All Night' which was to remain a mystery, although the girls did make a number of different suggestions, all of which I thought highly unlikely to be served in a restaurant. We were all so full that not one of us could do justice to a sweet and that did include Caroline and myself, much to everybody's amazement. Although I must admit I was very tempted to try 'Up All Night' just to find out what was to be served. Despite considerable encouragement from the girls I managed to resist the temptation.

Our quiet drive back to Indies Suites, which took a quarter of the time taken just five hours earlier, was punctuated by some impressive flashes of lightning in the far distance. What had been one of the best days of the holiday was rounded off with a chat and drink at the poolside bar, where I spotted and was tempted to try once again the local Stingray beer, having seen the brewery on our drive around the island earlier in the day. My initial tasting had been on our sea trip with Captain Marvin and for some unaccountable reason I had failed to follow up that particular taste test. I decided that this omission needed to be rectified and ordered the local brew.

Temptation did get the better of me and one or two beers became three or four as we chatted about our day at Rum Point and told some new arrivals at the hotel that it was well worth a visit before they had to return home. Willpower has never been one of my strongest assets and sitting in very amiable surroundings with convivial company as we swapped stories of our experiences to date on Grand Cayman one didn't notice either the time as it slipped by into the early hours or the exact amount of drink that one needed to consume to keep the vocal cords lubricated. The new guests were an English couple, who were both employed by financial institutions and were on the island as guests of a locally based company, looking at property before making a final decision about taking up the opportunity of contracts on the island. They were obviously highly regarded and seemed keen to make the move provided they could get what they were looking for. She had been headhunted and was already negotiating her terms whilst he was still considering various options that were open to him in the Georgetown financial community. He was still far more in the holiday mode and thoroughly enjoying his tropical treat before having to concentrate too much on his next career move. At that time of the morning career development was the last thing on his mind. He could also have earned a living as a Jack Dee lookalike and had a very similar and dry sense of humour.

So ended a most entertaining evening and we were to meet up with our new found English friends around the poolside bar on a daily basis for the remainder of the holiday. Them to update us on their progress on the employment and house-hunting front and us on what chaos we had inflicted on the island's inhabitants on that particular day.

As we climbed the stairs to our rooms the lightning was now much closer as it lit up the night sky and seemed to fork down into the sea. The first claps of thunder could now be heard in the distance but before you could blink I had inserted my earplugs and was fast asleep within seconds of hitting the pillow. It's amazing how tired one becomes by relaxing and doing absolutely nothing. I slept so well that I was totally oblivious to the thunderstorm that raged through the remainder of the night.

CHAPTER 13

Money Laundering

We were now well and truly into the holiday with the arrival of 'W' Day plus six, and my morning run was delayed due to the remnants of the overnight thunderstorm. I awoke to the tail end of what had been a torrential downpour. I was able to take my time with my pre-run stretching exercises and application of embrocation.

For the first time since starting my morning running ritual I briefly considered that I wouldn't need to apply the usual coating of cream to protect me from the sun. Having lingered on the balcony and watched the rain disappear it quickly became apparent that that such an approach would be foolhardy. Despite the rainfall the heat was already drying the patio areas and there was no detectable change in the humidity. The sun was starting to poke through the disappearing clouds and the weather forecast on the television was for another hot and sunny day. Another tube of suntan cream was started. How long would this one last I speculated as I rubbed the protective coating onto my shoulders, arms and legs.

I eventually set off about eight am and wondered if I could have at least one uneventful morning run without encountering the likes of Double

M or scrawny chickens training to represent the Cayman Islands in the next Domestic Fowl Olympics. Although a number of puddles remained, where there were slight dips in the road surface, the remainder of the road was already dry and it was less than thirty minutes since it had stopped raining. I turned right out of Fosters Drive and headed north. As I did so I noticed a couple of other runners come from the forecourt of the Holiday Inn heading in the same direction. They both looked younger and fitter than me, although on both counts that is not too difficult. I pretended not to notice my running companions but could not overcome that competitive urge which has been a trait of my sporting escapades over the years. I set off at a slightly faster pace than I had on any of my previous morning jogs. In fact on this occasion I was definitely running and not jogging. I wasn't at all sure that this approach was sensible. On second thoughts I knew it wasn't sensible and I was sure to suffer on the return leg of the run. However, I wondered how far I could get before they overhauled me but I was equally determined not to look behind to let them know that I knew they were there. It was going to be at least another mile and a half before the bend in the road was such that would enable me to glance backwards without making it obvious. Would I be able to keep going at that pace for that distance? Were they already gaining on me? Whereas I tend to puff and pant whilst running I couldn't hear the sound of heavy breathing at all, not even footsteps pounding along. I didn't know whether that was a good or bad sign.

If I'm honest there was also another reason for my putting in a greater effort than usual that morning. The traffic was much heavier than normal and appeared to be backed up all the way from Georgetown. It was nose to tail and I therefore had a much larger audience than normal. It wasn't comparable to London commuter traffic jams but it did make me wonder where they all parked once they got into the capital. I was determined that even if I were to be caught and overtaken I would not disgrace myself so at least tried to portray a reasonable impression of a runner. I just hoped that Roadrunner wasn't lurking in the bushes awaiting my arrival before leaping out to embarrass me in front of my car-bound audience.

I kept my head up and looking forward and still hadn't been caught as the traffic was now beginning to thin out. Dare I ease off slightly? The sweat was already dripping from me and I was in danger of replenishing the puddles that were quickly disappearing. I kept going, past Cemetery Corner and the fire station, which was empty this morning, and decided that I couldn't maintain this pace if I wished to return to the hotel in one piece.

I started to slow down as the road began to curve towards the junction with Willie Farrington Drive. I could spy ahead of me a group of workmen in hard hats, albeit there was no sign of roadworks. By now I realised that I had started too quickly so that my return leg would be quite pedestrian in comparison. Curiosity at last got the better of me and as I jogged around the bend I decided to try and sneak a surreptitious glance backwards. Had I actually outpaced them and increased the distance between us or were they now about to sprint past me and leave me in their slipstream?

I took a quick glance over my left shoulder and did it with a swift flick of my left hand across my brow so that to the uninitiated it appeared that I was merely dispatching some unwanted beads of sweat from my brow onto the road surface below.

I was amazed. I was the only runner on the road. There was no sign of the two runners from the Holiday Inn. Where were they? I know I'm not that fast. Had they already turned back? Had they turned off along one of the side roads or decided to use the footpath to the beach? I will never know as I never saw them again. I was convinced they weren't a figment of my imagination but whoever they were, and if they ever read this they will have the satisfaction of knowing that without even trying they had made me run my fastest workout since arriving on Grand Cayman.

Am I the only jogger who hates to be overtaken, or who when spying another athlete in the distance (well not me, but perhaps a genuine runner) then tries to catch them to prove a totally meaningless point to himself? I was only glad I was not on a training run with Fran as she is one of the most competitive people I know. I could have envisaged that both of us would have reached the point of exhaustion as neither would be prepared to give in to the other in any sort of run. The fact it was just a morning training and fitness jog would not make one iota of difference. Neither of us would have lasted the fortnight if we had been running together. One of us would have capitulated early and I suspect it would have been me.

On this particular morning although not exhausted I was feeling pretty shattered and for the first time broke into a walk to take some water on board well before the halfway mark.

If I thought I had a problem it was nothing compared to the workmen that I could now see were in a predicament. There were six of them. Two appeared to be working whilst the other four had removed their hard hats and were in a heated discussion whilst scratching their heads and looking skywards. This very much reminded me of back home in the UK where one third do the work and the remainder talk about it whilst giving the odd piece of advice or instructions. This is obviously a well-known and prevalent worldwide workmen's culture.

I followed their gaze to see that the two workers had managed to entangle a telegraph pole amongst the overhead cables about forty odd feet in the air. They looked as perplexed as their companions and were operating what appeared to be a cherry picker without the platform. Balanced precariously on the extended arm was the wooden pole that was now sitting at a dangerously acute angle and seemed to be held in place purely because it was jammed between a number of the cables. I'm not sure if they were high voltage electricity cables or overhead telephone wires. This airborne description appeared about to change as the pole started to gently see-saw in the sky and the cables began to take more of its weight. What was more worrying was the pole, that was now aimed fairly and squarely in my direction as the wires became more taut. The four workmen on the ground moved swiftly to one side as their two colleagues played furiously with the levers on the cherry-picker in an attempt to stabilise their pole as it had begun to take on a life of its own and seemed determined to either take out all telegraphic communications or the electricity supply to this part of the island. Unfairly, I thought to myself at least they had a ready made excuse should any of the services be disrupted. They could easily blame it on the thunderstorm and spin the story that they were only repairing the damage which was much worse than they imagined. Very unjust, I know, but governments have been known to spin far worse stories.

Not wishing to interfere or become a victim of what was beginning to resemble a giant arrow that was about to be launched from a bow where the strings were becoming tauter by the second and were guaranteed to snap just as I passed underneath (my island running experiences to date made this an odds-on certainty), I crossed the road and accelerated from walking pace into a sprint in a matter of seconds not slowing down until I was a good hundred metres past the potential accident zone. Well if not a sprint then at least as fast as my short fat hairy legs would carry me following their earlier exertions.

I continued slowly to my halfway turning point where I gulped down the remainder of the water before heading back on the homeward leg of my morning jog.

Knowing I would have to re-pass the Cayman equivalent of the British Telecom Spidermen, although none of these were up the pole they just seemed to be up the creek, I stayed on the opposite side of the road. The scene had not changed dramatically although they had now stopped the pole swinging in the air. This had been achieved by managing to entwine all the wires around it so that it was firmly trapped between them in the equivalent of a telegraphic hairnet. Whether this had been a deliberate ploy or not I do not know but I was willing to give them the benefit of the doubt. Although it was no longer moving the pole looked decidedly unsafe and the six engineers had obviously come to the same conclusion as they had removed themselves from the dropping zone and were out of range, a good thirty yards away.

The discussion was continuing but was now much more animated with arms being waved in all directions and the four had become six having been joined by the two lever operators, although one of the workers was standing with arms akimbo as if by some magical illusion that would ensure the pole remained airborne. The cherry-picker had been abandoned as it was directly in the line of fire should the pole work loose and remaining at the controls would have provided too much of a Bull's-eye in the centre of what was a very inviting target for this giant javelin that was waiting to be launched back to earth. The old adage of 'what goes up must come down' was just waiting to be proven once again.

One of the men, who I suspected was the foreman, had moved to the side of the group and was talking earnestly into his mobile phone. One part of me wanted to remain to watch and wait for the outcome of this local drama, as I had a feeling that the entertainment was likely to continue for some time yet. Once again others' misfortune was beginning to provide great spectator sport as four or five interested bystanders were now making their way from a nearby bus stop and were gathering to watch the early morning distraction. For once common sense got the better of my curiosity as I knew if I stopped for too long my legs would seize up so I jogged slowly past the scene on the opposite side of the road but the participants were totally oblivious to my presence. Although the traffic was now much diminished I wasn't at all sure that it was safe to drive past although they seemed content to do so at their own peril. The danger was plain for all to see but nobody appeared unduly bothered. Health and safety regulations and risk assessments were not on their agenda that morning. Quite how the problem of the flying telegraph pole was finally resolved I would never know as I gently jogged back to the hotel. The sun was, by now, shining brightly and the road surface totally dry. Anybody venturing out at this time would not have dreamt that a thunderstorm had finished not much more than an hour earlier. Unfortunately the storm had not reduced the humidity and my running vest and shorts were in their usual soaked and unkempt state as my legs carried me wearily into the hotel. I dived straight into the pool to relax my aching muscles before breakfast. My return leg took a full five minutes longer than my outward journey. I vowed if I saw the Holiday Inn runners on a future morning I would totally ignore them. Wishful thinking.

Having carried out my normal ritual of washing the running gear, shaving, showering and towelling down it took me another ten minutes to stop leaking before changing into a fresh pair of shorts and tee-shirt and returning back downstairs to join the girls for what was to be a late breakfast around the pool.

The cold fresh orange juice was particularly welcome and I probably had more than my fair share but I seemed to need it more than most. Having acquainted the group with the story of my morning run this merely ensured that Carrie and Caroline would definitely not be venturing out with me for a spot of early morning exercise no matter what bribes I might offer. I was destined to be running on my own for the remainder of the holiday. Jan and Diane decided to go beach walking and didn't seem particularly keen for me to join them. In any event they headed off in the opposite direction and most unusually had disappeared before I had finished my breakfast. Diane wanted to make the most of her last day on Grand Cayman before packing and making her way on the long journey back home to Oz.

Having left my sports wear draped over a chair on the balcony, knowing that it would be dry and aired within the hour, I made my way back to the pool to relax after my earlier toils along Seven Mile Beach. I joined Caroline and Danielle, who were both now so tanned up they could have been mistaken for permanent residents.

That reminded me just how hot the sun could be and it was time for another coating of the good old suntan cream. I couldn't possibly compare with the girls but was more than content, and comfortable, with my lightly grilled complexion which I must admit still looked positively pale against their golden tans.

We were all catching up on some reading, although Caroline was no longer asking the meaning of any of the words. Strangely, although I had experienced my most strenuous exercise so far I wasn't feeling any after-effects and had recovered far more quickly than I had anticipated a couple of hours ago. I put this down to the therapeutic compounds contained in the local Stingray beer that had been last night's medication and decided that I would need a further supply for the remaining days of the holiday even if it wasn't available on prescription.

From time to time my mind wandered back to the six workmen and I wondered if they had yet released the pole from the tangled strands of cable or even how and why they had got it there in the first place. Had the north-west tip of the island had its electricity supply or telephone communications cut off yet or had they managed to avoid such disruption? From what I had seen it would owe more to luck than judgement.

As my mind wandered between reading my book and daydreaming on the pitfalls of erecting telegraph poles, Indie the hotel cat suddenly appeared as she padded alongside the pool to lap from a saucer of milk shaded by the overhanging roof of the poolside bar. Occasionally it was possible to glimpse a small furry head poke out from the camouflage of the shrubbery and quickly scan right and left to ensure that Mother hadn't wandered too far away before disappearing just as swiftly back into the sanctuary of the bushes. This would be followed a minute or two later by a different, but just as inquisitive, head that then followed the same routine. Indie and her kittens had survived the overnight storm.

Diane and Jan returned from their promenade along the beach and we all had time for a light lunch before we had to bid our farewells to Diane. For a change the lunch was light with the exception of the rum cake that was now being eaten at an extraordinary rate in what I thought was the forlorn hope of it all being devoured before the end of the holiday. Strangely the cache in the refrigerator was not getting any smaller. A certain young lady was replenishing supplies on a regular basis using the excuse that they were for friends and family back home in England. There now appeared every likelihood that Caroline's suitcase would be even heavier on the return journey with the distinct possibility that an excess baggage charge was in the offing.

Carl and Fran joined us for lunch having spent the morning shopping in Georgetown and Fran seemed even more bubbly and excited than usual. Shopping and women, what a combination. They decided to stay poolside for the afternoon with Caroline and Danielle as they needed to extract every last ounce of energy from the sun to ensure the tans remained topped up.

I offered to take Diane to the airport with Jan and Carrie who were then going to do some real shopping as opposed to the window-gazing variety. I concluded that I must take this opportunity to make a final decision about the pair of earrings and also return to the antique dealers to see if the Carlton Ware dish was still in the window. The price was so good compared to what I would have to pay at home I had already decided that provided it had not already been sold I would buy it, particularly if I could still obtain the ten percent discount. If only Diane were staying on she could pack it for me and there would be a chance that it would get back to England in one piece. She really was far too efficient and had already packed her one small suitcase ready for her return journey to Australia. Even at this stage, with the evidence neatly packed in front of them, I'm not sure that the girls really believed that Diane only had the one suitcase to spend three weeks away from home and travel halfway around the world. It was as if they were waiting for her to go and collect another case from her room which was now empty and being cleaned whilst awaiting occupation by the next guests. Caroline remained quite perplexed and for the one and only time on the holiday was lost for words. Now that was a first.

There was still plenty of time before we had to get our Antipodean golfing star to check in so I joined the girls in the pool to cool off before I needed to dry and get changed for the trip to the airport.

What I had managed to forget was that at lunchtime I had retrieved more than enough cash from the hotel safe in order that I could get a good deal at the antique dealers. I had slipped all of the notes into the pocket of my swimming trunks and completely forgotten about them. They were now with me in the water and I suddenly realised they were becoming a soggy mass. I left the pool a lot quicker than when I went in and having extricated the slimy notes from my pocket, much to the amusement of all at poolside, returned to my room to see how I could then manage a speed drying job. This was to be a simple exercise. It was just a matter of laying them flat and allowing nature to take its course, whilst I showered and dried off myself for the second time that day.

By the time I joined everybody at the minibus, as the girls were bidding farewell to Diane, I won't pretend that the notes were pristine or even totally dry but at least they were passable as genuine currency even if still slightly damp to the touch. At least they seemed a little cleaner than when I retrieved them from the safe. Hopefully, by the time I tendered them, they may have dried a little more and not give the impression of just having come off the printing press. I had no wish to be conspicuous or give the appearance of being the printer or passer of counterfeit banknotes.

We dropped Diane off at the airport where she was travelling, on the first leg of her long return journey to Australia, with Cayman Airways to Cuba. From there she was hopping to Mexico and then to the west coast of the United States of America before the long haul back across the Pacific. We said our farewells and left her in the departure hall to await the call to her flight.

We drove into the centre of Georgetown and found plenty of parking places near the port area. I still hadn't fathomed out where all the traffic that commutes into the town disappears to when it arrives and then suddenly reappears at the end of the day to travel home. Although the sun was now blisteringly hot the cruise ships had departed and it was very comfortable walking around the town dipping into the air-conditioned shops to momentarily cool off.

I left Jan and Carrie in one of the many jewellers looking at cabinets of watches whilst I took myself off to the antique dealers ready to barter for my bargain Carlton Ware Buttercup dish. The owner was serving some other customers whilst I busied myself browsing at various objets d'art that were on display. I was even tempted with one or two other items on offer but only had limited funds available and didn't wish to push my luck and then have to pay more than I need by using a credit card. I had already checked and made sure that the Buttercup dish hadn't been sold over the last few days. It remained in its original position in the window display. Having just made another sale the owner was in a good mood and remembered me. What seemed to be the sole West Indian cricket sunhat on Grand Cayman, although I had now removed it and left it resting on his counter, may just have had something to do with recognition. He was as good as his word and was willing to drop the price provided I could pay in cash. I put my hand into my pocket and brought out a small wad of crumpled bank notes that I hoped had by now, with the advantage of the sun and my body heat, dried sufficiently not to arouse any suspicion. Pushing my luck I tried to haggle a little further but could see that he was not willing to drop any more and in all honesty had to admit that I had a real bargain compared to what I would have had to pay back home. I flicked off some not very crisp notes and handed them over which to my amazement and relief he accepted without question. He then carefully bubble- and newspaper-wrapped my newly acquired bowl to assist me with its safe passage back home to England. We bade each other farewell, both happy with the afternoon's trading, and I left to rejoin the girls. For the first time in my life I had bought goods in a foreign country with genuinely laundered money and it had been totally above board and legal.

By now the girls had already moved on to yet another shop and were inspecting three different watches that a charming young Irishman had laid on a black velvet cloth for Carrie to examine. He had been there for two years and was enjoying his time on the island. He hailed from Dublin so for the second time in two days I was receiving yet more tips on what to do and where to go when I eventually visited Dublin. He was a typically friendly Irishman and the main difference in the advice that I had received on the previous day seemed to concentrate on the inevitable Irish Liffey water. He was obviously a connoisseur of the world-renowned Guinness.

For all his Irish charm, and there was no doubt that he was aiming this directly at Carrie, he obviously felt that Jan and I were an unnecessary distraction; although he was trying to sideline us as diplomatically as possible he was eventually unsuccessful in persuading her to purchase one of his many watches. This, not unnaturally, did not prevent him from asking further questions probing our location on the island, and I envisaged further phone calls enquiring after the whereabouts of one of the girls. This time Carrie. This was all a new experience for me. As a middle-aged gentleman – well, man at least – being on holiday for the first time with a group of pretty young ladies I was having to get used to the charms of flattering young men who were displaying more than a passing interest in our party. It is fair to say that the interest was not directed at Jan or myself. For whatever reason the expected phone calls did not materialise on this occasion. It wasn't until sometime afterwards that I realised that I hadn't actually heard Carrie tell him where we were staying. I'm not sure if Caroline was being a good or bad influence on her.

Having contented ourselves with a little more window-shopping (well Jan and Carrie led me into this further window-gazing and it came as no surprise that the windows hadn't changed a bit since we last looked) we decided it was time for a return visit to the ice cream parlour that we had found tucked away down one of the side streets. On this occasion small cornets were more than sufficient although we quickly learned small is relative. The cheerful girl who served us obviously enjoyed her job and I suspect also had a liking for the ice cream. She was not small. Although small was one of only two sizes displayed for sale I don't think small figured in her mind once she started to dip her ladle into the large freezer container. She seemed to be limited to three different measures that she scooped with some dexterity from the different flavoured cartons to be perched precariously onto the mouth of the wafer-type cones. They were large, extra large and enormous.

We wandered back towards the port area remaining in the shade and tried to consume the ice cream before it melted away in the heat. We certainly didn't attempt to enter any of the other shops whilst we licked our fast-disappearing cornets, so took a seat to watch the comings and goings from the busy port.

A number of both container-type lorries and construction trucks were plying to and fro from the dockside and through the town further into the island. We had not previously seen these when the cruise ships were in port and they perhaps restricted their haulage times to the off-peak periods in the capital. It occurred to me that a pedestrianised area in the town centre, with vehicles diverted around the outskirts, would provide a much safer area for the shoppers to walk around without having to concentrate on passing traffic as they moved between the shops. It might also provide a more attractive vista as the cruise passengers disembarked and might even persuade some of them to return for a longer holiday on the island as opposed to just paying a fleeting visit as part of a cruise itinerary. I had already been fortunate enough to experience the advantages of staying on Grand Cayman and I'm sure that with a little thought and some capital investment it would prove to be a real benefit for the visitors, residents and the local economy. Great minds must think alike as I understand the Department of Tourism are now considering such an approach and the sooner they can persuade everybody to go down this road, or from a traffic perspective avoid this road, the better for all concerned.

We finished our ice creams before they melted away, and decided to return to the foreshore jewellers that we had previously window-shopped on at least two occasions. Well, at least two that I was aware of. It wouldn't have surprised me if the girls had paid more visits on their other excursions into town.

This particular jeweller's overlooked Hog Sty Bay and Georgetown harbour and we started on the ground floor, having first removed the remnants of the ice cream from our lips and wiped our sticky fingers on the ready supply of moist paper wipes that the girls carried permanently in their handbags.

Carrie started viewing the wide selection of watches on display whilst Jan was searching for a birthday present for Diane. She didn't want it to be too large or heavy as it was going to be airmailed to Australia. I came to the conclusion that discretion was the better part of valour and decided not to ask why she hadn't bought it on one of her previous visits. Diane could then have taken it home with her. She would not have opened it until her birthday and would definitely have found room in her suitcase.

I remained with them for a while until it became obvious that their efforts at decision-making were likely to become protracted. This was hardly surprising due to the amount of merchandise available and the fact that it was two women discussing the possibilities, although I wasn't brave enough to say that to their faces. I can just imagine how long it would have taken had Fran, Caroline and Danielle also been with us. Thank goodness they had decided to remain at the hotel and sunbathe. Having seen their previous differences of opinion over the simple selection of which dress to wear for the evening they would never have come to a consensus concerning which piece of jewellery suited them, although I'm sure the staff would not have minded this. In fact I think they sometimes positively encourage it in order to make a more expensive sale. In fairness to the sales staff in this store they did not fit into that category.

The one thing that I did like about this store was the lack of any high-pressure salesmanship. The staff were visible but invisible if that is not a contradiction in terms. They were available to help and advise you and remove items from the presentation cabinets enabling you to examine the different goods closely before making any decisions. They then left you to saunter and browse around the contrasting displays without exerting any influence on you to buy any particular goods that might, or might not, enhance their bonus.

Mother and daughter were by now in fervent conversation over the merits of the different watches and ornaments that they were considering. It was obvious that they were unlikely to reach agreement and the thought occurred to me that if they split up and each just concentrated on their individual needs it might just be possible to conclude the afternoon's shopping before the store closed. The staff had obviously witnessed this scenario many times before and remained discreetly in the background. I meanwhile kept my thoughts to myself.

I decided to leave them and wander upstairs to where I had seen the numerous earrings on my previous reconnaissance visits, knowing full well that they would soon join me to proffer advice on what I should consider as a suitable present that I could take back home. I would listen patiently and politely and then still follow my own nose as I had done on many previous occasions. I should really admit that my hooter is not, and perhaps never has been, my best feature, having been broken no less than four times. Sometimes, I would probably be better served by following others' advice and putting my stubborn streak to one side.

I made my way over to the several cabinets containing the earrings, not wishing to be distracted by the array of other diamonds and stones on show. I knew what I wanted and intended to concentrate on that and that alone. This purchase was going to be swift and straightforward and, with luck, might even be concluded before the girls arrived with their words of wisdom.

The Bee Gees were playing softly on disc in the background and whereas previously I might have associated them with discos and *Saturday Night Fever* from now on I link them with mood music for jewellers. I approached the counter and was immediately recognised by Carole, a young and attractive assistant who came from Venezuela, and had spoken to me on my previous scouting mission. My West Indian sun hat, which I was carrying very carefully with the well-wrapped Carlton Ware, was proving to have more than its main and intended use of providing shade from the sun. It was providing me with an identity although I wasn't sure whether this was a good or bad thing.

However, she amazed me as she asked, "Was that you I saw running out along Seven Mile Beach this morning?"

Now, what I didn't know was, had she seen me on the outward leg when I could actually have resembled a runner or on the homeward trek when I looked more akin to a geriatric lump of arthritic lard about to expire? One thing was certain, the sun hat was not as prominent as I had imagined. I had never worn it for running.

I decided to try and be non-committal and replied, "Yes, I do go running some mornings."

"I thought it was you I saw," she said, "as I was driving into work this morning, you were running up towards West Bay, you looked quite hot, had you been far?"

At least she had seen me when I was trying to run and had been kind enough to describe my efforts as running and not jogging. If she had seen me on the return journey her description of 'quite hot' would have been generous, to say the least, and on a scaled thermometer, of whatever variety, at least fifty degrees below the reality.

"About five miles," I replied, being very economical with the truth as she was not to know whether she had seen me at the start or finish of my run.

"Do you do that every day? Only I've not seen you running before and I come along there every morning," she said.

I decided honesty was the best policy and replied, "No, I try and go for a run at least every other morning but this morning I was about an hour later than normal. I prefer running when it's slightly cooler but this morning I waited for the storm to pass over before going out. I must admit I'm not used to running in this heat. At home it's a lot cooler."

"That's why a lot of people go running early in the morning, it's far too hot later in the day," she replied. "I normally see the regular runners whilst I'm driving into work but I knew I hadn't seen you before."

"We've only got another two or three days before we return home so I will probably just have another couple of morning runs. What amazes me is the amount of traffic about at that time of the morning. Is it always that bad?" I asked.

"Pretty much, but lots of people want to get to work early before it gets too hot. You soon get used to it, though," she responded. "Anyway, you didn't come in to talk about the traffic did you? Would you like to see the trays of earrings you were looking at the other day?"

"Yes please," I replied.

She quickly produced a couple of trays that included a pair that I had taken a particular interest in on my previous visit, and left me to peruse the various gems at my leisure. I had pretty much made up my mind on sticking to my original choice but was also struck with a couple of others that I hadn't spotted previously. Both of which matched a necklace that I had bought for Lesley on a previous occasion.

It was at this stage I was joined by Jan and Carrie who had jointly decided that I was in urgent need of their assistance. They hadn't yet finally made up their own minds, but had come to help me. Why was I not surprised?

I showed them the three pairs that I was considering and told them that I had more or less decided on my original selection but was now contemplating one of the other pairs instead, as they matched some other jewellery back home. Experience should have made me realise that was a mistake. I really should have appreciated that at the time but as I've mentioned earlier, strange things happen to me on holiday and I don't always act in character.

This was to be one of those occasions. All three pairs were then scrutinised minutely and compared in both daylight and artificial light. They were held against ear lobes together, separately and also as mixed pairs and compared and contrasted against each other in both ovoid and circular mirrors so that eventually every possible combination had been examined and debated without resolving the impasse. Perhaps the girls were having a bad influence on me as I was displaying distinct symptoms of that female shopping trait, procrastination over selection and a final decision.

Meanwhile, the Bee Gees continued to strum their beat and having worked through their extensive repertoire were about to repeat the performance. Now I don't dislike the Bee Gees but I hadn't come into town to listen to a Bee Gees concert. It was make-your-mind-up time.

I had come to a conclusion. I was going to stick to my original decision and buy the pair of earrings that had taken my eye when I had first visited the shop. Cost did not seem to factor into the female agenda in such circumstances.

I decided, however, that I would also back my judgement both ways and moreover opt for a pair of the earrings that matched Lesley's necklace, in addition to my initial choice. The girls actually agreed that this was a sensible and wise decision. They would, two instead of one will always appeal to the female variety of the species when buying presents.

This may well be considered by some to be a cop out and it probably was, but it needed positive action to bring this particular shopping venture to an end and the prices on Grand Cayman are such that my unusual and uncharacteristic extravagance was not going to break the bank.

Carole asked if I would like the presents wrapped and I didn't need asking twice. Present wrapping has never been my forte and my efforts at Christmas seem to use inordinate amounts of brightly coloured paper bound with equally lengthy reels of sticky tape, silk ribbons and pre-made stick-on bows. As hard as I try, and I genuinely do, the finished article normally looks scruffy and bulbous and does not represent the amount of time and care that I put into it. I'm sure there is a market out there for a present wrapping service to cater for the likes of me at Christmas. I don't believe I'm the only individual who struggles to make presents appear inviting for others and there is a profit to be made for any enterprising youngsters who have the time and initiative to set up such a venture for the month leading up to Christmas. There would also be considerable savings on the wasted miles of paper and Sellotape that the likes of me need to complete our attempts to produce something that at least resembles a reasonably wrapped parcel.

Carole meanwhile had simply and effectively wrapped two small but very smart presents and attached matching ribbons and bows that provided an appropriate and fetching finishing touch.

In thinking that we were finished I was, of course, being far too optimistic for as we descended the stairs I realised that the girls had yet to make their decisions. We started at a counter that contained such a wide variety of watches I thought we were likely to remain until closing time. Fortunately Carrie had already cast her eye over the enormous selection and had narrowed the choice down to just a couple. It didn't take her long to decide and we moved across the store to examine a collection of glass figurines that Jan had spied before joining me upstairs. It didn't take too long for Jan to settle on a crystal miniature golfer that we were all sure Diane would appreciate and enjoy. I had stood back a little whilst the girls were coming to their conclusions as I didn't wish to cause any further delay by trying to influence them, until Jan asked for my opinion of the golfer and it was easy for me to reinforce their views to conclude the deal. They were both all too quick in reminding me that they had taken only about half the time that I had needed to make a decision. My response that they were more used to such expeditions appeared somewhat feeble but I wasn't too bothered as we had eventually finished our shopping. Or so I thought.

I was brought back down to earth as they reminded me that we needed to call into the supermarket on the way home to restock the fridge-freezer for our final three or four days on the island.

We had also, after ten days, managed to run out of the communal kitty which we had all contributed to on our first morning at the hotel. That now seemed a long time ago. Bearing in mind the amount of food and drink that we had consumed it had lasted a lot longer than we had been entitled to expect. Carrie, who was the party banker, or chief controller of the kitty purse, in addition to her role as wedding organiser, had proved to be a very thrifty shopper and had already decided that she would obtain a small top-up from everybody when we got back to the hotel, although she didn't think we would need to chip in very much to keep us in nibbles and tipples for the remainder of the holiday. The visit to Foster's Supermarket was the briefest yet as I think all three of us had decided that we had done enough shopping for the day. Although wine and beer featured in the shopping trolley the staple diet of bread and water was by far the most prominent, particularly the bottles of water that had been diminishing by the hour as we all drank a greater amount than normal to avoid dehydration in the heat.

On arrival back at the hotel we just had time to stash our provisions in the kitchen before the girls all wanted to examine our purchases from the jewellers. For two of the girls they were merely re-examining articles that they had pored over for well over thirty minutes back in the shop before making their final decisions. There followed the normal female debate of reconsidering if they had made the correct selection. I remained strictly neutral but amazingly did receive unanimous approval for my purchases of the earrings, in the plural. Fortunately the girls volunteered to repack my gifts so that they remained as presentable as when they left the jewellers.

For probably the first and only time in my life I had done something that received approval and plaudits from all the five women in my life at that particular moment. I had to make a mental note to remember to record such a momentous event in my travel journal. I just hoped it would receive the same acclamation in equal measure from the one woman who really mattered, when I returned home.

Having concluded the debate on the success of our shopping endeavours we still managed to have enough time to relax by the pool and enjoy a cocktail or two chatting to our two new English friends who had started the day house-hunting but after a good, and we learned fairly liquid, lunch had decided to spend the afternoon walking the beach. They had been impressed with the properties they had inspected but a number had been out of their price range, although they were returning to the South Sound area the following morning to continue their search.

Bearing in mind that two of the most stressful things in life can be a house move and a change of job they were both totally laid back about the whole situation, or if not were giving an excellent impression of being so. The fact that the move and job change were taking place simultaneously on to a different continent and thousands of miles from home did not seem to bother them one iota. In fact they seemed to be relishing the experience and were looking forward to the opportunity and change of scenery as if setting out on one of life's little adventures and were determined to enjoy this episode of their lives whatever the outcome. They seemed to be an ideally suited couple who were very good company and it was easy to imagine him being the life and soul of any party.

We left them by the pool to return to our rooms to spruce ourselves up for the evening where the rendezvous for the first part of the night was to be an Italian restaurant called Ragazzi, which is located in Buckingham Square off West Bay Road and is close to the Hyatt Regency complex.

Meeting up by the bar for our compulsory pre-dinner drink I was amazed to find that Caroline and Danielle were already waiting for us and chatting to our two new chums. This was the second time that they managed to achieve this particular feat and on consecutive nights. Quite how they had managed to shower and change, and make a decision about which dress and shoes to select for the evening, in such record time I did not know and was not brave enough to ask.

What was not so astonishing was that having achieved personal best times in washing and dressing and having knocked a comfortable twenty minutes off their previous best time they still looked as stunning as ever in their chic summer frocks which displayed their golden tans to great effect. Just think how much time they could save in their lives by reducing the unnecessary and wasted titivating routine on a daily basis. Having said that I'm equally sure that on this holiday much of that time had been spent chattering and comparing outfits, particularly when they had all got together and Carl and I had been forced to endure yet more wasted time, loitering in the vicinity of the bar. Fortunately we chaps used our initiative and always managed to put such downtime to good use by taste testing the various cocktails on offer.

However, this particular night was different as they had promised to take Carl and I clubbing after our meal. In Carl's case this was not at all unusual but it had been some years since I had been clubbing and the thought of me bopping the night away had been but a distant memory. I have to admit, very distant. The girls seemed to think that I had acquitted myself reasonably well at the wedding reception on the previous Saturday evening and any embarrassment I might cause was unlikely to do permanent harm to my, or more importantly their, reputations. They gave me the once over and obviously felt that I was suitably attired for such an adventure. They told me that after the meal we were all going on to the Royal Palms nightclub but I'm not sure that they had warned the Royal Palms.

Carrie had volunteered to drive and we were soon making our way back towards Georgetown, passing the ever-growing Ritz Carlton where there were still workmen beavering away under some floodlights. Every time we passed there seemed to be an army of workers scurrying about the building site which extended to both sides of the road and included a footbridge that looked as if it were to become a permanent feature of the complex, once it was complete, to ensure safe passage from the main hotel and apartment building to the remainder of the facilities. Bearing in mind the amount of traffic using the main road this appeared to be an essential amenity for the future guests and residents alike.

Ristorante Ragazzi was very busy and obviously extremely popular. It had been opened about five years previously and we had learned that it was one of the best restaurants on the island but that it wouldn't break the bank. We had already telephoned earlier to ensure that we could reserve a table. It offered fine food, a wide and varied selection of wines, apparently over three hundred and fifty, and described itself in the hotel's restaurant directory as 'Fantastico'. We were not to be disappointed.

A smart, smiling and helpful hostess ushered us to a reception area and bar where we were able to peruse the menu whilst awaiting our table reservation. We made ourselves comfortable on some stools to the side of the bar whilst contemplating the culinary delights on offer. This was necessarily assisted by some light lubrication of the vocal cords.

I've mentioned before that first impressions are important and I was immediately impressed with this restaurant. It had a friendly yet informal atmosphere with the staff achieving that fine balance of being attentive without appearing overbearing or oppressive. The wine waiter was extremely helpful without being in the slightest bit patronising as can be the case in some upmarket establishments particularly when dealing with young clientele or those lacking in knowledge or confidence. The menu was extensive with something to cater for all tastes.

It was while we were at the bar considering our options that we were approached by Brian, who the girls immediately recognised as the young lad who had been leading the group salsa lessons, at the Café Med, over a week ago.

We learned very quickly that he was fifteen years old and was on holiday with his family. He instantly displayed a confidence that belied his years and was swiftly arranging photographs of himself with the girls, whilst simultaneously trying to chat them up. I wish that I had been only half as bold at his age but I just would not have dreamt of chatting up girls in their twenties. In fact, if I'm honest, at the age of fifteen I was probably still much more interested in football than girls. I was obviously a bit slow on the uptake and at that age they were only just beginning to register on my dashboard. I would have been far too embarrassed to attempt to chat up young ladies in their twenties. In truth as a young teenager I was probably still rather shy although when I tell anybody that today they have difficulty in believing me. Compared with Brian I was obviously a slow developer.

It would have been easy to label Brian as precocious but he was, in reality, a bright and charming young man. We found out that his father was something big in the automotive industry and as a developing teenager it appeared that he was attempting to escape from the family environment for at least part of his holiday, which in my view is perfectly normal for a boy of that age. He had swiftly ascertained that we were all going clubbing after the meal and lost no time in trying to persuade the girls that he should accompany us. In fact he was so keen he was even willing to return to his hotel to change his shoes so that he could comfortably dance the night away. He had obviously decided that the salsa lessons had not been a wasted effort.

Whilst we continued to peruse the menu, Brian provided us with a synopsis of the ongoing presidential election campaign back home in the good old United States of America. Brian was proving not to be a 'Brian'. Having given us a pen picture of the candidates, of which he just about tended to favour the incumbent president, George W. Bush, he went on to present a commentary on the state of both the main political parties. If he was accurate in his assessment, and he was proving to be an astute young man, then his opinion of American politicians and the two main parties was not very flattering.

If he didn't follow his father into the motor industry, and at this stage in his life he wanted to design and race fast cars, it was easy to imagine him becoming a future politician with enough desire to change things for the better and ample ambition to go far enough to be successful. Equally, I'm sure he's not the first teenager to feel that way as a student but very few are lucky or good enough to bring their dreams to fruition in the cloudy and murky world of politics, where it seems necessary to adopt the wheeler-dealer backscratcher or backstabber culture if one wishes to change the political landscape. As one of the most intelligent, articulate and confident teenagers I have ever met I'm sure that whatever he wants to do he is likely to be successful, be that fast cars, politics or whatever else takes his fancy as he grows into adulthood. He certainly already had the ability to attract and hold an audience with a subject that none of us were particularly interested in and even less so whilst we were on holiday.

Although it was not uninteresting listening to young Brian we were by now quite hungry and more interested in choosing our meals. Whilst it was also obvious that the girls did not want a fifteen-year-old tagging along for the night they had no wish to embarrass him and wanted to let him down lightly. Fortunately his father had motioned him back to the family dining table as their main course had now arrived. It was apparent that he had great respect for his father, for although he would have preferred to remain and try and persuade the girls that he should join us at the night club he returned to his table without a hint of protest, where he rejoined what appeared to be at least three generations of his family. That, however, didn't prevent him from throwing the occasional long wistful glance towards the girls once we were seated for our own meal.

We all eventually selected our dinners from the extensive menu and took our seats at the large circular table, which was to the side of and at one end of the long rectangular table that seated Brian and what seemed to be a large family gathering including his parents, a younger sister and we guessed both sets of grandparents or other relatives. Brian was positioned with his back to the wall so that he could attract the attention of the girls from time to time. They meanwhile responded by trying to resolutely but politely ignore him. He was not to be put off by their seeming indifference.

Having seen the size of the meals that the early diners were now enjoying I decided to forego a starter and opted for just the main course choosing a grilled rack of lamb with caramelised onion, white truffle essence and potato laces. I must admit that I wondered exactly what potato laces were likely to be but decided that it would be difficult to spoil a potato and I couldn't exactly imagine the chef at this restaurant doing so. Even I can boil a mean potato without inflicting too much damage on the potato or the kitchen. By now the drink must have started to have some sort of effect as there followed a silly conversation about lacing shoes with mashed potatoes or chips. In the cold light of day this doesn't appear to be in the slightest bit comical. In fact it sounds just plain stupid. However, at the time we came to the conclusion that unless you used a string of French fries the chances of potato lacing a pair of shoes were pretty slim. We were already in a flippant mood and the night was still young. Fortunately for me Carrie was the evening's chauffeur so that I could enjoy a drink without having to concern myself about the journey home.

Carl, who enjoys his food, had decided to have a starter and selected blue crab spring rolls. He generously offered to share them with those of us abstaining from a first course and then swiftly managed to catapult one into Danielle's glass of wine. She didn't really fancy her roll marinated, albeit briefly, in Pinot Grigio.

As anticipated the main courses arrived, beautifully prepared and presented, on exceptionally large plates, and this course was less eventful with eating initially taking precedence over conversation. With Caroline at the table this was unlikely to last very long but she was severely censured by the whole group for actually mentioning the forbidden 'W' word. She suddenly mentioned the word 'work' as she started to tell us her plans once she returned home next week. We knew the holiday was drawing to a close but didn't yet wish to be reminded of this fact and certainly didn't want to think about work for a few days yet. That would come soon enough for all of us.

Caroline, Carl and Fran still had sufficient appetites to demand puddings and it was whilst we watched them tuck into their sweets that we realised just how serious young Brian had been about joining us after the meal and moving on to the nightclub.

His family having completed their own meal he suddenly joined us at the table and had indeed surreptitiously returned to his hotel and changed his shoes so that he would be more comfortable dancing the night away. He was also carrying a fist-sized wedge of notes as if to prove his credentials. He explained that he didn't expect us to pay for him and also wanted to buy us all a drink. Glancing across towards his parents it appeared that they were quite happy to leave him in our company, content that he would not come to any harm.

The girls were not so convinced and were unanimous in the view that he would not be coming with us. They were equally unanimous that none of them wanted to tell him this and I gradually became aware that they were all looking in my direction in the certain expectation that I was to be the one to do the dirty deed.

He had, meanwhile, returned to the family table awaiting us finishing our meals. Perversely, the girls were equally certain that they had no wish to upset him as he was a sweet boy, but much too young for them. What would it do to their reputations if they were to be seen in a night club with a fifteen-year-old? Carl and I assured them that, from the exhibition we had witnessed a week previously, he was likely to be a much better dancer than either of us but to no avail. These girls were adopting a Margaret Thatcher-like approach and were not for turning.

There was no other way around this; I had to lie to him. I approached their table and explained to Brian and his father that we had experienced a very long day (at least that bit was true) and I was now feeling very tired so that we would not now be going out but returning to our hotel. We chatted for a few minutes and exchanged pleasantries and whilst Brian was obviously disappointed he tried hard not to show it, as any teenage boy would do in those circumstances. We all shook hands and as I turned to leave Brian's father was smiling and I'm certain gave me a knowing wink as I made my way back to our table. We hastily paid the bill and took our leave. It was a pity that Brian didn't have a somewhat younger partner that could have accompanied him. I'm sure the girls would not have then objected. I'm just as sure that he would even more quickly forget that our paths ever crossed and it would not be long before he would be charming other young ladies onto the dance floor.

We meanwhile jumped aboard our trusty charabanc and took the short journey to the Royal Palms with everybody hoping that Brian would not turn up and realise what a nasty deceitful bunch we Brits really were. Remembering the look on his father's face I was pretty confident that would not happen.

The Royal Palms is a beachside bar, disco and club and Carrie found difficulty in finding a parking space for the minibus. After three circuits of the car park, during which she suffered a surfeit of unwanted and unnecessary back-seat-driver advice and abuse she managed to squeeze us into the tiniest of gaps at the end of one row of cars. At least by being tucked in a corner we were unlikely to be shunted by any driver leaving the club in a hurry, particularly if he had drunk more than was good for him.

We entered the club past the two obligatory bouncers, or door stewards in current parlance, who were friendly enough but, hardly surprisingly, also appeared big enough and fit enough to look after themselves should the need arise. What did surprise me was the fact that we did not have to pay to gain entry. It had been some years, well many years, since I had been a regular clubber but I seemed to recollect that in many clubs in the dim distant past there used to be an entrance fee. Not so at the Royal Palms.

The club was designed around a large covered bar area that had a wide patio and an even wider beach to its rear. Along one side was a paved expanse that was being used for dancing, whilst facing this and offset from the bar was a small stage where a local group were keeping the customers entertained with a good mix of modern and more traditional numbers interspersed with the musicians playing reggae, soca, salsa and calypso. I had heard of all of these with the one exception of soca. I soon learned that it was a combination of soul and calypso and was soon to be part of the nickname of the Trinidad and Tobago football team in the World Cup where they became popularly known as the Soca Warriors.

To the front of the bar was a verandah that had a number of tables and chairs but far too few for the numbers in the club that night. The rationale seemed to be get them drinking and dancing and then drinking a bit more. This was not the place to be if you wanted to sit peacefully and have a quiet, romantic or animated conversation.

Having joined the crowd at the bar to get our first drinks Carl and I were served surprisingly quickly with our selection of cocktails and beers. There seemed to be an unwritten rule of the house that whilst you could surround the bar to drink you moved aside to allow others to get close enough to the bar staff to shout your orders and carry your drinks away without spilling half of them. Whilst being served we suddenly realised that we were surrounded by individuals from most continents, all of whom were more than happy to talk to us. The guys, unsurprisingly, were more interested in our relationship with the girls, a number speculating, incorrectly, that I was the father, Jan the mother and Carl either a brother or boyfriend. We played our cards close to our chests but decided to update the girls with the all too obvious interest when we got back with their drinks. In that short space of time we spoke to an Austrian, a Canadian, an Irishman, two Aussies, two Jamaicans, a German, a couple of Americans, a pair from South Africa and another group of Brits. The Royal Palms was probably more cosmopolitan than any bar in Earls Court, albeit with a smaller proportion of Antipodean drinkers than you might find in London. Perhaps the United Nations should consider opening a Caribbean annexe in Georgetown. Although the place was packed to the proverbial rafters the atmosphere was jovial and friendly and not dissimilar to the party mood of the wedding reception that was now all of six days ago. They say time flies when you are enjoying yourselves and this was certainly the case on Grand Cayman.

We stood chatting and watching the dancing when we were joined by Ray, Cynthia and Huggy Junior, who had arrived from Ray's home in West Bay. As a group we were fairly representative of the club's clientele that evening. On the way to the club I had been a little concerned that I was likely to be their oldest customer. Not just that night, but possibly that year. I needn't have worried as my vision of being the oldest swinger in town was beaten by a fair few regulars who all seemed to know each other and were enjoying themselves gyrating around the dance floor in a display of Caribbean rhythm and calypso. Even in my younger days I was never particularly lithe or supple but one or two of these seemed to have India rubber legs and put a few of the youngsters to shame with a display of disco dancing that even young Brian would have been proud to emulate. There were other family groups who were all enjoying themselves and the dance floor was becoming quite congested, with ages ranging from school years to those who may well have qualified for pensionable service. I hope I have not done any of the more 'wrinkly' dancers an injustice, and I do include myself in that group, but I make the point merely to prove that it is possible for the different generations, and in this case different races, to enjoy an evening's entertainment together without the slightest hint of hostility or discord. I don't know if this was peculiar to the Royal Palms in particular, the Cayman Islands in general or whether this night was an exception but it made for a relaxing and enjoyable evening for everybody present. I'm not sure that I could say the same for a night-club back home in good old England where I had seen more than my fair share of violence both as a punter in my youth and a peacekeeper and law enforcement officer in my more advancing and maturing years. Although, to be honest, our efforts at restoring law and order were not always wanted and rarely appreciated, particularly when we then went on to provide some of the combatants with free and very secure accommodation for the night. This was normally followed by the offer of a fried breakfast, that was regularly declined prior to an appearance in the dock before the local magistrates. Although the majority of these resulted in not much more than the proverbial slap on the wrist.

Carl and I were happy to sip our drinks, ponder the forthcoming football season and be mere spectators as the girls joined the dancers. Ray had already taken the dance floor by storm and was 'shakin' what his momma gave him'. If they had such an event as *Strictly Come Dancing* in Grand Cayman then I would put my money on Ray. If for no other reason his enthusiastic approach and extrovert style would endear him to the audience and be a dead cert vote winner. In contrast the dazzling Darren Bennett or the smooth ballroom ability of Anton Du Beke, who both woo their partners and the judges with their professional ability, are but gifted and very talented youngsters when compared against the aptitude of twinkle-toed senior citizen Ray who had by now enticed Jan onto the dance floor and was spinning her like a whirling dervish in and out of the assembled throng until he managed to capture the centre of the floor. How they avoided colliding with anyone I do not know but Ray either had an innate sense of direction that guided him into each gap, however small, as it appeared or he possesses an inbuilt dancing satellite navigation system that goes into automatic pilot as soon as he hits any dance floor. She seemed quite relieved to escape and rejoin Carl and me sitting at ringside quietly watching the dancing, foot tapping to the music and becoming slowly but pleasantly intoxicated.

This was not to last. Carl was soon persuaded to join Fran and the girls dancing. Perhaps persuaded is not a totally accurate description as it was Fran doing the persuading and she was not going to take no for an answer. Carl reluctantly, but I have to admit very sensibly, was soon swinging and swaying to the local beat, with Fran in hot pursuit. (Everybody was hot, not just Fran, although I had not yet reached the drip-dry stage. That was about to change.)

I was thoroughly enjoying the evening but if I thought I was going to get away without demonstrating my inability to jig and jive with two left feet then I should have known better. The girls had furtively sneaked up on me and having surrounded me ushered me onto the dance floor and then made a determined effort to ensure that not only did I dance with all of them but also tried to manoeuvre me into position so that I was captured on the club video camera for posterity. Try as I might I was not going to escape so I joined Carl dancing with the girls. I might even have surprised them, for when an old Chubby Checker number was played I managed to dredge up the twist from a dim distant memory even if my dodgy knees and grating hips kept telling me that my teenage days were long since gone and forgotten, and come the morning I might just be regretting this twenty-first century knees-up. By now a mixture of the drink, the girls and the surroundings had got me into the party spirit and I joined in the mood by hopping and rocking the remainder of the night away, even if I didn't always know what I was doing. As the night wore on my memory became vaguer although I do recollect bopping away to one or two Boney M numbers, including 'The Rivers of Babylon' and I'm sure if it had been Christmas we would also have embraced 'Mary's Boy Child Jesus Christ' in our ever-extending repertoire. I do specifically remember being involved in a rendition of 'Michael Row the Boat Ashore' with the girls that seemed to go down well with the other dancers. This resulted in me ending up as the sole dancer in the middle of a large circle of others where I had unwittingly become the centre of attention.

This particular number had been made popular back in 1961 by The Highwaymen when I was just a callow youth, or budding teenager, which is a description I tend to prefer. Bearing in mind just how long ago this was I even surprised myself by remembering all the words and the liquid refreshment had certainly lubricated my vocal cords, to the extent that my virtuoso solo performance developed into involving the audience in each of the 'Hallelujah' choruses. In fairness they didn't need that much persuasion. From the clapping and shrieks of encouragement I gathered that I was, not unusually, and to the obvious amusement and amazement of everybody in our party, making a spectacle of myself.

Needless to say by this stage the humidity had once again taken its toll on my shirt which unsurprisingly soon resembled a well-used dish cloth and was no longer anything like the pristine, crisp, well-ironed article that had started the evening several hours ago. Unfortunately I had not taken the precaution of carrying a reserve on the bus, as I had done for the wedding. The one consolation was that I was not the only one in this condition and the dance floor contained its fair share of slippery bodies by the end of the evening's entertainment.

Having started the night with some reservations about going to a night-club I had to admit it had been really enjoyable, even if a little damp as the night wore on. However, that was par for the course on this holiday and was something we had all become used to. If only I could have remembered to make a mental note to travel with an additional shirt each evening. My first experience of an open-air night club was something I would not forget in a hurry and just a tad different to what I could remember in Essex and East London back in the mists of time of the swinging sixties. I much preferred the Grand Cayman experience.

Carrie, our driver, had remained sober and hydrated on copious amounts of mineral water and was the only sensible one in the minibus as she unsuccessfully tried to control a noisy but happy bunch of revellers on the journey home. For some strange reason, and not for the first time, she missed the turning to the hotel so that by the time she doubled back nature's call had become rather urgent so I needed to race up the stairs to the apartment and dash to the loo to avoid more than just a damp shirt.

Before going to bed I ensured that I drank at least a pint of water. This may give the impression of being rather perverse, or at least contradictory, having just rushed to the lavatory to relieve myself. I didn't particularly want to drink any more and it took some time to empty the glass but experience had taught me that it was worth the effort to avoid the possibility of a hangover. I far prefer to have to get up in the middle of the night and search for the bathroom rather than eventually awake with a sore head and a mouth resembling a sheet of coarse sandpaper that has just been used to rub down an untreated plank of weatherboard, or as I have heard it said, in less genteel circles, 'a gorilla's armpit'.

It was well after three as I hit my pillow, my latest night yet, and I couldn't help wondering if I would wake in time for my morning jog along Seven Mile Beach? The dancing and singing had also fortuitously taken their toll as I slept like a baby and had no need to make any further dashes to the lavatory during this particular night.

CHAPTER 14

A Room at The Ritz

To my amazement I was awake bright and early and before the alarm that I had set for eight o'clock. Well, it was the weekend and I had just had a late night so I thought an extra hour in bed wouldn't come amiss. I lay there watching the sun trying to peep between the blinds and must admit that it was an effort to crawl out of bed to don my shorts and running vest. It would have been easy, and it was very tempting, to give that morning's run a miss, and the thought did cross my mind more than once. Strangely for me I had enough willpower to continue to prepare myself for my stint of daily exercise. With the holiday fast coming to a close I had decided to make the run a daily routine for the remaining few days of our stay on the island. Perhaps the sun was starting to get to me and make me act more abnormally than is usual when I'm on holiday. Back home this just would not have happened.

Firstly it was the weekend, and that's the only occasion in the week when I have the time to have a coffee in bed whilst perusing the newspapers. I use newspapers in the plural not because we have more than the one paper but the number of weekend supplements that clatter through the letterbox and thump onto the hall mat provide enough reading material for the remainder of the week. Needless to say the majority are not read and by the Monday morning have found their way into the canvas recycling sack to await collection by the borough dustmen who must cart away literally tons of wasted weekend supplements on every round. If the majority of their readers are like me then I believe the weekend national newspapers could save on a considerable amount of newsprint – although the majority isn't news – and also make a greater contribution to saving the odd rainforest or two.

Secondly, for my personal time clock it was still early in the morning and the best I manage under all normal circumstances is a run normally in late afternoon or early evening and then, even in a good week, only every other day. After such a late, for me, night of drinking and dancing I just would not be in any state to contemplate such a run. In fact the thought would not even have entered my addled brain back home. If I had woken up at that time on a Saturday morning the best I would normally achieve would be to roll over, consider that as more than sufficient exercise for the day, and go back to sleep until the paper arrived.

This was different. It was Grand Cayman, the sun was shining brightly and we only had a further three full days of our holiday remaining. In any event I was beginning to enjoy my early morning escapades and by now I was intrigued to find out what surprises were waiting, or lurking in the bushes, to catch me out each morning.

There wasn't any noise coming from the other bedroom, so I kitted up as quietly as possible and carried out my pre-run ritual of stretching exercises on the balcony. Indie the cat was lapping from a saucer of milk that one of the hotel guests had left out for her and the kittens, although at this time of the morning there wasn't any sign of her offspring. She briefly glanced in my direction and with a lick of her lips and a disdainful shake of the head as she finished the last of her breakfast and sprayed droplets of milk in all directions turned and walked back into the shrubbery to rejoin her young family. Quite what she made of the strange figure limbering up on the balcony at that time on a Saturday morning would forever remain a feline mystery.

The sun was already climbing over the roof of the hotel and it promised to be another hot day. That was no surprise. I went through my customary rub down with what was probably my

third, or was it fourth, tube of suntan cream. Who was count-
ing? Collecting my frozen bottled water from the freezer I
set off with great expectations for my trot along Seven Mile
Beach.

Not unexpectedly, for the weekend, there was a lot less traffic heading
into Georgetown. If anything it was even warmer than usual but I was,
by now, ninety minutes later than normal for my jog. I have to admit, that
Saturday morning it was a jog and not a run.

Although we had now been on the island for twelve days and
become far more acclimatised I still hadn't got used to the heat of the sun
at that time of the morning. We just don't experience that type of heat and
humidity back home. My pace was slower than usual, if that's possible,
and I decided it was a combination of the heat and the morning after the
night before. Perhaps this morning's exercise was not such a good idea
after all. I had consumed the bottle of water by the turn and headed back
at a pace that could best be described as a gentle jog and would probably
have been overtaken by anybody walking at a brisk pace. Fortunately
there were not any power walkers out and about on this Saturday morning
so I was spared the embarrassment and indignity of being passed by
a speedy pedestrian. This outing proved to be the most uneventful to
date and I missed the familiar faces of the other runners, dog walkers or
cyclists who had become nodding acquaintances on weekday mornings.

The only incident of note was on the outward leg, when I still
had a vestige of energy in my lower limbs. I was overtaken by a rather
ancient JCB digger that was meandering along in the general direction
of West Bay with the driver seemingly having great difficulty in steering
it in a straight line. Whether he had also been drinking and dancing the
night before I do not know. He still had no difficulty in racing past me
and seemed oblivious to all around him as he sat in the cab wearing an
extraordinarily large pair of headphones. Whether these were to mask
the sound of the noisy engine that was puffing, panting, wheezing and
expelling more than its fair share of exhaust gases into the atmosphere,

or he was listening to his favourite music on a CD player or iPod, I don't know but he disappeared into the distance leaving me to puff and pant, somewhat more quietly, on my own for the remainder of that morning's monotonous and unmemorable run. A relaxing fifteen minutes in the pool, followed by a cold shower still allowed me ample time to dhobi out my running kit before wandering down to breakfast. The girls would be disappointed: with not one tale of adventure or derring-do to bring back from the morning's run: most unusual. What on earth would we find to talk about over breakfast?

I needn't have worried as girls being girls there was no lack of conversation over the fruit juice, croissants and coffee. Most of the chat seemed to be generally related to Friday night at the Royal Palms and specifically recounting my efforts on the dance floor the previous evening where it seemed I had given a very good impression of a middle-aged English gentleman (I use the word in its loosest sense and was reminded by the girls that *middle-aged* is a relative expression – their idea of middle-aged being somewhat younger than my own) trying to disco dance and failing dismally. This was not the first time that I had been told by an attractive twenty something young lady when trying to describe my swinging and swaying on the dance floor that 'Ooh, you dance just like my dad!'

I'm now quite accustomed to having my middle-aged ego dented but still persevere in trying to prove that I can rock and twist the night away just as I did in my teenage years. Is this the onset of a mid-life crisis I ask myself?

However, as far as last night was concerned, I learned that I had added to the entertainment value and concluded that I couldn't have been totally embarrassing as I was made to promise that we would all return to the Royal Palms before the holiday finished, for one last farewell performance.

I had already decided that Saturday was going to be a lazy day when I intended to lounge by the pool, catch up on some missed sleep from last night, try to finish reading the book that I had started on the plane and also write up the travel journal. On opening it I found that there were only two blank pages left which were swiftly completed with events from a couple of days previously. I could not believe that I had done quite so much writing whilst on holiday. I obtained some additional notepaper from hotel reception, together with copies of two local newspapers, which were editions from slightly earlier in the week. At least it would allow me the opportunity to browse through them later in the day to catch up on any local or international news, after I had managed to bring the diary up to date.

The additional sheets were appended to the back of the diary by a sorry-looking excuse for an elastic band that I had found in my wash-bag. Quite how it had got there, who had put it there and why it was there I do not know. It's my holiday wash-bag so I can only assume that I had placed it there on some previous trip and completely forgotten about it. Perhaps I was having one of those senior moments that seem to become more frequent as I get older but at least I had found a use for it. The extra pages became rather tatty around the edges over the next few days as whichever way I tried to fold them there were always a couple of overhanging sides that became crimped by the elastic band. They also gradually acquired an oily patina of suntan lotion that did nothing to enhance their appearance.

I made my way to the poolside to join Carl and the girls who were already collecting their ration of sun for the day. The girls all now sported golden tans whereas Carl and myself had been more circumspect and could best be described as lightly bronzed but remained delicately pale in comparison to the girls. We were the only ones around the pool apart from Indie and her brood who were still taking advantage of the shade offered by the shrubbery although Indie was tempted to appear from time to time to continue lapping some milk and try a light snack of cat biscuits that had been left conveniently close to their leafy camouflaged cover by one of the many cat-loving guests.

Time for a coating of skin protection cream from the sun's rays before settling down on the sun bed at the side of the pool.

There wasn't any sign of the different diving parties. We were aware that the four quiet and friendly Americans had already left for an early morning flight but we didn't know if Dick had managed to round up his gang or whether they were out on a dive or had already left to return home and regale their neighbours with noisy tales of daring dives in local Caymanian shipwrecked waters. It transpired that they must have departed as Dick and his entourage did not resurface again so that peace and serenity returned to the pool for the remainder of our stay at Indies Suites.

In fairness to Dick's friends they were not overly noisy themselves and for the majority of the time they were out of the hotel on their diving expeditions. It was just that their leader had to prove that he was the loudest on the island and impose himself on his team so that anybody poolside knew their future plans and scheduled itinerary down to each detailed minute. This was subsequently followed by a chapter and verse sermon on their most recent dive which encompassed who had done what to whom together with a comprehensive account of all aspects of the day's excursion. This was then repeated so that all within earshot – and this covered the majority of the hotel guests – were soon to discover the technical aspects and finer points of each dive. Perhaps Dick had been the equivalent of a United States Army regimental sergeant-major as I'm sure his gravelly and booming voice would have been able to silence and bring to attention any recalcitrant platoon of recruits on a parade ground. It was certainly effective around the swimming pool. Fortunately this only occurred infrequently, before and after diving trips, so that for the majority of the time the hotel was perfectly tranquil save for the occasional burst of noisy laughter from their British guests. This was normally when Carl and I decided to throw Caroline into the pool in retaliation for being splashed as we were either dozing or reading.

In retrospect I think we all missed Dick and his pals. His foghorn had become a daily source of entertainment and conversation and the very sight of him waddling onto his patio had set the girls off in fits of the giggles that proved impossible to restrain and normally started the rest of us off so that any disinterested spectator must have wondered what on earth was going on that was quite so funny. They would probably have put it down to that quaint and strange English sense of humour without even trying to understand it. Having said that, it would have been difficult for anybody to remain disinterested with Dick's decibel level piercing the eardrums and the more discerning in the audience would have been well aware of exactly who and what had been the source of our amusement.

Having spent some time in bringing the diary up to date, which was necessarily intermingled with the occasional doze in the sun, I remembered the newspapers that I had found in reception. It was time to catch up with the local news and I retrieved them from underneath the sun bed only to find that they were slightly damp but fortunately remained readable. The dampness was due solely to the efforts of a certain young lady in climbing in and out of the swimming pool to obtain liquid refreshment that was being supplemented by generous portions of rum cake. The preferred flavour of that particular morning being banana, albeit this was masked heavily by the rum content which was probably the reason that the rum cake was so popular. Before I settled down to read I needed a quick dip to cool off and together with Carl managed to inadvertently carry Caroline into the pool with us. She didn't appear overly concerned until she surfaced to spy Indie making a beeline for the remainder of the rum cake that had been left by her chair. She leapt out of the water far more quickly than she had entered and in three swift paces reached the rum cake in the nick of time to retrieve it from the fast approaching feline who was about to sample it and test whether it was suitable as kitten food. Indie would never know as it was snatched from under her nose and eaten immediately to ensure that no other predator would have the opportunity to steal what was becoming Caroline's staple diet.

The cat scampered away into the bushes whilst the rest of us were convulsed in laughter at the antics of the Rum Cake Kid or 'Kidette'. Every group holiday needs a good character who has the ability to keep everybody amused, even if it is sometimes unwittingly. Caroline was certainly proving to be the comedienne of our party and importantly she also possessed that other ingredient vital in a good comic – an ability to laugh at herself.

I climbed more slowly from the pool, as befits a middle-aged gentleman, and towelled myself off before settling down to read the island newspapers.

Having lost my protective seal whilst splashing about in the water it was necessary to re-apply a swift layer of cream to ensure that sunburn didn't spoil the last few days of the holiday. Would I need to buy any more suntan cream before the holiday was over or would I manage to eke out my meagre supply in the one remaining tube? This was a topic I pondered, as I was slightly more conservative than usual with this application, but perhaps my skin was also becoming more hardened to the sun-drenched climate.

The *Cayman Net News* reminded me very much of a local provincial newspaper although it devoted a couple of sheets to international news, almost as an afterthought as if to acknowledge there was another world outside the island.

My impression was of a newspaper very much for and of the local people. It included a column for 'Person of the Day'.

I settled down poolside on my sun bed and updated myself on the island news, which was led by a story of the Royal Cayman Islands Police Service receiving video training to prepare their officers for the forthcoming general election. Little did they, or I at that stage, suspect that this would be one of many events that would fall foul of the oncoming disaster. Circumstances eventually dictated that the election would need to be postponed until the following year.

Other prominent stories in the paper included the appointment of the Island's first ombudsman, albeit his official nomenclature was the Complaints Commissioner, together with an article about the selection of the government's initial cultural attaches to the United Kingdom and the United States of America.

Reading the last story brought back memories of the 'cultural attachés' based in the diplomatic missions during the Cold War years. The term became synonymous, certainly fictionally, for the well-accepted cover for the spies operating out of the different embassies. In some spy novels this cover was used by the Eastern bloc countries but I'm sure the diplomats of some of the Western nations also took advantage of such cultural opportunities. Somehow I could not envisage the Cayman Islands' representatives in London and Washington attempting to set up a network of spies throughout both capitals. The thought, however, did have me sitting poolside and smiling to myself. Quite what James Bond would have made of a cultural attaché from the Cayman Islands I don't know but I'm sure he would have enjoyed visiting the islands where his rum cocktails would have been shaken not stirred.

Having glanced at some of the overseas news and acquainted myself with the latest position on both International and local sporting events I happened across one other notice that took my attention.

I do use the word 'notice' deliberately. It was the quaint legal terminology that caught my eye together with the accompanying deadline, which by the time I was reading the paper had already expired. The notice had been inserted by the Cayman Water Company letting their customers know that 'all delinquent bills must be paid by 4.30 pm today to ensure continuance of service'.

As I've said the deadline had already expired on the same afternoon that the paper had been printed. Although I'm sure the posting of the notice is a legal requirement, I'm equally convinced that those individuals who had accumulated such delinquent bills are the least likely persons to bother to read the legal notices in any newspaper. It also made me wonder just how sad was I to be reading such a thing whilst on holiday. I should have brought my anorak with me.

I did, however, conjure up an image of this group of delinquents, whatever they may look like, turning on the water only to find their taps had run dry. I'm sure the Cayman Water Company was well prepared for the flood of calls informing them of the unexpected problems with water supply. I can imagine that they had a predetermined and stark response along the lines of an expectation of some cash up front before a normal service would be resumed. How many delinquents the advert was aimed at I do not know but instead of being tucked away in an Official Notices column it was on page three amongst some other adverts and underneath local news stories. Not the sort of item that one was likely to come across on page three of one of the tabloids back home.

Lunch was an unhurried affair taken on the balcony of our apartment. Jan and the girls had prepared a salad with ham, cheese or tuna together with some fresh bread from the supermarket for those who wanted it. This was to be followed by a variety of fresh fruit for those who wished to stick to a healthy diet. I wasn't particularly hungry but took my time over a plate of salad and ham and was tempted by a generous slice of the crusty bread. It wasn't intended to be a generous slice but the bread knife in the kitchen wasn't the sharpest I have ever used and my attempt at slicing the bread produced a number of uneven giant doorsteps. It didn't, however, stop them all being eaten.

The hungriest amongst us was, unsurprisingly, Caroline. It is fair to say that she managed double portions of almost everything on top of her earlier breakfast and the morning snacks of rum cake. How she can eat so much, yet remain so slim I do not know. We also managed to demolish a couple of bottles of wine and in fairness to Caroline I was the one who managed the double portions of vin blanc.

All the girls returned to their suntrap by the pool whilst Carl and I offered to tidy up and wash the dishes, which wasn't a particularly arduous task. We also managed to catch the last couple of holes in the third round of the British Open which we hadn't realised was on until we flicked through the television channels. The standard of play seemed appreciably better than our efforts earlier in the week but they didn't appear to be enjoying it as much as we had at Safehaven. There was a considerable difference in the scores though and we hadn't had the pressure of knowing that a missed putt might cost us tens of thousands of pounds. Having completed our chores and our channel hopping, with the remote control, which seems to be almost an exclusive male phenomenon, we both decided that lunchtime on the Sunday might just coincide with the conclusion of the Open. We would need to time lunch appropriately but with the girls lapping up the sun didn't anticipate any problems.

Having made our plans we left the girls at the hotel and went for a long walk along the beach, although for most of the time we walked and splashed in the shallow water. Not for the first time my West Indian sun hat received a number of admiring glances and on three occasions we were approached by different individuals wanting to know where they could buy it. Back home in England it is said that if you go out walking your dog it won't be long before it brings you into conversations with others. The Grand Cayman equivalent was to go walking with my sun hat. We ended up chatting to three different families who were spending the afternoon on the beach prior to having a sunset barbeque for their evening meal. We didn't have the nerve to warn them about the local Ant Army as we had no wish to spoil any expectations of their meal.

We walked past the Governor's residence and continued onto the embryonic Ritz Carlton which looked even more impressive from its perspective of sea-view and beachside apartments. This was to be a sprawling multi-storey complex and the tallest building on the island. We had heard the local rumour that Bill Gates, the Microsoft magnate, intended to buy a penthouse suite but this was unconfirmed. We speculated on which of the many balconied apartments he might select as we gazed up enviously at the concrete edifice. We both wondered what it looked like from the inside as we turned around and started to meander back towards our own much smaller and, we suspected, somewhat less expensive hotel. I was still very satisfied with the personal service and quality of accommodation that we were receiving from Indies Suites and didn't see the Ritz as being directly competitive. At that time I wasn't to know that I would get a much better insight into the Ritz Carlton the following day.

Our return trip along the beach was a very slow stroll and we were amazed to see a group of runners race past us and disappear into the distance. They appeared exceptionally fit and the heat didn't seem to bother them at all. I admired their athletic prowess but decided my morning jogs were much more sensible for somebody of my age and ability. It occurred to us later that they may have been the small but talented squad of the Cayman Islands Olympic Team on one of their pre-games training sessions.

Back at the hotel the girls continued to lap up the sun as I alternated between the Jacuzzi and the swimming pool before going back upstairs to shower and prepare for the evening meal. Meeting at the hotel bar for our regular pre-dinner cocktail, for the first and only time on the holiday we all arrived together. I wasn't sure whether it was me having dragged my heels in the swimming pool and taken my time in the bathroom or the girls, who once again looked eager for a night on the town, and had decided to surprise us by getting ready in record time. Their timekeeping was improving by the day and they were proving Carl and me wrong that they were capable of washing and dressing just as quickly as the rest of us if they really wanted to. Sipping the cocktail, and I hasten to add this was one of the hotel's non-alcoholic fruit cocktails as I was to be taxi driver for the night, I was willing to give the girls the benefit of the doubt and decided that it was their speed and not my tardiness as we left on time.

We made our way south along Seven Mile Highway towards Georgetown and our destination, Rackhams, which had views across the harbour and out to sea. Unfortunately we had not thought of phoning ahead and booking a table and the only one available was out on the patio. This would not normally have been a problem; indeed it would have been welcomed. However, as we sat down and made ourselves comfortable we felt the first few spots of rain and looking out across the water could see the beginnings of an electric storm brewing in the distance. The waitress arrived quickly with the menus and we ordered a round of pre-dinner drinks, which arrived just as promptly. We took our time scanning the menu whilst sipping our drinks. Looking out to sea we could see the storm moving closer and the lightning appeared quite spectacular as it forked down towards the water.

Our waitress arrived back at the table and asked if we wished to remain. She explained that there weren't any vacant tables inside the restaurant and we would have to remain outside. She was concerned that although we were under a canopy the oncoming storm would bring with it so much rain that we wouldn't be able to complete our meal without getting soaked. She was genuinely more interested in our comfort and welfare than just selling us a meal. We discussed our options and decided it would be both drier and safer to move to a different venue. Unfortunately, with only a couple of days of the holiday remaining, we never got the opportunity to return to Rackhams to sample what appeared a varied menu. By the time we climbed into our trusty team minibus it was obvious that we had made the right decision. The rain by now was teeming down and even the largest umbrella would not have saved us from a thorough soaking had we remained in our original position.

We headed back out of town towards Seven Mile Beach and the cover of the Outback Restaurant where we had eaten on night one of our sojourn in Grand Cayman.

The Outback has gained its reputation as a steakhouse but I selected an excellent salmon washed down with a glass of fine Australian dry white wine. This was more than sufficient to satisfy my appetite and I passed up the opportunity to sample such mouth-watering delights as Cheesecake Olivia, Cinnamon Oblivion or Sydney's Sinful Sundae although I was left wondering exactly what comprised the final offering. Amongst the other puddings on offer was one that appealed to the girl with the sweetest tooth in our party. In the absence of any Caymanian rum cake, Caroline selected the Chocolate Thunder From Down Under and although generous enough to offer each of us a portion, which we all declined, she managed to clear the dish with her customary aplomb. What an appetite!

We had to dash across the car park to avoid being drenched as the storm was now well and truly over the island with rain lashing down and bouncing back up from the pavements and roadways so that it took only a matter of seconds to be soaked to the skin. Consequently the atmosphere in the minibus was decidedly steamy on the short trip back to Indies Suites. For once I needed to switch on the air-conditioning to demist the windows and not just cool down the interior of the bus. All feeling a little damp we decided, for a change, not to retire to the bar but climbed the stairs to our rooms for a relatively early night. Standing on the balcony, before hitting the sack, the storm was raging and the sky was being lit almost as spectacularly as the firework display we had witnessed a few nights earlier. Within seconds of my head hitting the pillow I was totally unconscious and oblivious to the thunder and lightning above. Isn't it amazing how tired one can become doing absolutely nothing whilst lazing in the sunshine?

Although I had, once again, set the alarm for eight o'clock I was wide awake and found myself fully kitted up on the balcony, limbering up with stretching exercises and it wasn't yet ten past seven. There wasn't a peep from the other bedroom and the next door suite was a haven of silence. I knew that wouldn't last so wisely decided against waking all the girls and left them to their slumbers.

Time for a gentle massage with a small amount of the diminishing suntan cream before collecting the bottle of iced water and setting off for Seven Mile Beach.

At long last the lazy days of the holiday and my early morning runs were to pay dividends. I started at my usual gentle pace but was feeling so good that by the time I reached the fire station I was fairly galloping along. Okay, I exaggerate but for me it was one of those days that do come along from time to time, where my breathing was easy and running seemed effortless. Although it was hot perhaps the storm of the night before had cleared the air and somehow it didn't seem as humid as usual. I didn't need to sip the water until close to the halfway stage but was well aware of how important it is to take liquid on board before you really need it. I didn't even need to slow to walking pace to finish the bottle, although some splashed onto my vest, as I was having one of those runs where you don't want to stop. The morning's run was uneventful, with one notable exception. And what an exception!

On the return lap I actually overtook two other runners and I'm not sure who was more amazed, them or me.

They looked to be a father and son out for a gentle run before breakfast and I don't know how far they had run before I came across them but they both appeared younger and fitter then me. Well, if not fitter then certainly slimmer. Not difficult. Fortunately, I was in my last half-mile before turning left into the drive down to the hotel so was deliberately pushing myself to see just how quickly I could complete the daily run. I went past them with a polite, if gasping, "Good morning" as by now my lungs were approaching bursting point but the end was in sight. I think they were equally polite with their response but my puffing and panting drowned out exactly what they did say. Somehow I managed to keep up my own reasonable pace until the last few yards before the hotel entrance when I did gradually slow down to a walking pace to cool off and get my breath back. It was my fastest run of the holiday and I have to admit I was feeling quite pleased with myself as I got rid of my trainers and threw off my running vest before diving into the swimming pool to gently relax. Well, that's not strictly accurate. I slid into the pool still regaining my breath before slowly swimming a couple of very lethargic lengths to be followed by a lazy ten minutes of trying to float on the surface, at which I was now becoming gradually proficient.

Returning to the room for a shower and my daily kit-washing routine the girls were still not awake. However, I obviously don't shower quietly because by the time I emerged they were both up and sitting on the balcony and wondering out loudly why it is that men make so much noise in the bathroom. I can't recollect my exact response but am sure it was along the lines of men being fortunate to find the room vacant as once a woman enters that inner sanctum she remains for the duration so the poor man has to make the most of any opportunity that comes his way. In any event whilst I can shave and wash my running kit quietly I cannot control the noise from a power shower as the jets hit the tiles. The good-humoured banter continued for a while until the noises from the suite next door indicated that we were all now wide awake, well in our neighbours' case at least they were out of bed. Caroline and Danielle appeared on their balcony and we were all soon trooping downstairs for a relaxing Sunday morning breakfast.

There were three or four new faces at the breakfast tables, all of whom had flown in from America for a week's diving in the local waters. We all exchanged pleasantries and munched our way through a quiet breakfast. The only thing that the new guests seemed to have in common with the recently departed Dick was a love of diving. If we hadn't seen them we would not have known they were there. Perhaps we had experienced both the noisiest and quietest set of divers from America all in the same fortnight. The new arrivals were somewhat younger than Dick and his pals, extremely polite, in fact almost shy, but once we started chatting and became acquainted they were very interested in where we lived in England and how close we lived to London. Without exception all of them wanted to visit the capital and quizzed us about the best places to stay and which landmarks were worth a visit. Whilst I'm sure we were reasonably helpful in relation to the latter selecting somewhere to stay in London can be far more difficult as there can be so many variables. For instance, budget can be a factor and can range from plush and expensive to cheap and cheerful. Location can also influence the price so it really requires a bit of research to find a hotel that suits both the type of holiday you want and also the depth of your pockets. We left our new friends with plenty of food for thought and wished them a good day's diving.

We had all decided to spend another lazy morning around the pool as realisation dawned that our idyll in the Cayman Islands was drawing to a close.

I returned to our room to change into my swimming trunks and pick up my book. As I selected an as yet unused top hanging in the wardrobe I spied my suitcase standing upended in the corner where I had placed it on day one and forgotten about it until now. For a brief moment I pondered whether it was worth considering starting to pack my case. The thought didn't last for very long, as I would have ample time on Tuesday. However, I was well aware that on this occasion I didn't have Lesley there to assist me, or even do it for me. Bearing in mind it was bursting at the seams on the outward leg I did wonder if I would manage to pack everything back in. Everybody else had already made their way poolside so I left the case perched comfortably in the corner of the wardrobe for at least another twenty-four hours, before it would need to complete its relaxing fortnight in darkness and start to stretch itself until it was, once again, bursting at the seams. If suitcases were able to communicate with each other then mine and Caroline's would be bemoaning their misfortune, through the partitioned wall, at both being lumbered with 'Heavy' luggage labelled travellers whilst their Australian cousins were able to live a much smaller, slimmer and fitter lifestyle.

I still managed to find time for what by now had become a very light protective coating of suntan cream before I joined the bronzed Baywatch Beauties and Carl who were lapping up the sun. Whilst I'm not sure that it was possible it seemed even hotter than usual and as I took up my position on the sun-lounger there wasn't one speck of cloud in the bright blue sky.

The morning passed both quickly and, for once, quietly. It was a simple mix of sunbathing, reading, snoozing and dipping into the water to cool off. Everybody seemed to be taking this opportunity to catch up on some sleep but only Jan, Carl and myself were taking the precaution of doing so in the shade. As was the norm the girls continued to ensure that they would return home with golden tans that would be the envy of their pale colleagues in their various offices back in London and East Anglia.

As the morning wore on and lunchtime approached Carl and I magnanimously offered to go and prepare lunch. This gesture on our part did bring forth one or two quizzical glances, particularly from Fran in Carl's direction, and the not entirely unexpected request from Caroline to make sure that we included her favourite rum cake on the pudding menu. We made our way upstairs but were joined by Jan who decided that it would be wiser if she was on hand to guide our culinary efforts. Despite our assurances that we could hardly ruin a salad she accompanied us to the kitchen and promptly took charge, persuading us that she was somewhat more used to preparing lunch than us two guys. However willing we might have appeared she obviously didn't require the assistance of a couple of reluctant sous-chefs, which left us with little alternative other than to catch up on the final round of the British Open Golf Championship. Although we took it in turns to wander from the screen into the kitchen and offer to help she did at least allow us to set the table on the balcony, which removed any feelings of guilt that we might have harboured. Those didn't last long as the Open approached its climax. Both of us would have to plead guilty to the fact that until that moment neither of us had ever heard of this fellow called Todd Hamilton who was about to win his first major championship.

Whilst the girls joined Jan on the balcony for lunch Carl and I took our trays back into the lounge to watch the final few holes. I think the girls felt slightly miffed that we weren't joining them for lunch as we preferred to be watching television. Whilst daytime television is neither Carl's nor my cup of tea the climax of the British Open is different and was a magnet that we could not resist. The girls just couldn't comprehend we two sports junkies but that was perhaps understandable as, other than Jan, none of them had yet been married. They have a lot to learn when they do marry, particularly if the lucky guys are sports fanatics.

Carl and I meanwhile became engrossed in the golf. How is it that the professional golfer can make the most difficult shots look so simple? Annoyingly they also manage to make it appear almost effortless. As lunch finished it coincided with the conclusion of the final round of the one hundred and thirty-third British Open from Royal Troon in Ayrshire, on the west coast of Scotland. Two players were locked together and were to go head to head in a four hole play-off: the South African Ernie Els, three times winner of the Open, against the previously unheralded American, thirty-eight-year-old Todd Hamilton. Els had narrowly missed becoming outright champion by misreading a twelve-footer on the eighteenth green and was now thrust into the play off against Hamilton who a year previously didn't even have a Professional Golfer's Association tour card.

Jan and the girls were, of course, totally disinterested in all this and couldn't understand why Carl and I were still glued to the box. I'm sure if Diane had still been around she would have explained our childlike golf-addicted enthusiasm and excitement. They were anxious to go down to the beach but Carl and I were in no hurry. We both quickly agreed that they should take the crewbus and we would join them at Governor's Beach once we had seen the conclusion of the golf. There was a slight delay as Caroline had to finish her lunchtime ration of rum cake before they all disappeared and left the two of us on our own to enjoy watching the four hole play off and we were not disappointed.

The first hole was also the first on the course and both golfers hit par fours. Hole two replicated the first with again two par fours. The third play off hole was number seventeen on the course, a par three. Hamilton gained an advantage with a par whilst Els dropped a shot. The fourth and final hole was the eighteenth and Hamilton lined up to take what was about to become the most important tee shot of his career. He hit an iron to the right of and off the fairway, in much the same way that a club handicapper might, and landed where the thousands of spectators were walking. Fortunately he was allowed a free drop. Els also used an iron and placed it on the right of the fairway. Hamilton then selected a five iron from about two hundred and twenty yards to the hole and left it considerably short of the green. Els meanwhile rifled his approach shot about twelve feet below the hole. Hamilton then somehow manufactured an approach onto the green using a fairway wood as a sort of putter and placed the ball just two feet from the hole. What a recovery. The pressure was back on Els who missed his putt, which allowed Hamilton to tap in to become the 2004 champion.

Carl and I had missed an hour on the beach but we both felt it was worth it although we also accepted that the girls would never understand why. Having had our fill of British sport, albeit provided by an American and South African, we made our way to the beach where we played a number of imaginary bunker shots in the fine grained sand. This was very different to the sticky sodden sand in a bunker at Three Rivers on a wet winter's day. Having perfected our bunker shots (in our dreams) we gradually made our way south, splashing through the shallow water as we went.

We found Jan and the girls on Governor's Beach. Well, we found their towels and bags – the girls themselves were all in the water, and Carl and I swiftly joined them, having worked up a reasonable sweat on the walk from the hotel. The water itself was even warmer than the hotel swimming pool but I found it more comfortable than lying on the sand with the sun beating down, and unless you could get up close against the Governor's boundary fence there was very little shade to protect you from the sun's rays. This didn't bother the girls who by now were all lying back on their towels and, within minutes of leaving the water, were totally dry.

It wasn't long before I was the only one left in the water but I was happy paddling and floating around until I eventually decided to come out and join the group on the silver sand.

Time for my afternoon replenishment of suntan lotion and I was happy that my final tube would just about last me for one further day before we were to be heading back to the cooler climes of the good old UK.

By the time I had dried off, which didn't take long, and slipped on my beach shirt and sun hat both Danielle and Fran decided that they wanted to go and explore further along the beach and I was more than happy to join them. We wandered for some time before Dani decided that she had walked enough for one day and made her way back to the group. Fran and I continued in the general direction of Georgetown before we also eventually decided we would turn and make our way back. Our return was even slower whilst we took in the sights and as we approached the Ritz Carlton we realised that their reception area for prospective owners and guests was open. Both being of an inquisitive disposition we poked our heads around the door and tried to appear genuinely interested, which we accepted was somewhat unfair, but we are both nosy by nature. Anyway I'm sure there are many others who turned up for a viewing who also weren't in the slightest bit interested in buying a condo and if they were in a similar situation to ourselves were unlikely to be able to afford one.

Over the next hour or so I saw a side to Fran that I hadn't previously experienced. Early on in the holiday I had marked her out as the quiet one of the party. Petite and demure, she seemed the sort who might melt into the background in any large group and be happy to remain on the periphery of any activity. How wrong can one be?

I suppose the first glimpse of my exceedingly poor judgment of the female form of humanity came during the wedding reception when she took to the dance floor and whilst centre-stage demonstrated dance steps that I would not dare attempt, culminating in the splits whilst sliding the length and breadth of the dance floor. This was the initial manifestation of the extrovert nature of young Fran. I really didn't take too much notice of this as we had all consumed our share of celebratory drink and we all find it far too easy to let our hair down in such circumstances. I wouldn't have given it a second thought had it not been for her contribution to the community singing on our battle bus when she attacked every tune with gusto, even if she didn't know the words. She was determined to be the lead singer in the group and set about learning the words of a well-known rugby song so that she would be the soloist, and not just one of the chorus, within our own holiday version of the Three Degrees. She never did quite succeed in that particular venture. The one other facet of her character that came to the fore whenever we played any sort of game was the competitive nature that she displayed in trying to win whatever was at stake. I accept that I'm competitive and it's a streak that doesn't always bring out the best in me, as I'm often reminded by Lesley. I knew from our battle on the golf course that Carl was also competitive and we both played hard but fair in our efforts to win. However, compared with Fran we were mere novices and could not possibly match her desire to be a winner at everything. To watch her play Twister so that she ties others in knots ensuring that they fall over whilst she somehow manages to retain her equilibrium on just one hand or foot defies any rational explanation let alone the law of gravity. When this fails she is not averse to giving opponents a crafty nudge with a sharp elbow ensuring that they lose their balance and topple over leaving our Fran the last man standing. So, having already had to revise my initial opinion of this little firebrand I was about to experience yet another side to her that ten days earlier I would not have dreamed possible. I was about to learn that I would need to treat her with both care and respect for the remainder of the holiday, well, all two days of it.

The charming young salesman ushered us into the reception area of the Ritz Carlton and lost no time in informing us that eighty percent of the residential apartments were already taken and if we were interested we shouldn't lose any time in making our decision to buy, otherwise we might not get exactly what we wanted. He had a typical salesman's line in patter that would obviously appeal to those who were tempted to purchase their own small part of the hotel complex. He was smart and presentable but perhaps a little naïve and impressionable. At least he appeared to be impressed with Fran and she wasn't about to disillusion or disappoint him.

Now, whilst we never actually said that we were there as potential purchasers, we also didn't indicate that we weren't. We merely played along and I suppose were a little bit naughty in letting him think that we were interested in the different types of apartment that he had to offer. Although I remained non-committal Fran did appear to be much more enthusiastic than me. Now we will never know exactly what sort of relationship he thought I had with Fran. Bearing in mind the age gap is in excess of thirty years and her hair is jet black contrasting beautifully against a very smooth complexion whilst my hair has progressed to the silvery grey receding stage and my features are now nicely wrinkled, he seemed to think I was some sort of rich sugar daddy. I did say he was naïve. Young Fran played along with this charade with some aplomb and it wasn't long before we were being shown plans of the sort of apartments on offer together with scale models of the proposed finished complex and all its facilities. Very impressive it was too! Fran's acting was equally impressive.

In addition to the hotel accommodation the Ritz Carlton offered nearly seventy residences commanding panoramic views of the curving shoreline of Seven Mile Beach and its endless golden sands. These ocean front apartments ranged between two and four bedrooms and we were informed that the prices ranged from $2.9 million at the lower end of the market peaking at $25 million for a top-notch suite. Once again it was emphasised that if we wished to reserve one then we needed to act quickly, but this is all a normal part of a salesman's pitch in an effort to sell, meet his targets and gain a commission. Fran seemed to be enjoying her role and was even beginning to ask questions about the appliances that came with each apartment. I didn't have the heart to ask if the dollar price was the Cayman Islands or United States dollar as the actual denomination wouldn't have made a jot of difference because I couldn't even dream of buying one of their cheaper properties, short of winning a rollover lottery. Fortunately there weren't any other customers, genuine or otherwise, to occupy the salesman so I didn't feel particularly guilty about wasting his time and he seemed happy enough to have some potential clients to talk to and practise his sales spiel.

My partner in crime certainly didn't and was now playing her part so well that if I hadn't known better even I might have been persuaded that she really was interested in moving to paradise. She even engaged the poor chap in a lengthy conversation about the Wreck of the Ten Sails, a subject where she had certainly done her homework and was the acknowledged expert within our little holiday group. It quickly became apparent that her knowledge of the subject was far greater than his, which she used to her advantage in making him feel that he should have known more about the history of his homeland. It was almost as if she was using the story to endorse her credentials as a potential purchaser and it was certainly having the desired effect. What a wicked young lady!

Having satisfied herself that the kitchen equipment and fittings could be individually designed and arranged to meet her particular culinary needs she went even further and enquired about the possibility of selecting her own colour schemes. Not unexpectedly this would not prove to be a problem as she could be involved from the early design and decoration stage. She would be able to take and compare samples of different work surfaces and tiles to ensure they matched and were in keeping with her style and taste. She was even more interested to learn that if she were feeling a tad exhausted from her new lifestyle, and didn't feel up to cooking the evening meal, then there was a talented Dial-A-Chef facility on call should it be required. Somehow I just didn't see myself as ever being likely to be able to avail myself of such an opportunity. On reflection I am, perhaps, being unfair. I do have such a skill readily available and she was at home. My wife Lesley happens to be a very good cook who is never afraid to try experimental dishes that always turn out exceptionally well. (Call me a crawler if you like but I know where my bread's buttered and have no wish to permanently cook for myself in the future.)

Fran, who now obviously had visions of Jamie Oliver or Delia Smith's home-cooked meals was now prompted to ask exactly what other facilities were available on site should we decide to select one of these particular apartments.

I turned to give her a meaningful look and received a kick on my left ankle for my trouble. From his position at the other side of the table our salesman was unable to see this exchange but did glance quizzically at me as I let out a slight 'ouch' and then tried to turn it into a cough and pretend that I had a frog in my throat. I don't think I was particularly convincing but having been egged on by Fran, who I'm sure would make a good actress without the need to attend any sort of drama school, our budding estate agent wasn't going to let us escape without giving us a complete run down on what we could expect from our investment.

When complete, the entire complex will stretch for one hundred and forty-four acres across the whole width of the western arm of the island from Seven Mile Beach to North Sound.

One wing of the hotel and the residential apartments was situated at the western edge between the beach and West Bay Road and was connected to the remainder of the complex by a pedestrian bridge across the highway. We had already passed under this many times on our trips back and forth into Georgetown and the airport. The residential services included a pre-arrival butler, dedicated concierge, doormen and porters, private entrances and a twenty-four-hour valet parking service in addition to the Chef on tap which Fran indicated was particularly appealing. I made a mental note to let Carl and the girls know of how her expectations had reached new heights and wondered if East Anglia might ever be able to match them. By this stage I couldn't look Fran in the face because if I made eye contact I knew I would start roaring with laughter and I had no wish to be kicked on the other leg, or anywhere else for that matter.

Our friendly salesman by now was directing all of his interest at Fran in the same way that a car salesman concentrates on selling to the wife and not the husband and consequently directs his interest to the colour of the bodywork which is much more important than any of the mechanical, technical or safety aspects. She had meanwhile, in her mind's eye, already crossed the road and was into the remainder of the hotel with its ballroom and fine dining restaurants.

I wasn't particularly interested in the spa, tennis centre or even Jean-Michel Cousteau's Ambassadors of the Environment for the Ritz Kids although I thought the concept to be a brilliant way to occupy the children whilst their parents were off diving or sampling the shopping malls. Jean-Michel is the son of the famous marine ecologist Jacques Cousteau and his idea to provide a fun filled adventure experience for kids with an opportunity to discover the ocean and our responsibilities to protect that environment offers an excellent 'hands on' experience where they would learn far more than sitting behind a school desk and reading a book. I do have to admit, however, that my ears did prick up at the mention of a golf course to be designed and developed by the legendary Greg Norman. This was to be established around the inland waterways and inlets and incorporated the Phase Two villa development and marina. The plan of the course looked particularly impressive but as we had found on the two other courses that we had visited it also appeared to be full of traps for the careless or wayward golfer and I fitted comfortably into that category. Not unexpectedly, a fair proportion of the holes found you deliberately hitting over water hazards with a number of other fairways skirting the water's edge. Nonetheless I decided that it was an experience I would look forward should I return to Grand Cayman to try and pit my wits against the design of one of the world's best golfers. I could, at least, see three holes on the plan where I was fairly confident that my balls would remain on dry land: if you get my drift.

This apparent upsurge in interest on my part now seemed to both excite and confuse our new found friend, the salesman. Until the mention of the golf course I had tried to remain casually indifferent to his exhortations, leaving all of the running to my overly enthusiastic partner who he had recognised as the customer that needed to be won over. Now, he was no longer certain if his tactic of wooing the little lady was likely to be as successful as he first thought and consequently started to switch his attention to me. Fortunately his knowledge and appreciation of the finer points of golf were even less than his interest in the Wreck of the Ten Sails so that when I asked him what his handicap was I was met with a bemused gaze that was to conclude our conversation about Greg Norman and his golf course. From my perspective, even as a non-prospective purchaser, his particular handicap was his disinterest in and total lack of knowledge of golf. This would be unlikely to assist him with a genuine buyer who was attracted to the complex by the ready availability of a golf course.

He returned his attention to Fran with whom he obviously felt far more comfortable and started to return to some of the detail of the suites available allied to the dining and leisure facilities within the hotel and all of this situated on the beautiful Seven Mile Beach. He repeated how important it was to make an early decision as the apartments were fast disappearing at their present prices. This at last seemed to bring Fran back to the real world as she turned away from him to face me asking me what I thought and at the same time winking and motioning toward the door. All I now had to do was make our excuses and leave with a minimum amount of embarrassment. I truthfully told him that as much as I would love the penthouse at twenty five million it was some way beyond our means. I didn't go into the detail of just how far beyond our means and I made an effort to appear suitably disappointed whilst casting a meaningful glare at Fran.

Then, not wanting to make him feel that he had totally wasted his time on a couple of nosey Brits who never had any intention, or even vague possibility, of buying an apartment, I was actually dishonest for the first time by telling him that we were running out of time, as we needed to leave to rejoin some friends. I was still trying to be truthful at that stage but then went on to say that we wished to have some time to consider all of our options and it might be more appropriate to wait until Phase Two of the development is commenced before we came to any firm decision. We both knew that we could wait until Phase One Hundred and Two if we wished; it wouldn't make an iota of difference to our chances of owning and living in an apartment at the Ritz Carlton, with or without the provision of the Dial-a-Chef service.

In fairness he didn't seem particularly disappointed, as I'm sure he was used to many people making a variety of excuses before they took their leave. In our case we had probably taken leave of our senses about an hour earlier and I merely wanted to regain at least a modicum of sanity before the end of the holiday. With Fran in tow, and displaying a penchant for acting that a week earlier I would not have believed possible, that was always going to be difficult to achieve. Whilst, prior to the holiday, I would never have described her as shy I equally could not have imagined the extrovert who earlier in the week wanted to learn the words of a rugby song and now wanted to lead me into mischief at the partly constructed Ritz Carlton. They do say that you see a person's real character when you go on holiday with them. How true.

As we edged our way towards the door another couple were entering and our salesman friend started his sales pitch immediately as if we had suddenly become invisible and had never existed. I hope he had more luck with them than he did with us.

We ran back along the beach to join the others, not because we wanted to run but Fran could sense what I was going to do if I managed to catch up with her. She collapsed into a laughing giggling heap as she leapt onto the others, using them as a human shield to prevent me from grabbing hold of her and dragging her into the water. By the time she had finished telling them of our little adventure at the Ritz the whole group were convulsed in laughter so that passers-by were all looking on but couldn't see what on earth we all found so funny. For her Sunday afternoon performance Fran won my nomination for an Oscar as the best actress of the holiday. It was a close-run thing as young Caroline was a far more consistent and extrovert performer but Fran's matinee cameo was truly memorable and exceptional. I had never been on a holiday quite like this before.

Our trip back to Indies Suites was uneventful as was the nightly ritual of showers, changing into smart casual evening wear, and being tempted by pre-dinner cocktails at the poolside bar.

The Sunday night was going to be a quiet informal meal at a nearby eatery where we could relax before what was to be our final full day on Grand Cayman. We made our way to the Canton Chinese restaurant where we were joined by Ray, wearing a very natty disco-type outfit with a grandiose belt around his waist that had a huge golden clasp as the centrepiece that couldn't fail to attract attention, together with Huggy Junior and Cynthia, for our evening meal. Ordering a wide variety of differing dishes from the menu these were placed on the revolving Party Suzanne in the centre of our circular table so that we were able to take our time over selecting whatever took our fancy. Not surprisingly the portions were enormous and for once they even exceeded Caroline's appetite. This was to be our only experience of testing the local island oriental cuisine and, not surprisingly, it didn't disappoint. The food was well prepared, the service friendly and efficient and we were able to take our time and chat over the holiday to date.

Having already been witness to Ray's flair and nifty footwork on the dance floor we now experienced his ability at storytelling as we took our time and practised our chopstick skills over dinner. He kept us entertained and amused for the duration. Whilst Fran repeated the story of our afternoon escapade mulling over the benefits of living in a beachside apartment at the Ritz and more than once exaggerated my embarrassment and discomfort in trying to control her, Ray had a multitude of tales from both his early seafaring days and then onto his later commercial exploits in New York. Young Huggy listened with eyes wide open and in obvious awe of someone who had been involved in so many adventures. Whilst we certainly enjoyed his storytelling the remainder of us continued our meal and listened with a large pinch of salt for flavouring. Young Huggy would find Enid Blyton positively boring compared to Ray's stories.

I'm sure if he had been at sea a couple of centuries earlier his many scrapes with potential disaster could have made him a greater legend than the pirates that we now read about and watch at the cinema. Quite what he meant as his ocean travelling had him 'bunkering in every port' he left to our imagination. I must admit that whilst he regaled us with his numerous voyages of adventure he reminded me of an erstwhile Uncle Albert of *Only Fools and Horses* fame who used to eruditely navigate his many naval tales from port to port to the equally disbelieving Del Boy and Rodney. I'm sure I do Ray an injustice with my analogy of a Caribbean-style Uncle Albert as he bears no resemblance to the white-whiskered old rascal at all. Ray's stories were also unscripted and I'm certain Uncle Albert's ability as a waltzing. jiving, prancing, swirling master of the dance floor wasn't a patch on our Ray once he led his partner onto the floor.

Ray saved his best tale until last and this involved him in his days when he was running a store in New York. This was after he left the Merchant Navy and before he returned to work back on Grand Cayman.

One dark night as he was about to shut up shop he was attacked by a bunch of armed robbers with whom he fought a lone and frenzied battle and saw them off one by one before the arrival of the New York Police Department to mop up what was left of them, which from Ray's description was merely some injured and bloodied bits and pieces left lying on the sidewalk awaiting hospitalisation. Clint Eastwood, eat your heart out. Now, this was Ray's story, not mine, and whilst I would have to admit to a little journalistic licence as I have, to the best of my memory, relayed the story of the past two weeks I just cannot compete with 'Shake what your Mama gave you baby' Ray.

He was a master at the art of storytelling, and if he were ever to write a book I'm sure it would be a bestseller. However, I do think he was slightly wrong-footed by Caroline when she asked him if his belt was genuine gold. By this time we had consumed the odd bottle or four of wine and Caroline had lost her inhibitions. That is not strictly accurate as I have difficulty in recollecting when Caroline displayed any inhibitions. Ray, meanwhile, was being uncharacteristically coy which only increased Caroline's curiosity, who continued to quiz him about the authenticity of his elaborate waistband. He was unsuccessfully trying to change the subject but Caroline would have none of it. By this time I was being nudged under the table by Dani with whom I knew I had to avoid eye contact otherwise we would both have collapsed into fits of laughter and been suitably embarrassed unless we could quickly invent a plausible explanation. This was the second time this had happened to me in a matter of hours and, although it had taken them the best part of a fortnight, the girls had obviously identified a weak spot of mine and were determined to take advantage. Fortunately they were just as prone to fits of laughter as me. By now Jan had realised that Dani was about to crack up into a fit of the giggles and as she caught my eye realised I was going to disintegrate in a similar fashion. Luckily Ray and Caroline were oblivious to our plight as they continued their verbal joust.

Jan, as usual, saved the day by asking everybody what they all wanted to do on the last day of the holiday. I still couldn't look at Dani and excused myself as I went to the gentlemen's lavatory where for once I didn't actually need to go. I spent the time washing hands, combing hair and composing myself.

By the time I returned, with a deadpan face, Carrie, our ever-reliable banker and keeper of the petty cash, was paying the bill. Our hosts were a little concerned, as, most unusually for us, we had left a considerable share of the food. Jan explained that we were just full up and had not appreciated how large the portions were going to be. This prompted the offer of 'doggie bags' to take away our leftovers which we politely declined as we had more than enough food left in our refrigerators to last us another week let alone one day.

We said our goodnights to Ray, Cynthia and Jose (Huggy Junior) in the car park and within ten minutes were back at the hotel. For once the bar was empty so we decided that an early night was a good idea as we wanted to cram as much as possible into our final day. Not wanting to miss my last opportunity for an early morning run I set the alarm for seven o'clock and was soon sleeping soundly no longer even noticing the gentle hum of the air-conditioning in the background.

CHAPTER 15

Cocktails at the Treehouse

was up bright and early before the alarm clock went off and kitted up on the balcony ready for a light coating of sun cream on my face, head and shoulders. I was confident that by rolling up this tube, just as you do toothpaste, it would last for the next twenty-four hours, without the need for replenishments. I completed my stretching exercises with Indie looking up at me from the shade of her shrubbery before she lost interest and went in search of her breakfast bowl of milk. She wouldn't get another opportunity to see such a sight at that time of the morning.

I hadn't been able to persuade the girls to join me for the final morning run so for the last time I set off with the sun on my back and the glistening bright blue water of the Caribbean lapping the sandy beach to my left and I found my mind started to wander. I was recollecting some of the many features of the island that I had experienced over the past fortnight as I said my final "good mornings" to the passing cyclists and runners heading in towards Georgetown, all of whom had become friendly nodding acquaintances over the past two weeks.

I was making good progress and as my mind drifted from one event to another it eventually came to the inevitable and necessary task of packing for the journey home. This in turn brought me back down

319

to earth as I suddenly had this vision in my mind's eye of me running along the highways and byways, back home in the Essex countryside, later in the week. However attractive the banks of the River Crouch and its creeks and inlets might be on a glorious summer's day somehow they weren't going to be able to compete with West Bay and Seven Mile Beach at seven o'clock in the morning. The chances of the commuters of South Essex ever seeing me running at that time of the morning were non-existent in any event.

I had finished my bottle of iced water by the halfway turn and as expected slowed down for the return leg, although, for me, I was still running at a reasonable rate. Well, at least I thought so until a long-legged woman wearing a pair of the most lurid purple shorts I had ever seen overtook me with ease. She raced past me as if I was stationary and with every lengthening pace increased the gap between us. I couldn't believe anybody could run that quickly in that heat. I wouldn't have minded if it had been Paula Radcliffe but it wasn't. Anyway I'm sure Paula wouldn't have worn such a pair of shorts, even on a training run.

I continued at my own steady, if slow, pace and was delighted and amazed that having turned past Cemetery Corner for the last time I could see that in the distance the Purple Vision had slowed to a walking pace whilst she was taking on liquid. The worst side of my character suddenly took over and that devil of a competitive urge started to come to the fore yet again. For the one and only time on the second half of my regular holiday run I managed to quicken my pace and as this was to be my final run I stretched myself until my lungs were bursting. Unbelievably in less than sixty seconds I was gliding past the Purple Flash. I was actually puffing and panting past her, but past her I did go. I resisted the temptation to let out a squeal of delight if for no other reason than that with my heavy breathing the best I could have managed would have been a distorted grunt of satisfaction. Anyway it would have appeared most discourteous as she had smiled sweetly and said "Hi" as she left me standing just a few minutes earlier. I couldn't even have managed a gasped "Hi", and the smiling sweetly concept whilst I'm running has never been an attribute that I've been blessed with. The best I could manage was a strangled grimace. Now my mind was focused on the running, as I was determined she would not overtake me for a second time. No time now to daydream about the holiday or anything else for that matter.

I was gritting my teeth, head down, arms pumping and going as fast as my short fat hairy legs would carry me as I struggled to get to my turn-off to the hotel before she caught me. I allowed myself the luxury of a swift glance behind and I had managed to open up a reasonable distance whilst she had been drinking, although I could just glimpse that she had started running again. I only had about a quarter of a mile to go and was determined not to be beaten. I was sucking in air and the sweat was now dripping off me and stinging my eyes.

A final lung-bursting effort had me turning left into Fosters Drive just as she went past me for the second time. She was still smiling sweetly as she exhorted me to "Keep going" whilst she continued what appeared to be her effortless run past the Holiday Inn and on along Seven Mile Beach.

Unfortunately I was in no state to respond and must have given her the impression of being an overweight, elderly, unfriendly and rather rude runner. Whilst the first part is accurate I'm not normally unfriendly or rude to fellow runners, however good they are compared to my more prosaic pace. On that particular morning I didn't have any choice as I was by then gasping for breath and in no state to say even one word. Whilst in one way I was pleased with my final run as my stop watch indicated it was my fastest of the holiday I was also thinking why do I put myself through such agony when it's not necessary. That was the toughest run that I could remember for a long time and I could have continued at my normal pace and felt much better for it. I entered the hotel entrance at a very sedate jog and wasn't in the slightest bit bothered who saw me going so slowly. Why was it when I had promised myself earlier in the holiday that I wouldn't enter into any imaginary race with other runners I had managed to do so at any opportunity? That sort of promise stands as much chance of being kept as my annual New Year's resolution to go on a diet, which is broken with monotonous regularity by the 5th January every year, and that's in a good year. What is it that I have in my psyche that makes me want to compete even when I know that I am likely to come in a poor second? Perhaps it's been something to do with supporting Chelsea for the past fifty years, although in their case the last four or five years have really seen their fortunes change. Whatever the reason I suspect I'm now too old to change my ways, so for any of those other runners who see me jogging around the roads and lanes of Essex don't laugh too much when you overtake me. I'm not being rude when I ignore you; it's just me being me.

Whilst the Purple Ghost had now disappeared and was racing away towards Georgetown I was trudging my weary legs towards the ice machine at the far end of the hotel. I only wanted a bottle of water and then to plunge into the swimming pool.

My plunge into the pool was no more than a flop as the best I could do was a little more than a couple of lengths before just lying there and relaxing in the warm water, although I was pleasantly surprised at how quickly I recovered. My morning runs had obviously been doing me some good.

Back upstairs Jan, who is an early bird, was up and sitting on the balcony reading her book. Carrie was still in bed as I set about washing my running gear for the final time. Although I tried to do this as quietly as possible it wasn't long before Carrie joined me in the kitchen and she assured me that I hadn't woken her, although I'm not so sure. There wasn't any noise from the two sleeping beauties next door so having left my kit on the balcony the three of us left together for breakfast. We knew by the time we returned it would be dry and ready for packing.

No sooner had I started on my second orange juice than we were joined by Caroline and Danielle who started complaining about a noisy neighbour who kept waking them each morning as he hung his washing out to dry. This time I did manage to smile sweetly, as I tucked into a fresh croissant, and told them that they would miss me later in the week when they would have to rely on a more conventional alarm clock to wake them for work. For two young lassies from the genteel and rural county of Suffolk their reply was most unladylike.

We took our time over breakfast whilst waiting for Carl and Fran to join us. A couple of families had arrived to replace Dick and his chums but I would estimate that the hotel was no more than half full. Jan reminded me that this was not their high season and was one of the reasons why Carrie had been able to get us such a good deal.

Jan, Carrie and I opted for a final trip into Georgetown whilst the others decided to spend a lazy morning by the pool adding that final sheen to their already bronzed torsos. Before we left Caroline carried out an inventory check on the number of rum cakes remaining in the refrigerator and placed an order for another four which would allow her enough capacity to meet her rum cake dietary needs for the next twenty-four hours but also provide sufficient supplies for the journey home and holiday presents for friends and family. I'm not sure if she had considered the potential excess baggage charge at that stage but she didn't appear unduly concerned as her wardrobe was already going to attract the 'Heavy' label, with or without any additional presents, rum cake or otherwise.

I needed to call at a bank to change my final couple of travellers cheques so that I had enough cash to put my final share into the kitty that, after last night, was down to a last few dollars. I also needed enough to pay my contribution towards the hire of the minibus that was due to be returned tomorrow morning. Carrie had reminded us that we still needed to arrange that with the hire company, and we decided to call in and see them on the way back from Georgetown to arrange delivery and final payment.

By the time we were heading along West Bay Road traffic was minimal and although there were plenty of pedestrians in town the major-ity were from a couple of enormous cruise liners moored in the bay, so we quickly found a parking space close to the bank.

Our second and final experience at the Cayman National Bank mirrored our initial visit, albeit this was a different branch. The bank cashiers are not the speediest that I've ever come across but all three of us found them charming, polite and courteous. For them the customer mattered and they went out of their way to ensure that you left the bank satisfied with the service you had received. If you are somebody who is happy with the impersonal hole in the wall machine that might or might not eat your piece of rectangular plastic if you make an involuntary error with your PIN number, then you shouldn't bother to enter one of the banks on Grand Cayman. If, however, you have any other sort of transaction or require a service where you need, or would appreciate, a human being who is willing and able to respond to your needs then make sure that you allow yourself an extra five minutes and I'm sure you won't be disappointed.

I left, having cashed up my remaining travellers cheques, and started to make my way back to our holiday-mobile. I should have known better as, not for the first time, I was hijacked by Jan and Carrie to join them on what they promised me would be their last shopping sortie of the holiday. I learned a long time ago not to listen to any promises that any female makes about shopping and I certainly didn't believe that these two would last another twenty-four hours on the island without the need to enter some sort of emporium to purchase that vital ingredient that would be needed for the journey home and then carefully placed in a bag to be forgotten until it is found months later as you pack for your next holiday. I accepted my fate as we entered another shopping plaza where the two of them just happened to come across a counter displaying a whole variety of catty-type ornaments and knick-knacks. A persuasive assistant mugged me into buying a couple of cat books that I didn't recollect seeing in the ever-growing feline library back home together with a box of gift notelets that were adorned with different coloured breeds of cat posing around the edges. They didn't leave much space for writing any sort of lengthy letter but for brief thank-you notes or the like even I have found them quite useful and I know Lesley is always happy to have her stocks replenished.

The girls were back in their element, a shopping heaven, but I had already had more than my fill and told them I would wait for them outside where I found a shady seat and was more than content to sit and watch the hundreds of cruisers being ferried across the harbour and dropped off at the main jetty, to spend a few hours sampling the delights of Grand Cayman.

The majority were Americans and they came in all sorts of shapes, sizes and moods. One particular couple were having a blazing row and had obviously had a major difference of opinion about the merits of coming ashore into Georgetown. She had obviously wanted to experience the delights of the capital of the Cayman Islands whereas from both his expression and the verbal abuse that he was aiming in her direction I'm not at all sure that he even wanted to be on the cruise. Others in their party were obviously embarrassed and moving apart from the argumentative couple as quickly as they could. This only had the effect of making them more isolated and consequently the centre of attention for the best part of a hundred yards or more. Once it became apparent that everybody was watching them make a spectacle of themselves, the wife tried to calm her partner down by indicating that they were currently the main spectator sport in Georgetown. This initially didn't have any effect, in fact it only seemed to spur him into a greater frenzy, as he became redder in the face and seemed on the verge of giving himself a heart attack, or blowing the proverbial gasket. I don't know if he suffered from blood pressure but I was convinced that he wasn't doing himself a great deal of good. I know I'm overweight but if I were to have stood next to him, which I had no intention of doing, I would have looked positively slim and that takes a bit of doing. Equally he wasn't wearing a hat and a combination of the midday sun, no headgear, a pair of shorts that fitted where they touched and a temper that was reaching boiling point were all indicating that here was a coronary just waiting to happen.

Fortunately for the local accident and emergency department, one of his fellow passengers found the courage to intervene before he managed to blow the seal off the pressure cooker that had built up a head of steam.

They obviously knew each other and although I wasn't close enough to hear exactly what was said our newly arrived mediator was able to pour oil on the troubled waters to the extent that he was able to lead them away towards the coolness of one of the nearby air-conditioned shops where hopefully he could conciliate between the simmering couple and bring them, particularly him, to their senses.

Another American couple, who I would guess were well into their seventies and were sitting near me, picked up their bags, got up and as they left shrugged their shoulders as he looked at me and said, "Life's too short," before crossing the road and making their way back to the pier. I nodded in agreement as normality resumed and I could continue with my holiday hobby of people watching although the remaining twenty minutes waiting for Jan and Carrie were quite tranquil compared to the previous ten.

They joined me, carrying a number of small bags and one large one bearing the 'Tortuga Rum Cake' label which contained no fewer than six variously flavoured cakes that should appease even Caroline's appetite for this Caymanian delicacy. Having missed all the fuss I gave them a brief update on the Caribbean version of a minor American domestic civil war. They quickly loaded their goodies onto the back seat of our minibus and I immediately learned that my judgement of not trusting their promise of a final shopping foray was to prove to be accurate. Why was I not surprised?

They now wanted me to drive back to Pure Art where they wanted a final, final, final look at the bargains before we made our way home. Fortunately this wasn't too far out of town, although in the opposite direction to the hotel. I pulled up, off the main road in the small parking area at the side of the shop and had already decided that I would remain in the air-conditioned comfort of the van whilst the girls entered their Aladdin's Cave to search for yet more bargains. At this rate it wouldn't just be Caroline's case that would attract a 'Heavy' label.

As the girls went into the store another car pulled up next to me and out got our two evening drinking friends, our British neighbours from the hotel. They had been house hunting in the South Sound area and learned of Pure Art so thought they would call in before lunch. Not unusually in such circumstances we then experienced the perfectly normal commercial sexual divide. The three girls all disappeared to look for local arts, crafts or anything else that took their fancy whilst us two guys kept our distance and remained outside chatting about the housing market and their prospects of renting or buying on the island. We probably had time to carry out surveys and prepare comprehensive Home Information Packs on at least three extensive properties before the girls eventually re-joined us and much to my amazement they weren't even carrying one bag. How they could spend so much time examining and deliberating over what to buy and then not buy it, I do not know. We both came to the conclusion that it was a woman thing that fortunately hadn't yet managed to inflict itself upon the male genes of the human race.

They were off to find the highly recommended Lighthouse Restaurant for lunch whereas we were returning to the hotel to rejoin the gang for our final lunch around the pool. We made a stop at the car hire company to arrange the return of our minibus the following day and received a very pleasant surprise. Having paid our initial deposit at the beginning of the holiday we asked for the final bill, so that we could divide the total between the whole team, and pay our dues the following morning. Carrie had already worked out a rough estimate per person so that everybody was able to ensure they were solvent enough to pay their final bills. The actual amount was considerably less than Carrie's estimate. There were two reasons for this imbalance. Firstly we had not been given the original vehicle that Mel had ordered on our behalf and the hire company had very reasonably reduced the price as we had not had one of their higher quality vehicles, but the second reason for the saving was Ted's inaccurate calculation of the exchange rates between the pound sterling and the United States and Cayman dollars.

Whereas I had some initial reservations about our Prestige Motor when we had collected it the reality was that, although it wasn't the smartest car on the island, it had served our purpose admirably and never even looked like letting us down, even when I drove 'like a tourist'.

The bonus of a much smaller bill than anticipated just indicated that first impressions can, sometimes, be misleading. So, well done Prestige Motors. In future I won't judge a car solely by the scratches on the body-work. We picked up the news from a local radio station on the drive back to the hotel and it was more like a chat over the garden fence between two friends about what had been going on in the locality over the past couple of days. It included some minor crime and traffic incidents, much of which wouldn't have got anywhere near the newsdesk of a BBC local radio station in England but featured prominently here, and even the smaller-type crime is still considered newsworthy and contained the usual appeal for witnesses. It certainly put island crime into perspective compared to what I was used to back home.

I had time for a quick dip in the pool before a leisurely alfresco lunch which Jan and the girls had whistled up in no time at all. The lunch was also an informal committee meeting with the only item on the agenda being where we would have our final dinner of the holiday. Differing options were proposed with Jan and I favouring the Calypso Grill in Morgan's Harbour out in West Bay. We had heard some good reports of this particular restaurant and it was one place where we had not yet eaten. I think we could have persuaded the majority to try that particular establishment for our last night but for Fran who was absolutely insistent that we eat at the Treehouse Restaurant and we try and book the table overhanging the water's edge. So determined was she that she was not prepared to take no for an answer. Whilst I would have liked to sample the delights of the Calypso Grill I knew that it was pointless in arguing with Fran when she was in that sort of adamant frame of mind. It was as if she had instigated a three-line whip and woe betide any dissenters. In truth, we all knew that it wasn't going to be any sort of hardship to eat at the Treehouse so, with Fran exerting her considerable influence over the committee, the decision was eventually unanimous. Proposed, seconded and voted for by Fran with all other opinions totally ignored.

Carl and I volunteered to do the washing up whilst the girls made their way to the beach. It wasn't long before we joined them for a final wander along the sand, not as far as the Ritz after yesterday's experience, and leisurely float in the Caribbean.

> *I managed to eke out the final drops of suntan cream from the sorry-looking tube that was now rolled into a tiny crimpled piece of plastic to force the last droplets from the gooey open capped end, which for a change wasn't also encrusted with hundreds of grains of sand. There was just enough to provide a final coating for my arms, legs and shoulders before 'borrowing' a little of Caroline's to prevent the remainder of my torso basting in the afternoon sun.*

The girls were determined to make the most of the sun on their final afternoon but I, of the more delicate disposition, decided that you could have too much of a good thing and had no wish to be overcooked and uncomfortable on what was going to be a long journey home the following day. I left the rest of the team lapping up the sun and made my way back to Indies Suites to find some shade next to the pool.

After a few gentle lengths of the pool I settled down on a sun lounger and continued to read my book, although this was interspersed with occasional lapses where I drifted off into the land of nod so that I was in that comfortable and carefree almost semi-conscious state that one reaches just before going off to sleep. Fifty-odd years ago my grandmother used to call it 'forty winks' as she settled down for her regular afternoon nap by the fireside. There was certainly no fire but, although I was well shaded from the heat of the afternoon sun, it was probably a lot hotter than my old Nan was used to in her small and draughty terraced house in South West London.

My reverie was interrupted by a couple of young female voices chatting to each other who had come to occupy the two sun beds immediately next to mine. Initially I was a bit put out and wondered why they couldn't have chosen any of the numerous beds scattered around the pool as opposed to invading my space and interrupting my peace and quiet. However, like me, they wanted some shade so all three of us tucked ourselves into one corner of the pool close to the shrubbery that had become home to Indie and her brood.

They were both young medical students who occupied digs nearby but had an arrangement with the owner of the hotel that allowed them to use the pool when it was quiet. They also had part-time jobs to help them eke out their student grants. Ironically one of them was a waitress at the Calypso Grill in West Bay and she confirmed that all the reports that we had heard about the quality of this particular restaurant were correct. This only made me wonder why on earth the majority of us hadn't stuck to our guns and insisted that we have our last main meal of the holiday at the Calypso Grill. Why had we allowed the insistent Fran to cajole us into returning to the Treehouse when there were many others, including the Calypso, that we had not had time to sample? We had no argument with the Treehouse – indeed we had already enjoyed an excellent meal there – but variety is the spice of life and we had not been disappointed to date so, for me, the choice would have been preferable to try a different restaurant and chef and experience an alternative menu.

My new student friend had now whetted my taste buds with her description of some of the meals on the menu at the Calypso Grill, so that at that stage I was probably feeling a little disappointed with our decision to return to what we knew would be a safe choice. Why was Fran so determined to return there?

The two student doctors were each carrying large medical tomes which they were using to pose questions to each other and it was apparent that they were revising for some sort of future examination or test but neither seemed particularly confident and they gave me the impression, perhaps falsely and unfairly, that they were more interested in the social side of life on the island rather than immersing themselves in the workings of the upper urinary tract, cardiovascular disease or other such bodily malfunction. However, I'm equally sure they were no different to the vast majority of other young students the world over, who mix pleasure with study and still manage to graduate with very acceptable degrees. Much more than I ever did when I was their age.

We chatted generally about the island until they decided to refresh themselves with a swim in the pool. I would have been quite happy to join them until I saw just how good they were as they completed length after length at a considerable rate of knots, taking it in turns to do many underwater. It wouldn't have surprised me if they had suddenly demonstrated their ability at synchronised swimming they were so at ease in the water. Realising that my efforts would only have embarrassed me in their company I said my farewells and made my way back to our apartment to shave and shower and prepare for our final evening meal of the holiday together. Jan and the girls had already returned from the beach so, as it would be a little while before I could get into the bathroom, I busied myself tidying the clothes that I had left lying on my bed and starting, eventually, to pack the first few non-essential items of clothing back into my suitcase. It wasn't long before the girls indicated that the bathroom was free so that I could lose my twenty-four-hour stubble and clean off the final layer of sun cream before smartening myself up for dinner. Whilst I was in the bathroom I could hear numerous comings and goings from next door with Caroline's dulcet tones being prominent amongst the muffled mutterings coming from Jan and Carrie's bedroom. Leaving the bathroom, robed only in a wraparound towel, I found Caroline trying on one pair of shoes and carrying three others. She was engaged in an animated conversation with Carrie, requesting advice on which pair of shoes best matched one particular dress. To my uneducated eye it was readily apparent that the shoes she was wearing matched perfectly, although I had learned long ago that my opinion would be neither wanted nor valued. I wisely decided to keep my mouth shut, which I readily accept is unusual for me. Jan came out to join the conversation and to my surprise she and Carrie agreed with my silent thoughts that Caroline looked just delightful as she was and her outfit set off her golden tan superbly. Caroline was not totally convinced and seemed concerned that she had not yet had an opportunity to wear two of the ten pairs of shoes that had been transported across the Atlantic. However, she seemed slightly more settled having been reassured by Jan and Carrie whilst I, bravely, kept my counsel.

It didn't take long before we were ready to lock our room and wander downstairs to the bar for our evening ritual of pre-dinner cocktails. Across the landing there was still an inordinate amount of noise coming from the neighbours' apartment, although it wasn't difficult to detect one particular voice above the others, in the hubbub of humorous babble emanating through the door. We let them know that we were ready and made our way to the bar where we found our two friendly financial consultants and a number of other guests were already well into their first, or it could have been their second, cocktails.

After a short while we were joined by Carl and Fran who informed us that Caroline remained indecisive about the shoes and was now considering the merits of each of the ten against her chosen frock. We took our time over the first drink and had ordered another round when Dani and Caroline eventually made their entrance from the poolside. They looked as pretty and charming as ever but Caroline did look somewhat different to the picture we had expected. She was now wearing a completely different outfit to the one we had seen some thirty minutes earlier. Different dress, different shoes and different evening bag. If and when this girl gets married I will have some sympathy for her husband-to-be and will need to warn him that he should always allow an additional two hours, minimum, before an evening out.

There then followed some entertaining banter, regarding dress and accessory selection, between Jan, Carrie and Caroline, which if it had been a boxing bout would have been won by Jan on a narrow points majority verdict. To enter any sort of verbal joust against Caroline is above and beyond the call of duty and to win it is almost unheard of. Jan did have experience on her side and together with unanimous support from the assembled company persuaded Caroline to accept defeat graciously. Even our new financial advisor friends joined in the badinage so that Caroline could see she was fighting a losing battle.

Having taken our time at the bar we boarded our battle bus for almost the last time, and prepared for the ten-minute drive towards Georgetown and the Treehouse Restaurant. Carrie had volunteered to be our driver for the night and we had been in the minibus less than sixty seconds before Fran and Caroline started the community singing for the final evening's performance from the very temporary, and voluntary, Indies Suites Mixed Voice Choir. Once again Fran wanted to venture into the normally male-dominated world of rugby songs but still hadn't managed to master the tune, let alone the words. Carl and I promised that we would teach her on our way home, via the Royal Palms, if only she would quieten down now. This proved impossible and she was even more excitable on this our final night than at any time previously on the holiday. I put it down to the influence of the sun, the cocktails and Caroline but not necessarily in that order. I was wrong on every count.

We arrived at the Treehouse in a very happy mood and perused the menu by the open-air bar. Some early diners were just about to vacate our table, which was perched over the water, and we were told that it would be no more than a ten-minute wait. We weren't in any hurry as we made ourselves comfortable sipping our pre-dinner drinks and cocktails with Carl and I discussing the possibilities for the forthcoming football season and also once again ruminating on what might have been on the golf course if only our shot selection had been different. It's a golfing trait that players are able to remember all the shots in their last game and by selecting only the poor ones are then able, in their own mind, to reduce their overall score by at least half a dozen shots. Unfortunately when returning for the next game it's rarely possible to put the theory into practice. In my case whilst I might improve the odd poor shot I cannot be sure that a previous good shot will be repeated so that I remain one of those many golfers who are destined to have the odd good game scattered amongst the many that are mediocre and best forgotten. Somehow Carl was quieter than usual and whilst seeming very content with life appeared to be a little preoccupied. Carrie, Dani and Caroline meanwhile were entering into some light-hearted banter with the barman who just didn't realise what he was letting himself in for. Jan and Fran had drifted to the far end of the bar where they were deep in their own conversation which from the body language gave the impression of being very happy but it was obvious that they didn't want to be interrupted or overheard.

We were in for two surprises. The first would become obvious to us all in a matter of minutes. We would not personally experience the second but would follow its progress with bated breath once we were back home, safe and sound, in dear old England.

Little did any of us imagine, as we sat watching the sunset over the tranquil waters of the Caribbean, that we would be amongst the last groups of guests to eat in this idyllic and romantic spot. In less than two months' time the Treehouse Restaurant, and hundreds of other buildings, including our home for the past fortnight, Indies Suites, would cease to exist in the form that we had become accustomed to during our holiday and the shape that we saw them on that last night on the island. David and Mel's home would be wrecked although at the time they wouldn't be there to see it.

Disaster was lurking over the horizon. A natural disaster that would have a dramatic effect on Grand Cayman and a number of other islands in the Caribbean. As we sat drinking and chatting we just didn't dream of what was in store for our holiday isle and could not have comprehended the chaos and destruction that was waiting around the corner. Before too long we would all be made aware of the force and fury of Hurricane Ivan, albeit our understanding would be second-hand and initially reliant on very sketchy and unconfirmed media reports.

CHAPTER 16

Ivan the Terrible

On my return to work the following week I was relating some tales of the holiday on Grand Cayman to work colleagues. One, who is a very good friend and whom I've known for over thirty years, had previously paid a one-day visit to the island from one of the many cruise liners berthing at Georgetown. Dick, like myself a retired policeman – we had both represented Basildon Police at football back in the 1970/80s and won our fair share of trophies – is a seasoned traveller and has experienced a good proportion of the globe.

Strangely, he is the only person I have met who was less than complimentary about New Zealand. Everybody else I've spoken to thoroughly enjoyed their holiday, particularly the scenery on South Island, and were unanimous that they would be happy to pay a return visit. Dick was the exception to the rule, although good rules should not have exceptions. He had timed his trip to coincide with a British Lions tour and maybe he didn't experience the best of New Zealand's climate. In fact from his description of the weather he probably saw the worst of it, with rain eclipsing sunshine at a ratio of about four days to one. Equally the Lions' abject failure and their dismal rugby may have coloured his perspective of this particular part of the southern hemisphere. The victorious All Blacks, whilst entertaining the home supporters, only made his visit all the bleaker, or blacker, and ensured that he is unlikely to make another crossing of the Tasman Sea to pay a return visit to the land of the Maoris and Kiwis in the foreseeable future, if ever. He is a man who is quite prepared to voice his opinions even if they might upset some people. If he has a miserable holiday he is not afraid to say so.

Consequently when he told me that he had enjoyed his visit to Grand Cayman, particularly Stingray City, it was easy to believe that he had been impressed with what he saw on his very brief sojourn on the island as a day-tripping cruiser. He did go on to say with devastating prescience, "It's one of the flattest places I've ever been to. If a tidal wave were to hit it, it would probably sink."

How hideously prophetic his words would prove to be. Some six weeks later Grand Cayman would be hit by winds, rain and seas the likes of which it hadn't experienced for over seventy years.

Hurricane Ivan was to be the forerunner of a number of natural disasters that were to occur over the following twelve months, which brought home to mankind that the power of nature can be unstoppable and when faced with such force we will always come off second best. The intensity, energy and unpredictability of such events can totally overwhelm even the best prepared emergency plans and for those who are ill prepared the damage, destruction and loss of life can only be described as a human tragedy.

Not being on the island at the time of the hurricane all of my views and opinions are reliant upon others, having been gleaned from newspaper and television reports together with personal accounts told me by Mel and David, and their friends, who had returned to their home, near South Sound, following their honeymoon and second reception in the UK.

To have completed my jottings from what had been a most enjoyable and memorable stay on the island and to have ignored what then occurred would have been grossly negligent and unfair on all those who suffered at the hands of Hurricane Ivan and more importantly would be an undeserved snub to those who then worked heroically, in dreadful conditions, for many hours and days to rescue people and try and bring some sort of normality back to Grand Cayman.

Fortunately the island did have warning that Hurricane Ivan was likely to hit them.

Ironically about a month earlier another hurricane had passed close to the island but when speaking to Mel about how bad the weather had been her response of "a bit of a stiff breeze yesterday" was a masterly piece of understatement.

A stiff breeze during the hurricane season in the Caribbean can be the equivalent of a Force 10 gale back here in England. This particular stiff breeze was Hurricane Charley, which passed between Grand Cayman and Little Cayman during the morning of 12th August. It was the second major hurricane of the 2004 hurricane season and eventually reached Category 4 on the Saffir-Simpson scale and by the time it reached Cuba its winds were recorded at a hundred and twenty miles per hour. A total of fifteen deaths, in the United States and the Caribbean, were attributable to Hurricane Charley together with over US$14 billion worth of damage. Little did we know that Charley was merely the harbinger for what was hiding just around the corner.

Fortunately the hurricane season warning system is tried and tested so that the people of Grand Cayman had early warning of what to expect and were given an opportunity to take what precautions they could and prepare for the worst.

When I opened my emails on 10th September I found the following that had been sent by Mel, to friends and family in England, at eleven pm local time on the 9th September.

Hello Everyone

Just thought I would check in with you before the hurricane. We are on the path of Hurricane Ivan. This one is big. It is a category 5 which is the biggest going. They think it is going to hit Jamaica but we will get the edges of it, so we are in for a nasty weekend. David will have to go to work so I am going to go to school so I am not on my own. It should be fairly safe so don't worry. I will let you know what happens. Keep your fingers crossed that we don't get too much water in our bedroom!!

Speak to you all soon
Love
Mel

Unfortunately they were to experience much more than just water in their bedroom. Knowing Mel as I do – she is not prone to exaggeration – I, and others, realised just how serious a situation they were likely to be in on the island. When we had spoken previously of the wind and rain of the hurricane seasons she had always just shrugged them off as part of life in the Caribbean and never appeared unduly perturbed. Since she had started her teaching career on Grand Cayman we had not received such an email and it was obvious that Ivan was going to be very different to her previous experiences and was to put her, and thousands of others, through the most frightening two days of their lives. I tried to monitor the progress of Ivan through the media and the Internet but news from Grand Cayman was either non-existent or, at best, very sketchy. I was not to hear from Mel again until she was able to send her next email, from Miami, during the night of 16th September. She and David had survived but they had lost their home and many of their wedding presents. The rear wall of their house was blown out, together with many of their belongings, although they were not there to witness it personally and wouldn't become aware of the impact of the damage to their home, and their lives, for a few days.

Hurricane Ivan was the strongest hurricane of the 2004 hurricane season and at the time it became the sixth most intense Atlantic hurricane on record but has now been demoted to the ninth. The 2005 season recorded three further hurricanes, Wilma, Rita and Katrina, all of which were stronger but didn't have the same impact on Grand Cayman that Hurricane Ivan had visited on the island. Katrina, of course, gained worldwide notoriety for the death and destruction it brought to New Orleans, when the levees burst and large parts of the city were submerged for days and weeks on end.

Not unusually the foundations of Ivan began to build in a small way many thousands of miles to the east of Grand Cayman. On 2nd September 2004 a tropical depression formed from a large tropical wave south of the Cape Verde Islands in the Atlantic. As the storm moved to the west it increased in strength and by 5th September it was just over a thousand miles east of Tobago and had been named Hurricane Ivan becoming a Category 3 hurricane with winds of one hundred and twenty-five miles per hour. At this early stage in its development the National Hurricane Centre noted its rapid strengthening was unprecedented at such a low latitude in the Atlantic basin.

By 7th September it was rapidly intensifying and it battered several of the Windward Islands as it entered the Caribbean. It passed directly over Grenada killing thirty-nine people and causing catastrophic damage. The capital, St George's, was severely damaged and several notable buildings, including the Prime Minister's residence, were destroyed. Ivan also caused extensive damage to a local prison, enabling most of the inmates to escape. According to a member of the Grenadian parliament at least eighty-five percent of the small island was devastated. Whilst not in the eye of the storm over one hundred and fifty properties in Barbados were damaged and a Canadian woman drowned, whilst a pregnant woman was killed in Tobago when a tree fell onto her home.

Ivan continued to intensify and by the 9th September it was on a parallel path with the coast of Venezuela just north of the Antilles and Aruba and was now classed as a Category 5 hurricane with winds exceeding one hundred and sixty miles per hour wreaking further damage and causing three further deaths in Venezuela. It then started to track west-northwest towards Jamaica and as it approached the island, late on 10th September it began a westward jog that kept the eye of the storm and the strongest winds to the south and west of the island. However, hurricane force winds battered Jamaica for hours causing significant wind and flood damage. A total of seventeen people were killed and a further eighteen thousand left homeless as a result of floodwaters and high winds. It continued on its western path and by 11th September winds were recorded at over a hundred and seventy miles per hour. At this stage Mel's prediction in her email was proving alarmingly accurate but her hope that Grand Cayman would only see the edges of the hurricane were about to be devastatingly shattered over the next couple of days.

Ivan hit Grand Cayman during the night of Saturday 11th September and the pre-dawn hours of the following day and continued to pummel the island until the morning of Monday 13th September. By now Ivan had reached its peak strength and some reports noted sustained wind speeds that were clocked at one hundred and sixty-seven miles per hour for a period exceeding four hours with tornadic gusts of up to two hundred and twenty-five miles per hour. There was immediate and widespread flooding with reports that large areas of Grand Cayman disappeared from radar and became part of the sea for the duration of the storm, including the airport runway, which was underwater and more suitable for submarines and ducks than aircraft. Islanders clambered onto rooftops and into loft spaces, in fact anything available to seek refuge and escape the surging floodwaters whilst watching the carnage as the waters rose relentlessly hour after hour. Jim, a teaching colleague of Mel, told me that he was lucky as the water only reached waist height at his home. Damage across the island was described as catastrophic and it was said that a huge surge of water came from North Sound down through Georgetown to meet a similar surge coming in the opposite direction from South Sound in the area of Walkers Road, which I knew was close to Melanie's school. At one point the entire island seemed to be swamped by a tidal surge that some described as being between fifteen and twenty feet high.

Trees were ripped out of the ground, power lines were down and roofs stripped off, as if by an electric can opener, and blown away. Thousands of vehicles were destroyed and much of the island's vegetation overwhelmed by the ferocious winds and flooding. Entire residential complexes were completely wiped from the face of the island. I was to learn, some weeks later, that Indies Suites lost large chunks of its roof and floodwaters inundated the whole of the ground floor to waist height. A mixture of the wind, rain and floodwaters destroyed everything inside the building together with the cars parked outside. Indies Suites' life as a hotel came to a watery conclusion that weekend. It seemed hard to imagine, until I saw some photographs, that our secure and peaceful refuge for an idyllic holiday in July would no longer host tourists to the island.

Water on the island was shut off at six pm on the 11th and power supplies were gradually lost district by district during the night with families left stranded and helpless by the rising waters. This was the strongest storm ever to hit the islands exceeding even the legendary storm of 1932. On one of the three islands, tiny Cayman Brac, which didn't suffer as badly as its larger brother island Grand Cayman, residents swarmed into caves for shelter. The storm, while packing monstrous winds, was also slow-moving which prolonged the devastation. Winds whipped across the island all night Saturday then on into Sunday until the eye eventually passed when the winds then roared in from the south to continue battering the island and cause further damage.

Cuba was next on the path of Ivan where it started to brush the western tip of the island and cause extensive damage late on 13th September. With most of its central circulation remaining offshore Ivan was able to proceed and pass through the Yucatan Channel with no loss of strength.

Once over the Gulf of Mexico Ivan did lose some strength, dropping back to a Category 4 hurricane but the warm waters of the Gulf re-energised the ferocious winds and it continued to intensify until it struck the mainland of the United States of America near Gulf Shores, Alabama, about two am on 16th September, by which time the winds had dropped to one hundred and thirty miles per hour.

Maintaining hurricane strength it continued inland until it was over Central Alabama when the winds began to decrease down to ninety miles per hour, although this seemed of little consolation to those in its path.

Late on the 16th Ivan weakened to a tropical depression although low pressure continued to dump rain onto the eastern coast of the United States of America.

By 18th September Ivan had lost its tropical characteristics and appeared to be petering out but this proved to be a false dawn as it was merely taking a break whilst preparing for its second wave. On 18th September remnants of the low crossed the coast of New Jersey as the storm continued to lose strength. However, by 21st September the remnants combined with a low pressure system over Cape Breton Island, Nova Scotia, Canada and started to regain enough strength to fell trees, cause localised flooding and leave thousands without any power. By the following day Ivan had regained its tropical characteristics and reformed into a depression following a circular route through the south-eastern United States resulting in further widespread flooding before tracking its path in a loop back to the northern Gulf of Mexico. Fortunately the revived Ivan then began to lose its impetus as it returned to landfall over Louisiana as a low grade tropical storm and by the evening of 23rd September weakened quickly as it travelled overland into south-east Texas where it eventually dissipated and finally blew itself out and disappeared from the weathermen's radar.

The name Ivan was retired in the spring of 2005 by the World Meteorological Organisation and will be replaced by Igor in the 2010 season. One can only hope that Igor will be more climatically friendly than his terrible predecessor. Ivan was attributed with several hydrological records including generating the tallest and most intense ever ocean wave at ninety-one feet (twenty-seven metres), recorded by sensors as it passed over the Gulf of Mexico. It would have dwarfed a ten-storey building and had the power to snap a ship in half but fortunately this particular wave never reached land. Twenty-four oil rigs were damaged and seven sunk together with considerable damage to submarine pipelines. Scientists used the data to calculate the extreme waves created under the eye of the storm and they suspect that the instruments missed some waves that may have been as high as one hundred and thirty feet (forty metres), the equivalent of a fifteen-storey building, combined with the fastest seafloor current at 2.25 metres per second. By comparison, the tsunami that swept across the Indian Ocean the following December stood about thirty feet high as it hit the shorelines, although in some parts of Indonesia it was reported to have reached sixty-five feet. Whilst, purely statistically in geophysical terms, the tsunami may not have reached the heights of Ivan its terrifying consequences and incalculable death toll impacted over a far wider area and on a much greater scale than even those who experienced Ivan could have imagined. Occurring, as it did, over the Christmas holiday only added to the grief and increased the misery.

Quite what Ivan's giant wave would have looked or felt like, should anybody have been in its wake, is unimaginable. Even memories of fairly recent events in the United Kingdom such as the flash floods in Boscastle, Cornwall, where television cameras happened to be on site filming a documentary about a seaside parish with a female vicar and were able to capture the storm waters devastating the village and tossing cars into the sea, cannot compare to the wall of water that preceded Ivan. The presence of the cameras must have seemed like manna from heaven to the editors of the evening news broadcast who were able to screen live feed from the scene as it unfolded. Viewers were able to watch for themselves the actual event as opposed to just viewing the aftermath. In a strangely perverse way the pictures may have actually assisted in increasing donations to the disaster fund to get Boscastle back on its feet. Whilst devastating for the village and its residents its scale was minute when compared to Ivan.

Nearly two decades earlier, Britain's Great Storm, which arrived overnight on 15th/16th October 1987, battering the south-east of England, and which was described by many involved as the most frightening experience of their lives, was hardly comparable to a Caribbean hurricane. In England this became the most famous, or infamous, weather event of the twentieth century. A total of eighteen people were killed, an estimated fifteen million trees destroyed by winds exceeding ninety miles per hour, and property damage was assessed at one billion pounds. The BBC's national weather forecaster Michael Fish was castigated for failing to predict this in the evening forecast and then, following an enquiry from a viewer, informing the audience that there was not going to be a hurricane. In weather forecasting terms Michael Fish was actually accurate in his summary. The storm was not a hurricane, where winds have to reach at least a hundred and twenty miles per hour, and a hurricane would drop much more rainfall than occurred on that particularly exceptional and frightening night. The strength of the wind was actually forecast but what was not identified was the wind direction and its change of track. By the time it was realised that it was going to bear north of the English Channel and batter London and the Home Counties there was only time to warn the emergency services in the early hours of the morning. The rest of the nation were tucked up sleeping in their beds blissfully unaware of the storm that was about to be unleashed. Even if they had been warned it is doubtful if the majority would have been able to take sufficient precautions to minimise the damage due to the sheer strength of the gales. Both the dramatic weather patterns of Boscastle and the Great Storm of 1987, whilst extreme in the United Kingdom, were miniscule when compared to the power and destruction that Ivan heaped on the Caribbean and the United States. On a global scale time would dictate that Ivan would quickly pale into insignificance, although not for those personally involved. Compared to the tsunami that was to follow just over three months later or Hurricane Katrina that was to devastate New Orleans the following year, Ivan became just a brief news item that was quickly forgotten.

For the record Ivan killed sixty-four people in the Caribbean, mainly in Grenada and Jamaica, three in Venezuela and twenty-five in the United States, including fourteen in Florida. Tornadoes spawned by Ivan, that struck communities along the leading edge of the storm, were responsible for a further twenty-five deaths that were indirectly attributable to Ivan. That gives a total of one hundred and seventeen deaths, although there isn't any accurate record of the numbers who suffered serious or minor injuries, but hospitals and the emergency medical services dealt with numerous cuts, bruises and broken limbs. In pure financial terms damage to property resulted in insurance claims totalling US$28 billion, making Ivan one of the costliest natural disasters in history. For many, in addition to and perhaps more importantly than the pure financial cost, Ivan left a legacy of fear and anxiety that changed their lives forever.

Due to the early warning most people on Grand Cayman were able to take some precautions and only two deaths were initially reported as a result of Ivan. With local radio reports updating residents on the path and progress of Ivan many had to decide where they should seek shelter for the duration of the storm. As the reports forecast a direct hit at category 5 and a state of emergency was declared many thousands, particularly those worried about the construction of their houses, decided to flee their homes and seek refuge with family, friends, at their workplaces or public shelters. The public shelters housed over four thousand people for the duration of the storm although the last minute decision by some to use these shelters did put some additional pressure on their capacity late on the Saturday and at least one had to close early. Radio reports coming into the shelters became increasingly dramatic as homes were damaged and the winds increased as one of the biggest storms in history started to engulf one of the smallest country islands in the world. Conditions in the shelters became increasingly uncomfortable as the high winds damaged some roofs and water gained entry to some making life in the temporary refuges even more difficult. Fear of the unknown, worries about how their homes were faring in addition to the overcrowded conditions did not make it easy for the residents to cope as the eye of the storm approached.

Governor Bruce Dinwiddy described damage as 'very, very severe and widespread'. A quarter of the buildings on the island were reported to be uninhabitable, with at least eighty percent damaged to some extent. Much of the island still remained without power, water or sewerage facilities tens days after the storm. Six months later less than half the islands pre-Ivan hotel rooms were usable. Damage on Grand Cayman totalled almost two billion US dollars.

With David on duty and, in common with many other emergency service personnel, not knowing when he would be able to return home or even knowing if there would be a home to return to, Mel decided to join Nic and a small number of other staff members and their families at the school which for the duration became known as the CPHS Hotel as opposed to its more familiar nomenclature of the Cayman Preparatory High School. She arrived there on the Saturday morning and was unable to leave until the following Monday. This small party of five adults, two children and two dogs, gradually increased in number to over thirty, and were joined on the Saturday afternoon by two friends of Nic who were seeking shelter as it was no longer safe to remain in their own home. Leanne, who was heavily pregnant, and due to give birth to her first child on the Saturday, arrived with her husband Stephen and their three huskies. There was no room for her at the hospital despite an imminently scheduled Caesarean. She was in the beginnings of labour, and had to remain horizontal, so they found a sofa from the staff room and moved it to one of the classrooms where she lay on it for the duration of the storm and managed to hang on, so to speak, although it became touch and go. Whilst this bore little resemblance to a stable and a manger in Bethlehem it is probable that conditions were more basic, if less frenetic and possibly safer than the centre of a Caribbean hurricane. You would be unlikely to find either venue recommended, and certainly not selected, as ideal conditions for bringing a baby into this world. The school first aid kit does not cater for childbirth and although a search for further medical kit was unsuccessful it did reveal a pair of pliers, a screwdriver and some string. All of these seemed superfluous and probably useless in the event of the baby arriving. Later attempts to fabricate an obstetric tool from a pair of old shelf supports recycled as a retractor were innovative but fortunately never had to be put to the test. Despite their miserable conditions and the potential danger they managed to retain their sense of humour. At least the dogs would have plenty of company and if all else failed they could make a sledge and the huskies could haul them to safety. In three feet of snow that may well have been possible but in three feet of water they were being somewhat overly optimistic. An amusing thought and possible brief distraction from the parlous position in which they found themselves.

CPHS Hotel had adopted the 'no frills' policy now popular with many airlines so that the weekend's residents effectively had access to their cabin luggage and nothing else. If they hadn't brought it with them then it just wasn't available. A lack of pooper scoopers was an initial concern but as events unfolded these became an irrelevance and the dogs behaved exceptionally well throughout, albeit after the first night one room did begin to have an aroma more akin to a kennels than a school or even temporary hotel although the dogs seemed less concerned than the humans.

Despite numerous attempts to gain contact, family and friends back in England were unable to obtain any news of, or from, Mel or David. Both power lines and telegraph lines were down and it proved impossible to communicate by mobile phone through the various cell-net systems, either verbally or by text. Initially even the main news sources, including the BBC, were only able to provide very sketchy information from Grand Cayman. Communication with the island was problematic and although it was obvious that the situation was serious there was a lack of detail at that stage. News emanating from Grenada and to a lesser extent Jamaica provided a backdrop of a natural disaster that only made the lack of information and the uncertainty all the more worrying for those trying to make contact with loved ones on the island. Equally, those locked down in the school now appeared to be isolated and survival was very much in their own hands. They would have to assist and support each other to see out the storm as there wasn't going to be any external aid.

By late Saturday night sheets of galvanised roofing were seen flying past the school at a hundred miles per hour, accompanied by what sounded like gunshots but were in fact car windows imploding/exploding due to the wind strength and pressure differential. They survived the first half of the night in relative comfort and for the most part at that early stage were able to keep warm and dry.

The storm became much worse in the early hours of the Sunday morning when water started to come in through the roof, which resulted in ceiling tiles dropping down into the classroom. It was at this stage that the full force of Ivan hit Grand Cayman, ripping sheets and tiles from roofs, causing buildings to collapse and sending a surge wave across the island. The worst of the storm was around nine o'clock on the Sunday morning with winds gusting up to two hundred and twenty miles per hour but the island faced a relentless battering for the remainder of the day and well into the following night. Whilst initially the small group had a feeling of safety in numbers and the camaraderie created a feeling almost akin to excitement at that time, they still hadn't comprehended just how Ivan would unfold. Whilst they were well aware of the potential danger they had never experienced such a strong or catastrophic hurricane. By daylight on the Sunday morning they could see little or nothing through the horizontal sheets of driving rain carrying flying debris past their temporary CPHS shelter. Visibility was virtually no more than a few yards.

Any excitement had long since been replaced by a degree of fear as they did not know just what to expect next or for how long their ordeal was likely to continue. They witnessed the canteen roof being peeled back as easily and as quickly as you would take the lid off a can of sardines. The corner of the school hall, which had suffered some early damage, became progressively worse as the morning wore on. By this time they were left with just two usable toilets, which in itself wasn't a problem other than the fact that at one bucket per flush their water supplies were only likely to last for about another twenty-four hours.

Mel meanwhile had to move from room to room within the school as the hurricane winds began to tear parts of the roof away from the rafters and shatter a number of windows on one side of the school. One end of the main roof was disintegrating and equipment was being blown along the upper corridor.

The sanctuary of the school was becoming smaller by the hour as the tightly knit group sheltering inside gradually retreated from classroom to classroom into an inner corridor in the hope that the storm would pass before the whole of the roof was blown away and the school with it. At one stage water was entering their latest bolthole and coming up to about mid-calf so yet again they carried Leanne and the sofa to the far end of the corridor but by then tiles were dropping everywhere and what they thought would be their place of safety was becoming more saturated by the minute. After a while she became used to being shunted from one sanctuary to another in an effort to avoid the oncoming tide and the crashing ceiling tiles. Despite repeated efforts to sweep water outside, these were to prove as futile as Canute, as the oncoming water continued to creep forward and the hotel guests were becoming wetter and wetter, with water levels gradually and relentlessly rising.

Having retreated as far as they could into the bottom corridor the external doors were blown open and started flapping wildly on their hinges. The men in the group found some electrical wiring and managed to fasten them together in an attempt to anchor them to their frames. Whilst this do-it-yourself first aid was being administered to the doors the girls ventured into what they hoped was the haven of the computer room only to see, through the back window, the canteen roof and the art room roof peel off and disappear into the distance. This, of course, was relative as in reality they could not see for much more than a distance of eight to ten feet in the swirling wind and rain. The noise was just as frightening and was later described by Nic as just like a steam engine in a tunnel going around the school and this was non-stop for over twenty-four hours. Those of my generation can well remember the noise of two steam engines meeting and passing each other in a tunnel. Whilst I've no idea of the exact decibel level it was extremely noisy. For those of more tender years it might be compared to the sound of Concorde taking off. To imagine that incessant din accompanied by the wind, rain and flood waters must have been quite terrifying.

The school maintenance man and his family tried to join the small group in the middle of the storm because they just didn't have anywhere else to go. Unfortunately due to the sheer strength of the wind they were unable to open the doors so he and his family eventually sought refuge in the sports hall but even as they were doing so the roof was coming off and the doors blew out. They managed to find some space underneath the stage and this became their hidey-hole where they remained for the duration of the storm. They may well have suffered from a different form of stage fright to the thespians that normally tread the boards above them but it saved them from the worst of the storm. Although they were in cramped and damp conditions and were hoping and praying that the floodwaters didn't continue to rise, at least they were protected from ceiling tiles and flying debris falling on their heads.

By this time shutters were being blown from classroom windows and one set came crashing through the glass panes of the computer room. Once again the party withdrew back into the corridor locking the door behind them in the forlorn hope that this would hold back the oncoming wind and rain. The group decided that they would now remain in the corridor as it was of cement construction and they reasoned that it was likely to be the strongest part of the structure and would afford them the greatest protection. They went along the corridor locking all the class-room doors, and although they realised it was probably a futile gesture, psychologically it seemed to provide as much security as possible as they gathered all their crash mats in the one corridor. This rationale appeared quite logical and was perhaps not dissimilar to Londoners decamping to the safe haven of the Underground railway stations during the Blitz. Very different circumstances, but both experiences probably just as frightening.

By now even the corridor was in three inches of water and with no dry clothing everybody was feeling very uncomfortable in addition to being just a bit distressed. They had never experienced a hurricane of this scale and had no idea how long it was likely to continue or even if it had yet reached its peak.

Ironically, perhaps the saving grace was the presence of the children and the dogs. It made the adults talk to them and play with them pretend-ing that everything was perfectly fine and that it was just an adventure to be sleeping in the school corridor on crash mats even if they were damp and in some discomfort. As the Sunday wore on the wind direction changed to a more southerly direction although it didn't appear to diminish in strength. In fact, if anything, it seemed to be growing stronger. For a while visibility improved slightly so that they could see the apartments opposite the school on Walkers Road. Looking out from the school they appeared to have weathered the storm. What they could not see from the school was that the rear of their neighbouring buildings had been completely torn away and they were open to the elements. The Sunday night was much worse than Saturday with more noise than ever and everything upstairs seemingly being blown from one end of the building to the other and then back again as the hurricane buffeted the school. More shutters were being wrenched from their hinges and blown away. Their ordeal seemed that much worse in total darkness, with no communication with the outside world, as radio contact had been lost many hours before. There was little they could do other than support each other and hope that the storm would blow out sooner rather than later. Sleep that night was impossible, in spite of trying desks, chairs or anything above water level. Leanne was continuing to hang on in there despite frequent moves to safer spots. From time to time soaked ceiling tiles fell to the ground making a splash in the muddy water. This was described by one of the hotel's temporary guests as being akin to a huge cow-pat falling to the ground, ensuring that anyone who was trying to sleep through the storm really did get a rude awakening. Not that anyone got any opportunity to sleep, although by now exhaustion was also setting in as their ordeal became a real test of endurance. In a conventional hotel there may well have been the odd justified complaint to management the following morning but in the middle of the night survival until daylight was the main thought on everybody's mind and discomfort or inconvenience had become totally inconsequential. As the night wore on the wind speeds, almost imperceptibly at first, began slowly to decrease until they were at least at tolerable levels.

The group stayed together in the corridor to fortunately see out the remainder of the storm until David and two of his colleagues eventually arrived on the Monday morning. They were the first people they had seen or spoken to since their arrival at the school on Saturday lunchtime. The police officers had all been working for the duration and although fatigued were doing all they could to reassure everybody they came into contact with during this most extraordinary tour of duty. As a shift that seemed never-ending it was wholly exceptional and one that they had never previously experienced and didn't wish to repeat.

David advised them not to leave the school as large parts of the island had been devastated and it was not yet safe to venture out as the sea was still engulfing a significant area. When they did eventually venture out, later in the day, they found the waves were still breaking onto Walkers Road close to the school and almost half a mile from the shoreline. It was only now that they were able to appreciate the damage to the school as they looked onto the canteen and the hall and the remains of the roof together with debris, tossed from far and wide, strewn everywhere. They had experienced the devastation inside the school at first hand and they now had to brave the elements to return to their own homes to discover what fate awaited them. Which of their homes were still standing in one piece? Would they be able to retrieve their belongings and for those who would be preparing insurance claims how long would it be before they received compensation and their lives returned to some sort of normality? At least they were all safe and had survived Cayman's worst storm in living memory.

As Mel and Nic made their way towards their homes they saw some people actually swimming down Denham Thompson Drive, which had been swamped to a level of four or five feet for most of its length, in an effort to reach dry land. Homes in this small area had been totally destroyed. Their roofs had caved in and the water had gone straight through carrying everything in its wake. They had difficulty in believing what they were seeing with their own eyes. The devastation around them was total.

Nic had recently bought her house and although it was totally flooded it remained structurally sound. The house was relatively empty, as far as belongings were concerned, as she had ordered lots of new goods to fit into her new home, most of which were sitting in a container waiting to be delivered. Nic spent much of the storm thinking about this and hoping all her new things were safe and dry inside the container. It transpired that the container was not water-resistant, which resulted in many of the items for her new house, including a brand new television and VCR, going straight into the dustbin. Nic admitted that she didn't really care about her belongings. Having endured the ordeal with her friends she was just grateful that they had all escaped with their lives and without any injuries. She just appreciated the fact that they were still all alive. Having experienced the hurricane and come out of the school in one piece to see the devastation first hand put things into some sort of perspective.

The two girls, who when they arrived together on Grand Cayman to take up their new teaching positions would not have imagined in their wildest dreams what lay in wait for them, managed to walk as far as the five-storey Citrus Grove building, which was hurricane-rated, and where many had sheltered for the duration of the storm. Citrus Grove lived up to its rating and never lost power, had air-conditioning and gravity sewage throughout the storm. Those who managed to harbour in such buildings for the duration were more fortunate than others who tried to make do in their own homes.

Mel and David's home did not fare as well as Nic's. As soon as they saw it they realised it was no longer habitable. Apart from the severe flood damage to the ground floor all the ceilings had collapsed and the rear wall had disappeared. Although they were able to retrieve a few of their belongings many had gone the same way as the wall and been swept away in the wind and the floodwaters. They had hardly been back from their honeymoon a month and their first home together had been destroyed by the awesome natural power of Ivan.

Nic said later that everybody cried that day when they saw what had happened to their homes and their efforts to build a future on the island.

Having recovered from the initial shock and taken stock they all realised that it could have been much worse. They were all alive and had each other for help and support and from time to time a shoulder to cry on and in those early stages that's what kept them going. Back home in England reports were still sketchy and try as we might communication with Grand Cayman was impossible.

We eventually heard from Mel via an e-mail that we received on 17th September having been sent by her after ten at night on the 16th.

Hello Everyone

Just wanted to let you all know that David and I are safe. I spent the hurricane in the school with lots of other people, including young children, a heavily pregnant lady (Leanne was still pregnant when she left and Stephen was trying to get her air ambulanced off on Monday, she is fine) and several dogs – it was an interesting weekend. It was the scariest thing I have ever been through. David was at work so was at the station but it did mean I couldn't get in touch with him much and that made me very nervous!! He is fine – completely knackered as he is working constantly, but fine.

I am currently in Miami. I am officially an evacuee and no I don't have a label around my neck and a gas mask!! We have finally had a shower and a warm meal and a bed that isn't wet. We have no power or water in Cayman and only a few phone lines work but we are all OK. Nic and I are planning on going back in a few days when hopefully there will be water.

Please don't worry about us – we are all OK. I have no ceilings and David and I are moving in with his Dad as they suffered no damage to their house (about the only one on the island!!). Mark and Janine's house has a hole in the ceiling but is liveable – Janine has taken the girls to England. Lori's house is still standing but suffered major damage to all her belongings. And Nic's house is fine but was obviously under a lot of water. We are all getting sorted slowly.

I will try and contact you before I go back to Cayman. Dani – I would seriously postpone any plans to come here for a while, it looks like war torn Bosnia and really they don't want anyone there who is not absolutely necessary. The damage is beyond anything I could have imagined.

Everyone is fine, smelly but fine, you will hear from us all soon. Thank you for all your messages.

Others referred to in the message were friends and teaching colleagues of Mel's who I had met at the wedding. Dani, who had fallen in love with the island, had planned to have another holiday with Mel and David and experience Pirates Week but that was an idea that had to be postponed indefinitely. The regular exhortations in the email that 'We're now safe, we're now OK, we're fine' were, I think, together with the attempted humour at the end of the message, mainly for the benefit of Jan who had, as any mother would, worried herself sick until she could be certain that her daughter was safe. Although there is reference to others' houses in the email there is just the briefest mention of lack of ceilings in her home, completely omitting the fact the house was a scene of devastation and they had lost most of their worldly goods. Again I think that was to prevent any unnecessary worrying for Jan, Ted and Carrie. At that stage Ted and Sue were still in temporary accommodation waiting to return to their own home that was being repaired following the fire that gutted it whilst they were out at work, earlier in the summer. I don't think Mel wanted to tell him that she and David were now in the same boat. It could wait a while.

In common with others on the island whilst they had survived the storm it would still take them a considerable time to recover from their ordeal, assess the damage to their home and what options were open to them in the hope they could gradually return to some degree of normality.

Stephen's company managed to obtain an air ambulance and Leanne was flown off on the Tuesday morning. When they got her to hospital the doctors were able to delay the labour with medication and the baby was born on the following Friday in Fort Lauderdale. He weighed four pounds and is named Finn Nicholas. Apparently Leanne was heard to comment that she would never name any of her children Ivan!

Much much later when I had the chance to speak to Mel she described Hurricane Ivan as 'very wet, very windy and a little bit scary'. To an extent time had dimmed her immediate memory and at the time of that conversation she, David and the island were well on the road to recovery. When pressed she was honest enough to admit that at the time it was 'a big bit scary'.

The first news that most of us were able to obtain came courtesy of the *Cayman Net News* with an update that they posted on the Internet at twelve noon on Tuesday 14th September. It was succinct and didn't paint a very bright picture. They had been busy collecting and compiling as much intelligence as they could from government sources but communication on the island was very limited and in those early stages the lack of accurate information was simply due to the fact that in parts of the island it was just unobtainable. Normal communication links were broken and inoperable, roads were impassable, many vehicles were wrecked beyond repair so even on a small island it was impossible to ascertain the true scale of devastation other than a general awareness that it was massive. Those in Georgetown still had no detailed reports of conditions in North Side or East End which indicated that both had been badly hit. Initial accounts of bodies floating in the water were later reported as cadavers from graveyards that had been flooded and not islanders killed by the storm.

Even the Cayman Islands Tourism Office acknowledged that they were frustrated due to a lack of consistent updates but were doing their very best to verify information and distribute it as quickly as possible to friends and families. In common with any large scale public disaster the early stages were chaotic and many do not appreciate just how long and difficult it can be for the emergency services to regain control and provide accurate information to the media in press conferences and releases. Twenty-first century satellite technology and our thirst for news and real-time pictures to be beamed into our living rooms only piles added pressure onto already overworked, and in some cases exhausted, officials who are trying to implement contingency plans to cope with the extraordinary events of such a major incident. Unfortunately they now have to accept that this will forever remain another role that they will need to cover in their emergency plans. It is a pressure that they could do without but to ignore it would, in this day and age, be unrealistic and unprofessional. It is a service that the public now expect and in all fairness are probably now entitled to expect. In any event family and friends of victims and survivors have always pressed for immediate information so that, in one sense, the response to the media is an extension of the old-style Casualty Bureau, albeit a significant extension that assumes a life of its own with an unremitting thirst for more information.

The *Cayman Net News* tried to summarise in bullet point form the situation as it stood on the Tuesday lunchtime. It was brief but at least started to give a feel for what the situation was like on the island.

It included some of the following information:

Dozens of people remained unaccounted for on Grand Cayman.

The Cayman Islands remained under a state of emergency and a curfew was imposed.

Many homes on Grand Cayman were confirmed uninhabitable either due to flooding or roof destruction.

Owen Roberts International Airport was open for restricted flights only and initially for daytime landings with priority being given to medical evacuees such as dialysis patients bound for Miami where their medical treatment would continue. The runway had been submerged just two days earlier.

Cayman Airways were coordinating emergency flights into Grand Cayman from Houston, Tampa and Miami.

Land phone lines remained down.

Cellphones were working, although the volume of calls made it difficult to make contact as circuits were permanently busy. (This was not unusual in any sort of emergency or major incident and was not peculiar to Grand Cayman.)

The Cayman Islands US office was starting to coordinate relief efforts and although their own office was severely damaged and closed the Department of Tourism opened the Cayman Islands Hurricane Relief Fund together with assistance from banks and other partners.

The Tortuga Rum Company immediately set aside one of their ware-houses as a staging area to collect incoming relief supplies whilst the Cox Lumber Company in Tampa set up similar facilities as a collection and onward transmission point for emergency relief.

The islanders were in need of many of the essentials that we, and in normal circumstances they, take for granted. With water and electricity supplies still cut off living conditions were uncomfortable and basic.

Tortuga Imports warehouse were accepting the following priority items:

Drinking water
Canned foods
Can openers
Bread
Nappies/Diapers
Plastic Utensils/Plates/Cups/Buckets
Medical Supplies
Generators
Candles
BBQ Grills and Coal
Cleaning Supplies (Dustbin/garbage bags, brooms)

Tents & Tarpaulins
Pens and paper
Battery powered lanterns
Water filtration systems
Blankets
Plywood
Batteries
Chainsaws

These were but a few of the items required urgently from what was an endless and ever growing list, plus of course cash donations to purchase emergency supplies and in due course support the relief effort, together with what would eventually become a massive rebuilding programme.

At that stage we still hadn't heard from Mel and David and it was to be another two days before we received her first email. Official news reports were very limited and frankly didn't contain a great deal of news so we became very reliant in those early days upon the *Cayman Net News*. In fact it was our only source of real information.

Hilary Benn, the UK Secretary of State for International Development, made a brief statement in the House of Commons. It indicated that communication with the island authorities remained extremely difficult with unconfirmed reports of loss of life and injury. It appeared that ninety-five percent of homes had suffered and twenty-five percent of Grand Cayman was still under water. The sewage system was flooded and there had been no power since Saturday. However, HMS *Richmond* arrived in Cayman waters on Monday and would be assisting with the relief effort in any way it could as soon as sea conditions permitted. The Governor had requested immediate supplies including cots for small children, plastic sheeting and water purification equipment. They were going to be dispatched within the next day. There was also some concern about law and order and a curfew had been hastily imposed during the hours of darkness. They were also looking at any options to reinforce police capacity from neighbouring islands. An assessment team from the

Department for International Development were hoping to arrive on the island the following day.

At that stage the curfew prescribed under the Emergency Powers Regulations by the Governor required residents to remain at home, or in their shelters from six pm until six am.

Eighty officers and men from HMS *Richmond* were deployed on the island to assist with security, shelter management, water desalination and engineering and numerous other emergency relief tasks. They were supported by crew from the Royal Fleet Auxiliary ship *Wave Ruler*.

The most pressing need was for food, water and shelter. Where possible schools were commissioned to serve as temporary shelters to house those who had lost their homes and had briefly sought refuge in private offices and government buildings. Unfortunately many of the schools were just as badly affected so for the majority survival was the name of the game and this remained their sole objective over those first few days. For the various small groups huddled together in different parts of the island it was just not possible to think further ahead than the next few hours and how they would be able to eke out what meagre supplies of food and water were needed to carry them over into the next day. For them, at that stage, long term, or even medium term, planning was just not possible and would not become part of their thought process for some time.

At government level they were instigating what contingency planning they could and seeking aid from any source available but in those first few days even their priority was the here and now. Rescue, safety and security were the immediate concerns and, having achieved that minor miracle, for the time being tomorrow would have to take care of itself.

Over the course of those first few days the pace of the relief effort gradually increased. Bearing in mind that at one stage it had been completely submerged, work at the airport was on track to return it to its full operational capacity by the following Friday. Cayman Airways was already running a number of flights taking off medical evacuees and stranded visitors and returning with emergency supplies.

The assistance of the two Royal Navy ships and their crews who were able to provide some limited supplies and humanitarian aid in those first few days was appreciated by the islanders. HMS *Richmond*'s helicopter was able to carry out surveillance flights, once the worst of the winds had subsided, and this improved the flow of intelligence and aided the effective appraisal of priorities.

Reports continued to filter through of the devastation across the island and the conditions that residents had endured throughout the storm. However, it was going to take weeks and months before any accurate assessment of the damage could be estimated and life could begin to return to some degree of normality.

Although the Governor felt confident enough to lift the emergency powers on Monday 27th September, almost three weeks after the state of emergency and hurricane alert were issued, there remained a long road to travel in the recovery process. Whilst electricity had been restored to some areas and water was flowing through some taps, restrictions on visitors to Grand Cayman remained in place and the police did not yet feel confident enough to totally lift the curfew, which had been from six pm to six am but was now from ten pm until five am.

The main reason for the continuation of the curfew was public safety and the restoration of lighting would become a key factor in any decision to ultimately lift the curfew. Although the police were overseeing a gradual return to normality it was easier for criminals to thrive in darkness as opposed to well-lit areas. In the final week of September they had carried out arrests for drugs, unlicensed firearms, burglary, handling stolen goods and breach of curfew. There was also anticipation that when people were eventually able to return to their homes for the first time there would be further reports of burglary.

Whilst breach of curfew carried maximum penalties of a thousand-dollar fine and six months' imprisonment the reality was that the few offenders who chanced their arm on not being caught had fines ranging from \$50 to \$150 and one day's imprisonment. The primary concern for safety, security and crime prevention dictated that the curfew, albeit gradually reduced to twelve midnight to five am, was to remain in place until 9th December, a period of almost three months, and this did cause some debate with various commercial interests within the community who considered that it was hindering a return to routine and business as usual on the island.

By early October police officers from Bermuda, the British Virgin Islands and Turks and Caicos who had arrived to assist their colleagues in an immediate time of need were able to return to their own islands. Local police officers were slowly but surely returning to the more routine patrols but having to do so whilst coping with their own family issues of loss of belongings and in some cases homelessness. For any emergency service to retain morale in such circumstances is always difficult. Individual officers have to return to duty day after day with an air of independent objectivity and are expected, by the public, to carry out their regular tasks as if they had not been personally affected by the tragedy, disaster or major incident. This expectation is not unfair but more a historical inheritance of previous generations of police, fire and rescue and medical emergency teams going about their duty with a professional stoicism that perhaps belied their inner feelings. The truth is that many did not always know how they coped in those situations.

I'm sure the situation on Grand Cayman was no different and in addition to having to deal personally with incidents they might only experience once in their careers they also had the additional pressure of how their own families were going to survive the disaster and how they would be able to return to some sort of normality. Demands from loved ones in such situations can have a huge impact on those working in the emergency services arena and it is vital that senior staff build into their contingency plans the very necessary support and welfare provision for their own staff if they are to maintain the high level of professionalism and expertise that is expected from them in such conditions. Assisting others, many of whom will be total strangers, to survive the immediate crisis and providing support to aid their recovery from adversity when, perhaps, their own loved ones are in a similar or worse plight and not appearing to receive the same amount of care and assistance can cause considerable strain on close relationships. Families can, maybe unfairly, feel neglected and this can lead to unnecessary stress and conflict at a time when it is least wanted and most difficult to cope with and work through. That sort of pressure has been known to destroy families but the emergency services workers are expected to carry on regardless and continue to deliver a professional and dispassionate service of rescue and recovery however anxious they may be feeling about their own families.

Although the Royal Cayman Islands Police Service were able to cope using their own resources together with invaluable assistance from the Special Constabulary a welcome addition to aid the national clean-up campaign was the arrival of thirty-four troops from the Bermuda Regiment who provided an immediate and organised response to the early recovery programme.

News emanating through the British media remained very patchy and rightly or wrongly a perception was developing that the authorities on Grand Cayman were not being transparent enough with the reality of the situation on the island. My impression was that it was being made deliberately difficult to obtain accurate information and this was being done to protect the reputation of the island, whether it be for financial, tourism or other reasons. I may well have been wrong but inaccurate perceptions can be important unless they are corrected.

Whatever the truth of the situation sensationalist captions such as 'You Loot, We Shoot' in a British newspaper do nothing to enhance the standing of the island and could have had a detrimental effect both on the immediate need to persuade individuals and governments to provide aid and longer term investment in both the financial markets and tourism. Whilst the pressure to deal with the immediate aftermath of such an event is immense, it is vital to prepare a media strategy and appoint an official to liaise with the press and television crews keeping them updated at regular intervals. Failure to do so is now both naïve and counterproductive as they will inevitably go and find their own stories and be tempted to present a picture that could be both unflattering and unfair on the emergency teams and authorities and effectively publish an account that is not a true reflection of action on the ground. I don't know if that was the situation as the weeks progressed during September but it did leave unanswered questions in the mind of the reader or listener that possibly could have been avoided.

Rightly or wrongly I just had a feeling that it was a deliberate and cynical attempt by the authorities to protect the island's status as a tax haven. By denying access to the international press it left individual reporters to their own devices to obtain their copy and as a group they are both resourceful and determined in their ability to seek out a story. One BBC journalist climbed through a hole in the perimeter fence around the airport after being denied entry. How many others used similar tactics or different ploys to track down their own 'scoop' will never be known. You are then faced with an alienated, frustrated and potentially angry group of experienced hacks who will use whatever means at their disposal to find the truth, or any unscrupulous ones to find a good story even if it is necessary to use a liberal amount of journalistic licence.

Consequently, tittle-tattle abounded and the lack of official, accurate and impartial information, however scarce that might have been at the time, allowed them to trace and obtain their stories from anybody who had a tale to tell whether it be totally accurate, slightly embellished in the telling or even second-hand and potentially inaccurate, based on local gossip.

An example in the popular British press included such rumours as machete gangs running wild; thirty people being washed to their deaths in a yacht club; cholera, typhoid and hepatitis A breaking out; hundreds of corpses being concealed in local mortuaries; UN aid workers being refused entry, and last but not least, looting. Whilst it was accepted that rumours such as these can quickly gain currency, until such time as these reporters started filtering their stories to the media back home the vast majority of the British public had no idea of the true scale of the disaster on Grand Cayman, which remains a British dependency. Such stories can quickly gain a head of steam. For example a multitude of convicted criminals escaping from the Island's prison which in reality turned out to be two. In such circumstances truth and fact become exaggerated and can rapidly become casualties as fiction then gains credence if the rumour mongers are not swiftly put in their place by regular and accurate media briefings.

With no such news black out on Grenada or Jamaica everybody was aware of the true havoc Ivan had wreaked on both those islands. Unless you had a specific interest in the Cayman Islands, and picked up tit-bits from family, friends or the Internet, it wasn't until the persistence of those reporters who managed to get onto the island and see for themselves the true nature and scale of the devastation that the vast majority back home in the UK had any real idea of the actual extent of the disaster.

Although both the Governor and the island's government vehemently denied any cover-up, blaming the inability to properly assess the level of damage due to its enormity and a breakdown in communications, it left me wondering if they could have provided more information much earlier. Local residents seemed divided in their views. Some were more generous in their judgement than others, believing that it was a combination of ineptitude or policy or if it were a deliberate decision it was with the best of intentions to avoid damaging the reputation of the islands but effectively the decision, for whatever reason, badly rebounded on them. One was left to speculate why when a British Overseas Territory had been utterly overwhelmed by a natural disaster, and was in need of immediate aid and vital supplies just to sustain basic living conditions, didn't anybody in Britain know anything about it?

This, combined with a view, perhaps, in British government circles that it might be difficult to explain to British taxpayers why they were bailing out a tax haven that is perceived by many to be far more prosperous than parts of Britain, may go some way to explain why the initial aid was considered by many to be minimal and paltry, no matter how urgent the humanitarian need at the time.

Sitting some five thousand miles away and trying to view it independently and objectively, is difficult when one has friends personally involved. Although the vast majority of the rumours were shown to be false or with little foundation and access to the foreign press had not been denied – albeit there had been communication problems – I was left with a feeling that links with the media could have been handled better and improved at an earlier stage. Without knowing the stresses placed upon those in authority, which would have been considerable, together with a lack of sleep, it is perhaps unfair to be too critical of decisions they had to make in quick time all of which would have been under unrelenting pressure. Whilst we may never know the rationale for some of those decisions my hope would be that the whole incident has been thoroughly de-briefed and lessons that have been learned are not forgotten but included in revised contingency plans and regularly exercised by all the prominent players involved so that in the event of a similar occurrence in the future, and one would hope it would not be as devastating as Ivan, then everybody is well prepared to play their part in the survival and recovery plan. A simple lesson I learned from a very good, and well-respected, senior policeman many years ago was the simple dictum, failing to plan is planning to fail. In the modern world a media strategy forms an important part of any emergency plan.

By early October news was trickling through a little more frequently although it was still somewhat limited. Mel had eventually been able to return to Grand Cayman from Miami and taken back with her as many essentials as she could carry, that weren't yet readily available on the island. Crucial items at that time included the likes of flashlights, additional batteries and toilet rolls. At last I, and others, received another long-awaited email from Mel:

> Well after some fun and games trying to get back to Cayman I managed to have a final weekend off before school starts on Monday – assuming we have power and water that is!!

Thanks for all your thoughts and good wishes and your offers of help. I don't really know what to suggest but thanks for the offers.

We are all OK and getting sorted out finally. I'm now used to 2 hours of running water in the evening and morning and cold showers if I remember when the water will be on!!

Actually the cold showers are a blessing and I will never take air-conditioning for granted again. Am a little fed up with food from the barbecue but various bars now have some cold beer so it isn't all bad.

David and I have now moved in with his Dad in West Bay and the phone is working intermittently.

I will speak to you all when I can.

Love

Mel.

They had both by now had the opportunity to return to the wreckage of what had once been their home, albeit briefly, in an attempt to rescue anything they could find. The reality was that this proved to be a wasted journey as they were only able to find and salvage one or two bits and pieces and the vast majority of the wedding presents that we had seen them open and admire on that hot and sultry afternoon in July were now gone forever. It was difficult to comprehend that what had only been ten weeks earlier now seemed a lifetime away. The winds and the storm waters of Ivan that had lashed the island in such a dramatic fashion for a weekend, so that no resident will ever forget the experience, had taken their belongings and scattered them to the four corners of the Caribbean. In common with thousands of others Mel and David would have to start building their lives again from scratch. Life was not going to be easy for some time to come.

At least they had a temporary roof over their heads so Mel returned to what was left of the school to continue teaching in rather more basic accommodation than pupils and staff had been used to. David, meanwhile, donned his not quite so pristine uniform to, if not return to conventional duties, start to assist the recovery programme whilst providing some safety and security for all those inhabitants who were trying to piece their lives back together and return to some sort of normality.

Life had to go on but it would prove to be some time before the island was able to return to traditional and typical patterns of life. Flexibility became the order of the day and an early casualty of the aftermath of Ivan was the general election which had to be postponed until the following year. Voting in members of a new assembly was not an imperative; restoring public utilities and re-housing the homeless were. Electioneering and the run-up to voting day with the frenetic and partisan door-knocking and public meetings of the different candidates would have been an unnecessary distraction and diverted important resources away from the urgent need to restore the island to a modicum of orderliness where everybody had access to basic amenities in the short term. Time was also needed to develop medium and longer term plans so that the recovery strategy could proceed as quickly as possible within a realistic timetable so that salvage and rebuilding priorities commenced without too many unforeseen glitches delaying the revival process. There was a need to co-ordinate with the insurance companies, construction industry, together with the import and transport contractors, to bring in the raw materials. Additional specialists and skilled craftsmen would have to be found and persuaded to fly into Georgetown for a temporary period to assist the local population. This would create a transient population who also required short-term accommodation, and the usual immigration rules also had to be considered. This just gives a small flavour of the immediate problems facing the islanders, their leaders and the Governor and the potential logistical nightmare that they were facing.

The general election could wait and the decision to delay was apposite and sensible.

Recovery was slow but steady and whilst progress was not always readily apparent on a daily basis that should not have detracted from the efforts of all the different organisations, both public and private, and the individuals who were working all hours to achieve some sort of normality and return living conditions to an acceptable, if rudimentary, level.

Things were improving even if they weren't always noticeable. By January well over seven thousand temporary work permits had been issued; more than double the normal number. Education needed to go on. Apart from the damage to school buildings, estimated at eighteen million dollars, a huge amount of school equipment, such as computers, desks, chairs and books, had been lost or damaged beyond repair. The country's libraries had seen over ten thousand books destroyed by Ivan and the main library had to be relocated. The shortage of space in schools and lack of useable facilities was being addressed but rebuilding was being hampered by flood residue, dampness and mould. An immediate solution was the arrival of twenty temporary classrooms to be distributed to various sites so that by the New Year pupils could attend on a more regular basis obviating the need for a rota system of alternate and half day schooling. Whether all of the children appreciated the arrival of their temporary accommodation as opposed to their short term timetable (no pun intended) remained to be seen.

Even the stingrays weren't forgotten. With a total lack of tourists making for Stingray City there was a danger that the stingrays would start to look elsewhere for their food. Normally they can rely on the tourists from the cruise ship excursions to provide them with hundreds of pounds of squid each day. Without that regular food source they may well have drifted away from their famous home to find other areas with a greater supply of their natural diet. Fortunately the Foster's supermarket company donated a thousand pounds of squid which they willingly imported and stored for daily collection by the dive operators to distribute to their hungry customers at the Sandbar and Stingray City.

Whilst work continued to remove debris and speed up the import and restocking of vital supplies to repair the country's infrastructure many individuals and families could easily have been overwhelmed by the situation into which they had been thrust.

Valuables and belongings that had been acquired over a lifetime, many with huge sentimental value, were lost forever. Keepsakes that had been handed down from one generation to the next had been cast aside by the wind and the sea so that tangible, even if small, parts of family histories would no longer be seen, felt and appreciated by those whose birthright should have given them access to their ancestors. Some families were left sleeping, living and eating in just one room without basic cooking and washing facilities. The added distraction of trying to keep dry until the leaking roof could be repaired made life even more miserable for some.

In a number of cases either no insurance, inadequate cover or delays in settling claims meant that many could see no light at the end of the tunnel and were on the verge of despair. The fact that by early November the cruise ships were able to resume making limited visits to the island and bringing in much needed and essential revenue to the tourist and commercial sector was of little or no consolation or consequence to many who were struggling to survive on a day to day basis.

As important as it was to the island's recovery and future tourism potential the daily stopovers for the cruisers didn't actually assist many still recovering from their ordeal in the aftermath of Ivan. The sense of despair and distress was very personal amongst those struggling to survive at a local level. Strategic solutions, whilst vital to assist the long-term economic recovery, did little to ease the plight of victims in the short term.

Existing in the skeletal remains of a house without doors or windows; where furniture and rugs had been replaced by something resembling a sandy, slurry, debris ridden mucky beach and living in those conditions without the power to light or cook dictated that the immediate priority was just survival, however difficult that might prove to be.

It was said at the time that many went through the whole gamut of emotions, that would normally take a lifetime to experience, in just a couple of weeks. Fright, frustration, anger, despair and depression all lead to decreased levels of tolerance and increased levels of stress. In those long dark weeks and months the Cayman Islanders proved just how resilient they are as a race. Not just resilient but also very generous, caring and compassionate. Even in the midst of recovering from their own disaster once the true scale of the Indian Ocean tsunami on 26th December 2004 became apparent Caymanians donated thousands of dollars to appeals for relief funds for the victims in Asia.

Churches, clubs, business, schools, youth groups, Red Cross, local charities and Rotary to name but a few collected money from individuals all over the islands to be sent by UNICEF and other recognised charities to assist the relief effort in the tsunami-hit region. Grand Cayman had its own problems with many losing their homes and possessions during Ivan but the people recognised that the tragedy in Asia was much greater, particularly in terms of loss of life. Despite their own troubles they still remembered and gave willingly to assist their fellow human beings whose needs were greater many thousands of miles away.

Whether it was the links to their seafaring forefathers and the toughness, both physical and mental, that type of existence breeds or just a bloody-minded indomitable spirit the Caymanians were determined that they would recover from the devastation of Ivan and the havoc it wrought upon their communities.

With an irrepressible resolve they set about their twin aims of getting back to 'business as usual' but also enhancing their contingency planning to be better prepared for any such future disaster.

The latter involved both short- and long-term plans, initially to provide early warning and improved predictions of hurricane tracking, their scale and potential effects. This would progress into the implementation of a National Emergency Agency updating communications, shelters, temporary housing, management of the emergency services, government agency response and business continuity.

Eventually this would all be housed in a new Emergency Services Command Centre where all responses could be monitored and controlled, providing a coordinated response.

As a major source of income tourism always remained high on the agenda and it was a matter not simply of rebuilding with bricks and mortar but just as importantly restoring confidence so that in addition to the cruise ships the likes of myself as a resident tourist would return to the island.

Whilst initially progress seemed painfully slow the green shoots of recovery did eventually start to sprout and with a mixture of press conferences, multi-media presentations and targeted marketing by the Department of Tourism the efforts proved worthwhile. Increases in both cruise visits and 'stayovers' demonstrated a steady trend of visitors returning to Grand Cayman, with the majority from the United States, Canada and Europe.

British Airways played their part to help kick-start the programme and boost tourism by offering much reduced fares on direct flights from Heathrow to Georgetown to attract family, friends and tourists in both high and low season.

The burgeoning cruise market, with the introduction of even bigger and better floating hotels, also played its part. In little over a year after Ivan the government had to consider revising the schedule of cruise ship visits to provide an improved balance between high and low-volume days and minimise the impact on residents.

Such was the demand from the various cruise lines to visit the island that plans were developed to increase the number and availability of onshore activities to cater for the swelling numbers who now wanted to experience and enjoy Cayman hospitality. In the lead-up to Christmas there were even thoughts of enhancing night-time activities to encourage residents to shift to more late evening shopping, linked to entertainment and eating venues to ease congestion earlier in the day.

Ivan will never be forgotten, particularly by those who had to endure and live through it but Grand Cayman is now just as welcoming and ready to host any visitor who wants to come and enjoy the many attractions it has to offer.

I mentioned at the beginning of this chapter that my account is totally second-hand but to have completed the story without mentioning Ivan would have been negligent, uncaring and dismissive of what became a vital part of Cayman history.

My thanks to Mel, David, Nic and their friends at the school for their accounts and other impressions from the media, not least the *Cayman Net News* for providing a link with their coverage, particularly during those early days. I'm sure my description doesn't do justice to the event or to the many selfless acts and efforts of all involved to recover from the devastation reeked by Ivan during those two terrible days. If my research has not discovered the whole story then I apologise unreservedly to those involved.

Chapter 17

A Pleasant Surprise at the Treehouse

A s we sat sipping our pre-dinner drinks and perusing the menu we didn't dream of the drama about to unfold in less than two months' time. However, we were also unprepared – at least I was – for a much more imminent but far more pleasant surprise.

It wasn't long before our table was ready and we were all able to take our seats at the restaurant's signature table at the end of the small pier overhanging the calm waters of the Caribbean. We and the other diners watched enthralled as a waiter started to feed the hungry tarpon whilst they dived and skidded across the surface in search of their nightly meal. Who said fish don't have brains?

We had all selected and ordered what was to be the final dinner of the holiday and the atmosphere was already more than convivial, perhaps assisted by the earlier cocktails, with our small party determined to really enjoy this last evening at the restaurant before dancing and singing the night away at the Royal Palms.

No sooner had the waiter left the table with confirmation of our various orders than Fran suddenly arose and asked for a moment's silence. In normal circumstances particularly with Caroline, Carrie and myself in full flow that would have been impossible but there was something about her that on this occasion did make us all shut up. She swiftly broke into a huge grin and with Carl joining her she announced to the assembled company that she and Carl became engaged yesterday. Carl had taken her to the beach at Smith's Cove as the sun was setting and proposed on the sun-kissed sand. Needless to say Fran had accepted. Who said that Englishmen weren't romantic!

Unbeknown to the majority of the others and me they had visited the jewellers when they disappeared into Georgetown earlier in the day to buy the engagement ring. The one exception, of course, was Jan who had guessed what was going on. Women's intuition! That had been the subject of their confidential conversation at the side of the bar some fifteen minutes earlier and Fran had sworn Jan to secrecy until she could announce it herself when we were all seated at the table. Her reason for insisting that we chose that table and that restaurant was now obvious to all.

What a superb end to the holiday. More emotion, hugs, kisses and yes, more tears of joy.

A bottle of Moët quickly arrived and yet again the 'happy snappers' were flashing away amongst the bubbly. Final nights on holiday can sometimes be a bit of an anticlimax with only packing the suitcases and a long journey home to look forward to. The engagement made sure that our final night was one that would not be forgotten and really was enjoyed by all of us but Carl and Fran in particular. Quite what the tarpon made of the shrieks of delight and the kisses and cuddles that were going on above their heads I do not know but even they seemed to realise that they were no longer the main attraction and in deference quietly slipped away to allow their human cousins centre stage to the applause of some nearby diners.

The champagne flowed freely although I have to give credit and top marks to Carrie, our driver for the evening, who kept to just the one glass whilst the remainder of us drank her share. I'm not sure that in the circumstances I would have had her willpower and if it had been my turn to drive I may well have been paying for taxis to take everybody home. As it tends to be on such occasions the time flew and it seemed no sooner had we started our meal than we had consumed a variety of delicious puddings (Caroline had just the two) and we were ready to gyrate the night away at the Royal Palms. In current parlance we were off clubbing but as my old granny might have said we were off to celebrate with 'a real right old knees-up'.

The Royal Palms was much quieter than our last visit. The band was missing and the clientele more subdued, listening to music being played by the DJ. This didn't dampen our spirits. Nothing would have achieved that on that night. Whilst we acclimatised ourselves to the more sober nature of the club we did eventually settle for our final beachside drink with a spontaneous but rousing rendition of 'Old MacDonald's Farm', allowing Dani to star through a variety of animal noises and caricatures that defied belief. She must have spent weeks in rehearsal, but it was a fitting finale to our two weeks in Grand Cayman. She was accompanied by the visiting Indies Suites mixed voice choir who provided their unstinting and enthusiastic support free of charge. This unprepared cabaret had never been witnessed before by the Royal Palms audience. It had never been seen before by any audience, but such was its classical standard, or it might just have been novelty value, that they demanded an encore. Dani didn't need persuading. The quiet one of the group wasn't really an introvert but had transformed into a Disco Farmyard Diva. Having exhausted our limited repertoire we decided to head for home. A totally exhausted but ebullient bunch who would all have been happy to stay on and extend what had been a great holiday full of fun and surprises. Carl and I had one final effort to teach Fran, at her insistence, the words of a little-known but simple rugby ditty but it was to no avail. She would have to wait to learn it another day, but even if she ever became word perfect she would from now on always have to play second fiddle to Dani the Diva.

Our final morning arrived and we took our time over a late breakfast around the pool, which was already bathed in sunshine and inviting everybody in for a last dip. Indie was hovering close to some overhanging foliage where two of her offspring, who seemed to have grown considerably in the past few days, were darting in and out of the shadows playing a game of hide and seek. She kept a watchful eye and from time to time ushered them back into the shrubbery lest they venture too close to the pool.

Our flight wasn't until early evening and we were fortunate that we didn't have to rush to vacate our rooms as the next guests weren't due to arrive until the following day. I spent the day reading, updating my jottings and packing my suitcase. The girls were either talking or sleeping and Jan was fussing around the rooms ensuring that the housemaids wouldn't have anything to do save changing the bedding once we had left.

Carrie and I returned our hired auto back to its own home having been in our care for the duration of our visit to Grand Cayman. The return journey was less exciting than our initial expedition with no sign of toothless racing drivers trying to overtake into non-existent gaps. Perhaps we had become used to the rules of the road but we weren't in any rush as we dawdled back to the garage to settle our account and be pleasantly surprised to learn that we didn't owe as much as we expected. I bade our trusty steed farewell and I apologised if my initial view had been less than complimentary. It had proved more than worthy of carrying our motley crew around the island without the slightest hint of a problem. They even returned us to the hotel free of charge.

Unsurprisingly, but disappointingly, Tropicana Coaches arrived spot on time, and from my perspective all too soon, to collect us and our baggage and transport us for the last time along Seven Mile Highway into Georgetown and on to the airport for our flight to Heathrow. I gazed back upon the miles of beach, bringing back recollections of the past fortnight. Memories of Roadrunner, Machete Man, the Telegraphic Javelin and the Purple Flash returned to haunt me and I wondered if I would come back one day. Would the beach remain so unspoilt to let me repeat my early morning perambulations in such peaceful and beautiful surroundings but without those little interruptions that kept slowing me down? It couldn't possibly have been the heat allied to my weight that left me the slowest July Jogger in Cayman Island history.

Check-in at Owen Roberts International Airport was far less frenetic than Heathrow, in fact it couldn't have been more different. However, there was one similarity that I should have been expecting. Two of our party again managed to attract the 'Heavy' label for our suitcases. Whilst I was convinced that I was returning with less, the wedding presents remaining on Grand Cayman, it didn't make a jot of difference to how they categorised my weight. Joining me in the overweight department was none other than Caroline who had managed to cram enough rum cake into her suitcase to feed half of East Anglia. I'm sure our visit had increased the island's production of rum cake tenfold in just two weeks. We took our punishment on the chin albeit to the delight and mirth of the others whilst our cases were affixed with another sticky label to warn the baggage handlers that they needed to be careful if they wished to avoid getting a hernia whilst lifting our holiday necessities.

I was to suffer one more indignity which amazingly turned into a minor triumph and was witnessed by all the others so that Lesley could not believe I was making it up.

I was the only one in our party to be selected for a security check. This entailed opening my case to enable the security staff to search the contents. Fortunately, Jan was carrying the key to her case so that I was able to avoid the embarrassment of explaining that my key remained in England and prevent the need for them to jemmy it open. Such an excuse would have ensured the check was even more thorough and may well have resulted in me being patted down as well. My searcher happened to be a female who was swift, meticulous and efficient.

Having initially asked me if I had packed my own case, to which I answered in the affirmative, she gave me a very quizzical look on completing her task. She then said, "You did say you packed your own case?"

"Yes," I replied.

"Are you sure?" she responded without changing her expression.

"Certain," I said.

"Well," she said, "I was convinced a woman packed it. It's so neat and tidy," as a twinkle came into her eyes and she started to grin.

"No, it was definitely me," I said, now feeling much more relieved as she turned from a security jobsworth into a normal, friendly and humorous human being.

"That's the smartest suitcase I've seen this year. That's got all the hallmarks of being a woman's work. Men aren't that tidy," she said as she allowed me to place the tiny and worthless lock back in position.

By now I was smiling broadly as Jan and the girls had overheard all of this conversation and watched firstly my discomfort at having my possessions searched but then my delight with the outcome and the compliments that had been paid my packing ability.

The suitcase packer in our family is Lesley who is much better organised than me, a good deal tidier and far more methodical in her approach to such chores. I wisely remain in the background and have enough sense to avoid proffering any advice. It is normal for packing to commence four to six weeks prior to departure, with various items being neatly laid out on the spare bed, having been pressed and folded to ensure there will be minimum creases when eventually unpacked. The return experience is, of necessity, more hurried but nonetheless just as fastidious and systematic.

The only occasions when I need to pack for myself are when returning from trips that I have made on my own. I never have to worry about the outward leg as Lesley believes I'm incapable of doing it myself and she very kindly looks after my interests ensuring that I'm well prepared for any eventuality. I therefore always stand some chance of turning up at least half presentable provided I remember to unpack on arrival and place suits, shirts and trousers on hangers in a wardrobe to allow any travel creases to drop out.

My trip to Grand Cayman had now provided irrefutable evidence to prove that I was more than capable of packing my own suitcase and I had even been complimented on my efforts. Well, I think it was a compliment, even if backhanded.

Part of me couldn't wait to tell Lesley, whilst my wiser self counselled against it. Did I want to be responsible for all future packing?

In addition to the Caribbean Mixed International Golfing Event perhaps they would, in future, consider hosting an all-comers World Championship in Portmanteau Packing. Now that's a challenge where I might excel. On second thoughts perhaps not!

We wandered through to the duty free shopping area where with the benefit of our unexpected additional Cayman Islands dollars, thanks to Prestige Motors' very fair and unexpected price reduction and Ted's inability to accurately transpose the exchange rates, we were able to select one or two extra gifts to take home. Caroline managed to find some more rum cake that she would carry as hand luggage just in case she became a little peckish whilst in the air.

From the comfort of the air-conditioned departure lounge we were able to watch our plane land and see the handful of passengers who were to replace us on the island. Wherever they were heading they would have difficulty in enjoying themselves as much as we had in our all too brief sojourn before we had to return to the real world of work and mortgages. Regrettably the destination screen indicated that our flight was due to depart on time. I would have been delighted if the crew had discovered a mechanical fault that would have delayed us for a day or two but it was not to be. The plane and crew were ready to go and our holiday really was over.

We bade farewell to Carl and Fran who were catching an earlier flight to Miami before joining their connection to Heathrow.

That left just Jan, me and the three successful career girls, Carrie, Caroline and Danielle, who continued to eye the available talent whilst we awaited our boarding call. Taller, older, younger, smarter, none of these seemed to be too critical in their decision-making process. In fact, not one of these attributes would have been discarded, provided he's 'fit' and well-minted, which seemed to be the maxim. Remember, girls set standards NOT restrictions.

They didn't seem to find what they were looking for, although I learned long ago that to try and second-guess exactly what a woman is looking for can be a pointless exercise. Even if you find it she is liable to change her mind and don't even try being logical. Female logic is one of those mysteries of life that for us mere mortals of the opposite sex will always be totally incomprehensible.

However, little was I to know that their unsuccessful reconnaissance of the airport lounge was to be the prelude to ending up on the flight deck of a Boeing 767 with Jan, the bride's mother, who was now carrying a plentiful supply of needles and cotton together with the dresses and worrying if they would be cleaned in time for the Suffolk reception, and three much bronzed and very happy young ladies from Bury St Edmunds who were preparing to invade Suffolk with cartons of rum cake.

But that's another story!!